The Dramatized
New Testament

D1315295

The Dramatized New Testament

New International Version

Edited by Michael Perry

Baker Books

A Division of Baker Book House Co
Grand Rapids, Michigan 49516

Copyright 1993 by Michael Perry and Jubilate Hymns

Based on *The Dramatised Bible*, first published in 1989 by Marshall Pickering and Bible Society.
Marshall Pickering is an imprint of the Collins Religious Division, part of the Collins Publishing
Group, London. Copyright © 1989 by Michael Perry.

Printed in the United States of America

Library of Congress Cataloging-in-Publication Data

Bible. N.T. English. New International. 1993.
    The dramatized New Testament: New International Version/edited by
Michael Perry.
       p.   cm.
Includes indexes.
ISBN 0-8010-7123-2
1. Bible. N.T.—Liturgical use. I. Perry, Michael, 1942– . II. Title.
BS2095.N37   1993
225.5'208—dc20   93-23807

To Helen and Simon
for whom may the Book live
as it has for me.

Contents

Editor's Preface

The Dramatized Bible—here, the New Testament—creates the opportunity for a vivid presentation of Bible narrative and teaching. Generations of ministers, teachers, and youth and children's leaders have done it before—turned the Bible text into drama so that worshipers or students can become actively involved in its teaching. But publication has always been piecemeal. Episodes have been available previously in dramatized form (the events leading up to Easter in various books, and the Christmas story in Hope Publishing Company's *Carols for Today*), but never, so far as we are aware, all the Bible narrative.

It is remarkable how much of the Bible uses the device of "reported speech" and so lends itself to dramatic presentation. For instance, we would not immediately think of the Book of Jeremiah in this way. And yet Jeremiah has a narrative form quite as amenable to dramatic presentation as, say, Genesis. It is the Hebrew tradition of storytelling that makes the task so inviting and the outcome so effective.

Old Testament Precedent

We like to think that further encouragement is given to the exercise of dramatizing the Bible for worship by one special discovery. It does appear that the Hebrew people in temple worship used drama to rehearse the acts of God in their history—notably the crossing of the Red Sea and their deliverance from the slavery of Egypt. Such dramatic presentations were not entertainment—though they would have been marvelously entertaining. And they were far more than visual aids—though Hebrew faith did require each generation to recall, before the next, God's saving interventions, so that his mercy and his demands would not be forgotten. The Hebrew dramas had a teaching role, and they were acts of worship too—precedents of our own "anamnesis," that is, the calling to mind of the saving work of Christ in the drama we term, according to our Christian tradition, the Lord's Supper, the Holy Communion/the Eucharist, or the Mass.

Evidence for a more extended use of drama in Hebrew worship comes from the Psalms. We have only to look at Psalm 118 to see that it is neither a hymn nor merely a meditation. There are obvious character parts and choral parts. And there are even "stage" instructions embedded in the text. For example, verse 27—"With boughs in hand, join in the festal procession up to the horns of the altar"—which, in some traditions, we blindly *sing* as though the psalm were homogeneous. It does not take much imagination to see that what we are dealing with is the script of a drama or the libretto of an opera, set in the context of a magnificent act of worship. Here the intending (and noble?) worshiper approaches the door of the temple and asks to enter to give thanks for God's deliverance. The ministers/priests tell him righteousness is a prerequisite of an approach to God. And the drama progresses from there. Permeating the drama are the resonant choruses of the Hebrew liturgy:

Leader	Let Israel say:
All	His love endures forever.
Leader	Let the house of Aaron say:
All	His love endures forever.
Leader	Let those who fear the LORD say:
All	His love endures forever!

Finally, the worshiper is admitted ("Blessed is he who comes in the name of the LORD") and the celebration begins ("With boughs in hand . . . "). As long as we consider the Old Testament dour and prosaic, its exciting suggestions for our own worship practice will be missed.

New Testament

The New Testament is full of vivid narrative. For the most part dramatizing comes easily and is obviously appropriate. While we have not forced a dramatic pattern upon passages not amenable to such treatment, we have dramatized some of the teaching material where it might at first sight appear that only one voice is required. For instance, where Jesus' words are cast in the rabbinic style that preserved them through the oral period until they became written elements of the Gospels:

Teacher	Blessed are the poor in spirit:
Students	For theirs is the kingdom of heaven.

. . . the teaching of Jesus indeed—but thereafter used in catechetical pattern by the early Christians. We follow their very effective form of dramatizing, and in this way recover its first freshness.

Much of the epistolary material is intentionally omitted from *The Dramatized New Testament* as it is best left as straight prose to be read by a single voice. But there are exceptions; for instance, Saint Paul has his own style of "question and answer":

Question   What advantage is there in being a Jew . . . ?

Answer   Much in every way!

. . . positively inviting dramatization!

Barriers Broken

Much of my life's work has been in the interests of a clearer presentation of the facts of the faith in worship. Centrally within this context, *The Dramatized New Testament* brings the text of Scripture to life. Using *The Dramatized New Testament* means involving people in recalling and recounting their salvation history. The experience is memorable and challenging.

Those who listen to *The Dramatized New Testament* are drawn into the presentation. As the story moves from voice to voice it is very difficult for attention to wander. Useful in all forms of church worship, *The Dramatized New Testament* is especially an ideal focus for the "word" aspect of all-age (so-called family) worship. Even young children, who naturally grow restive during a long and uneventful reading, find their interest and imagination caught up in the narrative as the Scriptures are presented in dramatized form.

We confidently commend this book to churches, youth groups, schools, study groups, and all who work in the area of education. It may be that producers and presenters of religious programs for radio and television will also find inspiration here. We happily anticipate that *The Dramatized New Testament* will enrich our worship by granting us a clearer vision of God and a surer knowledge of the revelation of the eternal purpose for our world in Jesus Christ.

Michael Perry
Summer 1993

Preface to NIV

The New International Version is a completely new translation of the Holy Bible made by over a hundred scholars working directly from the best available Hebrew, Aramaic and Greek texts. It had its beginning in 1965 when, after several years of exploratory study by committees from the Christian Reformed Church and the National Association of Evangelicals, a group of scholars met at Palos Heights, Illinois, and concurred in the need for a new translation of the Bible in contemporary English. This group, though not made up of official church representatives, was transdenominational. Its conclusion was endorsed by a large number of leaders from many denominations who met in Chicago in 1966.

Responsibility for the new version was delegated by the Palos Heights group to a self-governing body of fifteen, the Committee on Bible Translation, composed for the most part of biblical scholars from colleges, universities and seminaries. In 1967 the New York Bible Society (now the International Bible Society) generously undertook the financial sponsorship of the project—a sponsorship that made it possible to enlist the help of many distinguished scholars. The fact that participants from the United States, Great Britain, Canada, Australia and New Zealand worked together gave the project its international scope. That they were from many denominations—including Anglican, Assemblies of God, Baptist, Brethren, Christian Reformed, Church of Christ, Evangelical Free, Lutheran, Mennonite, Methodist, Nazarene, Presbyterian, Wesleyan and other churches—helped to safeguard the translation from sectarian bias.

How it was made helps to give the New International Version its distinctiveness. The translation of each book was assigned to a team of scholars. Next, one of the Intermediate Editorial Committees revised the initial translation, with constant reference to the Hebrew, Aramaic or Greek. Their work then went to one of the General Editorial Committees, which checked it in detail and made another thorough revision. This revision in turn was carefully reviewed by the Committee on Bible Translation, which made further changes and then released the final version for publication. In this way the entire Bible underwent three revisions, during each of which the translation was examined for its faithfulness to the original languages and for its English style.

All this involved many thousands of hours of research and discussion regarding the meaning of the texts and the precise way of putting them into English. It may well be that no other translation has been made by a more thorough process of review and revision from committee to committee than this one.

From the beginning of the project, the Committee on Bible Translation held to certain goals for the New International Version: that it would be an accurate translation and one that would have clarity and literary quality and so prove suitable for public and private reading, teaching, preaching, memorizing and liturgical use. The Committee also sought to preserve some measure of continuity with the long tradition of translating the Scriptures into English.

In working toward these goals, the translators were united in their commitment to the authority and infallibility of the Bible as God's Word in written form. They believe that it contains the divine answer to the deepest needs of humanity, that it sheds unique light on our path in a dark world, and that it sets forth the way to our eternal well-being.

The first concern of the translators has been the accuracy of the translation and its fidelity to the thought of the biblical writers. They have weighed the significance of the lexical and grammatical details of the Hebrew, Aramaic and Greek texts. At the same time, they have striven for more than a word-for-word translation. Because thought patterns and syntax differ from language to language, faithful communication of the meaning of the writers of the Bible demands frequent modifications in sentence structure and constant regard for the contextual meanings of words.

A sensitive feeling for style does not always accompany scholarship. Accordingly the Committee on Bible Translation submitted the developing version to a number of stylistic consultants. Two on them read every book of both Old and New Testaments twice—once before and once after the last major revision—and made invaluable suggestions. Samples of the translation were tested for clarity and ease of reading by various kinds of people—young and old, highly educated and less well educated, ministers and laymen.

Concern for clear and natural English—that the New International Version should be idiomatic but not idiosyncratic, contemporary but not dated—motivated the translators and consultants. At the same time, they tried to reflect the differing styles of the biblical writers. In view of the international use of English, the translators sought to avoid obvious Americanisms on the one hand and obvious Anglicisms on the other. A British edition reflects the comparatively few differences of significant idiom and of spelling.

As for the traditional pronouns "thou," thee" and "thine" in reference to the Deity, the translators judged that to use these archaisms (along with the old verb forms such as "doest," "wouldest" and "hadst") would violate accuracy in translation. Neither Hebrew, Aramaic nor Greek uses special pronouns for the persons of the Godhead. A present-day translation is not enhanced by forms that in the time of the King James Version were used in everyday speech, whether referring to God or man.

For the Old Testament the standard Hebrew text, the Masoretic Text as published in the latest editions of *Biblia Hebraica,* was used throughout. The Dead Sea Scrolls contain material bearing on an earlier stage of the Hebrew text. They were consulted, as were the Samaritan Pentateuch and the ancient scribal traditions relating to textual changes. Sometimes a variant Hebrew reading in the margin of the Masoretic Text was followed instead of the text itself. Such instances, being variants within the Masoretic tradition, are not specified by footnotes. In rare cases, words in the consonantal text were divided differently from the way they appear in the Masoretic Text. Footnotes indicate this. The translators also consulted the more important early versions—the Septuagint; Aquila, Symmachus and Theodotion; the Vulgate; the Syriac Peshitta; the Targums; and for the Psalms the *Juxta Hebraica* of Jerome. Readings from these versions were occasionally followed where the Masoretic Text seemed doubtful and where accepted principles of textual criticism showed that one or more of these textual witnesses appeared to provide the correct reading. Such instances are footnoted. Sometimes vowel letters and vowel signs did not, in the judgment of the translators, represent the correct vowels for the original consonantal text. Accordingly some words were read with a different set of vowels. These instances are usually not indicated by footnotes.

The Greek text used in translating the New Testament was an eclectic one. No other piece of ancient literature has such an abundance of manuscript witnesses as does the New Testament. Where existing manuscripts differ, the translators made their choice of readings according to accepted principles of New Testament textual criticism. Footnotes call attention to places where there was uncertainty about what the original text was. The best current printed texts of the Greek New Testament were used.

There is a sense in which the work of translation is never wholly finished. This applies to all great literature and uniquely so to the Bible. In 1973 the New Testament in the New International Version was published. Since then, suggestions for corrections and revisions have been received from various sources. The Committee on Bible Translation carefully considered the suggestions and adopted a number of them. These were incorporated in the first printing of the entire Bible in 1978. Additional revisions were made by the Committee on Bible Translation in 1983 and appear in printings after that date.

As in other ancient documents, the precise meaning of the biblical texts is sometimes uncertain. This is more often the case with the Hebrew and Aramaic texts than with the Greek text. Although archaeological and linguistic discoveries in this century aid in understanding difficult passages, some uncertainties remain. The more significant of these have been called to the reader's attention in the footnotes.

In regard to the divine name *YHWH*, commonly referred to as the *Tetragrammaton,* the translators adopted the device used in most English versions of rendering that name as "Lord" in capital letters to distinguish it from *Adonai,* another Hebrew word rendered "Lord," for which small letters are used. Wherever the two names stand together in the Old Testament as a compound name of God, they are rendered "Sovereign Lord."

Because for most readers today the phrases "the Lord of hosts" and "God of hosts" have little meaning, this version renders them "the Lord Almighty" and "God Almighty." These renderings convey the sense of the Hebrew, namely, "he who is sovereign over all the 'hosts' (powers) in heaven and on earth, especially over the 'hosts' (armies) of Israel." For readers unacquainted with Hebrew this does not make clear the distinction between *Sabaoth* ("hosts" or "Almighty") and *Shaddai* (which can also be translated "Almighty"), but the latter occurs infrequently and is always footnoted. When *Adonai* and *YHWH Sabaoth* occur together, they are rendered "the Lord, the Lord Almighty."

As for other proper nouns, the familiar spellings of the King James Version are generally retained. Names traditionally spelled with "ch," except where it is final, are usually spelled in this translation with "k" or "c," since the biblical languages do not have the sound that "ch" frequently indicates in English—for example, in *chant.* For well-known names such as Zechariah, however, the traditional spelling has been retained. Variation in the spelling of names in the original languages has usually not been indicated. Where a person or place has two or more different names in the Hebrew, Aramaic or Greek texts, the more familiar one has generally been used, with footnotes where needed.

To achieve clarity the translators sometimes supplied words not in the original texts but required by the context. If there was uncertainty about such material, it is enclosed in brackets. Also for the sake of clarity or style, nouns, including some proper nouns, are sometimes substituted for pronouns, and vice versa. And though the Hebrew writers often shifted back and forth between first, second and third personal pronouns without change of antecedent, this translation often makes them uniform, in accordance with English style and without the use of footnotes.

Poetical passages are printed as poetry, that is, with indentation of lines and with separate stanzas. These are generally designed to reflect the structure of Hebrew poetry. This poetry is normally characterized by parallelism in balanced lines. Most of the poetry in the Bible is in the Old Testament, and scholars differ regarding the scansion of Hebrew lines. The translators determined the stanza divisions for the most part by analysis of the subject matter. The stanzas therefore serve as poetic paragraphs.

As an aid to the reader, italicized sectional headings are inserted in most of the books. They are not to be regarded as part of the NIV text, are not for oral reading, and are not intended to dictate the interpretation of the sections they head.

The footnotes in this version are of several kinds, most of which need no explanation. Those giving alternative translations begin with "Or" and generally introduce the alternative with the last word preceding it in the text, except when it is a single-word alternative; in poetry quoted in a footnote a slant mark indicates a line division. Footnotes introduced by "Or" do not have uniform significance. In some cases two possible translations were considered to have about equal validity. In other cases, though the translators were convinced that the translation in the text was correct, they judged that another interpretation was possible and of sufficient importance to be represented in a footnote.

In the New Testament, footnotes that refer to uncertainty regarding the original text are introduced by "Some manuscripts" or similar expressions. In the Old Testament, evidence for the reading chosen is given first and evidence for the alternative is added after a semicolon (for example: Septuagint; Hebrew *father*). In such notes the term "Hebrew" refers to the Masoretic Text.

It should be noted that minerals, flora and fauna, architectural details, articles of clothing and jewelry, musical instruments and other articles cannot always be identified with precision. Also measures of capacity in the biblical period are particularly uncertain (see the table of weights and measures following the text).

Like all translations of the Bible, made as they are by imperfect man, this one undoubtedly falls short of its goals. Yet we are grateful to God for the extent to which he has enabled us to realize these goals and for the strength he has given us and our colleagues to complete our task. We offer this version of the Bible to him in whose name and for whose glory it has been made. We pray that it will lead many into a better understanding of the Holy Scriptures and a fuller knowledge of Jesus Christ the incarnate Word, of whom the Scriptures so faithfully testify.

The Committee on Bible Translation

June 1978
(Revised August 1983)

Names of the translators and editors may be secured
from the International Bible Society,
translation sponsors of the New International Version,
P.O. Box 62970, Colorado Springs, Colorado 80962-2970

Acknowledgments

As editor of *The Dramatized New Testament* I gladly acknowledge the skills of the teams of experts who prepared the outstanding and now celebrated New International Version of the Bible. I have appreciated the advice of the Reverend Kathleen Bowe upon the translation of my Liturgical Psalms, of the Reverend Robert Backhouse on all aspects of dramatization and typesetting and of Miss Janet Henderson on matters of copyright. My thanks go to my typist, Ann, my secretary, Bunty, and my daughter, Helen, for their conscientious work on copy, proofs, and indexes. I am grateful to church leaders and other authorities for their kind commendations and encouragement. I am indebted to the friendly staff at Baker Book House. I know that all who have cooperated in its production will find great satisfaction in the enthusiasm with which I am confident *The Dramatized New Testament* will be received.

M.A.P.

Using *The Dramatized New Testament*

Welcome to a new and powerful resource! If you are a minister, teacher, or leader, you will want to know how you can use this book to the greatest effect.

Realism

In designing *The Dramatized New Testament* we have tried to be realistic about the pressure upon ministers, teachers, and leaders: on the whole they require a book that can be used spontaneously and without great forethought, preparation, or rehearsal. We suggest that each organization using *The Dramatized New Testament* eventually needs five copies because, on average, there are five characters to a script. Then, at a moment's notice, willing readers can be given a copy each and invited to fill a character part. All characters are listed at the foot of each reading.

Superfluous "he said"s and the like are already excised from the text (with the permission of the copyright holders). While appropriate in prose, they are intrusive—sometimes even humorous—in drama. Usually in *The Dramatized New Testament* they are left in at the beginning of the piece, in order to establish the character, and then omitted thereafter. Further phrases that for similar reasons might be thought to make performance stilted are enclosed in bold square brackets: [and]. But such phrases or sentences should not be omitted without considering the particular implications. To omit them may well enliven the drama, but it will require the cast to compensate for the omission. This can either be done visually, by turning to one of the other characters, or aurally, by a change of voice. The best solution will depend on the local circumstances, the initiative of the leader, and the ability of the participants. Therefore, a rule of thumb might be—*only when consultation or rehearsal is possible, omit phrases in bold square brackets.*

The proprietors of the NIV text have required the insertion of additional square brackets (not bold) to show where explanatory text has been added. Please distinguish between this and the phrases suitable for omission. Also, to aid in effective dramatic reading, words have been italicized for emphasis occasionally that do not appear in italics in the NIV. Please note that, unless they designate foreign words, all italics in the text have been added by us.

Shortening an Episode

Bold square brackets have a different function when they enclose one or more paragraphs: they indicate where the reading may sensibly be shortened. Unless a sermon, service, talk, or discussion requires use of these longer sections, they are best left out in the interests of lively presentation and greater impact upon an audience.

Local Reproduction

Applications for reproduction of material from *The Dramatized New Testament* in the world outside North America may be addressed to Hope Publishing Company, Carol Stream, Illinois 60188 (phone 708-665-3200, FAX 708-665-2552, WATS 800-323-1049). For further information see the copyright page.

Audibility

Use of *The Dramatized New Testament* has a positive effect on the attention that a reading is given by a congregation, class, youth group, or study group. It also makes the content of the reading more memorable—not least to those who have participated. Much depends on audibility; so care needs to be taken in larger buildings. In church, or in a school assembly hall, a stage holding a minimum of five people can be used to advantage. Where appropriate, a microphone with a wide field that will pick up all the speakers should be used; or separate microphones might be considered. This sort of preparation will enable the minister/leader to involve people whose voices are less clear and not so strong.

Casting

It is obviously important that a strong voice should be cast for any key character, such as the **Narrator**. In a church service, this part can most usefully be given to the person who would have taken the Scripture reading if it had not been dramatized, thus ensuring that no one feels usurped by what should be a welcome development in worship. It is worth noting that more male than female characters speak in the Bible. However, when using *The Drama-*

tized New Testament, a good balance can still be obtained by employing female voices for narration, for the frequent anonymous **Persons**, and in the teaching passages that divide into **Voice 1, Voice 2**. Here it is good to have a contrast between the speakers.

Where **Voices 1–3** or **Persons 1–3** are used, participants should stand together in a group. Where **the Lord** or **God** speaks as a prophetic utterance and not in direct conversation, it is best for the reader to stand apart from the rest—even to be unseen.

Actions

There will be occasions—both formal and informal—when participants can add actions to a presentation from *The Dramatized New Testament.* Then, prior agreement over what is to be done is a safeguard against unintended humorous accidents! A rehearsal will be necessary unless the actors are very confident and experienced. At the rehearsal it is sensible to have someone watching who is able to assess the drama's impact on the proposed audience, and for the cast to listen and respond to that person's objective criticism. When actions are used in the context of large gatherings, visibility and audibility (especially when the speaker turns away from the audience) are of utmost importance. In seminar and class work, or in small groups, carefully prepared actions will add a startlingly fresh dynamic.

The Gospel of Matthew

The Birth of Jesus Christ
Matthew 1:18–25

Narrator   This is how the birth of Jesus Christ came about: His mother Mary was pledged to be married to Joseph, but before they came together, she was found to be with child through the Holy Spirit. Because Joseph her husband was a righteous man and did not want to expose her to public disgrace, he had in mind to divorce her quietly.

            But after he had considered this, an angel of the Lord appeared to him in a dream:

Angel   Joseph son of David, do not be afraid to take Mary home as your wife, because what is conceived in her is from the Holy Spirit. She will give birth to a son, and you are to give him the name Jesus, because he will save his people from their sins.

Narrator   All this took place to fulfill what the Lord had said through the prophet:

Prophet   The virgin will be with child and will give birth to a son, and they will call him Immanuel—

Narrator   Which means, "God with us." (PAUSE) When Joseph woke up, he did what the angel of the Lord had commanded him and took Mary home as his wife. But he had no union with her until she gave birth to a son. And he gave him the name Jesus.

Cast: **Narrator, Angel, Prophet.** (See also Appendix: Christmas Readings, page 415.)

The Visit of the Magi
Matthew 2:1–11 [12]

Narrator   After Jesus was born in Bethlehem in Judea, during the time of King Herod, Magi from the east came to Jerusalem and asked:

Magi   Where is the one who has been born king of the Jews? We saw his star in the east and have come to worship him.

Narrator   When King Herod heard this he was disturbed, and all Jerusalem with him. When he had called together all the people's chief priests and teachers of the law, he asked them where the Christ was to be born. They replied:

Chief priest   In Bethlehem in Judea.

Teacher   For this is what the prophet has written:

Prophet	But you, Bethlehem, in the land of Judah,
	    are by no means least among the rulers of Judah;
	for out of you will come a ruler
	    who will be the shepherd of my people Israel.

Narrator	Then Herod called the Magi secretly and found out from them the exact time the star had appeared. He sent them to Bethlehem [and said]:
Herod	Go and make a careful search for the child. As soon as you find him, report to me, so that I too may go and worship him.
Narrator	After they had heard the king, they went on their way, and the star they had seen in the east went ahead of them until it stopped over the place where the child was. When they saw the star, they were overjoyed. On coming to the house, they saw the child with his mother Mary, and they bowed down and worshipped him. Then they opened their treasures and presented him with gifts of gold and of incense and of myrrh. [And having been warned in a dream not to go back to Herod, they returned to their country by another route.]

Cast: **Narrator, Magi, Chief priest, Teacher** (can be the same as Chief priest), **Prophet, Herod.**
((See also Appendix: Christmas Readings, page 416.)

The Escape to Egypt
Matthew 2:13–18

Narrator	When [the Magi] had gone, an angel of the Lord appeared to Joseph in a dream:
Angel	Get up, take the child and his mother and escape to Egypt. Stay there until I tell you, for Herod is going to search for the child to kill him.
Narrator	So he got up, took the child and his mother during the night and left for Egypt, where he stayed until the death of Herod. And so was fulfilled what the Lord had said through the prophet:
Prophet	Out of Egypt I called my son.
Narrator	When Herod realized that he had been outwitted by the Magi, he was furious, and he gave orders to kill all the boys in Bethlehem and its vicinity who were two years old and under, in accordance with the time he had learned from the Magi. Then what was said through the prophet Jeremiah was fulfilled:

Jeremiah	A voice is heard in Ramah,
	    weeping and great mourning,
	Rachel weeping for her children
	    and refusing to be comforted,
	because they are no more.

Cast: **Narrator, Angel, Prophet, Jeremiah.** (See also Appendix: Christmas Readings, pages 420–21.)

The Return to Nazareth
Matthew 2:19–23

Narrator After Herod died, an angel of the Lord appeared in a dream to Joseph in Egypt:

Angel Get up, take the child and his mother and go to the land of Israel, for those who were trying to take the child's life are dead.

Narrator So [Joseph] got up, took the child and his mother and went to the land of Israel. (PAUSE) But when he heard that Archelaus was reigning in Judea in place of his father Herod, he was afraid to go there. Having been warned in a dream, he withdrew to the district of Galilee, and he went and lived in a town called Nazareth. So was fulfilled what was said through the prophets:

Prophet He will be called a Nazarene.

Cast: **Narrator, Angel, Prophet.** (See also Appendix: Christmas Readings, page 421.)

John the Baptist Prepares the Way
Matthew 3:1–12

Narrator John the Baptist came, preaching in the Desert of Judea:

John Repent, for the kingdom of heaven is near.

Narrator This is he who was spoken of through the prophet Isaiah:

Isaiah A voice of one calling in the desert,
"Prepare the way for the Lord,
　make straight paths for him."

Narrator John's clothes were made of camel's hair, and he had a leather belt around his waist. His food was locusts and wild honey. People went out to him from Jerusalem and all Judea and the whole region of the Jordan. Confessing their sins, they were baptized by him in the Jordan River. (PAUSE)

But when [John] saw many of the Pharisees and Sadducees coming to where he was baptizing, he said to them:

John You brood of vipers! Who warned you to flee from the coming wrath? Produce fruit in keeping with repentance. And do not think you can say to yourselves, "We have Abraham as our father." I tell you that out of these stones God can raise up children for Abraham. The ax is already at the root of the trees, and every tree that does not produce good fruit will be cut down and thrown into the fire.

I baptize you with water for repentance. But after me will come one who is more powerful than I, whose sandals I am not fit to carry. He will baptize you with the Holy Spirit and with fire. His winnowing fork is in his hand, and he will clear his threshing floor, gathering his wheat into the barn and burning up the chaff with unquenchable fire.

Cast: **Narrator, John, Isaiah**

The Baptism of Jesus
Matthew 3:13–17

Narrator	Jesus came from Galilee to the Jordan to be baptized by John. But John tried to deter him:
John	I need to be baptized by you, and do you come to me?
[Narrator	Jesus replied:]
Jesus	Let it be so now; it is proper for us to do this to fulfill all righteousness.
Narrator	Then John consented. (PAUSE)
	As soon as Jesus was baptized, he went up out of the water. At that moment heaven was opened, and he saw the Spirit of God descending like a dove and lighting on him. And a voice from heaven said:
Voice	This is my Son, whom I love; with him I am well pleased.

Cast: **Narrator, John, Jesus, Voice**

The Temptation of Jesus
Matthew 4:1–11

Narrator	Jesus was led by the Spirit into the desert to be tempted by the devil. After fasting forty days and forty nights, he was hungry. The tempter came to him and said:
The Devil	If you are the Son of God, tell these stones to become bread.
[Narrator	Jesus answered:]
Jesus	It is written: "Man does not live on bread alone, but on every word that comes from the mouth of God."
Narrator	Then the devil took him to the holy city and had him stand on the highest point of the temple, [and said to him:]
The Devil	If you are the Son of God, throw yourself down. For it is written: "He will command his angels concerning you, and they will lift you up in their hands, so that you will not strike your foot against a stone."
Jesus	It is also written: "Do not put the Lord your God to the test."
Narrator	Again, the devil took him to a very high mountain and showed him all the kingdoms of the world and their splendor.

The Devil	All this I will give you, if you will bow down and worship me.
Jesus	Away from me, Satan! For it is written: "Worship the Lord your God, and serve him only."
Narrator	Then the devil left him, and angels came and attended him.

Cast: **Narrator, the Devil, Jesus**

Jesus Begins to Preach
Matthew 4:12–25

Narrator	When Jesus heard that John had been put in prison, he returned to Galilee. Leaving Nazareth, he went and lived in Capernaum, which was by the lake in the area of Zebulun and Naphtali—to fulfill what was said through the prophet Isaiah:

Isaiah	Land of Zebulun and land of Naphtali,
	    the way to the sea, along the Jordan,
	    Galilee of the Gentiles—
	the people living in darkness
	    have seen a great light;
	on those living in the land of the shadow of death
	    a light has dawned.

Narrator	From that time on Jesus began to preach:
Jesus	Repent, for the kingdom of heaven is near.
Narrator	As Jesus was walking beside the Sea of Galilee, he saw two brothers, Simon called Peter and his brother Andrew. They were casting a net into the lake, for they were fishermen. [Jesus said:]
Jesus	Come, follow me, and I will make you fishers of men.
Narrator	At once they left their nets and followed him. (PAUSE) Going on from there, he saw two other brothers, James son of Zebedee and his brother John. They were in a boat with their father Zebedee, preparing their nets. Jesus called them, and immediately they left the boat and their father and followed him. (PAUSE) Jesus went throughout Galilee, teaching in their synagogues, preaching the good news of the kingdom, and healing every disease and sickness among the people. News about him spread all over Syria, and people brought to him all who were ill with various diseases, those suffering severe pain, the demon-possessed, those having seizures, and the paralyzed, and he healed them. Large crowds from Galilee, the Decapolis, Jerusalem, Judea and the region across the Jordan followed him.

Cast: **Narrator, Isaiah, Jesus**

The Calling of the First Disciples
From John 1 and Matthew 4 and 9

Narrator	Jesus decided to leave for Galilee. Finding Philip, he said to him:
Jesus	Follow me.
Narrator	Philip found Nathanael [and told him:]
Philip	We have found the one Moses wrote about in the Law, and about whom the prophets also wrote—Jesus of Nazareth, the son of Joseph.
[Narrator	Nathanael asked:]
Nathanael	Nazareth! Can anything good come from there?
Philip	Come and see.
Narrator	When Jesus saw Nathanael approaching, he said of him:
Jesus	Here is a true Israelite, in whom there is nothing false.
Nathanael	How do you know me?
Jesus	I saw you while you were still under the fig tree before Philip called you.
Nathanael	Rabbi, you are the Son of God; you are the King of Israel.
Narrator	As Jesus was walking beside the Sea of Galilee, he saw two brothers, Simon called Peter and his brother Andrew. They were casting a net into the lake, for they were fishermen. [Jesus said:]
Jesus	Come, follow me, and I will make you fishers of men.
Narrator	At once they left their nets and followed him. (PAUSE)
	Going on from there, [Jesus] saw two other brothers, James son of Zebedee and his brother John. They were in a boat with their father Zebedee, preparing their nets. Jesus called them, and immediately they left the boat and their father and followed him. (PAUSE)
	As Jesus went on from there, he saw a man named Matthew sitting at the tax collector's booth. [He told him:]
Jesus	Follow me.
Narrator	Matthew got up and followed him. (PAUSE)
	While Jesus was having dinner at Matthew's house, many tax collectors and "sinners" came and ate with him and his disciples. When the Pharisees saw this, they asked his disciples:
Pharisee	Why does your teacher eat with tax collectors and "sinners"?
Narrator	On hearing this, Jesus said:

| Jesus | It is not the healthy who need a doctor, but the sick. But go and learn what this means: "I desire mercy, not sacrifice." For I have not come to call the righteous, but sinners. |

Cast: **Narrator, Jesus, Philip, Nathanael, Pharisee**

The Beatitudes
Matthew 5:3–12

Jesus	Blessed are the poor in spirit:
Students	for theirs is the kingdom of heaven.
Jesus	Blessed are those who mourn:
Students	for they will be comforted.
Jesus	Blessed are the meek:
Students	for they will inherit the earth.
Jesus	Blessed are those who hunger and thirst for righteousness:
Students	for they will be filled.
Jesus	Blessed are the merciful:
Students	for they will be shown mercy.
Jesus	Blessed are the pure in heart:
Students	for they will see God.
Jesus	Blessed are the peacemakers:
Students	for they will be called sons of God.
Jesus	Blessed are those who are persecuted because of righteousness:
Students	for theirs is the kingdom of heaven.
Jesus	Blessed are you when people insult you, persecute you and falsely say all kinds of evil against you because of me. Rejoice and be glad, because great is your reward in heaven, for in the same way they persecuted the prophets who were before you.

Cast: **Jesus, Students**. (This reading is set out to reflect classic rabbinical teaching method.)

Jesus' Teaching about Anger
Matthew 5:21–24

Jesus	You have heard that it was said to the people long ago:
Rabbi	Do not murder, and anyone who murders will be subject to judgment.
Jesus	But I tell you that anyone who is angry with his brother will be subject to judgment. Again, anyone who says to his brother:

Angry person	Raca!
Jesus	Is answerable to the Sanhedrin. But anyone who says:
Angry person	You fool!
Jesus	Will be in danger of the fire of hell.
	Therefore, if you are offering your gift at the altar and there remember that your brother has something against you, leave your gift there in front of the altar. First go and be reconciled to your brother; then come and offer your gift.

Cast: **Jesus, Rabbi, Angry person**

Jesus' Teaching about Adultery and Divorce
Matthew 5:27–32

Jesus	You have heard that it was said:
Rabbi	Do not commit adultery.
Jesus	But I tell you that anyone who looks at a woman lustfully has already committed adultery with her in his heart. If your right eye causes you to sin, gouge it out and throw it away. It is better for you to lose one part of your body than for your whole body to be thrown into hell. And if your right hand causes you to sin, cut it off and throw it away. It is better for you to lose one part of your body than for your whole body to go into hell. (PAUSE)
	It has been said:
Rabbi	Anyone who divorces his wife must give her a certificate of divorce.
Jesus	But I tell you that anyone who divorces his wife, except for marital unfaithfulness, causes her to become an adulteress, and anyone who marries the divorced woman commits adultery.

Cast: **Jesus, Rabbi**

Jesus' Teaching about Oaths
Matthew 5:33–37

Jesus	You have heard that it was said to the people long ago:
Rabbi	Do not break your oath, but keep the oaths you have made to the Lord.
Jesus	But I tell you, Do not swear at all: either by heaven, for it is God's throne; or by the earth, for it is his footstool; or by Jerusalem, for it is the city of the Great King. And do not swear by your head, for you can-

not make even one hair white or black. Simply let your "Yes" be "Yes," and your "No," "No"; anything beyond this comes from the evil one.

Cast: **Jesus, Rabbi**

Jesus' Teaching on Prayer [and Fasting]
Matthew 6:5–15 [16–18]

Jesus   When you pray, do not be like the hypocrites, for they love to pray standing in the synagogues and on the street corners to be seen by men. I tell you the truth, they have received their reward in full. But when you pray, go into your room, close the door and pray to your Father, who is unseen. Then your Father, who sees what is done in secret, will reward you. (PAUSE) And when you pray, do not keep on babbling like pagans, for they think they will be heard because of their many words. Do not be like them, for your Father knows what you need before you ask him. This, then, is how you should pray:

Leader   Our Father in heaven,

Students   hallowed be your name,

Leader   your kingdom come,

Students   your will be done on earth as it is in heaven.

Leader and **student**   Give us today our daily bread.

Leader   Forgive us our debts,

Students   as we also have forgiven our debtors.

Leader   And lead us not into temptation,

Students   but deliver us from the evil one.

Jesus   For if you forgive men when they sin against you, your heavenly Father will also forgive you. But if you do not forgive men their sins, your Father will not forgive your sins.

[When you fast, do not look somber as the hypocrites do, for they disfigure their faces to show men they are fasting. I tell you the truth, they have received their reward in full. But when you fast, put oil on your head and wash your face, so that it will not be obvious to men that you are fasting, but only to your Father, who is unseen; and your Father, who sees what is done in secret, will reward you.]

Cast: **Jesus, Leader** (can be the same as Jesus), **Students** (two or more). (This reading is arranged to reflect the rabbinic style of teaching. For a straightforward treatment see pages 169–70.)

Jesus' Teaching about God and Possessions
Matthew 6:24–34

Jesus   No one can serve two masters. Either he will hate the one and love the other, or he will be devoted to the one and despise the other. You cannot serve both God and Money.

Therefore I tell you, do not worry about your life, what you will eat or drink; or about your body, what you will wear. Is not life more important than food, and the body more important than clothes? Look at the birds of the air; they do not sow or reap or store away in barns, and yet your heavenly Father feeds them. Are you not much more valuable than they? Who of you by worrying can add a single hour to his life?

And why do you worry about clothes? See how the lilies of the field grow. They do not labor or spin. Yet I tell you that not even Solomon in all his splendor was dressed like one of these. If that is how God clothes the grass of the field, which is here today and tomorrow is thrown into the fire, will he not much more clothe you, O you of little faith? So do not worry [, saying]:

Person 1   What shall we eat?

Person 2   What shall we drink?

Person 3   What shall we wear?

Jesus   For the *pagans* run after all these things, and your heavenly Father knows that you need them. But seek first his kingdom and his righteousness, and all these things will be given to you as well. Therefore do not worry about tomorrow, for tomorrow will worry about itself. Each day has enough trouble of its own.

Cast: **Jesus, Person 1, Person 2, Person 3** (can be the same as Persons 1 and 2)

Judging Others
Matthew 7:1–5

Jesus   Do not judge, or you too will be judged. For in the same way you judge others, you will be judged, and with the measure you use, it will be measured to you. (PAUSE)

Why do you look at the speck of sawdust in your brother's eye and pay no attention to the plank in your own eye? How can you say to your brother:

Person   Let me take the speck out of your eye—

| Jesus | When all the time there is a plank in your own eye? You hypocrite, first take the plank out of your own eye, and then you will see clearly to remove the speck from your brother's eye. |

Cast: **Jesus, Person**

I Never Knew You
Matthew 7:21–23

Jesus	Not everyone who says to me:
Person 1	Lord!
Person 2	Lord!
Jesus	Will enter the kingdom of heaven, but only he who does the will of my Father who is in heaven. Many will say to me on that day:
Person 1	Lord!
Person 2	Lord!
Person 1	Did we not prophesy in your name?
Person 2	And in your name drive out demons?
Person 1	And perform many miracles?
Jesus	Then I will tell them plainly:
Jesus as Judge	I never knew you. Away from me, you evildoers!

Cast: **Jesus, Person 1, Person 2, Jesus as Judge** (can be the same as Jesus)

Jesus' Parable of the Wise and Foolish Builders
Matthew 7:24–29

Voice 1	Everyone who hears these words of mine and puts them into practice is like a wise man who built his house on the rock.
Voice 2	The rain came down, the streams rose, and the winds blew and beat against that house; yet it did not fall, because it had its foundation on the rock.
Voice 1	But everyone who hears these words of mine and does not put them into practice is like a foolish man who built his house on sand.
Voice 2	The rain came down, the streams rose, and the winds blew and beat against that house, and it fell with a great crash.

| Narrator | When Jesus had finished saying these things, the crowds were amazed at his teaching, because he taught as one who had authority, and not as their teachers of the law. |

Cast: **Voice 1, Voice 2, Narrator**

Jesus Heals People
Matthew 8:1–13 [14–17]

Narrator	When [Jesus] came down from the mountainside, large crowds followed him. A man with leprosy came and knelt before him.
Man	Lord, if you are willing, you can make me clean.
Narrator	Jesus reached out his hand and touched the man.
Jesus	I am willing. Be clean!
Narrator	Immediately he was cured of his leprosy.
Jesus	See that you don't tell anyone. But go, show yourself to the priest and offer the gift Moses commanded, as a testimony to them. (PAUSE)
Narrator	When Jesus had entered Capernaum, a centurion came to him, asking for help.
Centurion	Lord, my servant lies at home paralyzed and in terrible suffering.
Jesus	I will go and heal him.
Centurion	Lord, I do not deserve to have you come under my roof. But just say the word, and my servant will be healed. For I myself am a man under authority, with soldiers under me. I tell this one, "Go," and he goes; and that one, "Come," and he comes. I say to my servant, "Do this," and he does it.
Narrator	When Jesus heard this, he was astonished and said to those following him:
Jesus (to crowd)	I tell you the truth, I have not found anyone in Israel with such great faith. I say to you that many will come from the east and the west, and will take their places at the feast with Abraham, Isaac and Jacob in the kingdom of heaven. But the subjects of the kingdom will be thrown outside, into the darkness, where there will be weeping and gnashing of teeth.
Jesus (to centurion)	Go! It will be done just as you believed it would.
Narrator	And his servant was healed at that very hour. (PAUSE)
	[When Jesus came into Peter's house, he saw Peter's mother-in-law lying in bed with a fever. He touched her hand and the fever left her, and she got up and began to wait on him.

When evening came, many who were demon-possessed were brought to him, and he drove out the spirits with a word and healed all the sick. This was to fulfill what was spoken through the prophet Isaiah:

Isaiah He took up our infirmities
and carried our diseases.]

Cast: **Narrator, Man, Jesus, Centurion,** [**Isaiah** (can be the same as Narrator)]

The Cost of Following Jesus (i)
Matthew 8:18–22

Narrator When Jesus saw the crowd around him, he gave orders to cross to the other side of the lake. Then a teacher of the law came to him [and said:]

Lawyer Teacher, I will follow you wherever you go.

[Narrator Jesus replied:]

Jesus Foxes have holes and birds of the air have nests, but the Son of Man has no place to lay his head.

Narrator Another disciple said to him:

Disciple Lord, first let me go and bury my father.

Narrator But Jesus told him:

Jesus
(to disciple) Follow me, and let the dead bury their own dead.

Cast: **Narrator, Lawyer, Jesus, Disciple**

Jesus Calms the Storm
Matthew 8:23–27

Narrator [Jesus] got into the boat and his disciples followed him. Without warning, a furious storm came up on the lake, so that the waves swept over the boat. But Jesus was sleeping. The disciples went and woke him:

Disciples Lord, save us! We're going to drown!

[Narrator He replied:]

Jesus You of little faith, why are you so afraid?

Narrator Then he got up and rebuked the winds and the waves, and it was completely calm. The men were amazed:

Disciples What kind of man is this? Even the winds and the waves obey him!

Cast: **Narrator, Disciples, Jesus**

The Healing of Two Demon-possessed Men
Matthew 8:28–34

Narrator	When [Jesus] arrived . . . in the region of the Gadarenes, two demon-possessed men coming from the tombs met him. They were so violent that no one could pass that way.
Man 1	What do you want with us, Son of God?
Man 2	Have you come here to torture us before the appointed time?
Narrator	Some distance from them a large herd of pigs was feeding. The demons begged Jesus:
Demon	If you drive us out, send us into the herd of pigs.
Narrator	He said to them:
Jesus	Go!
Narrator	So they came out and went into the pigs, and the whole herd rushed down the steep bank into the lake and died in the water. (PAUSE) Those tending the pigs ran off, went into the town and reported all this, including what had happened to the demon-possessed men. Then the whole town went out to meet Jesus. And when they saw him, they pleaded with him to leave their region.

Cast: **Narrator, Man 1, Man 2, Demon, Jesus**

Jesus Heals a Paralytic
Matthew 9:1–8

Narrator	Jesus stepped into a boat, crossed over and came to his own town. Some men brought to him a paralytic, lying on a mat. When Jesus saw their faith, he said to the paralytic:
Jesus	Take heart, son; your sins are forgiven.
Narrator	At this, some of the teachers of the law said to themselves:
Lawyer	This fellow is blaspheming!
Narrator	Knowing their thoughts, Jesus said:
Jesus	Why do you entertain evil thoughts in your hearts? Which is easier: to say, "Your sins are forgiven," or to say, "Get up and walk"? But so that you may know that the Son of Man has authority on earth to forgive sins. . . .
[Narrator	Then he said to the paralytic:]
Jesus (to man)	Get up, take your mat and go home.

| Narrator | And the man got up and went home. When the crowd saw this, they were filled with awe; and they praised God, who had given such authority to men. |

Cast: **Narrator, Jesus, Lawyer**

The Calling of Matthew
Matthew 9:9–13

Narrator	[Jesus] saw a man named Matthew sitting at the tax collector's booth. [He told him:]
Jesus	Follow me.
Narrator	And Matthew got up and followed him. While Jesus was having dinner at Matthew's house, many tax collectors and "sinners" came and ate with him and his disciples. When the Pharisees saw this, they asked his disciples:
Pharisee	Why does your teacher eat with tax collectors and "sinners"?
Narrator	On hearing this, Jesus said:
Jesus	It is not the healthy who need a doctor, but the sick. But go and learn what this means:
Hosea	I desire mercy, not sacrifice.
Jesus	For I have not come to call the righteous, but sinners.

Cast: **Narrator, Jesus, Pharisee, Hosea** (can be the same as Jesus). (See also comprehensive text on pages 28–29 and 214–16.)

Jesus Questioned about Fasting
Matthew 9:14–17

Narrator	John's disciples came and asked [Jesus]:
Person	How is it that we and the Pharisees fast, but your disciples do not fast?
[Narrator	Jesus answered:]
Jesus	How can the guests of the bridegroom mourn while he is with them? The time will come when the bridegroom will be taken from them; then they will fast.
	No one sews a patch of unshrunk cloth on an old garment, for the patch will pull away from the garment, making the tear worse. Neither do men pour new wine into old wineskins. If they do, the skins will burst, the wine will run out and the wineskins will be ruined. No, they pour new wine into new wineskins, and both are preserved.

Cast: **Narrator, Person, Jesus**

A Dead Girl
and a Sick Woman
Matthew 9:18–26

Narrator   A ruler came and knelt before [Jesus] and said:

Ruler   My daughter has just died. But come and put your hand on her, and she will live.

Narrator   Jesus got up and went with him, and so did his disciples. (PAUSE)

Just then a woman who had been subject to bleeding for twelve years came up behind him and touched the edge of his cloak. [She said to herself:]

Woman   If I only touch his cloak, I will be healed.

Narrator   Jesus turned and saw her. [He said:]

Jesus   Take heart, daughter, your faith has healed you.

Narrator   And the woman was healed from that moment.

When Jesus entered the ruler's house and saw the flute players and the noisy crowd, he said:

Jesus   Go away. The girl is not dead but asleep.

Narrator   But they laughed at him. After the crowd had been put outside, he went in and took the girl by the hand, and she got up. News of this spread through all that region.

Cast: **Narrator, Ruler, Woman, Jesus**

Jesus Heals More People
Matthew 9:27–38

Narrator   Two blind men followed [Jesus,] calling out:

Blind man 1
(shouting)   Son of David!

Blind man 2
(shouting)   Have mercy on us!

Narrator   When [Jesus] had gone indoors, the blind men came to him, and he asked them:

Jesus   Do you believe that I am able to do this?

Blind men
1 and 2   Yes, Lord!

Narrator   Then he touched their eyes.

Jesus   According to your faith will it be done to you.

Narrator	And their sight was restored. (PAUSE) Jesus warned them sternly:
Jesus	See that no one knows about this.
Narrator	But they went out and spread the news about him all over that region. (PAUSE)
	While they were going out, a man who was demon-possessed and could not talk was brought to Jesus. And when the demon was driven out, the man who had been mute spoke. The crowd was amazed.
Person	Nothing like this has ever been seen in Israel.
Narrator	But the Pharisees said:
Pharisee	It is by the prince of demons that he drives out demons. (PAUSE)
Narrator	Jesus went through all the towns and villages, teaching in their synagogues, preaching the good news of the kingdom and healing every disease and sickness. When he saw the crowds, he had compassion on them, because they were harassed and helpless, like sheep without a shepherd. [Then he said to his disciples:]
Jesus	The harvest is plentiful but the workers are few. Ask the Lord of the harvest, therefore, to send out workers into his harvest field.

Cast: **Narrator**, **Blind man 1**, **Blind man 2** (can be the same as Blind man 1), **Jesus**, **Person**, **Pharisee**

Jesus Sends Out the Twelve
Matthew 10:1–8a [8b–15]

Narrator	[Jesus] called his twelve disciples to him and gave them authority to drive out evil spirits and to heal every disease and sickness.
	These are the names of the twelve apostles: first, Simon—
Commentator	Who is called Peter.
Narrator	And his brother Andrew; James son of Zebedee, and his brother John; Philip and Bartholomew; Thomas and Matthew—
Commentator	The tax collector.
Narrator	James son of Alphaeus, and Thaddaeus; Simon the Zealot and Judas Iscariot—
Commentator	Who betrayed [Jesus].
Narrator	These twelve Jesus sent out with the following instructions:
Jesus	Do not go among the Gentiles or enter any town of the Samaritans. Go rather to the lost sheep of Israel. As you go, preach this message: "The kingdom of heaven is near." Heal the sick, raise the dead, cleanse those who have leprosy, drive out demons.

[Freely you have received, freely give. Do not take along any gold or silver or copper in your belts; take no bag for the journey, or extra tunic, or sandals or a staff; for the worker is worth his keep.

Whatever town or village you enter, search for some worthy person there and stay at his house until you leave. As you enter the home, give it your greeting. If the home is deserving, let your peace rest on it; if it is not, let your peace return to you. If anyone will not welcome you or listen to your words, shake the dust off your feet when you leave that home or town. I tell you the truth, it will be more bearable for Sodom and Gomorrah on the day of judgment than for that town.]

Cast: **Narrator, Commentator, Jesus**

The Cost of Following Jesus (ii)

Matthew 10:32–39

Jesus   Whoever acknowledges me before men, I will also acknowledge him before my Father in heaven. But whoever disowns me before men, I will disown him before my Father in heaven.

Do not suppose that I have come to bring peace to the earth. I did not come to bring peace, but a sword. For I have come to turn:

Micah   A man against his father,
        a daughter against her mother,
    a daughter-in-law against her mother-in-law—
        a man's enemies will be the members of his own household.

Jesus   Anyone who loves his father or mother more than me is not worthy of me; anyone who loves his son or daughter more than me is not worthy of me; and anyone who does not take his cross and follow me is not worthy of me. Whoever finds his life will lose it, and whoever loses his life for my sake will find it.

Cast: **Jesus, Micah**

Jesus and John the Baptist

Matthew 11:1–10

Narrator   After Jesus had finished instructing his twelve disciples, he went on . . . to teach and preach in the towns of Galilee.

When John heard in prison what Christ was doing, he sent his disciples to ask him:

Disciple 1   Are you the one who was to come—

Disciple 2	Or should we expect someone else?
Jesus (to disciples)	Go back and report to John what you hear and see: The blind receive sight, the lame walk, those who have leprosy are cured, the deaf hear, the dead are raised, and the good news is preached to the poor. Blessed is the man who does not fall away on account of me.
Narrator	As John's disciples were leaving, Jesus began to speak to the crowd about John:
Jesus (to crowd)	What did you go out into the desert to see? A reed swayed by the wind? If not, what did you go out to see? A man dressed in fine clothes? No, those who wear fine clothes are in kings' palaces. Then what did you go out to see? A prophet? Yes, I tell you, and more than a prophet. This is the one about whom it is written:
Malachi	I will send my messenger ahead of you, who will prepare your way before you.

Cast: **Narrator, Disciple 1, Disciple 2, Jesus, Malachi**

Jesus Speaks of John the Baptist
Matthew 11:11–19

Jesus	I tell you the truth: Among those born of women there has not risen anyone greater than John the Baptist; yet he who is least in the kingdom of heaven is greater than he. From the days of John the Baptist until now, the kingdom of heaven has been forcefully advancing, and forceful men lay hold of it. For all the Prophets and the Law prophesied until John. And if you are willing to accept it, he is the Elijah who was to come. He who has ears, let him hear.
	To what can I compare this generation? They are like children sitting in the marketplaces and calling out to others:
Child 1	We played the flute for you,
Child 2	And you did not dance;
Child 3	We sang a dirge,
Child 4	And you did not mourn.
Jesus	For John came neither eating nor drinking, and they say:
Person 1	He has a demon.
Jesus	The Son of Man came eating and drinking, and they say:
Person 2	Here is a glutton and a drunkard—
Person 1	A friend of tax collectors and "sinners."

| Jesus | But wisdom is proved right by her actions. |

Cast: **Jesus, Child 1, Child 2** (can be the same as Child 1), **Child 3, Child 4** (can be the same as Child 3), **Person 1, Person 2** (can be the same as Person 1)

Woe on Unrepentant Cities

Matthew 11:20–24

| Narrator | Jesus began to denounce the cities in which most of his miracles had been performed, because they did not repent. |
| Jesus | Woe to you, Korazin! Woe to you, Bethsaida! If the miracles that were performed in you had been performed in Tyre and Sidon, they would have repented long ago in sackcloth and ashes. But I tell you, it will be more bearable for Tyre and Sidon on the day of judgment than for you. And you, Capernaum, will you be lifted up to the skies? No, you will go down to the depths. If the miracles that were performed in you had been performed in Sodom, it would have remained to this day. But I tell you that it will be more bearable for Sodom on the day of judgment than for you. |

Cast: **Narrator, Jesus**

Rest for the Weary

Matthew 11:25–30

Narrator	Jesus said:
Jesus (in prayer)	I praise you, Father, Lord of heaven and earth, because you have hidden these things from the wise and learned, and revealed them to little children. Yes, Father, for this was your good pleasure.
Jesus	All things have been committed to me by my Father. No one knows the Son except the Father, and no one knows the Father except the Son and those to whom the Son chooses to reveal him.
Jesus (to crowd)	Come to me, all you who are weary and burdened, and I will give you rest. Take my yoke upon you and learn from me, for I am gentle and humble in heart, and you will find rest for your souls. For my yoke is easy and my burden is light.

Cast: **Narrator, Jesus**

Lord of the Sabbath
Matthew 12:1–14

Narrator   Jesus went through the grainfields on the Sabbath. His disciples were hungry and began to pick some heads of grain and eat them. When the Pharisees saw this, they said to him:

Pharisee   Look! Your disciples are doing what is unlawful on the Sabbath.

Narrator   [Jesus] answered:

Jesus   Haven't you read what David did when he and his companions were hungry? He entered the house of God, and he and his companions ate the consecrated bread—which was not lawful for them to do, but only for the priests. Or haven't you read in the Law that on the Sabbath the priests in the temple desecrate the day and yet are innocent? I tell you that one greater than the temple is here. If you had known what these words mean, "I desire mercy, not sacrifice," you would not have condemned the innocent. For the Son of Man is Lord of the Sabbath.

Narrator   Going on from that place, he went into their synagogue, and a man with a shriveled hand was there. Looking for a reason to accuse Jesus, they asked him:

Pharisee   Is it lawful to heal on the Sabbath?

Jesus   If any of you has a sheep and it falls into a pit on the Sabbath, will you not take hold of it and lift it out? How much more valuable is a man than a sheep! Therefore it is lawful to do good on the Sabbath.

[Narrator   Then he said to the man:]

Jesus   Stretch out your hand.

Narrator   So he stretched it out and it was completely restored, just as sound as the other. But the Pharisees went out and plotted how they might kill Jesus.

Cast: **Narrator, Pharisee, Jesus**

God's Chosen Servant
Matthew 12:15–21

Narrator   Many followed [Jesus,] and he healed all their sick, warning them not to tell who he was. This was to fulfill what was spoken through the prophet Isaiah:

Isaiah   Here is my servant whom I have chosen,
    the one I love, in whom I delight;
I will put my Spirit on him,
    and he will proclaim justice to the nations.
He will not quarrel or cry out;

no one will hear his voice in the streets.
A bruised reed he will not break,
and a smoldering wick he will not snuff out,
till he leads justice to victory.
In his name the nations will put their hope.

Cast: **Narrator, Isaiah**

Jesus and Beelzebub
Matthew 12:22–32

Narrator   [Some people] brought [Jesus] a demon-possessed man who was blind and mute, and Jesus healed him, so that he could both talk and see. All the people were astonished and said:

Person(s)   Could this be the Son of David?

Narrator   But when the Pharisees heard this, they said:

Pharisee   It is only by Beelzebub, the prince of demons, that this fellow drives out demons.

Narrator   Jesus knew their thoughts and said to them:

Jesus   Every kingdom divided against itself will be ruined, and every city or household divided against itself will not stand. If Satan drives out Satan, he is divided against himself. How then can his kingdom stand? And if I drive out demons by Beelzebub, by whom do your people drive them out? So then, they will be your judges. But if I drive out demons by the Spirit of God, then the kingdom of God has come upon you.

Or again, how can anyone enter a strong man's house and carry off his possessions unless he first ties up the strong man? Then he can rob his house.

He who is not with me is against me, and he who does not gather with me scatters. (PAUSE) And so I tell you, every sin and blasphemy will be forgiven men, but the blasphemy against the Spirit will not be forgiven. Anyone who speaks a word against the Son of Man will be forgiven, but anyone who speaks against the Holy Spirit will not be forgiven, either in this age or in the age to come.

Cast: **Narrator, Person(s), Pharisee, Jesus**

The Sign of Jonah
Matthew 12:38–41 [42]

Narrator   Some of the Pharisees and teachers of the law said to [Jesus]:

Pharisee   Teacher, we want to see a miraculous sign from you.

[Narrator   He answered:]

Jesus	A wicked and adulterous generation asks for a miraculous sign! But none will be given it except the sign of the prophet Jonah. For as Jonah was three days and three nights in the belly of a huge fish, so the Son of Man will be three days and three nights in the heart of the earth. The men of Nineveh will stand up at the judgment with this generation and condemn it; for they repented at the preaching of Jonah, and now one greater than Jonah is here. [The Queen of the South will rise at the judgment with this generation and condemn it; for she came from the ends of the earth to listen to Solomon's wisdom, and now one greater than Solomon is here.]

Cast: **Narrator, Pharisee, Jesus.** (This reading is short and may be linked with the previous one, in which case it is desirable to omit the narrator's line in bold square brackets.)

The Return of the Evil Spirit
Matthew 12:43–45

Jesus	When an evil spirit comes out of a man, it goes through arid places seeking rest and does not find it. Then it says:
Evil spirit	I will return to the house I left.
Jesus	When it arrives, it finds the house unoccupied, swept clean and put in order. Then it goes and takes with it seven other spirits more wicked than itself, and they go in and live there. And the final condition of that man is worse than the first. (PAUSE)
(slowly)	That is how it will be with this wicked generation.

Cast: **Jesus, Evil spirit**

Jesus' Mother and Brothers
Matthew 12:46–50

Narrator	While Jesus was . . . talking to the crowd, his mother and brothers stood outside, wanting to speak to him.
Person 1	Your mother and brothers are standing outside.
Person 2	[They want] to speak to you.
[Narrator	[Jesus] replied:]
Jesus	Who is my mother, and who are my brothers?
Narrator	Pointing to his disciples, he said:
Jesus	Here are my mother and my brothers. For whoever does the will of my Father in heaven is my brother and sister and mother.

Cast: **Narrator, Person 1, Person 2** (can be the same as Person 1), **Jesus**

45

The Parable of the Sower
Matthew 13:1–9, 18–23*

Narrator	Jesus . . . sat by the lake. Such large crowds gathered around him that he got into a boat and sat in it, while all the people stood on the shore. Then he told them many things in parables.
Storyteller	A farmer went out to sow his seed.
Interpreter	Listen then to what the parable of the sower means.
Storyteller	As he was scattering the seed, some fell along the path, and the birds came and ate it up.
Interpreter	When anyone hears the message about the kingdom and does not understand it, the evil one comes and snatches away what was sown in his heart. This is the seed sown along the path. (PAUSE)
Storyteller	Some fell on rocky places, where it did not have much soil. It sprang up quickly, because the soil was shallow. But when the sun came up, the plants were scorched, and they withered because they had no root.
Interpreter	The one who received the seed that fell on rocky places is the man who hears the word and at once receives it with joy. But since he has no root, he lasts only a short time. When trouble or persecution comes because of the word, he quickly falls away. (PAUSE)
Storyteller	Other seed fell among thorns, which grew up and choked the plants.
Interpreter	The one who received the seed that fell among the thorns is the man who hears the word, but the worries of this life and the deceitfulness of wealth choke it, making it unfruitful. (PAUSE)
Storyteller	Still other seed fell on good soil, where it produced a crop—a hundred, sixty or thirty times what was sown.
Interpreter	But the one who received the seed that fell on good soil is the man who hears the word and understands it. He produces a crop, yielding a hundred, sixty or thirty times what was sown.
Narrator	[And Jesus concluded,] "He who has ears, let him hear."

Cast: **Narrator, Storyteller, Interpreter.** (*The parable of the sower is set out sequentially where it occurs at Mark 4:1–9 and Luke 8:4–15. Here in Matthew, parable and interpretation are intermixed for teaching purposes.)

The Purpose of the Parables
Matthew 13:10–17

Narrator	The disciples came to [Jesus] and asked:

Disciple	Why do you speak to the people in parables?
Jesus	The knowledge of the secrets of the kingdom of heaven has been given to you, but not to them. Whoever has will be given more, and he will have an abundance. Whoever does not have, even what he has will be taken from him. This is why I speak to them in parables:

Though seeing, they do not see;
   though hearing, they do not hear or understand.
In them is fulfilled the prophecy of Isaiah:

Isaiah	You will be ever hearing but never understanding;

   you will be ever seeing but never perceiving.
For this people's heart has become calloused;
   they hardly hear with their ears,
   and they have closed their eyes.
Otherwise they might see with their eyes,
   hear with their ears,
   understand with their hearts
and turn, and I would heal them.

Jesus	But blessed are your eyes because they see, and your ears because they hear. For I tell you the truth, many prophets and righteous men longed to see what you see but did not see it, and to hear what you hear but did not hear it.

Cast: **Narrator, Disciple, Jesus, Isaiah**

The Parable of the Weeds
Matthew 13:24–30, 37–43

Storyteller	The kingdom of heaven is like a man who sowed good seed in his field.
Interpreter	The one who sowed the good seed is the Son of Man.
Storyteller	But while everyone was sleeping, his enemy came and sowed weeds among the wheat, and went away.
Interpreter	The field is the world, and the good seed stands for the sons of the kingdom. The weeds are the sons of the evil one, and the enemy who sows them is the devil.
Storyteller	When the wheat sprouted and formed heads, then the weeds also appeared. The owner's servants came to him [and said]:
Servant	Sir, didn't you sow good seed in your field? Where then did the weeds come from?
[Storyteller	He replied:]
Man	An enemy did this.
Servant	Do you want us to go and pull them up?

Man	No, because while you are pulling the weeds, you may root up the wheat with them. Let both grow together until the harvest. At that time I will tell the harvesters: First collect the weeds and tie them in bundles to be burned; then gather the wheat and bring it into my barn.
Interpreter	The harvest is the end of the age, and the harvesters are angels. As the weeds are pulled up and burned in the fire, so it will be at the end of the age. The Son of Man will send out his angels, and they will weed out of his kingdom everything that causes sin and all who do evil. They will throw them into the fiery furnace, where there will be weeping and gnashing of teeth. Then the righteous will shine like the sun in the kingdom of their Father. He who has ears, let him hear.

Cast: **Storyteller, Interpreter, Servant, Man.** (The parable and its interpretation are intermixed for teaching purposes.)

Parables of the Kingdom
Matthew 13:31–35, 44–52

Narrator	[Jesus] told them another parable: [the parable of the mustard seed.]
Jesus	The kingdom of heaven is like a mustard seed, which a man took and planted in his field. Though it is the smallest of all your seeds, yet when it grows, it is the largest of garden plants and becomes a tree, so that the birds of the air come and perch in its branches.

Narrator	He told them still another parable: [the parable of the yeast.]
Jesus	The kingdom of heaven is like yeast that a woman took and mixed into a large amount of flour until it worked all through the dough.
Narrator	Jesus spoke all these things to the crowd in parables; he did not say anything to them without using a parable. So was fulfilled what was spoken through the prophet:
Psalmist	I will open my mouth in parables, I will utter things hidden since the creation of the world.

[Narrator	The parable of the hidden treasure. (PAUSE)]
Jesus	The kingdom of heaven is like treasure hidden in a field. When a man found it, he hid it again, and then in his joy went and sold all he had and bought that field.

[Narrator	The parable of the pearl. (PAUSE)]

Jesus	Again, the kingdom of heaven is like a merchant looking for fine pearls. When he found one of great value, he went away and sold everything he had and bought it.

[Narrator	The parable of the net. (PAUSE)]
Jesus	Once again, the kingdom of heaven is like a net that was let down into the lake and caught all kinds of fish. When it was full, the fishermen pulled it up on the shore. Then they sat down and collected the good fish in baskets, but threw the bad away. This is how it will be at the end of the age. The angels will come and separate the wicked from the righteous and throw them into the fiery furnace, where there will be weeping and gnashing of teeth.

Narrator	[New truths and old. (PAUSE)] [Jesus asked:]
Jesus	Have you understood all these things?
Disciple(s)	Yes.
Jesus	Therefore every teacher of the law who has been instructed about the kingdom of heaven is like the owner of a house who brings out of his storeroom new treasures as well as old.

Cast: **Narrator, Jesus, Psalmist** (can be the same as Narrator or can be the same as Jesus), Disciple(s)

A Prophet without Honor
Matthew 13:54–58

Narrator	Coming to his hometown, [Jesus] began teaching the people in their synagogue, and they were amazed.
Person 1	Where did this man get this wisdom?
Person 2	And [what about] these miraculous powers?
Person 3	Isn't this the carpenter's son?
Person 1	Isn't his mother's name Mary?
Person 2	And aren't his brothers James, Joseph, Simon and Judas?
Person 1	Aren't all his sisters with us?
Person 3	Where then did this man get all these things?
Narrator	And they took offense at him. (PAUSE) But Jesus said to them:
Jesus	Only in his hometown and in his own house is a prophet without honor.

| Narrator | He did not do many miracles there because of their lack of faith. |

Cast: **Narrator, Person 1** (preferably female), **Person 2, Person 3, Jesus**

John the Baptist Beheaded
Matthew 14:1–12

Narrator	Herod the tetrarch heard the reports about Jesus, and he said to his attendants:
Herod	This is John the Baptist; he has risen from the dead! That is why miraculous powers are at work in him.
Narrator	Now Herod had arrested John and bound him and put him in prison because of Herodias, his brother Philip's wife, for John had been saying to him:
John	It is not lawful for you to have her.
Narrator	Herod wanted to kill John, but he was afraid of the people, because they considered him a prophet. (PAUSE)
	On Herod's birthday the daughter of Herodias danced for them and pleased Herod so much that he promised:
Herod	[I swear that I will give you whatever you ask!]
Narrator	Prompted by her mother, she said:
Daughter	Give me here on a platter the head of John the Baptist.
Narrator	The king was distressed, but because of his oaths and his dinner guests, he ordered that her request be granted and had John beheaded in the prison. His head was brought in on a platter and given to the girl, who carried it to her mother. John's disciples came and took his body and buried it. Then they went and told Jesus.

Cast: **Narrator, Herod, John, Daughter**

Jesus Feeds the Five Thousand
Matthew 14:13–21

Narrator	Jesus heard what had happened [to John the Baptist, and] he withdrew by boat privately to a solitary place. Hearing of this, the crowds followed him on foot from the towns. When Jesus landed and saw a large crowd, he had compassion on them and healed their sick.
	As evening approached, the disciples came to him [and said:]
Disciple 1	This is a remote place, and it's already getting late. Send the crowds away, so they can go to the villages and buy themselves some food.
[Narrator	Jesus replied:]

Jesus	They do not need to go away. You give them something to eat.
Disciple 2	We have here only five loaves of bread and two fish.
Jesus	Bring them here to me.
Narrator	[Jesus] directed the people to sit down on the grass. Taking the five loaves and the two fish and looking up to heaven, he gave thanks and broke the loaves. Then he gave them to the disciples, and the disciples gave them to the people. They all ate and were satisfied, and the disciples picked up twelve basketfuls of broken pieces that were left over. The number of those who ate was about five thousand men, besides women and children.

Cast: **Narrator, Disciple 1, Jesus, Disciple 2** (can be the same as Disciple 1)

Jesus Walks on the Water
Matthew 14:22–33

Narrator	Jesus made the disciples get into the boat and go on ahead of him to the other side, while he dismissed the crowd. After he had dismissed them, he went up on a mountainside by himself to pray. (PAUSE) When evening came, he was there alone, but the boat was already a considerable distance from land, buffeted by the waves because the wind was against it. (PAUSE) During the fourth watch of the night Jesus went out to them, walking on the lake. When the disciples saw him walking on the lake, they were terrified.
Disciple	It's a ghost!
Narrator	And [they] cried out in fear. But Jesus immediately said to them:
Jesus	Take courage! It is I. Don't be afraid.
[Narrator	Peter spoke up:]
Peter	Lord, if it's you, tell me to come to you on the water.
Jesus	Come!
Narrator	Then Peter got down out of the boat, walked on the water and came toward Jesus. But when he saw the wind, he was afraid and, beginning to sink, cried out:
Peter	Lord, save me!
Narrator	Immediately Jesus reached out his hand and caught him.
Jesus	You of little faith, why did you doubt?
Narrator	When they climbed into the boat, the wind died down. Then those who were in the boat worshiped him.

Disciple	Truly you are the Son of God.

Cast: **Narrator, Disciple, Jesus, Peter**

The Teaching of the Ancestors
Matthew 15:1–9

Narrator	Some Pharisees and teachers of the law came to Jesus from Jerusalem and asked:
Pharisee	Why do your disciples break the tradition of the elders?
Lawyer	They don't wash their hands before they eat!
[Narrator	Jesus replied:]
Jesus	And why do you break the command of God for the sake of your tradition? For God said, "Honor your father and mother" and "Anyone who curses his father or mother must be put to death." But you say that if a man says to his father or mother, "Whatever help you might otherwise have received from me is a gift devoted to God," he is not to "honor his father" with it. Thus you nullify the word of God for the sake of your tradition. You hypocrites! Isaiah was right when he prophesied about you:

Isaiah	These people honor me with their lips,
	    but their hearts are far from me.
	They worship me in vain;
	    their teachings are but rules taught by men.

Cast: **Narrator, Pharisee, Lawyer** (can be the same as Pharisee), **Jesus, Isaiah**

Clean and Unclean
Matthew 15:10–20

Narrator	Jesus called the crowd to him and said:
Jesus (to crowd)	Listen and understand. What goes into a man's mouth does not make him "unclean," but what comes out of his mouth, that is what makes him "unclean."
Narrator	Then the disciples came to him and asked:
Disciple	Do you know that the Pharisees were offended when they heard this?
Jesus (to disciples)	Every plant that my heavenly Father has not planted will be pulled up by the roots. Leave them; they are blind guides. If a blind man leads a blind man, both will fall into a pit.
[Narrator	Peter spoke up:]

Peter	Explain the parable to us.
Jesus	Are you still so dull? Don't you see that whatever enters the mouth goes into the stomach and then out of the body? But the things that come out of the mouth come from the heart, and these make a man "unclean." For out of the heart come evil thoughts, murder, adultery, sexual immorality, theft, false testimony, slander. These are what make a man "unclean"; but eating with unwashed hands does not make him "unclean."

Cast: **Narrator, Jesus, Disciple, Peter** (can be the same as Disciple, in which case words in brackets may be omitted)

The Faith of the Canaanite Woman
Matthew 15:21–28

Narrator	Jesus withdrew to the region of Tyre and Sidon. A Canaanite woman from that vicinity came to him:
Woman (crying out)	Lord, Son of David, have mercy on me! My daughter is suffering terribly from demon-possession.
Narrator	Jesus did not answer a word. So his disciples came to him and urged him:
Disciple 1	Send her away!
Disciple 2	For she keeps crying out after us.
Narrator	[Jesus] answered:
Jesus	I was sent only to the lost sheep of Israel.
Narrator	The woman came and knelt before him.
Woman	Lord, help me!
Jesus	It is not right to take the children's bread and toss it to their dogs.
Woman	Yes, Lord, but even the dogs eat the crumbs that fall from their masters' table.
Jesus	Woman, you have great faith! Your request is granted.
Narrator	And her daughter was healed from that very hour.

Cast: **Narrator, Woman, Disciple 1, Disciple 2** (can be the same as Disciple 1), **Jesus**

Jesus Feeds the Four Thousand
Matthew 15:29–39

Narrator	Jesus . . . went up on a mountainside and sat down. Great crowds came to him, bringing the lame, the blind, the crippled, the mute and many

others, and laid them at his feet; and he healed them. The people were amazed when they saw the mute speaking, the crippled made well, the lame walking and the blind seeing. And they praised the God of Israel. (PAUSE)

Jesus called his disciples to him:

Jesus	I have compassion for these people; they have already been with me three days and have nothing to eat. I do not want to send them away hungry, or they may collapse on the way.
[Narrator	His disciples answered:]
Disciple	Where could we get enough bread in this remote place to feed such a crowd?
Jesus	How many loaves do you have?
Disciple	Seven, and a few small fish.
Narrator	[Jesus] told the crowd to sit down on the ground. Then he took the seven loaves and the fish, and when he had given thanks, he broke them and gave them to the disciples, and they in turn to the people. They all ate and were satisfied. Afterward the disciples picked up seven basketfuls of broken pieces that were left over. The number of those who ate was four thousand, besides women and children. (PAUSE) After Jesus had sent the crowd away, he got into [a] boat, and went to the vicinity of Magadan.

Cast: **Narrator, Jesus, Disciple**

The Demand for a Sign
Matthew 16:1–4

Narrator	The Pharisees and Sadducees came to Jesus and tested him by asking him to show them a sign from heaven. He replied:
Jesus	When evening comes, you say:
Person 1	It will be fair weather, for the sky is red.
Jesus	And in the morning [you say]:
Person 2	Today it will be stormy, for the sky is red and overcast.
Jesus	You know how to interpret the appearance of the sky, but you cannot interpret the signs of the times. A wicked and adulterous generation looks for a miraculous sign, but none will be given it except the sign of Jonah.
Narrator	Jesus then left them and went away.

Cast: **Narrator, Jesus, Person 1, Person 2** (can be the same as Person 1)

The Yeast of the Pharisees and Sadducees
Matthew 16:5–12

Narrator	When [the disciples went across the lake, they] forgot to take bread. Jesus said to them:
Jesus	Be careful. Be on your guard against the yeast of the Pharisees and Sadducees.
Narrator	They discussed this among themselves and said:
Disciple	It is because we didn't bring any bread.
Narrator	Aware of their discussion, Jesus asked:
Jesus	You of little faith, why are you talking among yourselves about having no bread? Do you still not understand? Don't you remember the five loaves for the five thousand, and how many basketfuls you gathered? Or the seven loaves for the four thousand, and how many basketfuls you gathered? How is it you don't understand that I was not talking to you about bread? But be on your guard against the yeast of the Pharisees and Sadducees.
Narrator	Then they understood that he was not telling them to guard against the yeast used in bread, but against the teaching of the Pharisees and Sadducees.

Cast: **Narrator**, **Jesus**, **Disciple**

Peter's Confession of Christ
Matthew 16:13–20

Narrator	When Jesus came to the region of Caesarea Philippi, he asked his disciples:
Jesus	Who do people say the Son of Man is?
[Narrator	They replied:]
Disciple 1	Some say John the Baptist.
Disciple 2	Others say Elijah—
Disciple 3	And still others, Jeremiah or one of the prophets.
Jesus	But what about you? Who do you say I am?
Narrator	Simon Peter answered:
Peter	You are the Christ, the Son of the living God.
Jesus	Blessed are you, Simon son of Jonah, for this was not revealed to you by man, but by my Father in heaven. And I tell you that you are Peter, and on this rock I will build my church, and the gates of Hades will not overcome it. I will give you the keys of the kingdom of heaven; whatever

you bind on earth will be bound in heaven, and whatever you loose on earth will be loosed in heaven.

Narrator   Then he warned his disciples not to tell anyone that he was the Christ.

Cast: **Narrator, Jesus, Disciple 1, Disciple 2, Disciple 3** (can be the same as Disciple 1), **Peter** (can be the same as Disciple 2)

Jesus Predicts His Death
Matthew 16:21–28

Narrator   Jesus began to explain to his disciples:

Jesus   [I] must go to Jerusalem and suffer many things at the hands of the elders, chief priests and teachers of the law. [I] must be killed and on the third day be raised to life.

Narrator   Peter took him aside and began to rebuke him.

Peter   Never, Lord! This shall never happen to you!

[Narrator   Jesus turned and said to Peter:]

Jesus (to Peter)   Get behind me, Satan! You are a stumbling block to me; you do not have in mind the things of God, but the things of men.

Narrator   Then Jesus said to his disciples:

Jesus   If anyone would come after me, he must deny himself and take up his cross and follow me. For whoever wants to save his life will lose it, but whoever loses his life for me will find it. What good will it be for a man if he gains the whole world, yet forfeits his soul? Or what can a man give in exchange for his soul? For the Son of Man is going to come in his Father's glory with his angels, and then he will reward each person according to what he has done. I tell you the truth, some who are standing here will not taste death before they see the Son of Man coming in his kingdom.

Cast: **Narrator, Jesus, Peter**

The Transfiguration
Matthew 17:1–13

Narrator   Jesus took with him Peter, James and John the brother of James, and led them up a high mountain by themselves. There he was transfigured before them. His face shone like the sun, and his clothes became as white as the light. Just then there appeared before them Moses and Elijah, talking with Jesus. Peter said to Jesus:

Peter   Lord, it is good for us to be here. If you wish, I will put up three shelters—one for you, one for Moses and one for Elijah.

Narrator	While he was still speaking, a bright cloud enveloped them, and a voice from the cloud said:
Voice	This is my Son, whom I love; with him I am well pleased. Listen to him!
Narrator	When the disciples heard this, they fell facedown to the ground, terrified. But Jesus came and touched them.
Jesus	Get up. Don't be afraid.
Narrator	When they looked up, they saw no one except Jesus.
	As they were coming down the mountain, Jesus instructed them:
Jesus	Don't tell anyone what you have seen, until the Son of Man has been raised from the dead.
Narrator	The disciples asked him:
Disciple	Why then do the teachers of the law say that Elijah must come first?
Jesus	To be sure, Elijah comes and will restore all things. But I tell you, Elijah has already come, and they did not recognize him, but have done to him everything they wished. In the same way the Son of Man is going to suffer at their hands.
Narrator	Then the disciples understood that he was talking to them about John the Baptist.

Cast: **Narrator, Peter, Voice, Jesus, Disciple**

The Healing of a Boy with a Demon
Matthew 17:14–20

Narrator	A man approached Jesus and knelt before him:
Man	Lord, have mercy on my son! He has seizures and is suffering greatly. He often falls into the fire or into the water. I brought him to your disciples, but they could not heal him.
[Narrator	Jesus replied:]
Jesus	O unbelieving and perverse generation, how long shall I stay with you? How long shall I put up with you? Bring the boy here to me.
Narrator	Jesus rebuked the demon, and it came out of the boy, and he was healed from that moment.
	Then the disciples came to Jesus in private and asked:
Disciple	Why couldn't we drive it out?

Jesus	Because you have so little faith. I tell you the truth, if you have faith as small as a mustard seed, you can say to this mountain, "Move from here to there" and it will move. Nothing will be impossible for you.

Cast: **Narrator, Man, Jesus, Disciple**

The Greatest in the Kingdom of Heaven
Matthew 18:1–5, 10; 19:13–15

Narrator	The disciples came to Jesus and asked:
Disciple	Who is the greatest in the kingdom of heaven?
Narrator	He called a little child and had him stand among them. [And he said:]
Jesus	I tell you the truth, unless you change and become like little children, you will never enter the kingdom of heaven. Therefore, whoever humbles himself like this child is the greatest in the kingdom of heaven.
	And whoever welcomes a little child like this in my name welcomes me. . . .
	See that you do not look down on one of these little ones. For I tell you that their angels in heaven always see the face of my Father in heaven. . . .
Narrator	Then little children were brought to Jesus for him to place his hands on them and pray for them. But the disciples rebuked those who brought them. Jesus said:
Jesus	Let the little children come to me, and do not hinder them, for the kingdom of heaven belongs to such as these.
Narrator	When he had placed his hands on them, he went on from there.

Cast: **Narrator, Disciple, Jesus**

The Parable of the Unmerciful Servant
Matthew 18:21–35

Narrator	Peter came to Jesus [and asked]:
Peter	Lord, how many times shall I forgive my brother when he sins against me? Up to seven times?
[Narrator	Jesus answered:]
Jesus	I tell you, not seven times, but seventy-seven times.
	Therefore, the kingdom of heaven is like a king who wanted to settle accounts with his servants. As he began the settlement, a man who owed him ten thousand talents was brought to him. Since he was not able to

pay, the master ordered that he and his wife and his children and all that he had be sold to repay the debt.

The servant fell on his knees before him.

Servant	Be patient with me, and I will pay back everything.
Jesus	The servant's master took pity on him, canceled the debt and let him go. But when that servant went out, he found one of his fellow servants who owed him a hundred denarii. He grabbed him and began to choke him.
Servant (roughly)	Pay back what you owe me!
Jesus	His fellow servant fell to his knees and begged him:
Fellow servant (pleading)	Be patient with me, and I will pay you back.
Jesus	But he refused. Instead, he went off and had the man thrown into prison until he could pay the debt. When the other servants saw what had happened, they were greatly distressed and went and told their master everything that had happened.

Then the master called the servant in.

King	You wicked servant, I canceled all that debt of yours because you begged me to. Shouldn't you have had mercy on your fellow servant just as I had on you?
Jesus	In anger his master turned him over to the jailers to be tortured, until he should pay back all he owed. (PAUSE)
(looking around)	This is how my heavenly Father will treat each of you unless you forgive your brother from your heart.

Cast: **Narrator, Peter, Jesus, Servant, Fellow servant, King**

Divorce
Matthew 19:1–12

Narrator	Jesus . . . left Galilee and went into the region of Judea to the other side of the Jordan. Large crowds followed him, and he healed them there.
	Some Pharisees came to him to test him. They asked:
Pharisee 1	Is it lawful for a man to divorce his wife for any and every reason?
[Narrator	[Jesus] replied:]
Jesus	Haven't you read that at the beginning the Creator "made them male and female," and said:

59

God	For this reason a man will leave his father and mother and be united to his wife, and the two will become one flesh.
Jesus	So they are no longer two, but one. Therefore what God has joined together, let man not separate.
[Narrator	The Pharisees asked him:]
Pharisee 2	Why then, did Moses command that a man give his wife a certificate of divorce and send her away?
Jesus	Moses permitted you to divorce your wives because your hearts were hard. But it was not this way from the beginning. I tell you that anyone who divorces his wife, except for marital unfaithfulness, and marries another woman commits adultery.
Narrator	The disciples said to him:
Disciple	If this is the situation between a husband and wife, it is better not to marry.
Jesus	Not everyone can accept this word, but only those to whom it has been given. For some are eunuchs because they were born that way; others were made that way by men; and others have renounced marriage because of the kingdom of heaven. The one who can accept this should accept it.

Cast: **Narrator, Pharisee 1, Jesus, God** (can be the same as Jesus), **Pharisee 2, Disciple**

The Little Children and Jesus
Matthew 19:13–15

Narrator	Little children were brought to Jesus for him to place his hands on them and pray for them. But the disciples rebuked those who brought them. Jesus said:
Jesus	Let the little children come to me, and do not hinder them, for the kingdom of heaven belongs to such as these. (PAUSE)
Narrator	When he had placed his hands on them, he went on from there.

Cast: **Narrator, Jesus**

The Rich Young Man
Matthew 19:16–30

Narrator	Now a man came up to Jesus and asked:
Man	Teacher, what good thing must I do to get eternal life?
[Narrator	Jesus replied:]

Jesus	Why do you ask me about what is good? There is only One who is good. If you want to enter life, obey the commandments.
Man	Which ones?
Jesus	Do not murder, do not commit adultery, do not steal, do not give false testimony, honor your father and mother, and love your neighbor as yourself.
Man	All these I have kept. What do I still lack?
Jesus	If you want to be perfect, go, sell your possessions and give to the poor, and you will have treasure in heaven. Then come, follow me.
Narrator	When the young man heard this, he went away sad, because he had great wealth. [Then Jesus said to his disciples:]
Jesus	I tell you the truth, it is hard for a rich man to enter the kingdom of heaven. Again I tell you, it is easier for a camel to go through the eye of a needle than for a rich man to enter the kingdom of God.
Narrator	When the disciples heard this, they were greatly astonished and asked:
Disciple	Who then can be saved?
Narrator	Jesus looked at them and said:
Jesus (looking hard)	With man this is impossible, but with God all things are possible.
Narrator	Peter answered him:
Peter	We have left everything to follow you! What then will there be for us?
Jesus	I tell you the truth, at the renewal of all things, when the Son of Man sits on his glorious throne, you who have followed me will also sit on twelve thrones, judging the twelve tribes of Israel. And everyone who has left houses or brothers or sisters or father or mother or children or fields for my sake will receive a hundred times as much and will inherit eternal life. But many who are first will be last, and many who are last will be first.

Cast: **Narrator, Man, Jesus, Disciple, Peter**

The Parable of the Workers in the Vineyard
Matthew 20:1–16

Jesus	The kingdom of heaven is like a landowner who went out early in the morning to hire men to work in his vineyard. He agreed to pay them a denarius for the day and sent them into his vineyard.
	About the third hour he went out and saw others standing in the marketplace doing nothing. He told them:

61

Owner	You also go and work in my vineyard, and I will pay you whatever is right.
Jesus	So they went. (PAUSE) He went out again about the sixth hour and the ninth hour and did the same thing. About the eleventh hour he went out and found still others standing around. [He asked them:]
Owner	Why have you been standing here all day long doing nothing?
Man 3	Because no one has hired us.
Owner	You also go and work in my vineyard.
Jesus	When evening came, the owner of the vineyard said to his foreman:
Owner	Call the workers and pay them their wages, beginning with the last ones hired and going on to the first.
Jesus	The workers who were hired about the eleventh hour came and each received a denarius. So when those came who were hired first, they expected to receive more. But each one of them also received a denarius. When they received it, they began to grumble against the landowner:
Man 1 (grumbling)	These men who were hired last worked only one hour.
Man 2	You have made them equal to us who have borne the burden of the work and the heat of the day.
Owner (to Man 1)	Friend, I am not being unfair to you. Didn't you agree to work for a denarius? Take your pay and go. I want to give the man who was hired last the same as I gave you. Don't I have the right to do what I want with my own money? Or are you envious because I am generous? (PAUSE)
Jesus (looking around)	So the last will be first, and the first will be last.

Cast: **Jesus** (as Narrator), **Owner**, **Man 3**, **Man 1**, **Man 2** (can be the same as Man 1)

Jesus Again Predicts His Death
Matthew 20:17–19

Narrator	As Jesus was going up to Jerusalem, he took the twelve disciples aside and said to them:
Jesus	We are going up to Jerusalem, and the Son of Man will be betrayed to the chief priests and the teachers of the law. They will condemn him to death and will turn him over to the Gentiles to be mocked and flogged and crucified. On the third day he will be raised to life!

Cast: **Narrator, Jesus**

A Mother's Request
Matthew 20:20–28

Narrator	The mother of Zebedee's sons came to Jesus with her sons and, kneeling down, asked a favor of him:
Jesus	What is it you want?
Mother	Grant that one of these two sons of mine may sit at your right and the other at your left in your kingdom.
[Narrator	Jesus said to them:]
Jesus (to the sons)	You don't know what you are asking. Can you drink the cup I am going to drink?
[Narrator	They answered:]
Sons	We can.
Jesus	You will indeed drink from my cup, but to sit at my right or left is not for me to grant. These places belong to those for whom they have been prepared by my Father.
Narrator	When the [other] ten [disciples] heard about this, they were indignant with the two brothers. [So] Jesus called them [all] together:
Jesus	You know that the rulers of the Gentiles lord it over them, and their high officials exercise authority over them. Not so with you. Instead, whoever wants to become great among you must be your servant, and whoever wants to be first must be your slave—just as the Son of Man did not come to be served, but to serve, and to give his life as a ransom for many.

Cast: **Narrator, Jesus, Mother, Sons** (two)

Two Blind Men Receive Sight
Matthew 20:29–34

Narrator	As Jesus and his disciples were leaving Jericho, a large crowd followed him. (PAUSE) Two blind men were sitting by the roadside, and when they heard that Jesus was going by, they shouted:
Blind man 1	Lord, Son of David!
Blind man 2	Have mercy on us!

63

Narrator	The crowd rebuked them and told them to be quiet, but they shouted all the louder:
Blind men 1 and 2	Lord, Son of David, have mercy on us!
Narrator	Jesus stopped and called them.
Jesus	What do you want me to do for you?
Blind man 1	Lord, we want our sight.
Narrator	Jesus had compassion on them and touched their eyes. Immediately they received their sight and followed him.

Cast: **Narrator, Blind man 1, Blind man 2, Jesus**

The Triumphal Entry
Matthew 21:1–11

Narrator	As [Jesus and his disciples] approached Jerusalem and came to Bethphage on the Mount of Olives, Jesus sent two disciples, saying to them:
Jesus	Go to the village ahead of you, and at once you will find a donkey tied there, with her colt by her. Untie them and bring them to me. If anyone says anything to you, tell him that the Lord needs them, and he will send them right away.
Narrator	This took place to fulfill what was spoken through the prophet:
Zechariah	Say to the Daughter of Zion, "See, your king comes to you, gentle and riding on a donkey, on a colt, the foal of a donkey."
Narrator	The disciples went and did as Jesus had instructed them. They brought the donkey and the colt, placed their cloaks on them, and Jesus sat on them. A very large crowd spread their cloaks on the road, while others cut branches from the trees and spread them on the road. The crowds that went ahead of him and those that followed shouted:
Person 1	Hosanna to the Son of David!
Person 2	Blessed is he who comes in the name of the Lord! Hosanna in the highest!
Narrator	When Jesus entered Jerusalem, the whole city was stirred [and asked:]
Person 3	Who is this?

[Narrator	The crowds answered:]
Persons 1 **and 2**	This is Jesus, the prophet from Nazareth in Galilee.

Cast: **Narrator, Jesus, Zechariah** (can be the same as Narrator), **Person 1, Person 2, Person 3**

Jesus at the Temple
Matthew 21:12–16 [17]

Narrator	Jesus entered the temple area and drove out all who were buying and selling there. He overturned the tables of the money changers and the benches of those selling doves. [He said to them:]
Jesus	It is written, "My house will be called a house of prayer," but you are making it a "den of robbers."
Narrator	The blind and the lame came to him at the temple, and he healed them. But when the chief priests and the teachers of the law saw the wonderful things he did and the children shouting in the temple area, . . . they were indignant.
Children	Hosanna to the Son of David!
[Narrator	So they asked Jesus:]
Chief priest (to Jesus)	Do you hear what these children are saying?
Jesus	Yes. Have you never read, "From the lips of children and infants you have ordained praise"?
[Narrator	[Jesus] left them and went out of the city to Bethany, where he spent the night.]

Cast: **Narrator, Jesus, Children** (at least two), **Chief priest**

The Fig Tree Withers
Matthew 21:18–22

Narrator	Early in the morning, as [Jesus] was on his way back to the city, he was hungry. Seeing a fig tree by the road, he went up to it but found nothing on it except leaves. Then he said to it:
Jesus	May you never bear fruit again!
Narrator	Immediately the tree withered. When the disciples saw this, they were amazed.
Disciple	How did the fig tree wither so quickly?

Jesus	I tell you the truth, if you have faith and do not doubt, not only can you do what was done to the fig tree, but also you can say to this mountain, "Go, throw yourself into the sea," and it will be done. If you believe, you will receive whatever you ask for in prayer.

Cast: **Narrator, Jesus, Disciple**

The Authority of Jesus Questioned
Matthew 21:23–27

Narrator	Jesus entered the temple courts, and, while he was teaching, the chief priests and the elders of the people came to him.
Chief priest	By what authority are you doing these things?
Elder	And who *gave* you this authority?
[Narrator	Jesus replied:]
Jesus	I will also ask you one question. If you answer me, I will tell you by what authority I am doing these things. John's baptism—where did it come from? Was it from heaven, or from men?
Narrator	They discussed it among themselves and said:
[Elder	What shall we say?]
Chief priest	If we say, "From heaven," he will ask, "Then why didn't you believe him?"
Elder	But if we say, "From men"—we are afraid of the people, for they all hold that John was a prophet.
Narrator	So they answered Jesus:
Chief priest and **Elder**	We don't know.
[Narrator	Then he said:]
Jesus	Neither will I tell you by what authority I am doing these things.

Cast: **Narrator, Chief priest, Elder, Jesus**

The Parable of the Two Sons
Matthew 21:28–32

Jesus	What do you think? There was a man who had two sons. He went to the first [and said]:
Father	Son, go and work today in the vineyard.
[Jesus	He answered:]
Elder son	I will not.

Jesus	But later he changed his mind and went. (PAUSE) Then the father went to the other son and said the same thing. He answered:
Younger son	I will, sir.
Jesus	But he did not go. (PAUSE) Which of the two did what his father wanted?
Person	The first.
Jesus	I tell you the truth, the tax collectors and the prostitutes are entering the kingdom of God ahead of you. For John came to you to show you the way of righteousness, and you did not believe him, but the tax collectors and the prostitutes did. And even after you saw this, you did not repent and believe him.

Cast: **Jesus, Father, Elder son, Younger son, Person**

The Parable of the Tenants
Matthew 21:33–46

[Narrator	Jesus said:]
Jesus	Listen to another parable: (PAUSE) There was a landowner who planted a vineyard. He put a wall around it, dug a winepress in it and built a watchtower. Then he rented the vineyard to some farmers and went away on a journey. When the harvest time approached, he sent his servants to the tenants to collect his fruit.
	The tenants seized his servants; they beat one, killed another, and stoned a third. Then he sent other servants to them, more than the first time, and the tenants treated them the same way. Last of all, he sent his son to them. [He said:]
Landowner	They will respect my son.
Jesus	But when the tenants saw the son, they said to each other:
Tenant 1	This is the heir.
Tenant 2	Come, let's kill him and take his inheritance!
Jesus	So they took him and threw him out of the vineyard and killed him. (PAUSE)
	Therefore, when the owner of the vineyard comes, what will he do to those tenants?
Person 1	He will bring those wretches to a wretched end—
Person 2	And he will rent the vineyard to other tenants—
Person 1	Who will give him his share of the crop at harvest time.
Jesus	Have you never read [what] the Scriptures [say]?

Psalmist	The stone the builders rejected
	    has become the capstone;
	the Lord has done this,
	    and it is marvelous in our eyes.

Jesus	Therefore I tell you that the kingdom of God will be taken away from you and given to a people who will produce its fruit. He who falls on this stone will be broken to pieces, but he on whom it falls will be crushed.
Narrator	When the chief priests and the Pharisees heard Jesus' parables, they knew he was talking about them. They looked for a way to arrest him, but they were afraid of the crowd because the people held that he was a prophet.

Cast: **Narrator, Jesus, Landowner, Tenant 1, Tenant 2, Person 1, Person 2** (can be the same as Person 1), **Psalmist** (can be the same as Jesus)

The Parable of the Wedding Banquet
Matthew 22:1–14

[Narrator	Jesus spoke to them again in parables:]
Jesus	The kingdom of heaven is like a king who prepared a wedding banquet for his son. He sent his servants to those who had been invited to the banquet to tell them to come, but they refused to come. Then he sent some more servants and said:
King	Tell those who have been invited that I have prepared my dinner: My oxen and fattened cattle have been butchered, and everything is ready. Come to the wedding banquet.
Jesus	But they paid no attention and went off—one to his field, another to his business. The rest seized his servants, mistreated them and killed them. (PAUSE) The king was enraged. He sent his army and destroyed those murderers and burned their city. [Then he said to his servants:]
King	The wedding banquet is ready, but those I invited did not deserve to come. Go to the street corners and invite to the banquet anyone you find.
Jesus	So the servants went out into the streets and gathered all the people they could find, both good and bad, and the wedding hall was filled with guests. (PAUSE) But when the king came in to see the guests, he noticed a man there who was not wearing wedding clothes. [The king asked him:]
King	Friend, how did you get in here without wedding clothes?
Jesus	The man was speechless. Then the king told the attendants:

King	Tie him hand and foot, and throw him outside, into the darkness, where there will be weeping and gnashing of teeth.
Jesus (slowly)	For many are invited, but few are chosen.

Cast: [**Narrator**,] **Jesus, King**

Paying Taxes to Caesar
Matthew 22:15–22

Narrator	Then the Pharisees went out and laid plans to trap [Jesus] in his words. They sent their disciples to him along with the Herodians. [They said:]
Spy 1	Teacher, we know you are a man of integrity and that you teach the way of God in accordance with the truth.
Spy 2	You aren't swayed by men, because you pay no attention to who they are.
Spy 1	Tell us then, what is your opinion? Is it right to pay taxes to Caesar or not?
Narrator	But Jesus, knowing their evil intent, said:
Jesus	You hypocrites, why are you trying to trap me? Show me the coin used for paying the tax.
Narrator	They brought him a denarius. (PAUSE)
Jesus	Whose portrait is this? And whose inscription?
Spies 1 and 2	Caesar's.
Jesus	Give to Caesar what is Caesar's, and to God what is God's.
Narrator	When they heard this, they were amazed. So they left him and went away.

Cast: **Narrator, Spy 1, Spy 2, Jesus**

Marriage at the Resurrection
Matthew 22:23–33

Narrator	The Sadducees, who say there is no resurrection, came to [Jesus] with a question:
Sadducee 1	Teacher, Moses told us that if a man dies without having children, his brother must marry the widow and have children for him.
Sadducee 2	Now there were seven brothers among us. The first one married and died, and since he had no children, he left his wife to his brother.
Sadducee 1	The same thing happened to the second and third brother, right on down to the seventh.

Sadducee 2	Finally, the woman died.
Sadducee 1	Now then, at the resurrection, whose wife will she be of the seven?
Sadducee 2	Since all of them were married to her.
[Narrator	Jesus replied:]
Jesus	You are in error because you do not know the Scriptures or the power of God. At the resurrection people will neither marry nor be given in marriage; they will be like the angels in heaven. But about the resurrection of the dead—have you not read what God said to you?
Voice	I am the God of Abraham, the God of Isaac, and the God of Jacob.
Jesus	He is not the God of the dead but of the living.
Narrator	When the crowds heard this, they were astonished at his teaching.

Cast: **Narrator, Sadducee 1, Sadducee 2, Jesus, Voice** (can be the same as Jesus)

The Greatest Commandment
Matthew 22:34–40

Narrator	Hearing that Jesus had silenced the Sadducees, the Pharisees got together. One of them, an expert in the law, tested him with this question:
Pharisee (to Jesus)	Teacher, which is the greatest commandment in the Law?
[Narrator	Jesus replied:]
Jesus	"Love the Lord your God with all your heart and with all your soul and with all your mind." This is the first and greatest commandment. And the second is like it: "Love your neighbor as yourself." All the Law and the Prophets hang on these two commandments.

Cast: **Narrator, Pharisee, Jesus**

Whose Son Is the Christ?
Matthew 22:41–46

Narrator	While the Pharisees were gathered together, Jesus asked them:
Jesus	What do you think about the Christ? Whose son is he?
[Narrator	They replied:]
Pharisee	The son of David.
Jesus	How is it then that David, speaking by the Spirit, calls him "Lord"? For he says:

Psalmist	The Lord said to my Lord:
	"Sit at my right hand
	until I put your enemies under your feet."

Jesus	If then David calls him "Lord," how can he be his *son?*

Narrator	No one could say a word in reply, and from that day on no one dared to ask him any more questions.

Cast: **Narrator, Jesus, Pharisee, Psalmist** (can be the same as Jesus)

Jesus Warns against the Teachers of the Law and the Pharisees (i)
Matthew 23:1–12

Narrator	Jesus said to the crowds and to his disciples:

Jesus	The teachers of the law and the Pharisees sit in Moses' seat. So you must obey them and do everything they tell you. But do not do what they do, for they do not practice what they preach. They tie up heavy loads and put them on men's shoulders, but they themselves are not willing to lift a finger to move them.
	Everything they do is done for men to see: They make their phylacteries wide and the tassels on their garments long; they love the place of honor at banquets and the most important seats in the synagogues; they love to be greeted in the marketplaces and to have men call them:

Persons 1 and 2 (ingratiatingly)	Rabbi!

Jesus	But you are not to be called "Rabbi," for you have only one Master and you are all brothers. And do not call anyone on earth:

Person 1	Father!

Jesus	For you have one Father, and he is in heaven. Nor are you to be called:

Person 2	Teacher!

Jesus	For you have one Teacher, the Christ. The greatest among you will be your servant. (PAUSE) For whoever exalts himself will be humbled, and whoever humbles himself will be exalted.

Cast: **Narrator, Jesus, Person 1, Person 2**

Jesus Warns against the Teachers of the Law and the Pharisees (ii)
Matthew 23:[1], 13–22

[Narrator	Jesus said to the crowds and to his disciples:]

71

Jesus	Woe to you, teachers of the law and Pharisees, you hypocrites! You shut the kingdom of heaven in men's faces. You yourselves do not enter, nor will you let those enter who are trying to. Woe to you, teachers of the law and Pharisees, you hypocrites! You travel over land and sea to win a single convert, and when he becomes one, you make him twice as much a son of hell as you are.
	Woe to you, blind guides! (PAUSE) [You say:]
Lawyer	If anyone swears by the temple, it means nothing.
Pharisee	But if anyone swears by the gold of the temple, he is bound by his oath.
Jesus	You blind fools! Which is greater: the gold, or the temple that makes the gold sacred? (PAUSE) [You also say:]
Lawyer	If anyone swears by the altar, it means nothing.
Pharisee	But if anyone swears by the gift on it, he is bound by his oath.
Jesus	You blind men! Which is greater: the gift, or the altar that makes the gift sacred? Therefore, he who swears by the altar swears by it and by everything on it. And he who swears by the temple swears by it and by the one who dwells in it. And he who swears by heaven swears by God's throne and by the one who sits on it.

Cast: [**Narrator**] (should be omitted when this reading continues from the previous one), **Jesus**, **Lawyer**, **Pharisee**

Jesus' Love for Jerusalem
Matthew 23:37–39

Jesus	O Jerusalem, Jerusalem, you who kill the prophets and stone those sent to you, how often I have longed to gather your children together, as a hen gathers her chicks under her wings, but you were not willing. Look, your house is left to you desolate. For I tell you, you will not see me again until you say:
Persons	Blessed is he who comes in the name of the Lord.

Cast: **Jesus**, **Persons** (three or more)

Signs of the End of the Age
Matthew 24:1–14

Narrator	Jesus left the temple and was walking away when his disciples came up to him to call his attention to its buildings. He asked:
Jesus	Do you see all these things? I tell you the truth, not one stone here will be left on another; every one will be thrown down.

Narrator	As Jesus was sitting on the Mount of Olives, the disciples came to him privately.
Disciple 1 (to Jesus)	Tell us, when will this happen—
Disciple 2	And what will be the sign of your coming and of the end of the age?
Jesus	Watch out that no one deceives you. For many will come in my name, claiming, "I am the Christ," and will deceive many. You will hear of wars and rumors of wars, but see to it that you are not alarmed. Such things must happen, but the end is still to come. Nation will rise against nation, and kingdom against kingdom. There will be famines and earthquakes in various places. All these are the beginning of birth pains.
	Then you will be handed over to be persecuted and put to death, and you will be hated by all nations because of me. At that time many will turn away from the faith and will betray and hate each other, and many false prophets will appear and deceive many people. Because of the increase of wickedness, the love of most will grow cold, but he who stands firm to the end will be saved. And this gospel of the kingdom will be preached in the whole world as a testimony to all nations, and then the end will come.

Cast: **Narrator, Jesus, Disciple 1, Disciple 2** (can be the same as Disciple 1)

Jesus Speaks of Things to Come
Matthew 24:15–27

Jesus	When you see standing in the holy place "the abomination that causes desolation," spoken of through the prophet Daniel—
Narrator	Let the reader understand—
Jesus	Then let those who are in Judea flee to the mountains. Let no one on the roof of his house go down to take anything out of the house. Let no one in the field go back to get his cloak. How dreadful it will be in those days for pregnant women and nursing mothers! Pray that your flight will not take place in winter or on the Sabbath. For then there will be great distress, unequaled from the beginning of the world until now— and never to be equaled again. If those days had not been cut short, no one would survive, but for the sake of the elect those days will be shortened. (PAUSE) At that time if anyone says to you:
Person 1	Look, here is the Christ!
Jesus	Or:
Person 2	There he is!
Jesus	Do not believe it. For false Christs and false prophets will appear and perform great signs and miracles to deceive even the elect—if that were possible. See, I have told you ahead of time. (PAUSE)

73

	So if anyone tells you:
Person 1	There he is, out in the desert!
Jesus	Do not go out. Or:
Person 2	Here he is, in the inner rooms.
Jesus	Do not believe it. For as lightning that comes from the east is visible even in the west, so will be the coming of the Son of Man.

Cast: **Jesus, Narrator** (can be the same as Jesus), **Person 1, Person 2**

The Coming of the Son of Man
Matthew 24:29–31

Reader 1	Immediately after the distress of those days, "the sun will be darkened,
Reader 2	and the moon will not give its light;
Reader 3	the stars will fall from the sky,
Reader 4	and the heavenly bodies will be shaken."
Reader 1	At that time the sign of the Son of Man will appear in the sky.
Reader 2	All the nations of the earth will mourn.
Reader 3	They will see the Son of Man coming on the clouds of the sky, with power and great glory.
Reader 4	He will send his angels with a loud trumpet call.
Reader 1	And they will gather his elect from the four winds, from one end of the heavens to the other.

Cast: **Reader 1, Reader 2, Reader 3, Reader 4**

Jesus Teaches the Lesson of the Fig Tree
Matthew 24:32–35

Reader 1	Learn this lesson from the fig tree:
Reader 2	As soon as its twigs get tender and its leaves come out, you know that summer is near.
Reader 1	Even so, when you see all these [signs], you know that [the coming of the Son of Man] is near, right at the door.
Reader 2	I tell you the truth, this generation will certainly not pass away until all these things have happened.
Reader 1	Heaven and earth will pass away, but my words will never pass away.

Cast: **Reader 1, Reader 2**

The Day and Hour Unknown
Matthew 24:36–44

Reader 1   No one knows about that day or hour, not even the angels in heaven, nor the Son, but only the Father.

Reader 2   As it was in the days of Noah, so it will be at the coming of the Son of Man. For in the days before the flood, people were eating and drinking, marrying and giving in marriage, up to the day Noah entered the ark; and they knew nothing about what would happen until the flood came and took them all away. That is how it will be at the coming of the Son of Man.

Reader 1   Two men will be in the field; one will be taken and the other left. Two women will be grinding with a hand mill; one will be taken and the other left.

Reader 2   Therefore keep watch, because you do not know on what day your Lord will come. But understand this: If the owner of the house had known at what time of night the thief was coming, he would have kept watch and would not have let his house be broken into.

Reader 1   So you also must be ready, because the Son of Man will come at an hour when you do not expect him.

Cast: **Reader 1, Reader 2**

The Parable of the Ten Virgins
Matthew 25:1–13

Jesus   The kingdom of heaven will be like ten virgins who took their lamps and went out to meet the bridegroom. Five of them were foolish and five were wise. The foolish ones took their lamps but did not take any oil with them. The wise, however, took oil in jars along with their lamps. The bridegroom was a long time in coming, and they all became drowsy and fell asleep. At midnight the cry rang out:

Voice   Here's the bridegroom! Come out to meet him!

Jesus   Then all the virgins woke up and trimmed their lamps. The foolish ones said to the wise:

Foolish virgin 1   Give us some of your oil.

Foolish virgin 2   Our lamps are going out.

[Jesus   The wise ones answered:]

Wise virgin 1   No, there may not be enough for both us and you.

Wise virgin 2   Instead, go to those who sell oil and buy some for yourselves.

Jesus	But while they were on their way to buy the oil, the bridegroom arrived. The virgins who were ready went in with him to the wedding banquet. And the door was shut. Later the others also came.
Foolish virgin 1 (crying out)	Sir!
Foolish virgin 2 (crying out)	Sir!
Foolish virgins 1 and 2	Open the door for us!
Jesus	But he replied:
Bridegroom	I tell you the truth, I don't know you.
Jesus	Therefore keep watch, because you do not know the day or the hour.

Cast: **Jesus, Voice** (at a distance), **Foolish virgin 1, Foolish virgin 2, Wise virgin 1, Wise virgin 2** (can be the same as Wise virgin 1), **Bridegroom** (can be the same as Voice)

The Parable of the Talents
Matthew 25:14–30

Jesus	[The kingdom of heaven] will be like a man going on a journey, who called his servants and entrusted his property to them. To one he gave five talents of money, to another two talents, and to another one talent, each according to his ability. Then he went on his journey. The man who had received the five talents went at once and put his money to work and gained five more. So also, the one with the two talents gained two more. But the man who had received the one talent went off, dug a hole in the ground and hid his master's money. (PAUSE) After a long time the master of those servants returned and settled accounts with them. The man who had received the five talents brought the other five.
Servant 1	Master, you entrusted me with five talents. See, I have gained five more.
Jesus	His master replied:
Master	Well done, good and faithful servant! You have been faithful with a few things; I will put you in charge of many things. Come and share your master's happiness! (PAUSE)
Jesus	The man with the two talents also came.
Servant 2	Master, you entrusted me with two talents; see, I have gained two more.

Master	Well done, good and faithful servant! You have been faithful with a few things; I will put you in charge of many things. Come and share your master's happiness! (PAUSE)
Jesus	Then the man who had received the one talent came.
Servant 3	Master, I knew that you are a hard man, harvesting where you have not sown and gathering where you have not scattered seed. So I was afraid and went out and hid your talent in the ground. See, here is what belongs to you.
Master	You wicked, lazy servant! So you knew that I harvest where I have not sown and gather where I have not scattered seed? Well then, you should have put my money on deposit with the bankers, so that when I returned I would have received it back with interest.
	Take the talent from him and give it to the one who has the ten talents.
Jesus (slowly)	For everyone who has will be given more, and he will have an abundance. Whoever does not have, even what he has will be taken from him.
Master	And throw that worthless servant outside, into the darkness, where there will be weeping and gnashing of teeth.

Cast: **Jesus, Servant 1, Master, Servant 2, Servant 3**

The Sheep and the Goats
Matthew 25:31–46

Jesus	When the Son of Man comes in his glory, and all the angels with him, he will sit on his throne in heavenly glory. All the nations will be gathered before him, and he will separate the people one from another as a shepherd separates the sheep from the goats. He will put the sheep on his right and the goats on his left.
	Then the King will say to those on his right:
The King	Come, you who are blessed by my Father; take your inheritance, the kingdom prepared for you since the creation of the world. For I was hungry and you gave me something to eat, I was thirsty and you gave me something to drink, I was a stranger and you invited me in, I needed clothes and you clothed me, I was sick and you looked after me, I was in prison and you came to visit me.
Jesus	Then the righteous will answer him:
Righteous person 1	Lord, when did we see you hungry and feed you, or thirsty and give you something to drink?

Righteous person 2	When did we see you a stranger and invite you in, or needing clothes and clothe you?
Righteous person 3	When did we see you sick or in prison and go to visit you?
The King (to Righteous persons)	I tell you the truth, whatever you did for one of the least of these brothers of mine, you did for me.
Jesus	Then he will say to those on his left:
The King (to Person under a curse)	Depart from me, you who are cursed, into the eternal fire prepared for the devil and his angels. For I was hungry and you gave me nothing to eat, I was thirsty and you gave me nothing to drink, I was a stranger and you did not invite me in, I needed clothes and you did not clothe me, I was sick and in prison and you did not look after me.
Jesus	They also will answer:
Person under a curse	Lord, when did we see you hungry or thirsty or a stranger or needing clothes or sick or in prison, and did not help you?
Jesus	He will reply:
The King	I tell you the truth, whatever you did not do for one of the least of these, you did not do for me.
Jesus	Then they will go away to eternal punishment, but the righteous to eternal life.

Cast: **Jesus, the King, Righteous person 1, Righteous person 2** (can be the same as Righteous person 1), **Righteous Person 3** (can be the same as Righteous person 1), **Person under a curse**

The Plot against Jesus
Matthew 26:1–5, 14–16

Narrator	Jesus . . . said to his disciples:
Jesus	As you know, the Passover is two days away—and the Son of Man will be handed over to be crucified. (PAUSE)
Narrator	Then the chief priests and the elders of the people assembled in the palace of the high priest, whose name was Caiaphas, and they plotted to arrest Jesus in some sly way and kill him. **[They said:]**
Chief priest	But not during the Feast, or there may be a riot among the people. . . .

Narrator	Then one of the Twelve—the one called Judas Iscariot—went to the chief priests [and asked]:
Judas Iscariot	What are you willing to give me if I hand him over to you?
Narrator	So they counted out for him thirty silver coins. From then on Judas watched for an opportunity to hand [Jesus] over.

Cast: **Narrator, Jesus, Chief priest, Judas Iscariot**

Jesus Anointed at Bethany
Matthew 26:6–13

Narrator	While Jesus was in Bethany in the home of a man known as Simon the Leper, a woman came to him with an alabaster jar of very expensive perfume, which she poured on his head as he was reclining at the table. When the disciples saw this, they were indignant:
Disciple 1	Why this waste?
Disciple 2	This perfume could have been sold at a high price and the money given to the poor.
Narrator	Aware of this, Jesus said to them:
Jesus	Why are you bothering this woman? She has done a beautiful thing to me. The poor you will always have with you, but you will not always have me. When she poured this perfume on my body, she did it to prepare me for burial. I tell you the truth, wherever this gospel is preached throughout the world, what she has done will also be told, in memory of her.

Cast: **Narrator, Disciple 1, Disciple 2** (can be the same as Disciple 1), **Jesus**

Jesus Eats the Passover Meal with His Disciples
Matthew 26:17–25

Narrator	On the first day of the Feast of Unleavened Bread, the disciples came to Jesus and asked:
Disciple	Where do you want us to make preparations for you to eat the Passover?
[Narrator	He replied:]
Jesus	Go into the city to a certain man and tell him, "The Teacher says: My appointed time is near. I am going to celebrate the Passover with my disciples at your house." (PAUSE)
Narrator	So the disciples did as Jesus had directed them and prepared the Passover. (PAUSE)

When evening came, Jesus was reclining at the table with the Twelve. And while they were eating, he said: |

79

Jesus	I tell you the truth, one of you will betray me.
Narrator	They were very sad and began to say to him one after the other:
Disciple	Surely not I, Lord?
Jesus	The one who has dipped his hand into the bowl with me will betray me. The Son of Man will go just as it is written about him. But woe to that man who betrays the Son of Man! It would be better for him if he had not been born.
Narrator	Then Judas, the one who would betray him, said:
Judas	Surely not I, Rabbi?
Jesus (slowly)	Yes, it is you.

Cast: **Narrator, Disciple, Jesus, Judas**

The Lord's Supper
Matthew 26:26–30

Narrator	While they were eating, Jesus took bread, gave thanks and broke it, and gave it to his disciples, saying:
Jesus	Take and eat; this is my body.
Narrator	Then he took the cup, gave thanks and offered it to them, saying:
Jesus	Drink from it, all of you. This is my blood of the covenant, which is poured out for many for the forgiveness of sins. (PAUSE) I tell you, I will not drink of this fruit of the vine from now on until that day when I drink it anew with you in my Father's kingdom.
Narrator	When they had sung a hymn, they went out to the Mount of Olives.

Cast: **Narrator, Jesus**

Jesus Predicts Peter's Denial
Matthew 26:31–35

Narrator	Jesus told [his disciples]:
Jesus	This very night you will all fall away on account of me, for it is written:
Zechariah	I will strike the shepherd, and the sheep of the flock will be scattered.
Jesus	But after I have risen, I will go ahead of you into Galilee.
Narrator	Peter replied:
Peter (to Jesus)	Even if all fall away on account of you, I never will.

Jesus	I tell you the truth, this very night, before the rooster crows, you will disown me three times.
Peter	Even if I have to die with you, I will never disown you. (PAUSE)
Narrator	And all the other disciples said the same.

Cast: **Narrator**, **Jesus**, **Zechariah** (can be the same as Jesus), **Peter**

Gethsemane
Matthew 26:36–46

Narrator	Jesus went with his disciples to a place called Gethsemane, and he said to them:
Jesus	Sit here while I go over there and pray.
Narrator	He took Peter and the two sons of Zebedee along with him, and he began to be sorrowful and troubled.
Jesus	My soul is overwhelmed with sorrow to the point of death. Stay here and keep watch with me.
Narrator	Going a little farther, he fell with his face to the ground and prayed:
Jesus	My Father, if it is possible, may this cup be taken from me. Yet not as I will, but as you will.
Narrator	Then he returned to his disciples and found them sleeping. He asked Peter:
Jesus	Could you men not keep watch with me for one hour? Watch and pray so that you will not fall into temptation. The spirit is willing, but the body is weak.
Narrator	He went away a second time and prayed:
Jesus	My Father, if it is not possible for this cup to be taken away unless I drink it, may your will be done.
Narrator	When he came back, he again found them sleeping, because their eyes were heavy. So he left them and went away once more and prayed the third time, saying the same thing. (PAUSE) Then he returned to the disciples [and said to them:]
Jesus	Are you still sleeping and resting? Look, the hour is near, and the Son of Man is betrayed into the hands of sinners. Rise, let us go! Here comes my betrayer!

Cast: **Narrator**, **Jesus**

Jesus Arrested
Matthew 26:47–56

Narrator Judas, one of the Twelve, arrived. With him was a large crowd armed with swords and clubs, sent from the chief priests and the elders of the people. Now the betrayer had arranged a signal with them:

Judas Iscariot The one I kiss is the man; arrest him.

Narrator Going at once to Jesus, Judas said:

Judas Iscariot Greetings, Rabbi!

Narrator And kissed him. Jesus replied:

Jesus Friend, do what you came for.

Narrator Then the men stepped forward, seized Jesus and arrested him. With that, one of Jesus' companions reached for his sword, drew it out and struck the servant of the high priest, cutting off his ear.

[Jesus said to him:]

Jesus Put your sword back in its place, for all who draw the sword will die by the sword. Do you think I cannot call on my Father, and he will at once put at my disposal more than twelve legions of angels? But how then would the Scriptures be fulfilled that say it must happen in this way?

Narrator At that time Jesus said to the crowd:

Jesus Am I leading a rebellion, that you have come out with swords and clubs to capture me? Every day I sat in the temple courts teaching, and you did not arrest me. But this has all taken place that the writings of the prophets might be fulfilled.

Narrator Then all the disciples deserted him and fled.

Cast: **Narrator, Judas Iscariot, Jesus**

Jesus before the Sanhedrin
Matthew 26:57–68

Narrator Those who had arrested Jesus took him to Caiaphas, the high priest, where the teachers of the law and the elders had assembled. But Peter followed him at a distance, right up to the courtyard of the high priest. He entered and sat down with the guards to see the outcome.

The chief priests and the whole Sanhedrin were looking for false evidence against Jesus so that they could put him to death. But they did not find any, though many false witnesses came forward.

Finally two came forward and declared:

Man 1 This fellow said, "I am able to destroy the temple of God—

Man 2	And rebuild it in three days."
Narrator	Then the high priest stood up and said to Jesus:
High priest (to Jesus)	Are you not going to answer? (PAUSE) What is this testimony that these men are bringing against you?
Narrator	But Jesus remained silent. (PAUSE) The high priest said to him:
High priest	I charge you under oath by the living God: Tell us if you are the Christ, the Son of God.
[Narrator	Jesus replied:]
Jesus	Yes, it is as you say. But I say to all of you: In the future you will see the Son of Man sitting at the right hand of the Mighty One and coming on the clouds of heaven.
Narrator	Then the high priest tore his clothes and said:
High priest	He has spoken blasphemy! Why do we need any more witnesses? Look, now you have heard the blasphemy. What do you think?
Man 1	He is worthy of death.
[Man 2	He must die.]
Narrator	Then they spit in his face and struck him with their fists. Others slapped him and said:
Man 1 (cynically)	Prophesy to us, Christ.
Man 2	Who hit you?

Cast: **Narrator**, **Man 1**, **Man 2**, **High priest**, **Jesus**

Peter Disowns Jesus
Matthew 26:69–75

Narrator	Peter was sitting out in the courtyard, and a servant girl came to him. [She said:]
Girl 1	You also were with Jesus of Galilee.
Narrator	But he denied it before them all:
Peter	I don't know what you're talking about.
Narrator	Then he went out to the gateway, where another girl saw him and said to the people there:
Girl 2 (to men)	This fellow was with Jesus of Nazareth.
Narrator	He denied it again, with an oath:

Peter	I don't know the man!
Narrator	After a little while, those standing there went up to Peter and said:
Man 1	Surely you are one of them.
Man 2	For your accent gives you away.
[Narrator	Then he began to call down curses on himself and he swore to them:]
Peter	I don't know the man!
Narrator	Immediately a rooster crowed. Then Peter remembered the word Jesus had spoken:
Voice of Jesus (far away)	Before the rooster crows, you will disown me three times.
Narrator	And he went outside and wept bitterly.

Cast: **Narrator, Girl 1, Peter, Girl 2, Man 1, Man 2, Voice of Jesus** (far away)

Jesus before Pilate
Matthew 27:1–2, 11–14

Narrator	Early in the morning, all the chief priests and the elders of the people came to the decision to put Jesus to death. They bound him, led him away and handed him over to Pilate, the governor. . . .
	[Later] Jesus stood before the governor, and the governor asked him:
Pilate	Are you the king of the Jews?
[Narrator	Jesus replied:]
Jesus	Yes, it is as you say.
Narrator	When he was accused by the chief priests and the elders, he gave no answer. (PAUSE) Then Pilate asked him:
Pilate	Don't you hear the testimony they are bringing against you?
Narrator	But Jesus made no reply, not even to a single charge—to the great amazement of the governor.

Cast: **Narrator, Pilate, Jesus**

Judas Hangs Himself
Matthew 27:3–10

Narrator	When Judas, who had betrayed him, saw that Jesus was condemned, he was seized with remorse and returned the thirty silver coins to the chief priests and the elders.
Judas Iscariot	I have sinned, for I have betrayed innocent blood.
[Narrator	They replied:]
Chief priest	What is that to us?

Elder	That's your responsibility.
Narrator	So Judas threw the money into the temple and left. Then he went away and hanged himself.
	The chief priests picked up the coins and said:
Chief priest	It is against the law to put this into the treasury, since it is blood money.
Narrator	So they decided to use the money to buy the potter's field as a burial place for foreigners. That is why it has been called the Field of Blood to this day. Then what was spoken by Jeremiah the prophet was fulfilled:
Jeremiah (distant voice)	They took the thirty silver coins, the price set on him by the people of Israel, and they used them to buy the potter's field, as the Lord commanded me.

Cast: **Narrator, Judas Iscariot, Chief priest, Elder, Jeremiah** (distant voice)

Jesus Is Sentenced to Death
Matthew 27:15–26]

Narrator	Now it was the governor's custom at the Feast to release a prisoner chosen by the crowd. At that time they had a notorious prisoner, called Barabbas. So when the crowd had gathered, Pilate asked them:
Pilate	Which one do you want me to release to you: Barabbas, or Jesus who is called Christ?
Narrator	For he knew it was out of envy that they had handed Jesus over to him.
	While Pilate was sitting on the judge's seat, his wife sent him this message:
Pilate's wife	Don't have anything to do with that innocent man, for I have suffered a great deal today in a dream because of him.
Narrator	But the chief priests and the elders persuaded the crowd to ask for Barabbas and to have Jesus executed. [Pilate asked the crowd:]
Pilate	Which of the two do you want me to release to you?
Person 1 (calling)	Barabbas.
Pilate	What shall I do, then, with Jesus who is called Christ?
Person 2 (calling)	Crucify him!
Pilate	Why? What crime has he committed?
Narrator	But they shouted all the louder:
Persons 1 and 2	Crucify him!

Narrator	When Pilate saw that he was getting nowhere, but that instead an uproar was starting, he took water and washed his hands in front of the crowd.
Pilate	I am innocent of this man's blood. It is your responsibility!
[Narrator	All the people answered:]
Person 1	Let his blood be on us—
Person 2	And on our children!
Narrator	Then he released Barabbas to them. But he had Jesus flogged, and handed him over to be crucified.

Cast: **Narrator, Pilate, Pilate's wife, Person 1, Person 2**

The Crucifixion
Matthew 27:27–44

Narrator	[Pilate's] soldiers took Jesus into the Praetorium and gathered the whole company of soldiers around him. They stripped him and put a scarlet robe on him, and then twisted together a crown of thorns and set it on his head. They put a staff in his right hand and knelt in front of him and mocked him.
Soldier(s)	Hail, king of the Jews!
Narrator	They spit on him, and took the staff and struck him on the head again and again. After they had mocked him, they took off the robe and put his own clothes on him. Then they led him away to crucify him. (PAUSE) As they were going out, they met a man from Cyrene, named Simon, and they forced him to carry the cross. They came to a place called Golgotha (which means:
Voice (slowly)	The Place of the Skull).
Narrator	There they offered Jesus wine to drink, mixed with gall; but after tasting it, he refused to drink it. When they had crucified him, they divided up his clothes by casting lots. And sitting down, they kept watch over him there. Above his head they placed the written charge against him:
Voice	This is Jesus, the King of the Jews.
Narrator	Two robbers were crucified with him, one on his right and one on his left. (PAUSE) Those who passed by hurled insults at him, shaking their heads and saying:
Person 1	You who are going to destroy the temple and build it in three days, save yourself!
Person 2	Come down from the cross, if you are the Son of God!

86

Narrator	In the same way the chief priests, the teachers of the law and the elders mocked him:
Priest (cynically)	He saved others, but he can't save himself!
Lawyer (with sarcasm)	He's the King of Israel!
Elder (mocking)	Let him come down now from the cross, and we will believe in him.
Priest (challeng-ing)	He trusts in God. Let God rescue him now if he wants him, for he said, "I am the Son of God."
Narrator (slowly)	In the same way the robbers who were crucified with him also heaped insults on him.

Cast: **Narrator**, **Soldier(s)**, **Voice** (can be the same as Narrator), **Person 1**, **Person 2**, **Priest**, **Lawyer**, **Elder**

The Death of Jesus
Matthew 27:45–56

Narrator	From the sixth hour until the ninth hour darkness came over all the land. About the ninth hour Jesus cried out in a loud voice:
Jesus	*Eloi, Eloi, lama sabachthani?* . . . My God, my God, why have you forsaken me?
Narrator	When some of those standing there heard this, they said:
Person 1	He's calling Elijah.
Narrator	Immediately one of them ran and got a sponge. He filled it with wine vinegar, put it on a stick, and offered it to Jesus to drink. The rest said:
Person 2	Now leave him alone. Let's see if Elijah comes to save him.
Narrator	And when Jesus had cried out again in a loud voice, he gave up his spirit. (PAUSE)
	At that moment the curtain of the temple was torn in two from top to bottom. The earth shook and the rocks split. The tombs broke open and the bodies of many holy people who had died were raised to life. They came out of the tombs, and after Jesus' resurrection they went into the holy city and appeared to many people.
	When the centurion and those with him who were guarding Jesus saw the earthquake and all that had happened, they were terrified, and exclaimed:
Centurion	Surely he was the Son of God!

| Narrator | Many women were there, watching from a distance. They had followed Jesus from Galilee to care for his needs. Among them were Mary Magdalene, Mary the mother of James and Joses, and the mother of Zebedee's sons. |

Cast: **Narrator, Jesus, Person 1, Person 2, Centurion**

The Burial of Jesus
Matthew 27:57–66

| Narrator | As evening approached, there came a rich man from Arimathea, named Joseph, who had himself become a disciple of Jesus. Going to Pilate, he asked for Jesus' body, and Pilate ordered that it be given to him. Joseph took the body, wrapped it in a clean linen cloth, and placed it in his own new tomb that he had cut out of the rock. He rolled a big stone in front of the entrance to the tomb and went away. Mary Magdalene and the other Mary were sitting there opposite the tomb. (PAUSE)

The next day, the one after Preparation Day, the chief priests and the Pharisees went to Pilate [and said:] |
Priest	Sir, we remember that while he was still alive that deceiver said, "After three days I will rise again." So give the order for the tomb to be made secure until the third day. Otherwise, his disciples may come and steal the body and tell the people that he has been raised from the dead. This last deception will be worse than the first.
[Narrator	Pilate told them:]
Pilate	Take a guard. Go, make the tomb as secure as you know how.
Narrator	So they went and made the tomb secure by putting a seal on the stone and posting the guard.

Cast: **Narrator, Priest, Pilate**

The Resurrection
Matthew 28:1–10

| Narrator | After the Sabbath, at dawn on the first day of the week, Mary Magdalene and the other Mary went to look at the tomb.

There was a violent earthquake, for an angel of the Lord came down from heaven and, going to the tomb, rolled back the stone and sat on it. His appearance was like lightning, and his clothes were white as snow. The guards were so afraid of him that they shook and became like dead men. The angel said to the women: |
| Angel | Do not be afraid, for I know that you are looking for Jesus, who was crucified. He is not here; he has risen, just as he said. Come and see the place where he lay. Then go quickly and tell his disciples, "He has risen |

	from the dead and is going ahead of you into Galilee. There you will see him." Now I have told you.
Narrator	So the women hurried away from the tomb, afraid yet filled with joy, and ran to tell his disciples. Suddenly Jesus met them:
Jesus	Greetings.
Narrator	They came to him, clasped his feet and worshiped him.
Jesus	Do not be afraid. Go and tell my brothers to go to Galilee; there they will see me.

Cast: **Narrator, Angel, Jesus**

The Guards' Report
Matthew 28:11–15

Narrator	While the women were on their way, some of the guards went into the city and reported to the chief priests everything that had happened. When the chief priests had met with the elders and devised a plan, they gave the soldiers a large sum of money, telling them:
Priest	You are to say, "His disciples came during the night and stole him away while we were asleep." If this report gets to the governor, we will satisfy him and keep you out of trouble.
Narrator	So the soldiers took the money and did as they were instructed. And this story has been widely circulated among the Jews to this very day.

Cast: **Narrator, Priest.** (This reading is short and preferably linked with the preceding one.)

The Great Commission
Matthew 28:16–20

Narrator	The eleven disciples went to Galilee, to the mountain where Jesus had told them to go. When they saw him, they worshiped him; but some doubted. Then Jesus came to them and said:
Jesus	All authority in heaven and on earth has been given to me. Therefore go and make disciples of all nations, baptizing them in the name of the Father and of the Son and of the Holy Spirit, and teaching them to obey everything I have commanded you. And surely I am with you always, to the very end of the age.

Cast: **Narrator, Jesus**

See also the Passion Readings, beginning on page 423, and the Easter Readings, beginning on page 466.

The Gospel of Mark

John the Baptist Prepares the Way
Mark 1:1–8

Narrator	[This is] the beginning of the gospel about Jesus Christ, the Son of God. (PAUSE) It is written in Isaiah the prophet:

Prophet	[God said:]
	I will send my messenger ahead of you,
	  who will prepare your way—
	a voice of one calling in the desert,
	"Prepare the way for the Lord,
	  make straight paths for him."

Narrator	And so John came, baptizing in the desert region and preaching:
[John	Turn away from your sins and be baptized, and God will forgive your sins.]
Narrator	The whole Judean countryside and all the people of Jerusalem went out to him. Confessing their sins, they were baptized by him in the Jordan River. (PAUSE) John wore clothing made of camel's hair, with a leather belt around his waist, and he ate locusts and wild honey. And this was his message:
John	After me will come one more powerful than I, the thongs of whose sandals I am not worthy to stoop down and untie. I baptize you with water, but *he* will baptize you with the Holy Spirit.

Cast: **Narrator, Prophet, John**

The Baptism and Temptation of Jesus
Mark 1:9–13

Narrator	[*At that time] Jesus came from Nazareth in Galilee and was baptized by John in the Jordan. As Jesus was coming up out of the water, he saw heaven being torn open and the Spirit descending on him like a dove. And a voice came from heaven:
Voice	You are my Son, whom I love; with you I am well pleased.
Narrator	At once the Spirit sent him out into the desert, and he was in the desert forty days, being tempted by Satan. He was with the wild animals, and angels attended him.

Cast: **Narrator, Voice.** (*This link is retained when the reading is used with the previous one.)

The Calling of the First Disciples
Mark 1:14–20

Narrator	After John was put in prison, Jesus went into Galilee, proclaiming the good news of God:
Jesus	The time has come. The kingdom of God is near. Repent and believe the good news!
Narrator	As Jesus walked beside the Sea of Galilee, he saw Simon and his brother Andrew casting a net into the lake, for they were fishermen. Jesus said:
Jesus	Come, follow me, and I will make you fishers of men.
Narrator	At once they left their nets and followed him.
	When he had gone a little farther, he saw James son of Zebedee and his brother John in a boat, preparing their nets. Without delay he called them, and they left their father Zebedee in the boat with the hired men and followed him.

Cast: **Narrator, Jesus**

Jesus Drives Out an Evil Spirit
Mark 1:21–28

Narrator	[Jesus and his disciples] went to Capernaum, and when the Sabbath came, Jesus went into the synagogue and began to teach. The people were amazed at his teaching, because he taught them as one who had authority, not as the teachers of the law. (PAUSE) Just then a man in their synagogue who was possessed by an evil spirit cried out:
Man	What do you want with us, Jesus of Nazareth? Have you come to destroy us? I know who you are—the Holy One of God!
[Narrator	Jesus ordered the spirit:]
Jesus	Be quiet! Come out of him!
Narrator	The evil spirit shook the man violently and came out of him with a shriek. (PAUSE) The people were all so amazed that they asked each other:
Person 1	What is this?
Person 2	A new teaching—
Person 1	And with authority! He even gives orders to evil spirits.
Person 2	And they obey him.
Narrator	News about him spread quickly over the whole region of Galilee.

Cast: **Narrator, Man, Jesus, Person 1, Person 2**

Jesus Preaches in Galilee
Mark 1:35–45

Narrator	Very early in the morning, while it was still dark, Jesus got up, left the house and went off to a solitary place, where he prayed. Simon and his companions went to look for him, and when they found him, they exclaimed:
Disciple	Everyone is looking for you!
Narrator	Jesus replied:
Jesus	Let us go somewhere else—to the nearby villages—so I can preach there also. That is why I have come.
Narrator	So he traveled throughout Galilee, preaching in their synagogues and driving out demons. (PAUSE) A man with leprosy came to him and begged him on his knees:
Man	If you are willing, you can make me clean.
Narrator	Filled with compassion, Jesus reached out his hand and touched the man.
Jesus	I am willing. Be clean!
Narrator	Immediately the leprosy left him and he was cured. Jesus sent him away at once with a strong warning:
Jesus	See that you don't tell this to anyone. But go, show yourself to the priest and offer the sacrifices that Moses commanded for your cleansing, as a testimony to them.
Narrator	Instead [the man] went out and began to talk freely, spreading the news. As a result, Jesus could no longer enter a town openly but stayed outside in lonely places. Yet the people still came to him from every-where.

Cast: **Narrator, Disciple, Jesus, Man**

Jesus Heals a Paralytic
Mark 2:1–12

Narrator	When Jesus . . . entered Capernaum, the people heard that he had come home. So many gathered that there was no room left, not even outside the door, and he preached the word to them. Some men came, bringing to him a paralytic, carried by four of them. Since they could not get him to Jesus because of the crowd, they made an opening in the roof above Jesus and, after digging through it, lowered the mat the

	paralyzed man was lying on. When Jesus saw their faith, he said to the paralytic:
Jesus	Son, your sins are forgiven.
Narrator	Now some teachers of the law were sitting there, thinking to themselves:
Lawyer 1	Why does this fellow talk like that?
Lawyer 2	He's blaspheming!
Lawyer 3	Who can forgive sins but God alone?
Narrator	Immediately Jesus knew in his spirit that this was what they were thinking in their hearts [and he said to them]:
Jesus	Why are you thinking these things? Which is easier: to say to the paralytic, "Your sins are forgiven," or to say, "Get up, take your mat and walk"? But that you may know that the Son of Man has authority on earth to forgive sins. . . .
Narrator	He said to the paralytic:
Jesus	I tell you, get up, take your mat and go home.
Narrator	[The man] got up, took his mat and walked out in full view of them all. This amazed everyone and they praised God, saying:
Person	We have never seen anything like this!

Cast: **Narrator, Jesus, Lawyer 1, Lawyer 2, Lawyer 3, Person** (can be the same as Lawyer 1, or Lawyers 1 and 2 can be the same)

The Calling of Levi
Mark 2:13–17

Narrator	Once again Jesus went out beside the lake. A large crowd came to him, and he began to teach them. As he walked along, he saw Levi son of Alphaeus sitting at the tax collector's booth. [Jesus told him:]
Jesus	Follow me.
Narrator	And Levi got up and followed him. (PAUSE)
	While Jesus was having dinner at Levi's house, many tax collectors and "sinners" were eating with him and his disciples, for there were many who followed him. When the teachers of the law who were Pharisees saw him eating with the "sinners" and tax collectors, they asked his disciples:
Pharisee	Why does he eat with tax collectors and "sinners"?
Narrator	On hearing this, Jesus said to them:

Jesus	It is not the healthy who need a doctor, but the sick. I have not come to call the righteous, but sinners.

Cast: **Narrator, Jesus, Pharisee**

Jesus Questioned about Fasting
Mark 2:18–22

Narrator	Now John's disciples and the Pharisees were fasting. Some people came and asked Jesus:
Person	How is it that John's disciples and the disciples of the Pharisees are fasting, but yours are not?
[Narrator	Jesus answered:]
Jesus	How can the guests of the bridegroom fast while he is with them? They cannot, so long as they have him with them. (PAUSE) But the time will come when the bridegroom will be taken from them, and on that day they will fast.
	No one sews a patch of unshrunk cloth on an old garment. If he does, the new piece will pull away from the old, making the tear worse. And no one pours new wine into old wineskins. If he does, the wine will burst the skins, and both the wine and the wineskins will be ruined. No, he pours new wine into new wineskins.

Cast: **Narrator, Person, Jesus**

Lord of the Sabbath
Mark 2:23–28

Narrator	One Sabbath Jesus was going through the grainfields, and as his disciples walked along, they began to pick some heads of grain. The Pharisees said to him:
Pharisee	Look, why are they doing what is unlawful on the Sabbath?
[Narrator	He answered:]
Jesus (to Pharisee)	Have you never read what David did when he and his companions were hungry and in need? In the days of Abiathar the high priest, he entered the house of God and ate the consecrated bread, which is lawful only for priests to eat. And he also gave some to his companions.
	The Sabbath was made for man, not man for the Sabbath. So the Son of Man is Lord even of the Sabbath.

Cast: **Narrator, Pharisee, Jesus**

The Man with a Paralyzed Hand
Mark 3:1–6

Narrator	Another time [Jesus] went into the synagogue, and a man with a shriveled hand was there. Some of [the people] were looking for a reason to accuse Jesus, so they watched him closely to see if he would heal him on the Sabbath. Jesus said to the man with the shriveled hand:
Jesus	Stand up in front of everyone.
Narrator	Then Jesus asked [the people]:
Jesus	Which is lawful on the Sabbath: to do good or to do evil, to save life or to kill?
Narrator	But they remained silent. (PAUSE) He looked around at them in anger and, deeply distressed at their stubborn hearts, said to the man:
Jesus	Stretch out your hand.
Narrator	He stretched it out, and his hand was completely restored. Then the Pharisees went out and began to plot with the Herodians how they might kill Jesus.

Cast: **Narrator, Jesus**

Crowds Follow Jesus
Mark 3:7–12

Narrator 1	Jesus withdrew with his disciples to the lake, and a large crowd from Galilee followed.
Narrator 2	When they heard all he was doing, many people came to him from Judea, Jerusalem, Idumea, and the regions across the Jordan and around Tyre and Sidon.
Narrator 1	Because of the crowd he told his disciples to have a small boat ready for him, to keep the people from crowding him.
Narrator 2	For he had healed many, so that those with diseases were pushing forward to touch him.
Narrator 1	Whenever the evil spirits saw him, they fell down before him and cried out:
Evil spirit (loudly)	You are the Son of God.
Narrator 2	But he gave them strict orders not to tell who he was.

Cast: **Narrator 1, Narrator 2** (can be the same as Narrator 1 when this reading is linked to the previous one), **Evil spirit**

The Appointing of the Twelve Apostles
Mark 3:13–19

Narrator	Jesus went up on a mountainside and called to him those he wanted, and they came to him. He appointed twelve—designating them apostles. [He told them:]
Jesus	[I have appointed you to be with me. I will also send you] out to preach and to have authority to drive out demons.
Narrator	These are the twelve he appointed: Simon—
Commentator	To whom he gave the name Peter.
Narrator	James son of Zebedee and his brother John.
Commentator	To them he gave the name Boanerges, which means Sons of Thunder.
Narrator	Andrew, Philip, Bartholomew, Matthew, Thomas, James—
Commentator	[The] son of Alphaeus.
Narrator	Thaddaeus, Simon—
Commentator	The Zealot.
Narrator	And Judas Iscariot—
Commentator	Who betrayed [Jesus].

Cast: **Narrator, Jesus, Commentator**

Jesus and Beelzebub
Mark 3:20–30

Narrator	Jesus entered a house, and again a crowd gathered, so that he and his disciples were not even able to eat. When his family heard about this, they went to take charge of him, for they said:
Person	He is out of his mind.
Narrator	And the teachers of the law who came down from Jerusalem said:
Lawyer 1	He is possessed by Beelzebub!
Lawyer 2	By the prince of demons he is driving out demons.
Narrator	So Jesus called them and spoke to them in parables:
Jesus	How can Satan drive out Satan? If a kingdom is divided against itself, that kingdom cannot stand. If a house is divided against itself, that house cannot stand. And if Satan opposes himself and is divided, he cannot stand; his end has come. (PAUSE) In fact, no one can enter a strong man's house and carry off his possessions unless he first ties up the strong man. Then he can rob his house.

I tell you the truth, all the sins and blasphemies of men will be forgiven them. But whoever blasphemes against the Holy Spirit will never be forgiven; he is guilty of an eternal sin.

| Narrator | [Jesus] said this because they were saying, "He has an evil spirit." |

Cast: **Narrator, Person, Lawyer 1, Lawyer 2** (can be the same as Lawyer 1), **Jesus**

Jesus' Mother and Brothers
Mark 3:31–35

Narrator	Jesus' mother and brothers arrived. Standing outside, they sent someone in to call him. A crowd was sitting around him, and they told him:
Person 1	Your mother and brothers are outside looking for you.
Person 2	[They want you.]
Narrator	[Jesus] asked:
Jesus	Who are my mother and my brothers?
Narrator	Then he looked at those seated in a circle around him and said:
Jesus	Here are my mother and my brothers! Whoever does God's will is my brother and sister and mother.

Cast: **Narrator, Person 1, Person 2** (can be the same as Person 1), **Jesus**

The Parable of the Sower
Mark 4:1–20

Narrator	Again Jesus began to teach by the lake. The crowd that gathered around him was so large that he got into a boat and sat in it out on the lake, while all the people were along the shore at the water's edge. He taught them many things by parables, and in his teaching said:
Jesus	Listen! A farmer went out to sow his seed. As he was scattering the seed, some fell along the path, and the birds came and ate it up. Some fell on rocky places, where it did not have much soil. It sprang up quickly, because the soil was shallow. But when the sun came up, the plants were scorched, and they withered because they had no root. Other seed fell among thorns, which grew up and choked the plants, so that they did not bear grain. Still other seed fell on good soil. It came up, grew and produced a crop, multiplying thirty, sixty, or even a hundred times.
Narrator	Then Jesus said:
Jesus	He who has ears to hear, let him hear.
Narrator	When he was alone, the Twelve and the others around him asked him about the parables. [He told them:]

Jesus	The secret of the kingdom of God has been given to you. But to those on the outside everything is said in parables so that, [as Isaiah says:]
Isaiah	They may be ever seeing but never perceiving, and ever hearing but never understanding; otherwise they might turn and be forgiven!
[Narrator	Then Jesus said to them:]
Jesus	Don't you understand this parable? How then will you understand any parable? The farmer sows the word. Some people are like seed along the path, where the word is sown. As soon as they hear it, Satan comes and takes away the word that was sown in them.
	Others, like seed sown on rocky places, hear the word and at once receive it with joy. But since they have no root, they last only a short time. When trouble or persecution comes because of the word, they quickly fall away.
	Still others, like seed sown among thorns, hear the word; but the worries of this life, the deceitfulness of wealth and the desires for other things come in and choke the word, making it unfruitful.
	Others, like seed sown on good soil, hear the word, accept it, and produce a crop—thirty, sixty or even a hundred times what was sown.

Cast: **Narrator, Jesus, Isaiah.** (See two quite different dramatizations of this parable at Matthew 13:1 and Luke 8:4.)

Parables of the Kingdom
Mark 4:21–34

Narrator	[Jesus] said to [the Twelve and the others around him]:
Jesus	Do you bring in a lamp to put it under a bowl or a bed? Instead, don't you put it on its stand? For whatever is hidden is meant to be disclosed, and whatever is concealed is meant to be brought out into the open. If anyone has ears to hear, let him hear.
Narrator	[He continued:]
Jesus	Consider carefully what you hear. With the measure you use, it will be measured to you—and even more. Whoever has will be given more; whoever does not have, even what he has will be taken from him.
Narrator	He also said:
Jesus	This is what the kingdom of God is like. A man scatters seed on the ground. Night and day, whether he sleeps or gets up, the seed sprouts and grows, though he does not know how. All by itself the soil produces grain—first the stalk, then the head, then the full kernel in the head. As soon as the grain is ripe, he puts the sickle to it, because the harvest has come. (PAUSE)

Narrator	Again he said:
Jesus	What shall we say the kingdom of God is like, or what parable shall we use to describe it? It is like a mustard seed, which is the smallest seed you plant in the ground. Yet when planted, it grows and becomes the largest of all garden plants, with such big branches that the birds of the air can perch in its shade.
Narrator	With many similar parables Jesus spoke the word to them, as much as they could understand. He did not say anything to them without using a parable. But when he was alone with his own disciples, he explained everything.

Cast: **Narrator, Jesus**

Jesus Calms the Storm [and Walks on the Water]
Mark 4:35–41 [6:45–51]

Narrator	[Jesus] said to his disciples:
Jesus	Let us go over to the other side [of the lake.]
Narrator	Leaving the crowd behind, they took him along, just as he was, in the boat. There were also other boats with him. A furious squall came up, and the waves broke over the boat, so that it was nearly swamped. Jesus was in the stern, sleeping on a cushion. The disciples woke him and said to him:
Disciples 1 and 2	Teacher!
Disciple 1	Don't you care if we drown?
Narrator	[Jesus got up and] rebuked the wind:
Jesus	Quiet!
Narrator	And [he] said to the waves:
Jesus	Be still!
Narrator	Then the wind died down and it was completely calm. He said to his disciples:
Jesus	Why are you so afraid? Do you still have no faith?
Narrator	They were terrified and asked each other:
Disciple 1	Who is this?
Disciple 2	Even the wind and the waves obey him!
[Narrator	Immediately Jesus made his disciples get into the boat and go on ahead of him to Bethsaida, while he dismissed the crowd. After leaving them, he went up on a mountainside to pray.

When evening came, the boat was in the middle of the lake, and he was alone on land. He saw the disciples straining at the oars, because the wind was against them. About the fourth watch of the night he went out to them, walking on the lake. He was about to pass by them, but when they saw him walking on the lake, they [cried out:

Disciples
1 and **2**
(hoarse
whisper)   It's a ghost!]

Narrator   They all saw him and were terrified. (PAUSE) Immediately he spoke to them and said:

Jesus   Take courage! It is I. Don't be afraid.

Narrator   Then he climbed into the boat with them, and the wind died down. They were completely amazed.]

Cast: **Narrator, Jesus, Disciple 1, Disciple 2** (can be the same as Disciple 1)

The Healing of a Demon-possessed Man
Mark 5:1–20

Narrator   [Jesus and his disciples] went across the lake to the region of the Gerasenes. When Jesus got out of the boat, a man with an evil spirit came from the tombs to meet him. This man lived in the tombs, and no one could bind him any more, not even with a chain. For he had often been chained hand and foot, but he tore the chains apart and broke the irons on his feet. No one was strong enough to subdue him. Night and day among the tombs and in the hills he would cry out and cut himself with stones.

When he saw Jesus from a distance, he ran and fell on his knees in front of him. He shouted at the top of his voice:

Man   What do you want with me, Jesus, Son of the Most High God? Swear to God that you won't torture me!

Narrator   For Jesus had said to him:

Jesus   Come out of this man, you evil spirit!

Narrator   Then Jesus asked him:

Jesus   What is your name?

Man   My name is Legion, for we are many.

Narrator   And he begged Jesus again and again not to send [the demons] out of the area. (PAUSE) A large herd of pigs was feeding on the nearby hillside. The demons begged Jesus:

Demon   Send us among the pigs; allow us to go into them.

Narrator	He gave them permission, and the evil spirits came out and went into the pigs. The herd, about two thousand in number, rushed down the steep bank into the lake and were drowned. (PAUSE)
	Those tending the pigs ran off and reported this in the town and countryside, and the people went out to see what had happened. When they came to Jesus, they saw the man who had been possessed by the legion of demons, sitting there, dressed and in his right mind; and they were afraid. Those who had seen it told the people what had happened to the demon-possessed man—and told about the pigs as well. Then the people began to plead with Jesus to leave their region.
	As Jesus was getting into the boat, the man who had been demon-possessed begged to go with him. Jesus did not let him, but said:
Jesus	Go home to your family and tell them how much the Lord has done for you, and how he has had mercy on you.
Narrator	So the man went away and began to tell in the Decapolis how much Jesus had done for him. And all the people were amazed.

Cast: **Narrator, Man, Jesus, Demon**

A Dead Girl and a Sick Woman
Mark 5:21–43

Narrator	When Jesus had again crossed over by boat to the other side of the lake, a large crowd gathered around him while he was by the lake. Then one of the synagogue rulers, named Jairus, came there. Seeing Jesus, he fell at his feet and pleaded earnestly with him:
Jairus	My little daughter is dying. Please come and put your hands on her so that she will be healed and live.
Narrator	So Jesus went with him.
	A large crowd followed and pressed around him. And a woman was there who had been subject to bleeding for twelve years. She had suffered a great deal under the care of many doctors and had spent all she had, yet instead of getting better she grew worse. When she heard about Jesus, she came up behind him in the crowd and touched his cloak, because she thought:
Woman	If I just touch his clothes, I will be healed.
Narrator	Immediately her bleeding stopped and she felt in her body that she was freed from her suffering.
	At once Jesus realized that power had gone out from him. He turned around in the crowd and asked:
Jesus	Who touched my clothes?
Narrator	His disciples answered:

Disciple 1	You see the people crowding against you.
Disciple 2	And yet you can ask, "Who touched me?"
Narrator	But Jesus kept looking around to see who had done it. Then the woman, knowing what had happened to her, came and fell at his feet and, trembling with fear, told him the whole truth. He said to her:
Jesus	Daughter, your faith has healed you. Go in peace and be freed from your suffering.
Narrator	While Jesus was still speaking, some men came from the house of Jairus, the synagogue ruler [and said:]
Messenger (to Jairus)	Your daughter is dead. Why bother the teacher any more?
Narrator	Ignoring what they said, Jesus told the synagogue ruler:
Jesus	Don't be afraid; just believe.
Narrator	He did not let anyone follow him except Peter, James and John the brother of James. When they came to the home of the synagogue ruler, Jesus saw a commotion, with people crying and wailing loudly. He went in and said to them:
Jesus	Why all this commotion and wailing? The child is not dead but asleep.
Narrator	But they laughed at him.
	After he put them all out, he took the child's father and mother and the disciples who were with him, and went in where the child was. He took her by the hand and said to her:
Jesus	*Talitha koum!* Little girl, I say to you, get up!
Narrator	Immediately the girl stood up and walked around (she was twelve years old). At this they were completely astonished. He gave strict orders not to let anyone know about this, and told them:
[Jesus	Give her something to eat.]

Cast: **Narrator, Jairus, Woman, Jesus, Disciple 1, Disciple 2** (can be the same as Jairus), **Messenger**

A Prophet without Honor
Mark 6:1–6

Narrator	Jesus . . . went to his hometown, accompanied by his disciples. When the Sabbath came, he began to teach in the synagogue, and many who heard him were amazed.
Person 1	Where did this man get these things?
Person 2	What's this wisdom that has been given him?

Person 1	He even does miracles!
Person 2	Isn't this the carpenter? Isn't this Mary's son?
Person 1	The brother of James, Joseph, Judas and Simon?
Person 2	Aren't his sisters here with us?
Narrator	And they took offense at him. (PAUSE)
	Jesus said to them:
Jesus (to Persons 1 and 2)	Only in his hometown, among his relatives and in his own house is a prophet without honor.
Narrator	He could not do any miracles there, except lay his hands on a few sick people and heal them. And he was amazed at their lack of faith.

Cast: **Narrator, Person 1, Person 2, Jesus**

Jesus Sends Out the Twelve
Mark 6:6–13

Narrator	Jesus went around teaching from village to village. Calling the Twelve to him, he sent them out two by two and gave them authority over evil spirits. (PAUSE) These were his instructions:
Jesus	Take nothing for the journey except a staff—no bread, no bag, no money in your belts. Wear sandals but not an extra tunic. Whenever you enter a house, stay there until you leave that town. And if any place will not welcome you or listen to you, shake the dust off your feet when you leave, as a testimony against them.
Narrator	They went out and preached that people should repent. They drove out many demons and anointed many sick people with oil and healed them.

Cast: **Narrator, Jesus**

John the Baptist Beheaded
Mark 6:14–29

Narrator	King Herod heard about [Jesus, for his] name had become well known. Some were saying:
Person 1	John the Baptist has been raised from the dead, and that is why miraculous powers are at work in him.
Narrator	Others said:
Person 2	He is Elijah.

Narrator	And still others claimed:
Person 1	He is a prophet, like one of the prophets of long ago.
Narrator	But when Herod heard this, he said:
Herod (frightened)	John, the man I beheaded, has been raised from the dead!
Narrator	For Herod himself had given orders to have John arrested, and he had him bound and put in prison. He did this because of Herodias, his brother Philip's wife, whom he had married. For John had been saying to Herod:
John	It is not lawful for you to have your brother's wife.
Narrator	So Herodias nursed a grudge against John and wanted to kill him. But she was not able to, because Herod feared John and protected him, knowing him to be a righteous and holy man. When Herod heard John, he was greatly puzzled; yet he liked to listen to him.
	Finally the opportune time came. On his birthday Herod gave a banquet for his high officials and military commanders and the leading men of Galilee. When the daughter of Herodias came in and danced, she pleased Herod and his dinner guests. (PAUSE) The king said to the girl:
Herod	Ask me for anything you want, and I'll give it to you.
Narrator	And he promised her with an oath:
Herod	Whatever you ask I will give you, up to half my kingdom.
Narrator	She went out and said to her mother:
Girl	What shall I ask for?
[Narrator	She answered:]
Herodias (with malice)	The head of John the Baptist.
Narrator	At once the girl hurried in to the king with the request:
Girl	I want you to give me right now the head of John the Baptist on a platter.
Narrator	The king was greatly distressed, but because of his oaths and his dinner guests, he did not want to refuse her. So he immediately sent an executioner with orders to bring John's head. The man went, beheaded John in the prison, and brought back his head on a platter. He presented it to the girl, and she gave it to her mother. On hearing of this, John's disciples came and took his body and laid it in a tomb.

Cast: **Narrator, Person 1, Person 2, Herod, John** (the Baptist, can be the same as Narrator), **Girl, Herodias**

Jesus Feeds the Five Thousand
Mark 6:30–44

Narrator	The apostles gathered around Jesus and reported to him all they had done and taught. Then, because so many people were coming and going that they did not even have a chance to eat, he said to them:
Jesus	Come with me by yourselves to a quiet place and get some rest.
Narrator	So they went away by themselves in a boat to a solitary place. (PAUSE) But many who saw them leaving recognized them and ran on foot from all the towns and got there ahead of them. When Jesus landed and saw a large crowd, he had compassion on them, because they were like sheep without a shepherd. So he began teaching them many things.
	By this time it was late in the day, so his disciples came to him.
Disciple 1	This is a remote place, and it's already very late.
Disciple 2	Send the people away.
Disciple 1	[Let them] go to the surrounding countryside and villages and buy themselves something to eat.
Jesus	You give them something to eat.
Disciple 1	That would take eight months of a man's wages! Are we to go and spend that much on bread and give it to them to eat?
Jesus	How many loaves do you have? Go and see.
Narrator	When they found out, they said:
Disciple 2	Five—and two fish.
Narrator	Then Jesus directed them to have all the people sit down in groups on the green grass. So they sat down in groups of hundreds and fifties. Taking the five loaves and the two fish and looking up to heaven, he gave thanks and broke the loaves. Then he gave them to his disciples to set before the people. He also divided the two fish among them all. They all ate and were satisfied, and the disciples picked up twelve basketfuls of broken pieces of bread and fish. (PAUSE) The number of the men who had eaten was five thousand.

Cast: **Narrator, Jesus, Disciple 1, Disciple 2**

Jesus Walks on the Water
Mark 6:45–56

Narrator	Jesus made his disciples get into the boat and go on ahead of him to Bethsaida, while he dismissed the crowd. After leaving them, he went up on a mountainside to pray.

When evening came, the boat was in the middle of the lake, and he was alone on land. He saw the disciples straining at the oars, because the wind was against them. About the fourth watch of the night he went out to them, walking on the lake. He was about to pass by them, but when they saw him walking on the lake, they . . . cried out:

Disciples 1 and 2 (hoarse whisper)	[It's a ghost!]
Narrator	They all saw him and were terrified. Immediately he spoke to them and said:
Jesus	Take courage! It is I. Don't be afraid.
Narrator	Then he climbed into the boat with them, and the wind died down. They were completely amazed, for they had not understood about the loaves; their hearts were hardened.
	When they had crossed over, they landed at Gennesaret and anchored there. As soon as they got out of the boat, people recognized Jesus. They ran throughout that whole region and carried the sick on mats to wherever they heard he was. And wherever he went—into villages, towns or countryside—they placed the sick in the marketplaces. They begged him to let them touch even the edge of his cloak, and all who touched him were healed.

Cast: **Narrator, Disciple 1, Disciple 2** (can be the same as Disciple 1), **Jesus.** (See also the composite version on pages 99–100.)

The Teaching of the Elders
Mark 7:1–13

Narrator	The Pharisees and some of the teachers of the law who had come from Jerusalem gathered around Jesus and saw some of his disciples eating food with hands that were "unclean," that is, unwashed. (The Pharisees and all the Jews do not eat unless they give their hands a ceremonial washing, holding to the tradition of the elders. When they come from the marketplace they do not eat unless they wash. And they observe many other traditions, such as the washing of cups, pitchers and kettles.)
	So the Pharisees and teachers of the law asked Jesus:
Lawyer	Why don't your disciples live according to the tradition of the elders instead of eating their food with "unclean" hands?
Narrator	[Jesus] replied:
Jesus	Isaiah was right when he prophesied about you hypocrites; as it is written:

106

Isaiah	These people honor me with their lips,
	    but their hearts are far from me.
	They worship me in vain;
	    their teachings are but rules taught by men.

Jesus	You have let go of the commands of God and are holding on to the traditions of men.
	You have a fine way of setting aside the commands of God in order to observe your own traditions! For Moses said:
Moses	Honor your father and your mother. Anyone who curses his father or mother must be put to death.
Jesus	But you say that if a man says to his father or mother: "Whatever help you might otherwise have received from me is Corban"—
Narrator (aside)	That is, a gift devoted to God—
Jesus	Then you no longer let him do anything for his father or mother. Thus you nullify the word of God by your tradition that you have handed down. And you do many things like that.

Cast: **Narrator, Lawyer, Jesus, Isaiah, Moses**

Clean and Unclean
Mark 7:14–23

Narrator	Jesus called the crowd to him and said:
Jesus	Listen to me, everyone, and understand this. Nothing outside a man can make him "unclean" by going into him. Rather, it is what comes out of a man that makes him "unclean."
Narrator	After he had left the crowd and entered the house, his disciples asked him about this parable.
Jesus	Are you so dull? Don't you see that nothing that enters a man from the outside can make him "unclean"? For it doesn't go into his heart but into his stomach, and then out of his body.
Narrator	In saying this, Jesus declared all foods "clean." He went on:
Jesus	What comes out of a man is what makes him "unclean." For from within, out of men's hearts, come evil thoughts, sexual immorality, theft, murder, adultery, greed, malice, deceit, lewdness, envy, slander, arrogance and folly. All these evils come from inside and make a man "unclean."

Cast: **Narrator, Jesus**

The Faith of a Syrophoenician Woman
Mark 7:24–30

Narrator   Jesus . . . went to the vicinity of Tyre. He entered a house and did not want anyone to know it; yet he could not keep his presence secret. In fact, as soon as she heard about him, a woman whose little daughter was possessed by an evil spirit came and fell at his feet. The woman was a Greek, born in Syrian Phoenicia. She begged Jesus to drive the demon out of her daughter.

Jesus   First let the children eat all they want, for it is not right to take the children's bread and toss it to their dogs.

Woman   Yes, Lord, but even the dogs under the table eat the children's crumbs.

Jesus   For such a reply, you may go; the demon has left your daughter.

Narrator   She went home and found her child lying on the bed, and the demon gone.

Cast: **Narrator, Jesus, Woman**

The Healing of a Deaf and Mute Man
Mark 7:31–37

Narrator   Jesus left the vicinity of Tyre and went through Sidon, down to the Sea of Galilee and into the region of the Decapolis. There some people brought to him a man who was deaf and could hardly talk, and they begged him to place his hand on the man.

After he took him aside, away from the crowd, Jesus put his fingers into the man's ears. Then he spit and touched the man's tongue. He looked up to heaven and with a deep sigh said to him:

Jesus   *Ephphatha!* Be opened!

Narrator   At this, the man's ears were opened, his tongue was loosened and he began to speak plainly.

Jesus commanded [the people] not to tell anyone. But the more he did so, the more they kept talking about it. [They] were overwhelmed with amazement.

Person 1   He has done everything well.

Person 2   He even makes the deaf hear and the mute speak.

Cast: **Narrator, Jesus, Person 1, Person 2** (can be the same as Person 1)

Jesus Feeds the Four Thousand
Mark 8:1–10

Narrator	Another large crowd gathered. Since they had nothing to eat, Jesus called his disciples to him and said:
Jesus	I have compassion for these people; they have already been with me three days and have nothing to eat. If I send them home hungry, they will collapse on the way, because some of them have come a long distance.
Narrator	His disciples answered:
Disciple	But where in this remote place can anyone get enough bread to feed them?
Jesus	How many loaves do you have?
Disciple	Seven.
Narrator	He told the crowd to sit down on the ground. When he had taken the seven loaves and given thanks, he broke them and gave them to his disciples to set before the people, and they did so. They had a few small fish as well; he gave thanks for them also and told the disciples to distribute them. The people ate and were satisfied. Afterward the disciples picked up seven basketfuls of broken pieces that were left over. About four thousand men were present. And having sent them away, he got into the boat with his disciples and went to the region of Dalmanutha.

Cast: **Narrator, Jesus, Disciple**

The Pharisees Ask for a Miracle
Mark 8:11–21

Narrator	The Pharisees came and began to question Jesus. To test him, they asked him for a sign from heaven. He sighed deeply [and said:]
Jesus	Why does this generation ask for a miraculous sign? I tell you the truth, no sign will be given to it.
Narrator	Then he left them, got back into the boat and crossed to the other side [of the lake]. (PAUSE)
	The disciples had forgotten to bring bread, except for one loaf they had with them in the boat. Jesus warned them:
Jesus	Be careful. Watch out for the yeast of the Pharisees and that of Herod.
Narrator	They discussed this with one another and said:
Disciple (aside)	It is because we have no bread.
Narrator	Aware of their discussion, Jesus asked them:

Jesus	Why are you talking about having no bread? Do you still not see or understand? Are your hearts hardened? Do you have eyes but fail to see, and ears but fail to hear? And don't you remember? When I broke the five loaves for the five thousand, how many basketfuls of pieces did you pick up?
Disciple	Twelve.
Jesus	And when I broke the seven loaves for the four thousand, how many basketfuls of pieces did you pick up?
Disciple	Seven.
Jesus	Do you *still* not understand?

Cast: **Narrator, Jesus, Disciple**

The Healing of a Blind Man at Bethsaida
Mark 8:22–26

Narrator	[Jesus and his disciples] came to Bethsaida, and some people brought a blind man and begged Jesus to touch him. He took the blind man by the hand and led him outside the village. When he had spit on the man's eyes and put his hands on him, Jesus asked:
Jesus	Do you see anything?
Narrator	He looked up and said:
Man	I see people; they look like trees walking around.
Narrator	Once more Jesus put his hands on the man's eyes. Then his eyes were opened, his sight was restored, and he saw everything clearly. Jesus sent him home, saying:
Jesus	Don't go into the village.

Cast: **Narrator, Jesus, Man**

Peter's Confession of Christ
Mark 8:27–30

Narrator	Jesus and his disciples went on to the villages around Caesarea Philippi. On the way he asked them:
Jesus	Who do people say I am?
Disciple	Some say John the Baptist; others say Elijah; and still others, one of the prophets.
Jesus	But what about you? Who do you say I am?
Narrator	Peter answered:

Peter	You are the Christ.
[Narrator	Jesus warned them:]
Jesus (to disciples)	[Do not tell anyone about me.]

Cast: **Narrator, Jesus, Disciple, Peter**

Jesus Predicts His Death
Mark 8:31–38

Narrator	[Jesus] began to teach [his disciples]:
Jesus	The Son of Man must suffer many things and be rejected by the elders, chief priests and teachers of the law. He must be killed and after three days rise again.
Narrator	He spoke plainly about this, and Peter took him aside and began to rebuke him.
	But when Jesus turned and looked at his disciples, he rebuked Peter.
Jesus	Get behind me, Satan! You do not have in mind the things of God, but the things of men.
Narrator	Then he called the crowd to him along with his disciples and said:
Jesus	If anyone would come after me, he must deny himself and take up his cross and follow me. For whoever wants to save his life will lose it, but whoever loses his life for me and for the gospel will save it. What good is it for a man to gain the whole world, yet forfeit his soul? Or what can a man give in exchange for his soul? If anyone is ashamed of me and my words in this adulterous and sinful generation, the Son of Man will be ashamed of him when he comes in his Father's glory with the holy angels.

Cast: **Narrator, Jesus**

The Transfiguration
Mark 9:2–13

Narrator	Jesus took Peter, James and John with him and led them up a high mountain, where they were all alone. There he was transfigured before them. His clothes became dazzling white, whiter than anyone in the world could bleach them. And there appeared before them Elijah and Moses, who were talking with Jesus. Peter said to Jesus:
Peter	Rabbi, it is good for us to be here. Let us put up three shelters—one for you, one for Moses and one for Elijah.

Narrator	(He did not know what to say, they were so frightened.) Then a cloud appeared and enveloped them, and a voice came from the cloud:
Voice (at a distance)	This is my Son, whom I love. Listen to him!
Narrator	Suddenly, when they looked around, they no longer saw anyone with them except Jesus. (PAUSE) As they were coming down the mountain, Jesus gave them orders:
Jesus	[Do not tell anyone what you have seen until the Son of Man has] risen from the dead.
Narrator	They kept the matter to themselves, discussing [it.]
Disciple 1	What [does] "rising from the dead" [mean]?
Narrator	And they asked him:
Disciple 2	Why do the teachers of the law say that Elijah must come first?
Jesus	To be sure, Elijah does come first, and restores all things. Why then is it written that the Son of Man must suffer much and be rejected? But I tell you, Elijah has come, and they have done to him everything they wished, just as it is written about him.

Cast: **Narrator**, **Peter**, **Voice** (at a distance), **Jesus**, **Disciple 1**, **Disciple 2**

The Healing of a Boy with an Evil Spirit
Mark 9:14–29

Narrator	When [Peter, James and John came with Jesus] to the other disciples, they saw a large crowd around them and the teachers of the law arguing with them. As soon as all the people saw Jesus, they were overwhelmed with wonder and ran to greet him. [Jesus asked his disciples:]
Jesus	What are you arguing with them about?
Narrator	A man in the crowd answered:
Father	Teacher, I brought you my son, who is possessed by a spirit that has robbed him of speech. Whenever it seizes him, it throws him to the ground. He foams at the mouth, gnashes his teeth and becomes rigid. I asked your disciples to drive out the spirit, but they could not.
Jesus	O unbelieving generation, how long shall I stay with you? How long shall I put up with you? Bring the boy to me.
Narrator	So they brought him. When the spirit saw Jesus, it immediately threw the boy into a convulsion. He fell to the ground and rolled around, foaming at the mouth. Jesus asked the boy's father:
Jesus	How long has he been like this?

Father	From childhood. It has often thrown him into fire or water to kill him. But if you can do anything, take pity on us and help us.
Jesus	"If you can"? Everything is possible for him who believes.
Narrator	Immediately the boy's father exclaimed:
Father (crying out)	I do believe; help me overcome my unbelief!
Narrator	When Jesus saw that a crowd was running to the scene, he rebuked the evil spirit.
Jesus	You deaf and mute spirit, I command you, come out of him and never enter him again.
Narrator	The spirit shrieked, convulsed him violently and came out. The boy looked so much like a corpse that many said:
Father and **Disciple**	He's dead.
Narrator	But Jesus took him by the hand and lifted him to his feet, and he stood up. (PAUSE) After Jesus had gone indoors, his disciples asked him privately:
Disciple	Why couldn't we drive it out?
Jesus	This kind can come out only by prayer.

Cast: **Narrator, Jesus, Father, Disciple**

Jesus and His Disciples
Mark 9:30–41

Jesus Speaks Again about His Suffering and Death (Mark 9:30–32)

Narrator	[Jesus and his disciples] . . . passed through Galilee. Jesus did not want anyone to know where they were, because he was teaching his disciples. He said to them:
Jesus	The Son of Man is going to be betrayed into the hands of men. They will kill him, and after three days he will rise.
Narrator	But they did not understand what he meant and were afraid to ask him about it.

Who Is the Greatest? (Mark 9:33–37)

Narrator	They came to Capernaum. When he was in the house, he asked them:
Jesus	What were you arguing about on the road?
Narrator	But they kept quiet because on the way they had argued about who was the greatest. Sitting down, Jesus called the Twelve and said:

113

Jesus	If anyone wants to be first, he must be the very last, and the servant of all.
Narrator	He took a little child and had him stand among them. Taking him in his arms, he said to them:
Jesus	Whoever welcomes one of these little children in my name welcomes me; and whoever welcomes me does not welcome me but the one who sent me.

Whoever Is Not against Us Is for Us (Mark 9:38–41)

Narrator	[John said to Jesus:]
John	Teacher, we saw a man driving out demons in your name and we told him to stop, because he was not one of us.
Jesus	Do not stop him. No one who does a miracle in my name can in the next moment say anything bad about me, for whoever is not against us is for us. I tell you the truth, anyone who gives you a cup of water in my name because you belong to Christ will certainly not lose his reward.

Cast: **Narrator, Jesus, John**

Causing to Sin
Mark 9:42–50

Teacher	If anyone causes one of these little ones who believe in me to sin, it would be better for him to be thrown into the sea with a large millstone tied around his neck.
Reader 1	If your hand causes you to sin, cut it off.
Teacher	It is better for you to enter life maimed than with two hands to go into hell, where the fire never goes out.
Reader 2	And if your foot causes you to sin, cut it off.
Teacher	It is better for you to enter life crippled than to have two feet and be thrown into hell.
Reader 3	And if your eye causes you to sin, pluck it out.
Teacher	It is better for you to enter the kingdom of God with one eye than to have two eyes and be thrown into hell.
Isaiah	Where their worm does not die, and the fire is not quenched.
Teacher	Everyone will be salted with fire.
Readers 1 and 2	Salt is good—
Reader 3	But if it loses its saltiness, how can you make it salty again?

Teacher	Have salt in yourselves, and be at peace with each other.

Cast: **Teacher, Reader 1, Reader 2, Reader 3, Isaiah**

Divorce
Mark 10:1–12

Narrator	Jesus . . . went into the region of Judea and across the Jordan. Again crowds of people came to him, and as was his custom, he taught them.
	Some Pharisees came and tested him by asking:
Pharisee	Is it lawful for a man to divorce his wife?
Narrator	[Jesus answered with a question:]
Jesus	What did Moses command you?
Pharisee	Moses permitted a man to write a certificate of divorce and send her away.
Jesus	It was because your hearts were hard that Moses wrote you this law. But at the beginning of creation God "made them male and female." "For this reason a man will leave his father and mother and be united to his wife, and the two will become one flesh." So they are no longer two, but one. Therefore what God has joined together, let man not separate.
Narrator	When they were in the house again, the disciples asked Jesus about this. He answered:
Jesus	Anyone who divorces his wife and marries another woman commits adultery against her. And if she divorces her husband and marries another man, she commits adultery.

Cast: **Narrator, Pharisee, Jesus**

The Little Children and Jesus
Mark 10:[1], 13–16

Narrator	[Jesus . . . went into the region of Judea and across the Jordan. Again crowds of people came to him, and as was his custom, he taught them.]
	People were bringing little children to Jesus to have him touch them, but the disciples rebuked them. When Jesus saw this, he was indignant. He said to them:
Jesus	Let the little children come to me, and do not hinder them, for the kingdom of God belongs to such as these. I tell you the truth, anyone who will not receive the kingdom of God like a little child will never enter it.

Narrator	And he took the children in his arms, put his hands on them and blessed them.

Cast: **Narrator, Jesus**

The Rich Young Man
Mark 10:17–31

Narrator	As Jesus started on his way, a man ran up to him and fell on his knees before him.
Man	Good teacher, what must I do to inherit eternal life?
[Narrator	Jesus answered:]
Jesus	Why do you call me good? No one is good—except God alone. You know the commandments: "Do not murder, do not commit adultery, do not steal, do not give false testimony, do not defraud, honor your father and mother."
Man	Teacher, all these I have kept since I was a boy.
Narrator	Jesus looked at him and loved him.
Jesus	One thing you lack. Go, sell everything you have and give to the poor, and you will have treasure in heaven. Then come, follow me.
Narrator	At this the man's face fell. He went away sad, because he had great wealth. (PAUSE)

Jesus looked around and said to his disciples: |
Jesus	How hard it is for the rich to enter the kingdom of God!
Narrator	The disciples were amazed at his words. But Jesus said again:
Jesus	Children, how hard it is to enter the kingdom of God! It is easier for a camel to go through the eye of a needle than for a rich man to enter the kingdom of God.
Narrator	The disciples were even more amazed, and said to each other:
Disciple (aside)	Who then can be saved?
Narrator	Jesus looked at them and said:
Jesus	With man this is impossible, but not with God; all things are possible with God.
Narrator	Peter said to him:
Peter	We have left everything to follow you!
Jesus	I tell you the truth, no one who has left home or brothers or sisters or mother or father or children or fields for me and the gospel will fail to

receive a hundred times as much in this present age (homes, brothers, sisters, mothers, children and fields—and with them, persecutions) and in the age to come, eternal life. But many who are first will be last, and the last first.

Cast: **Narrator, Man, Jesus, Disciple, Peter**

Jesus Again Predicts His Death
Mark 10:32–34

Narrator   [Jesus and his disciples] were on their way up to Jerusalem, with Jesus leading the way, and the disciples were astonished, while those who followed were afraid. Again he took the Twelve aside and told them what was going to happen to him.

Jesus   We are going up to Jerusalem, and the Son of Man will be betrayed to the chief priests and teachers of the law. They will condemn him to death and will hand him over to the Gentiles, who will mock him and spit on him, flog him and kill him. Three days later he will rise.

Cast: **Narrator, Jesus**

The Request of James and John
Mark 10:35–45

Narrator   James and John, the sons of Zebedee, came to him. [They said:]

James   Teacher, we want you to do for us whatever we ask.

Jesus   What do you want me to do for you?

John   Let one of us sit at your right and the other at your left in your glory.

Jesus   You don't know what you are asking. Can you drink the cup I drink or be baptized with the baptism I am baptized with?

James and **John**   We can.

Jesus   You will drink the cup I drink and be baptized with the baptism I am baptized with, but to sit at my right or left is not for me to grant. These places belong to those for whom they have been prepared.

Narrator   When the ten heard about this, they became indignant with James and John. Jesus called them together and said:

Jesus   You know that those who are regarded as rulers of the Gentiles lord it over them, and their high officials exercise authority over them. Not so with you. Instead, whoever wants to become great among you must be your servant, and whoever wants to be first must be slave of all. For even

117

the Son of Man did not come to be served, but to serve, and to give his life as a ransom for many.

Cast: **Narrator, James, Jesus, John**

Blind Bartimaeus Receives His Sight
Mark 10:46–52

Narrator	Then they came to Jericho. As Jesus and his disciples, together with a large crowd, were leaving the city, a blind man, Bartimaeus (that is, the Son of Timaeus), was sitting by the roadside begging. When he heard that it was Jesus of Nazareth, he began to shout:
Bartimaeus	Jesus, Son of David, have mercy on me!
Narrator	Many rebuked him and told him to be quiet, but he shouted all the more:
Bartimaeus	Son of David, have mercy on me!
Narrator	Jesus stopped and said:
Jesus	Call him.
Narrator	So they called to the blind man:
Person 1	Cheer up!
Person 2	On your feet! He's calling you.
Narrator	Throwing his cloak aside, he jumped to his feet and came to Jesus.
Jesus	What do you want me to do for you?
Bartimaeus	Rabbi, I want to see.
Jesus	Go, your faith has healed you.
Narrator	Immediately he received his sight and followed Jesus along the road.

Cast: **Narrator, Bartimaeus, Jesus, Person 1, Person 2** (can be the same as Person 1)

The Triumphal Entry
Mark 11:1–11

Narrator	As they approached Jerusalem and came to Bethphage and Bethany at the Mount of Olives, Jesus sent two of his disciples, saying to them:
Jesus	Go to the village ahead of you, and just as you enter it, you will find a colt tied there, which no one has ever ridden. Untie it and bring it here. If anyone asks you, "Why are you doing this?" tell him, "The Lord needs it and will send it back here shortly."

Narrator	They went and found a colt outside in the street, tied at a doorway. As they untied it, some people standing there asked:
Bystanders 1 and 2	What are you doing—
Bystander 1	untying that colt?
Narrator	They answered as Jesus had told them to, and the people let them go. When they brought the colt to Jesus and threw their cloaks over it, he sat on it. Many people spread their cloaks on the road, while others spread branches they had cut in the fields. Those who went ahead and those who followed shouted:
Persons 1 and 2	Hosanna!
Person 1	Blessed is he who comes in the name of the Lord!
Person 2	Blessed is the coming kingdom of our father David!
Persons 1 and 2	Hosanna in the highest!
Narrator	Jesus entered Jerusalem and went to the temple. He looked around at everything, but since it was already late, he went out to Bethany with the Twelve.

Cast: **Narrator, Jesus, Bystander 1, Bystander 2** (can be the same as Bystander 1), **Person 1, Person 2** (can be the same as Bystander 2)

The Withered Fig Tree
Mark 11:12–14, 20–25

Narrator	The next day as they were leaving Bethany, Jesus was hungry. Seeing in the distance a fig tree in leaf, he went to find out if it had any fruit. When he reached it, he found nothing but leaves, because it was not the season for figs. Then he said to the tree:
Jesus	May no one ever eat fruit from you again.
Narrator	And his disciples heard him say it. . . . (PAUSE)
	In the morning, as they went along, they saw the fig tree withered from the roots. Peter remembered and said to Jesus:
Peter	Rabbi, look! The fig tree you cursed has withered!
Jesus	Have faith in God. I tell you the truth, if anyone says to this mountain, "Go, throw yourself into the sea," and does not doubt in his heart but believes that what he says will happen, it will be done for him. Therefore I tell you, whatever you ask for in prayer, believe that you have received it, and it will be yours. And when you stand praying, if you hold

119

anything against anyone, forgive him, so that your Father in heaven may forgive you your sins.

Cast: **Narrator, Jesus, Peter**

Jesus Clears the Temple
Mark 11:15–19, 27–33

Narrator   On reaching Jerusalem, Jesus entered the temple area and began driving out those who were buying and selling there. He overturned the tables of the money changers and the benches of those selling doves, and would not allow anyone to carry merchandise through the temple courts. And as he taught them, he said:

Jesus   Is it not written:
"My house will be called
a house of prayer for all nations"?
But you have made it "a den of robbers."

Narrator   The chief priests and the teachers of the law heard this and began looking for a way to kill him, for they feared him, because the whole crowd was amazed at his teaching.

When evening came, they went out of the city. . . . (PAUSE)

[The next day] they arrived again in Jerusalem, and while Jesus was walking in the temple courts, the chief priests, the teachers of the law and the elders came to him [and asked]:

Lawyer 1   By what authority are you doing these things?

Lawyer 2   And who gave you authority to do this?

Jesus   I will ask you one question. Answer me, and I will tell you by what authority I am doing these things. John's baptism—was it from heaven, or from men? Tell me!

Narrator   They discussed it among themselves and said:

Lawyer 2   If we say, "From heaven," he will ask, "Then why didn't you believe him?"

Lawyer 1   But if we say, "From men". . .

Narrator   (They feared the people, for everyone held that John really was a prophet.) So they answered Jesus:

Lawyer 1   We don't know.

Jesus (firmly)   Neither will I tell you by what authority I am doing these things.

Cast: **Narrator, Jesus, Lawyer 1, Lawyer 2**

The Parable of the Tenants
Mark 12:1–12

Narrator	[Jesus] then began to speak to [the chief priests, the teachers of the law and the elders] in parables:
Jesus	A man planted a vineyard. He put a wall around it, dug a pit for the winepress and built a watchtower. Then he rented the vineyard to some farmers and went away on a journey. At harvest time he sent a servant to the tenants to collect from them some of the fruit of the vineyard. But they seized him, beat him and sent him away empty-handed. Then he sent another servant to them; they struck this man on the head and treated him shamefully. He sent still another, and that one they killed. He sent many others; some of them they beat, others they killed.
	He had one left to send, a son, whom he loved. He sent him last of all, saying:
Owner	They will respect my son.
Jesus	But the tenants said to one another:
Tenant 1	This is the heir.
Tenant 2	Come, let's kill him, and the inheritance will be ours.
Jesus	(PAUSE) So they took him and killed him, and threw him out of the vineyard.
	What then will the owner of the vineyard do? He will come and kill those tenants and give the vineyard to others. Haven't you read this scripture?
Psalmist	The stone the builders rejected has become the capstone; the Lord has done this, and it is marvelous in our eyes.
Narrator	Then they looked for a way to arrest him because they knew he had spoken the parable against them. But they were afraid of the crowd; so they left him and went away.

Cast: **Narrator, Jesus, Owner, Tenant 1, Tenant 2, Psalmist**

Paying Taxes to Caesar
Mark 12:13–17

Narrator	Some of the Pharisees and Herodians [tried to trap Jesus with questions]. They came to him and said:

121

Herodian	Teacher, we know you are a man of integrity. You aren't swayed by men, because you pay no attention to who they are.
Pharisee	But you teach the way of God in accordance with the truth.
Herodian	Is it right to pay taxes to Caesar or not? Should we pay or shouldn't we?
Narrator	But Jesus knew their hypocrisy.
Jesus	Why are you trying to trap me? Bring me a denarius and let me look at it.
Narrator	They brought the coin, and he asked them:
Jesus	Whose portrait is this? And whose inscription?
Pharisee and **Herodian**	Caesar's.
Jesus	Give to Caesar what is Caesar's and to God what is God's.
Narrator	And they were amazed at him.

Cast: **Narrator, Herodian, Pharisee, Jesus**

Marriage at the Resurrection
Mark 12:18–27

Narrator	The Sadducees, who say there is no resurrection, came to [Jesus] with a question. They said:
Sadducee 1	Teacher, Moses wrote for us:
Sadducee 2	If a man's brother dies and leaves a wife but no children, the man must marry the widow and have children for his brother.
Sadducee 1	Now there were seven brothers. The first one married and died without leaving any children.
Sadducee 2	The second one married the widow, but he also died, leaving no child.
Sadducee 1	It was the same with the third.
Sadducee 2	In fact, none of the seven left any children.
Sadducee 1	Last of all, the woman died too.
Sadducee 2	At the resurrection whose wife will she be, since the seven were married to her?
Narrator	Jesus replied:
Jesus	Are you not in error because you do not know the Scriptures or the power of God? When the dead rise, they will neither marry nor be given in marriage; they will be like the angels in heaven. Now about the dead rising—have you not read in the book of Moses, in the account of the bush, how God said to him, "I am the God of Abraham, the God of

Isaac, and the God of Jacob"? He is not the God of the dead, but of the living. You are badly mistaken!

Cast: **Narrator, Sadducee 1, Sadducee 2** (can be the same as Sadducee 1), **Jesus**

The Greatest Commandment
Mark 12:28–34

Narrator	One of the teachers of the law came and heard [the Sadducees] debating. Noticing that Jesus had given them a good answer, he asked him:
Lawyer	Of all the commandments, which is the most important?
[Narrator	Jesus answered:]
Jesus	The most important one is this: "Hear, O Israel, the Lord our God, the Lord is one. Love the Lord your God with all your heart and with all your soul and with all your mind and with all your strength." The second is this: "Love your neighbor as yourself." There is no commandment greater than these.
Lawyer	Well said, teacher. You are right in saying that God is one and there is no other but him. To love him with all your heart, with all your understanding and with all your strength, and to love your neighbor as yourself is more important than all burnt offerings and sacrifices.
Narrator	When Jesus saw that he had answered wisely, he said to him:
Jesus	You are not far from the kingdom of God.
Narrator	And from then on no one dared ask him any more questions.

Cast: **Narrator, Lawyer, Jesus**

Whose Son Is the Christ?
Mark 12:35–40

Narrator	While Jesus was teaching in the temple courts, he asked:
Jesus	How is it that the teachers of the law say that the Christ is the son of David? David himself, speaking by the Holy Spirit, declared:
David	The Lord said to my Lord: "Sit at my right hand until I put your enemies under your feet."
Jesus	David himself calls him "Lord." How then can he be his son?
Narrator	The large crowd listened to him with delight. As he taught, Jesus said:
Jesus	Watch out for the teachers of the law. They like to walk around in flowing robes and be greeted in the marketplaces, and have the most impor-

tant seats in the synagogues and the places of honor at banquets. They devour widows' houses and for a show make lengthy prayers. Such men will be punished most severely.

Cast: **Narrator, Jesus, David** (can be the same as Jesus)

The Widow's Offering
Mark 12:41–44

Narrator   Jesus sat down [in the temple] opposite the place where the offerings were put and watched the crowd putting their money into the temple treasury. Many rich people threw in large amounts. But a poor widow came and put in two very small copper coins, worth only a fraction of a penny. Calling his disciples to him, Jesus said:

Jesus   I tell you the truth, this poor widow has put more into the treasury than all the others. They all gave out of their wealth; but she, out of her poverty, put in everything—all she had to live on.

Cast: **Narrator, Jesus**

Jesus Speaks of Troubles
Mark 13:1–13

Narrator   As [Jesus] was leaving the temple, one of his disciples said to him:

Disciple   Look, Teacher! What massive stones! What magnificent buildings!

[Narrator   Jesus replied:]

Jesus   Do you see all these great buildings? Not one stone here will be left on another; every one will be thrown down. (PAUSE)

Narrator   As Jesus was sitting on the Mount of Olives opposite the temple, Peter, James, John and Andrew asked him privately:

Disciple   Tell us, when will these things happen? And what will be the sign that they are all about to be fulfilled?

Jesus   Watch out that no one deceives you. Many will come in my name, claiming, "I am he," and will deceive many. When you hear of wars and rumors of wars, do not be alarmed. Such things must happen, but the end is still to come. Nation will rise against nation, and kingdom against kingdom. There will be earthquakes in various places, and famines. These are the beginning of birth pains.

You must be on your guard. You will be handed over to the local councils and flogged in the synagogues. On account of me you will stand before governors and kings as witnesses to them. And the gospel must first be preached to all nations. Whenever you are arrested and brought to trial, do not worry beforehand about what to say. Just say whatever is given you at the time, for it is not you speaking, but the Holy Spirit.

Brother will betray brother to death, and a father his child. Children will rebel against their parents and have them put to death. All men will hate you because of me, but he who stands firm to the end will be saved.

Cast: **Narrator, Disciple, Jesus**

Jesus Speaks of the Abomination
Mark 13:14–23

Jesus   When you see "the abomination that causes desolation" standing where it does not belong—

Narrator   Let the reader understand—

Jesus   Then let those who are in Judea flee to the mountains. Let no one on the roof of his house go down or enter the house to take anything out. Let no one in the field go back to get his cloak. How dreadful it will be in those days for pregnant women and nursing mothers! Pray that this will not take place in winter, because those will be days of distress unequaled from the beginning, when God created the world, until now—and never to be equaled again. If the Lord had not cut short those days, no one would survive. But for the sake of the elect, whom he has chosen, he has shortened them. (PAUSE) At that time if anyone says to you:

Person 1   Look, here is the Christ!

Jesus   Or,

Person 2   Look, there he is!

Jesus   Do not believe it. For false Christs and false prophets will appear and perform signs and miracles to deceive the elect—if that were possible. So be on your guard; I have told you everything ahead of time.

Cast: **Jesus, Narrator, Person 1, Person 2**

Jesus' Warnings about the End
Mark 13:24–37

Teacher 1   In those days, following that distress,

"the sun will be darkened,
and the moon will not give its light;
the stars will fall from the sky,
and the heavenly bodies will be shaken."

At that time men will see the Son of Man coming in clouds with great power and glory. And he will send his angels and gather his elect from the four winds, from the ends of the earth to the ends of the heavens.

Teacher 2	Now learn this lesson from the fig tree: As soon as its twigs get tender and its leaves come out, you know that summer is near. Even so, when you see these things happening, you know that it is near, right at the door. I tell you the truth, this generation will certainly not pass away until all these things have happened. Heaven and earth will pass away, but my words will never pass away.
Teacher 1	No one knows about that day or hour, not even the angels in heaven, nor the Son, but only the Father. Be on guard! Be alert! You do not know when that time will come.
Teacher 2	It's like a man going away: He leaves his house and puts his servants in charge, each with his assigned task, and tells the one at the door to keep watch.
	Therefore keep watch because you do not know when the owner of the house will come back—whether in the evening, or at midnight, or when the rooster crows, or at dawn. If he comes suddenly, do not let him find you sleeping.
[Teacher 1	What I say to you, I say to everyone:]
Teachers 1 and 2	Watch!

Cast: **Teacher 1, Teacher 2**

Jesus in Danger
Mark 14:1–11

The Plot against Jesus (Mark 14:1–2)

Narrator	Now the Passover and the Feast of Unleavened Bread were only two days away, and the chief priests and the teachers of the law were looking for some sly way to arrest Jesus and kill him.
Priest	But not during the Feast.
Lawyer	The people may riot.

Jesus Anointed at Bethany (Mark 14:3–9)

Narrator	While he was in Bethany, reclining at the table in the home of a man known as Simon the Leper, a woman came with an alabaster jar of very expensive perfume, made of pure nard. She broke the jar and poured the perfume on his head. (PAUSE) Some of those present were saying indignantly to one another:
Person 1	Why this waste of perfume?
Person 2	It could have been sold for more than a year's wages and the money given to the poor.
Narrator	And they rebuked her harshly. [But Jesus said:]

126

Jesus	Leave her alone. Why are you bothering her? She has done a beautiful thing to me. The poor you will always have with you, and you can help them any time you want. But you will not always have me. She did what she could. She poured perfume on my body beforehand to prepare for my burial. I tell you the truth, wherever the gospel is preached throughout the world, what she has done will also be told, in memory of her.

Judas Agrees to Betray Jesus (Mark 14:10–11)

Narrator	Then Judas Iscariot, one of the Twelve, went to the chief priests to betray Jesus to them. They were delighted to hear this and promised to give him money. So he watched for an opportunity to hand him over.

Cast: **Narrator, Priest, Lawyer** (can be the same as Priest), **Person 1, Person 2** (can be the same as Person 1), **Jesus**

Jesus Eats the Passover Meal with His Disciples
Mark 14:12–21

Narrator	On the first day of the Feast of Unleavened Bread, when it was customary to sacrifice the Passover lamb, Jesus' disciples asked him:
Disciple	Where do you want us to go and make preparations for you to eat the Passover?
Narrator	So he sent two of his disciples, telling them:
Jesus	Go into the city, and a man carrying a jar of water will meet you. Follow him. Say to the owner of the house he enters, "The Teacher asks: Where is my guest room, where I may eat the Passover with my disciples?" He will show you a large upper room, furnished and ready. Make preparations for us there.
Narrator	The disciples left, went into the city and found things just as Jesus had told them. So they prepared the Passover. (PAUSE) When evening came, Jesus arrived with the Twelve. While they were reclining at the table eating, he said:
Jesus	I tell you the truth, one of you will betray me—one who is eating with me.
Narrator	They were saddened, and one by one they said to him:
Disciple	Surely not I?
Jesus	It is one of the Twelve, one who dips bread into the bowl with me. The Son of Man will go just as it is written about him. But woe to that man who betrays the Son of Man! It would be better for him if he had not been born.

Cast: **Narrator, Disciple, Jesus**

The Lord's Supper
Mark 14:22–26

Narrator	While [the Twelve] were eating, Jesus took bread, gave thanks and broke it, and gave it to his disciples, saying:
Jesus	Take it; this is my body.
Narrator	Then he took the cup, gave thanks and offered it to them, and they all drank from it. [He said to them:]
Jesus	This is my blood of the covenant, which is poured out for many. I tell you the truth, I will not drink again of the fruit of the vine until that day when I drink it anew in the kingdom of God.
Narrator	When they had sung a hymn, they went out to the Mount of Olives.

Cast: **Narrator, Jesus**

Jesus Predicts Peter's Denial
Mark 14:27–31

Narrator	Jesus told them:
Jesus	You will all fall away, for it is written:

"I will strike the shepherd,
   and the sheep will be scattered."

But after I have risen, I will go ahead of you into Galilee.

Narrator	Peter declared:
Peter	Even if all fall away, I will not.
Jesus (to Peter)	I tell you the truth, today—yes, tonight—before the rooster crows twice you yourself will disown me three times.
Peter (insistently)	Even if I have to die with you, I will never disown you.
Narrator	And all the others said the same.

Cast: **Narrator, Jesus, Peter**

Gethsemane
Mark 14:32–42

Narrator	They went to a place called Gethsemane, and Jesus said to his disciples:
Jesus	Sit here while I pray.

Narrator	He took Peter, James and John along with him, and he began to be deeply distressed and troubled.
Jesus	My soul is overwhelmed with sorrow to the point of death. Stay here and keep watch.
Narrator	Going a little farther, he fell to the ground and prayed that if possible the hour might pass from him.
Jesus	*Abba*, Father, everything is possible for you. Take this cup from me. Yet not what I will, but what you will.
Narrator	Then he returned to his disciples and found them sleeping. He said to Peter:
Jesus	Simon, are you asleep? Could you not keep watch for one hour?
Narrator	[And he said to them:]
Jesus (looking around)	Watch and pray so that you will not fall into temptation. The spirit is willing, but the body is weak.
Narrator	Once more he went away and prayed the same thing. (PAUSE) When he came back, he again found them sleeping, because their eyes were heavy. They did not know what to say to him. (PAUSE) Returning the third time, he said to them:
Jesus	Are you still sleeping and resting? Enough! The hour has come. Look, the Son of Man is betrayed into the hands of sinners. Rise! Let us go! Here comes my betrayer!

Cast: **Narrator, Jesus**

Jesus Arrested
Mark 14:43–52

Narrator	Just as [Jesus] was speaking, Judas, one of the Twelve, appeared. With him was a crowd armed with swords and clubs, sent from the chief priests, the teachers of the law, and the elders. (PAUSE) Now the betrayer had arranged a signal with them:
Judas	The one I kiss is the man; arrest him and lead him away under guard.
Narrator	Going at once to Jesus, Judas said:
Judas	Rabbi!
Narrator	. . . and kissed him. The men seized Jesus and arrested him. Then one of those standing near drew his sword and struck the servant of the high priest, cutting off his ear.
Jesus	Am I leading a rebellion, that you have come out with swords and clubs to capture me? Every day I was with you, teaching in the temple courts, and you did not arrest me. But the Scriptures must be fulfilled.

129

Narrator	Then everyone deserted him and fled. (PAUSE)
	A young man, wearing nothing but a linen garment, was following Jesus. When they seized him, he fled naked, leaving his garment behind.

Cast: **Narrator, Judas, Jesus**

Before the Sanhedrin
Mark 14:53–65

Narrator	[The crowd] took Jesus to the high priest, and all the chief priests, elders and teachers of the law came together. Peter followed him at a distance, right into the courtyard of the high priest. There he sat with the guards and warmed himself at the fire.
	The chief priests and the whole Sanhedrin were looking for evidence against Jesus so that they could put him to death, but they did not find any. Many testified falsely against him, but their statements did not agree.
	Then some stood up and gave this false testimony against him:
Man	We heard him say, "I will destroy this man-made temple and in three days will build another, not made by man."
Narrator	Yet even then their testimony did not agree.
	Then the high priest stood up before them and asked Jesus:
High priest	Are you not going to answer? What is this testimony that these men are bringing against you?
Narrator	But Jesus remained silent and gave no answer. Again the high priest asked him:
High priest	Are you the Christ, the Son of the Blessed One?
Narrator	Jesus [answered:]
Jesus	I am. And you will see the Son of Man sitting at the right hand of the Mighty One and coming on the clouds of heaven.
Narrator	The high priest tore his clothes.
High priest	Why do we need any more witnesses? You have heard the blasphemy. What do you think?
Narrator	They all condemned him as worthy of death. (PAUSE) Then some began to spit at him; they blindfolded him, struck him with their fists, and said:
Man	Prophesy! [Guess who hit you!]

130

Narrator	And the guards took him and beat him.

Cast: **Narrator, Man, High priest, Jesus**

Peter Disowns Jesus
Mark 14:66–72

Narrator	While Peter was below in the [high priest's] courtyard, one of the servant girls of the high priest came by. When she saw Peter warming himself, she looked closely at him.
Girl	You also were with that Nazarene, Jesus.
Narrator	But he denied it:
Peter	I don't know or understand what you're talking about.
Narrator	And [he] went out into the entryway.[Just then a cock crowed.] (PAUSE)
	When the servant girl saw him there, she said again to those standing around:
Girl	This fellow is one of them.
Narrator	Again he denied it. After a little while, those standing near said to Peter:
Bystander	Surely you are one of them, for you are a Galilean.
Narrator	He began to call down curses on himself, and he swore to them.
Peter	I don't know this man you're talking about.
Narrator	Immediately the rooster crowed the second time. Then Peter remembered the word Jesus had spoken to him: "Before the rooster crows twice you will disown me three times." And he broke down and wept.

Cast: **Narrator, Girl, Peter, Bystander**

Jesus before Pilate
Mark 15:1–15

Narrator	Very early in the morning, the chief priests, with the elders, the teachers of the law and the whole Sanhedrin, reached a decision. They bound Jesus, led him away and handed him over to Pilate. [Pilate asked:]
Pilate	Are you the king of the Jews?
[Narrator	Jesus replied:]
Jesus	Yes, it is as you say.
Narrator	The chief priests accused him of many things. So again Pilate asked him:
Pilate	Aren't you going to answer? See how many things they are accusing you of.

Narrator	But Jesus still made no reply, and Pilate was amazed.
	Now it was the custom at the Feast to release a prisoner whom the people requested. A man called Barabbas was in prison with the insurrectionists who had committed murder in the uprising. The crowd came up and asked Pilate to do for them what he usually did.
Pilate (calling)	Do you want me to release to you the king of the Jews?
Narrator	[He knew] it was out of envy that the chief priests had handed Jesus over to him. (PAUSE) But the chief priests stirred up the crowd to have Pilate release Barabbas instead. Pilate [spoke again to the crowd]:
Pilate	What shall I do, then, with the one you call the king of the Jews?
[Narrator	They shouted:]
Crowd	Crucify him!
Pilate	Why? What crime has he committed?
[Narrator	But they shouted all the louder:]
Crowd	Crucify him!
Narrator	Wanting to satisfy the crowd, Pilate released Barabbas to them. He had Jesus flogged, and handed him over to be crucified.

Cast: **Narrator, Pilate, Jesus, Crowd** (two or more persons)

The Crucifixion
Mark 15:16–32

Narrator	The soldiers led Jesus away into the palace (that is, the Praetorium) and called together the whole company of soldiers. They put a purple robe on him, then twisted together a crown of thorns and set it on him. And they began to call out to him:
Soldier(s)	Hail, king of the Jews!
Narrator	Again and again they struck him on the head with a staff and spit on him. Falling on their knees, they paid homage to him. And when they had mocked him, they took off the purple robe and put his own clothes on him. Then they led him out to crucify him.
	A certain man from Cyrene, Simon, the father of Alexander and Rufus, was passing by on his way in from the country, and they forced him to carry the cross. They brought Jesus to the place called Golgotha (which means The Place of the Skull). Then they offered him wine mixed with myrrh, but he did not take it. And they crucified him. Dividing up his clothes, they cast lots to see what each would get.

It was the third hour when they crucified him. The written notice of the charge against him read:

Voice of
Pilate
(slowly) THE KING OF THE JEWS.

Narrator They crucified two robbers with him, one on his right and one on his left. Those who passed by hurled insults at him, shaking their heads and saying:

Persons 1
and 2 So!

Person 1 You who are going to destroy the temple and build it in three days.

Person 2 Come down from the cross and save yourself!

Narrator In the same way the chief priests and the teachers of the law mocked him among themselves.

Lawyer 1 He saved others, but he can't save himself!

Lawyer 2 Let this Christ, this King of Israel, come down now from the cross, that we may see and believe.

Narrator Those crucified with him also heaped insults on him.

Cast: **Narrator**, **Soldier(s)** (one or more persons—can be supplemented by Lawyers 1 and 2), **Voice of Pilate**, **Person 1**, **Person 2**, **Lawyer 1**, **Lawyer 2**

The Death of Jesus
Mark 15:33–39

Narrator At the sixth hour darkness came over the whole land until the ninth hour. And at the ninth hour Jesus cried out in a loud voice:

Jesus *Eloi, Eloi, lama sabachthani?*

Narrator Which means, "My God, my God, why have you forsaken me?" (PAUSE) When some of those standing near heard this, they said:

Person 1 Listen, he's calling Elijah.

Narrator One man ran, filled a sponge with wine vinegar, put it on a stick, and offered it to Jesus to drink. [He said:]

Person 2 Now leave him alone. Let's see if Elijah comes to take him down. (PAUSE)

Narrator With a loud cry, Jesus breathed his last. (PAUSE)

The curtain of the temple was torn in two from top to bottom. And when the centurion, who stood there in front of Jesus, heard his cry and saw how he died, he said:

133

| Centurion | Surely this man was the Son of God! |

Cast: **Narrator, Jesus, Person 1, Person 2, Centurion**

The Burial of Jesus
Mark 15:40–47

| Narrator 1 | Some women were watching from a distance. Among them were Mary Magdalene, Mary the mother of James the younger and of Joses, and Salome. In Galilee these women had followed him and cared for his needs. Many other women who had come up with him to Jerusalem were also there. |

| Narrator 2 | It was Preparation Day. |

| Commentator | That is, the day before the Sabbath. |

| Narrator 2 | So as evening approached, Joseph of Arimathea, a prominent member of the Council, who was himself waiting for the kingdom of God, went boldly to Pilate and asked for Jesus' body. Pilate was surprised to hear that he was already dead. Summoning the centurion, he asked him if Jesus had already died. When he learned from the centurion that it was so, he gave the body to Joseph. So Joseph bought some linen cloth, took down the body, wrapped it in the linen, and placed it in a tomb cut out of rock. Then he rolled a stone against the entrance of the tomb. |

| Narrator 1 | Mary Magdalene and Mary the mother of Joses saw where he was laid. |

Cast: **Narrator 1, Narrator 2, Commentator** (can be the same as Narrator 1)

The Resurrection
Mark 16:1–8

| Narrator | When the Sabbath was over, Mary Magdalene, Mary the mother of James, and Salome bought spices so that they might go to anoint Jesus' body. Very early on the first day of the week, just after sunrise, they were on their way to the tomb and they asked each other: |

| Mary | Who will roll the stone away from the entrance of the tomb? |

| Narrator | But when they looked up, they saw that the stone, which was very large, had been rolled away. (PAUSE) As they entered the tomb, they saw a young man dressed in a white robe sitting on the right side, and they were alarmed. He said: |

| Young man | Don't be alarmed. You are looking for Jesus the Nazarene, who was crucified. He has risen! He is not here. See the place where they laid him. (PAUSE) But go, tell his disciples and Peter, "He is going ahead of you into Galilee. There you will see him, just as he told you." |

Narrator	Trembling and bewildered, the women went out and fled from the tomb. They said nothing to anyone, because they were afraid.

Cast: **Narrator, Mary, Young man**

Jesus Appears to His Disciples and Is Taken up to Heaven
Mark 16:9–20*

Narrator 1	When Jesus rose early on the first day of the week, he appeared first to Mary Magdalene, out of whom he had driven seven demons. She went and told those who had been with him and who were mourning and weeping. When they heard that Jesus was alive and that she had seen him, they did not believe it.
Narrator 2	Afterward Jesus appeared in a different form to two of them while they were walking in the country. These returned and reported it to the rest; but they did not believe them either.
Narrator 1	Later Jesus appeared to the Eleven as they were eating; he rebuked them for their lack of faith and their stubborn refusal to believe those who had seen him after he had risen. He said to them:
Jesus	Go into all the world and preach the good news to all creation. Whoever believes and is baptized will be saved, but whoever does not believe will be condemned. And these signs will accompany those who believe: In my name they will drive out demons; they will speak in new tongues; they will pick up snakes with their hands; and when they drink deadly poison, it will not hurt them at all; they will place their hands on sick people, and they will get well.
Narrator 2	After the Lord Jesus had spoken to them, he was taken up into heaven and he sat at the right hand of God. Then the disciples went out and preached everywhere, and the Lord worked with them and confirmed his word by the signs that accompanied it.

Cast: **Narrator 1, Narrator 2, Jesus.** (*The earliest manuscripts and some other ancient witnesses do not have Mark 16:9–20.)

See also the Passion Readings, beginning on page 423, and the Easter Readings, beginning on page 466.

The Gospel of Luke

The Birth of John the Baptist Foretold
Luke 1:5–25

Narrator 1 In the time of Herod king of Judea there was a priest named Zechariah, who belonged to the priestly division of Abijah; his wife Elizabeth was also a descendant of Aaron.

Narrator 2 Both of them were upright in the sight of God, observing all the Lord's commandments and regulations blamelessly. But they had no children, because Elizabeth was barren; and they were both well along in years. (PAUSE)

Narrator 1 Once when Zechariah's division was on duty, he was serving as priest before God.

Narrator 2 He was chosen by lot, according to the custom of the priesthood, to go into the temple of the Lord and burn incense.

Narrator 1 And when the time for the burning of incense came, all the assembled worshipers were praying outside.

Then an angel of the Lord appeared to him, standing at the right side of the altar of incense. When Zechariah saw him, he was startled and was gripped with fear. But the angel said to him:

Angel Do not be afraid, Zechariah; your prayer has been heard. Your wife Elizabeth will bear you a son, and you are to give him the name John. He will be a joy and delight to you, and many will rejoice because of his birth, for he will be great in the sight of the Lord. He is never to take wine or other fermented drink, and he will be filled with the Holy Spirit even from birth. Many of the people of Israel will he bring back to the Lord their God. And he will go on before the Lord, in the spirit and power of Elijah, to turn the hearts of the fathers to their children and the disobedient to the wisdom of the righteous—to make ready a people prepared for the Lord.

Narrator 1 Zechariah asked the angel:

Zechariah How can I be sure of this? I am an old man and my wife is well along in years.

Angel I am Gabriel. I stand in the presence of God, and I have been sent to speak to you and to tell you this good news. And now you will be silent and not able to speak until the day this happens, because you did not believe my words, which will come true at their proper time.

Narrator 2 Meanwhile, the people were waiting for Zechariah and wondering why he stayed so long in the temple.

Narrator 1	When he came out, he could not speak to them. They realized he had seen a vision in the temple, for he kept making signs to them but remained unable to speak.
Narrator 2	When his time of service was completed, he returned home. After this his wife Elizabeth became pregnant and for five months remained in seclusion. She said:
Elizabeth	The Lord has done this for me. In these days he has shown his favor and taken away my disgrace among the people.

Cast: **Narrator 1, Narrator 2, Angel, Zechariah, Elizabeth**

The Birth of Jesus Foretold

Luke 1:26–38

Narrator	In the sixth month, God sent the angel Gabriel to Nazareth, a town in Galilee, to a virgin pledged to be married to a man named Joseph, a descendant of David. The virgin's name was Mary. The angel went to her and said:
Angel	Greetings, you who are highly favored! The Lord is with you.
Narrator	Mary was greatly troubled at his words and wondered what kind of greeting this might be. [But the angel said to her:]
Angel	Do not be afraid, Mary, you have found favor with God. You will be with child and give birth to a son, and you are to give him the name Jesus. He will be great and will be called the Son of the Most High. The Lord God will give him the throne of his father David, and he will reign over the house of Jacob forever; his kingdom will never end.
[Narrator	Mary asked the angel:]
Mary	How will this be, since I am a virgin?
Angel	The Holy Spirit will come upon you, and the power of the Most High will overshadow you. So the holy one to be born will be called the Son of God. (PAUSE) [Even Elizabeth your relative is going to have a child in her old age, and she who was said to be barren is in her sixth month. For nothing is impossible with God.]
[Narrator	Mary answered:]
Mary	I am the Lord's servant. May it be to me as you have said.
Narrator	Then the angel left her.

Cast: **Narrator, Angel, Mary.** (See also Appendix: Christmas Readings, pages 416–17.)

Mary Visits Elizabeth
Luke 1:39–56

Narrator   [After the angel left her,] Mary got ready and hurried to a town in the hill country of Judea, where she entered Zechariah's home and greeted Elizabeth. When Elizabeth heard Mary's greeting, the baby leaped in her womb, and Elizabeth was filled with the Holy Spirit. In a loud voice she exclaimed:

Elizabeth
(delighted)   Blessed are you among women, and blessed is the child you will bear! But why am I so favored, that the mother of my Lord should come to me? As soon as the sound of your greeting reached my ears, the baby in my womb leaped for joy. Blessed is she who has believed that what the Lord has said to her will be accomplished!

Narrator   And Mary said:

Mary   My soul glorifies the Lord
  and my spirit rejoices in God my Savior,
for he has been mindful of the humble state of his servant.
From now on all generations will call me blessed,
  for the Mighty One has done great things for me—
  holy is his name.
His mercy extends to those who fear him,
  from generation to generation.
He has performed mighty deeds with his arm;
  he has scattered those who are proud in their inmost thoughts.
He has brought down rulers from their thrones
  but has lifted up the humble.
He has filled the hungry with good things
  but has sent the rich away empty.
He has helped his servant Israel,
  remembering to be merciful
to Abraham and his descendants forever,
  even as he said to our fathers.

Narrator   Mary stayed with Elizabeth for about three months and then returned home.

Cast: **Narrator, Elizabeth, Mary.** (See also Appendix: Christmas Readings, pages 417–18.)

The Birth of John the Baptist
Luke 1:57–80

Narrator   When it was time for Elizabeth to have her baby, she gave birth to a son. Her neighbors and relatives heard that the Lord had shown her great mercy, and they shared her joy. (PAUSE)

On the eighth day they came to circumcise the child, and they were going to name him after his father Zechariah, but his mother spoke up and said:

Elizabeth   No! He is to be called John.

[Narrator   They said to her:]

Relative   There is no one among your relatives who has that name.

Narrator   Then they made signs to his father, to find out what he would like to name the child. He asked for a writing tablet, and to everyone's astonishment he wrote:

Zechariah*   His name is John.

Narrator   Immediately his mouth was opened and his tongue was loosed, and he began to speak, praising God. The neighbors were all filled with awe, and throughout the hill country of Judea people were talking about all these things. Everyone who heard this wondered about it, asking:

Relative   What then is this child going to be?

Narrator   For the Lord's hand was with him.

His father Zechariah was filled with the Holy Spirit and prophesied:

Zechariah   Praise be to the Lord, the God of Israel,
                    because he has come and has redeemed his people.
                He has raised up a horn of salvation for us
                    in the house of his servant David
                (as he said through his holy prophets of long ago),
                salvation from our enemies
                    and from the hand of all who hate us—
                to show mercy to our fathers
                    and to remember his holy covenant,
                    the oath he swore to our father Abraham:
                to rescue us from the hand of our enemies,
                    and to enable us to serve him without fear
                    in holiness and righteousness before him all our days.

                And you, my child, will be called a prophet of the Most High;
                    for you will go on before the Lord to prepare the way for him,
                to give his people the knowledge of salvation
                    through the forgiveness of their sins,
                because of the tender mercy of our God,
                    by which the rising sun will come to us from heaven
                to shine on those living in darkness
                    and in the shadow of death,
                to guide our feet into the path of peace.

139

| Narrator | And the child grew and became strong in spirit; and he lived in the desert until he appeared publicly to Israel. |

Cast: **Narrator, Elizabeth, Relative, Zechariah** (*At this point it is better if Zechariah does not speak, but holds up a previously written sign bearing the words "His name is John.")

The Birth of Jesus
Luke 2:1–7

| Narrator | In those days Caesar Augustus issued a decree that a census should be taken of the entire Roman world. |

| Commentator | (This was the first census that took place while Quirinius was governor of Syria.) |

| Narrator | And everyone went to his own town to register. |
| | So Joseph also went up from the town of Nazareth in Galilee to Judea, to Bethlehem the town of David, because he belonged to the house and line of David. |

| Commentator | He went there to register with Mary, who was pledged to be married to him and was expecting a child. |

| Narrator | While they were there, the time came for the baby to be born, and she gave birth to her firstborn, a son. She wrapped him in cloths and placed him in a manger, because there was no room for them in the inn. |

Cast: **Narrator, Commentator.** (See also Appendix: Christmas Readings, pages 418–19.)

The Angels Announce the Birth of Jesus
Luke 2:8–14

| Narrator | There were shepherds living out in the fields [near Bethlehem], keeping watch over their flocks at night. An angel of the Lord appeared to them, and the glory of the Lord shone around them, and they were terrified. But the angel said to them: |

| Angel | Do not be afraid. I bring you good news of great joy that will be for all the people. Today in the town of David a Savior has been born to you; he is Christ the Lord. This will be a sign to you: You will find a baby wrapped in cloths and lying in a manger. |

| Narrator | Suddenly a great company of the heavenly host appeared with the angel, praising God and saying: |

| Chorus (joyfully) | Glory to God in the highest, and on earth peace to men on whom his favor rests. |

Cast: **Narrator, Angel, Chorus** (three or more, including Angel). (See also Appendix: Christmas Readings, page 419.)

The Shepherds Find the Baby
Luke 2:15–20

Narrator   When the angels had left them and gone into heaven, the shepherds said to one another:

Shepherd 1   Let's go to Bethlehem—

Shepherd 2   And see this thing that has happened—

Shepherd 3   Which the Lord has told us about.

Narrator   So they hurried off and found Mary and Joseph, and the baby, who was lying in the manger. When they had seen him, they spread the word concerning what had been told them about this child, and all who heard it were amazed at what the shepherds said to them. But Mary treasured up all these things and pondered them in her heart. The shepherds returned, glorifying and praising God for all the things they had heard and seen, which were just as they had been told.

Cast: **Narrator, Shepherd 1, Shepherd 2, Shepherd 3** (can be the same as Shepherd 1 and/or Shepherd 2). (See also Appendix: Christmas Readings, page 419.)

Jesus Presented in the Temple
Luke 2:22–38

Narrator   When the time of their purification according to the Law of Moses had been completed, Joseph and Mary took [Jesus] to Jerusalem to present him to the Lord . . .

Lawyer   (As it is written in the Law of the Lord: "Every firstborn male is to be consecrated to the Lord.")

Narrator   . . . and [they went] to offer a sacrifice in keeping with what is said in the Law of the Lord:

Lawyer   "A pair of doves or two young pigeons."

Narrator   Now there was a man in Jerusalem called Simeon, who was righteous and devout. He was waiting for the consolation of Israel, and the Holy Spirit was upon him. It had been revealed to him by the Holy Spirit that he would not die before he had seen the Lord's Christ. Moved by the Spirit, he went into the temple courts. When the parents brought in the child Jesus to do for him what the custom of the Law required, Simeon took him in his arms and praised God, saying:

Simeon   Sovereign Lord, as you have promised,
    you now dismiss your servant in peace.
For my eyes have seen your salvation,
    which you have prepared in the sight of all people,
a light for revelation to the Gentiles
    and for glory to your people Israel.

Narrator	The child's father and mother marveled at what was said about him. Then Simeon blessed them and said to Mary, his mother:
Simeon	This child is destined to cause the falling and rising of many in Israel, and to be a sign that will be spoken against, so that the thoughts of many hearts will be revealed. And a sword will pierce your own soul too.
Narrator	There was also a prophetess, Anna, the daughter of Phanuel, of the tribe of Asher. She was very old; she had lived with her husband seven years after her marriage, and then was a widow until she was eighty-four. She never left the temple but worshiped night and day, fasting and praying. Coming up to them at that very moment, she gave thanks to God and spoke about the child to all who were looking forward to the redemption of Jerusalem.

Cast: **Narrator, Lawyer, Simeon.** (See also Appendix: Christmas Readings, pages 421–22.)

Jesus as a Boy
Luke 2:39–52

Narrator	When Joseph and Mary had done everything required by the Law of the Lord, they returned to Galilee to their own town of Nazareth. And the child grew and became strong; he was filled with wisdom, and the grace of God was upon him. (PAUSE)
	Every year his parents went to Jerusalem for the Feast of the Passover. When he was twelve years old, they went up to the Feast, according to the custom. After the Feast was over, while his parents were returning home, the boy Jesus stayed behind in Jerusalem, but they were unaware of it. Thinking he was in their company, they traveled on for a day. Then they began looking for him among their relatives and friends. When they did not find him, they went back to Jerusalem to look for him. After three days they found him in the temple courts, sitting among the teachers, listening to them and asking them questions. Everyone who heard him was amazed at his understanding and his answers. When his parents saw him, they were astonished. His mother said to him:
Mary	Son, why have you treated us like this? Your father and I have been anxiously searching for you.
[Narrator	He asked:]
Jesus	Why were you searching for me? Didn't you know I had to be in my Father's house?
Narrator	But they did not understand what he was saying to them. (PAUSE) Then he went down to Nazareth with them and was obedient to them. But

his mother treasured all these things in her heart. And Jesus grew in wisdom and stature, and in favor with God and men.

Cast: **Narrator, Mary, Jesus** (as a boy)

John the Baptist Prepares the Way
Luke 3:[1], 2–14

Narrator [In the fifteenth year of the reign of Tiberius Caesar—when Pontius Pilate was governor of Judea, Herod tetrarch of Galilee, his brother Philip tetrarch of Iturea and Traconitis, and Lysanias tetrarch of Abilene—] during the high priesthood of Annas and Caiaphas, the word of God came to John son of Zechariah in the desert. He went into all the country around the Jordan, preaching a baptism of repentance for the forgiveness of sins. As is written in the book of the words of Isaiah the prophet:

Isaiah A voice of one calling in the desert,
"Prepare the way for the Lord,
   make straight paths for him.
Every valley shall be filled in,
   every mountain and hill made low.
The crooked roads shall become straight,
   the rough ways smooth.
And all mankind will see God's salvation."

Narrator John said to the crowds coming out to be baptized by him:

John You brood of vipers! Who warned you to flee from the coming wrath? Produce fruit in keeping with repentance. And do not begin to say to yourselves, "We have Abraham as our father." For I tell you that out of these stones God can raise up children for Abraham. The ax is already at the root of the trees, and every tree that does not produce good fruit will be cut down and thrown into the fire.

Narrator The crowd asked:

Person What should we do then?

John The man with two tunics should share with him who has none, and the one who has food should do the same.

Narrator Tax collectors also came to be baptized. They asked:

Tax collector Teacher, what should we do?

John Don't collect any more than you are required to.

Narrator Then some soldiers asked him:

Soldier And what should we do?

143

| John | Don't extort money and don't accuse people falsely—be content with your pay. |

Cast: **Narrator, Isaiah, John, Person, Tax collector, Soldier**

John the Baptist and the Baptism of Jesus
Luke 3:15–22

Narrator	The people were waiting expectantly and were all wondering in their hearts if John might possibly be the Christ. John answered them all:
John	I baptize you with water. But one more powerful than I will come, the thongs of whose sandals I am not worthy to untie. He will baptize you with the Holy Spirit and with fire. His winnowing fork is in his hand to clear his threshing floor and to gather the wheat into his barn, but he will burn up the chaff with unquenchable fire.
Narrator	And with many other words John exhorted the people and preached the good news to them.
	But when John rebuked Herod the tetrarch because of Herodias, his brother's wife, and all the other evil things he had done, Herod added this to them all: He locked John up in prison. (PAUSE)
	When all the people were being baptized, Jesus was baptized too. And as he was praying, heaven was opened and the Holy Spirit descended on him in bodily form like a dove. And a voice came from heaven:
Voice	You are my Son, whom I love; with you I am well pleased.

Cast: **Narrator, John, Voice** (from a distance)

The Temptation of Jesus
Luke 4:1–15

Narrator	Jesus, full of the Holy Spirit, returned from the Jordan and was led by the Spirit in the desert, where for forty days he was tempted by the devil. He ate nothing during those days, and at the end of them he was hungry. The devil said to him:
Devil	If you are the Son of God, tell this stone to become bread.
[Narrator	Jesus answered:]
Jesus	It is written: "Man does not live on bread alone."
Narrator	The devil led him up to a high place and showed him in an instant all the kingdoms of the world. And he said to him:

144

Devil	I will give you all their authority and splendor, for it has been given to me, and I can give it to anyone I want to. So if you worship me, it will all be yours.
Jesus	It is written: "Worship the Lord your God and serve him only."
Narrator	The devil led him to Jerusalem and had him stand on the highest point of the temple.
Devil	If you are the Son of God, throw yourself down from here. For it is written:

"He will command his angels concerning you
    to guard you carefully;
they will lift you up in their hands,
    so that you will not strike your foot against a stone."

Jesus	It says: "Do not put the Lord your God to the test."
Narrator	When the devil had finished all this tempting, he left him until an opportune time.
	Jesus returned to Galilee in the power of the Spirit, and news about him spread through the whole countryside. He taught in their synagogues, and everyone praised him.

Cast: **Narrator, Devil, Jesus**

Jesus Rejected at Nazareth
Luke 4:16–30

Narrator	[Jesus] went to Nazareth, where he had been brought up, and on the Sabbath day he went into the synagogue, as was his custom. And he stood up to read. The scroll of the prophet Isaiah was handed to him. Unrolling it, he found the place where it is written:
Jesus	The Spirit of the Lord is on me,
because he has anointed me
to preach good news to the poor.
He has sent me to proclaim freedom for the prisoners
and recovery of sight for the blind,
to release the oppressed,
to proclaim the year of the Lord's favor.
Narrator	Then [Jesus] rolled up the scroll, gave it back to the attendant and sat down. The eyes of everyone in the synagogue were fastened on him, and he began by saying to them:
Jesus	Today this scripture is fulfilled in your hearing.
Narrator	All spoke well of him and were amazed at the gracious words that came from his lips.
Worshiper	Isn't this Joseph's son?

145

Jesus	Surely you will quote this proverb to me: "Physician, heal yourself! Do here in your hometown what we have heard that you did in Capernaum."
	I tell you the truth, no prophet is accepted in his hometown. (PAUSE) I assure you that there were many widows in Israel in Elijah's time, when the sky was shut for three and a half years and there was a severe famine throughout the land. Yet Elijah was not sent to any of them, but to a widow in Zarephath in the region of Sidon. And there were many in Israel with leprosy in the time of Elisha the prophet, yet not one of them was cleansed—only Naaman the Syrian.
Narrator	All the people in the synagogue were furious when they heard this. They got up, drove him out of the town, and took him to the brow of the hill on which the town was built, in order to throw him down the cliff. But he walked right through the crowd and went on his way.

Cast: **Narrator, Jesus, Worshiper**

Jesus Drives Out an Evil Spirit
Luke 4:31–37

Narrator	[Jesus] went down to Capernaum, a town in Galilee, and on the Sabbath began to teach the people. They were amazed at his teaching, because his message had authority.
	In the synagogue there was a man possessed by a demon, an evil spirit. He cried out at the top of his voice:
Man (loudly)	Ha! What do you want with us, Jesus of Nazareth? Have you come to destroy us? I know who you are—the Holy One of God!
Narrator	Jesus [ordered the spirit]:
Jesus (firmly)	Be quiet! Come out of him!
Narrator	Then the demon threw the man down before them all and came out without injuring him. (PAUSE) All the people were amazed and said to each other:
Person 1	What is this teaching?
Person 2	With authority and power he gives orders to evil spirits.
Person 1	And they come out!
Narrator	And the news about him spread throughout the surrounding area.

Cast: **Narrator, Man, Jesus, Person 1, Person 2**

Jesus Heals and Preaches
Luke 4:38–44

Narrator   Jesus left the synagogue and went to the home of Simon. Now Simon's mother-in-law was suffering from a high fever, and they asked Jesus to help her. So he bent over her and rebuked the fever, and it left her. She got up at once and began to wait on them.

When the sun was setting, the people brought to Jesus all who had various kinds of sickness, and laying his hands on each one, he healed them. Moreover, demons came out of many people, shouting:

Demon   You are the Son of God!

Narrator   But he rebuked them and would not allow them to speak, because they knew he was the Christ. (PAUSE)

At daybreak Jesus went out to a solitary place. The people were looking for him and when they came to where he was, they tried to keep him from leaving them. But he said:

Jesus   I must preach the good news of the kingdom of God to the other towns also, because that is why I was sent.

Narrator   And he kept on preaching in the synagogues of Judea.

Cast: **Narrator, Demon, Jesus**

The Calling of the First Disciples
Luke 5:1–11

Narrator   One day as Jesus was standing by the Lake of Gennesaret, with the people crowding around him and listening to the word of God, he saw at the water's edge two boats, left there by the fishermen, who were washing their nets. He got into one of the boats, the one belonging to Simon, and asked him to put out a little from shore. Then he sat down and taught the people from the boat. (PAUSE)

When he had finished speaking, he said to Simon:

Jesus   Put out into deep water, and let down the nets for a catch.

[Narrator   Simon answered:]

Simon   Master, we've worked hard all night and haven't caught anything. But because you say so, I will let down the nets.

Narrator   When they had done so, they caught such a large number of fish that their nets began to break. So they signaled their partners in the other boat to come and help them, and they came and filled both boats so full that they began to sink. When Simon Peter saw this, he fell at Jesus' knees and said:

147

Simon	Go away from me, Lord; I am a sinful man!
Narrator	For he and all his companions were astonished at the catch of fish they had taken, and so were James and John, the sons of Zebedee, Simon's partners. [Then Jesus said to Simon:]
Jesus (to Simon)	Don't be afraid; from now on you will catch men.
Narrator	So they pulled their boats up on shore, left everything and followed him.

Cast: **Narrator, Jesus, Simon**

The Man with Leprosy
Luke 5:12–16

Narrator	While Jesus was in one of the towns, a man came along who was covered with leprosy. When he saw Jesus, he fell with his face to the ground and begged him:
Man	Lord, if you are willing, you can make me clean.
Narrator	Jesus reached out his hand and touched the man.
Jesus	I am willing. Be clean!
Narrator	And immediately the leprosy left him. Then Jesus ordered him:
Jesus	Don't tell anyone, but go, show yourself to the priest and offer the sacrifices that Moses commanded for your cleansing, as a testimony to them.
Narrator	Yet the news about him spread all the more, so that crowds of people came to hear him and to be healed of their sicknesses. But Jesus often withdrew to lonely places and prayed.

Cast: **Narrator, Man, Jesus**

Jesus Heals a Paralytic
Luke 5:17–26

Narrator	One day as [Jesus] was teaching, Pharisees and teachers of the law, who had come from every village of Galilee and from Judea and Jerusalem, were sitting there. And the power of the Lord was present for him to heal the sick. Some men came carrying a paralytic on a mat and tried to take him into the house to lay him before Jesus. When they could not find a way to do this because of the crowd, they went up on the roof and lowered him on his mat through the tiles into the middle of the crowd, right in front of Jesus. When Jesus saw their faith, he said:
Jesus	Friend, your sins are forgiven.

148

Narrator	The Pharisees and the teachers of the law began thinking to themselves:
Lawyer	Who is this fellow who speaks blasphemy? Who can forgive sins but God alone?
Narrator	Jesus knew what they were thinking and asked:
Jesus	Why are you thinking these things in your hearts? Which is easier: to say, "Your sins are forgiven," or to say, "Get up and walk"? But that you may know that the Son of Man has authority on earth to forgive sins. . . .
Narrator	He said to the paralyzed man:
Jesus	I tell you, get up, take your mat and go home.
Narrator	Immediately he stood up in front of them, took what he had been lying on and went home praising God. Everyone was amazed and gave praise to God. They were filled with awe and said:
Person	We have seen remarkable things today.

Cast: **Narrator, Jesus, Lawyer, Person**

The Calling of Levi
Luke 5:27–32

Narrator	Jesus . . . saw a tax collector by the name of Levi sitting at his tax booth. [Jesus said to him:]
Jesus	Follow me.
Narrator	Levi got up, left everything and followed him. Then Levi held a great banquet for Jesus at his house, and a large crowd of tax collectors and others were eating with them. But the Pharisees and the teachers of the law who belonged to their sect complained to his disciples:
Pharisee	Why do you eat and drink with tax collectors and "sinners"?
Narrator	Jesus answered them:
Jesus	It is not the healthy who need a doctor, but the sick. I have not come to call the righteous, but sinners to repentance.

Cast: **Narrator, Jesus, Pharisee**

Jesus Questioned about Fasting
Luke 5:33–39

Narrator	[Some people said to Jesus:]
Person 1	John's disciples often fast and pray.

149

Person 2	And so do the disciples of the Pharisees.
Person 1	But yours go on eating and drinking.
Narrator	Jesus answered:
Jesus	Can you make the guests of the bridegroom fast while he is with them? But the time will come when the bridegroom will be taken from them; in those days they will fast.
Narrator	He told them this parable:
Jesus	No one tears a patch from a new garment and sews it on an old one. If he does, he will have torn the new garment, and the patch from the new will not match the old. And no one pours new wine into old wineskins. If he does, the new wine will burst the skins, the wine will run out and the wineskins will be ruined. No, new wine must be poured into new wineskins. And no one after drinking old wine wants the new, for he says, "The old is better."

Cast: **Narrator, Person 1, Person 2** (can be the same as Person 1), **Jesus**

Lord of the Sabbath
Luke 6:1–11

Narrator	One Sabbath Jesus was going through the grainfields, and his disciples began to pick some heads of grain, rub them in their hands and eat the kernels. Some of the Pharisees asked:
Pharisee	Why are you doing what is unlawful on the Sabbath?
Narrator	Jesus answered them:
Jesus	Have you never read what David did when he and his companions were hungry? He entered the house of God, and taking the consecrated bread, he ate what is lawful only for priests to eat. And he also gave some to his companions. The Son of Man is Lord of the Sabbath.
Narrator	On another Sabbath he went into the synagogue and was teaching, and a man was there whose right hand was shriveled. The Pharisees and the teachers of the law were looking for a reason to accuse Jesus, so they watched him closely to see if he would heal on the Sabbath. But Jesus knew what they were thinking and said to the man with the shriveled hand:
Jesus	Get up and stand in front of everyone.
Narrator	So he got up and stood there. Then Jesus said to them:
Jesus	I ask you, which is lawful on the Sabbath: to do good or to do evil, to save life or to destroy it?
Narrator	He looked around at them all, and then said to the man:

Jesus	Stretch out your hand.
Narrator	He did so, and his hand was completely restored. But they were furious and began to discuss with one another what they might do to Jesus.

Cast: **Narrator, Pharisee, Jesus**

The Twelve Apostles
Luke 6:12–19

Narrator 1	[One day] Jesus went out to a mountainside to pray, and spent the night praying to God. When morning came, he called his disciples to him and chose twelve of them, whom he also designated apostles: Simon—
Narrator 2	whom he named Peter;
Narrator 1	Andrew—
Narrator 2	his brother;
Narrator 1	James, John, Philip, Bartholomew, Matthew, Thomas, James—
Narrator 2	son of Alphaeus;
Narrator 1	Simon—
Narrator 2	who was called the Zealot;
Narrator 1	Judas—
Narrator 2	son of James;
Narrator 1	and Judas Iscariot—
Narrator 2	who became a traitor.
Narrator 1	He went down with them and stood on a level place. A large crowd of his disciples was there.
Narrator 2	And a great number of people from all over Judea, from Jerusalem, and from the coast of Tyre and Sidon [were there.]
Narrator 1	[They] had come to hear him and to be healed of their diseases.
Narrator 2	Those troubled by evil spirits were cured.
Narrator 1	The people all tried to touch him, because power was coming from him and healing them all.

Cast: **Narrator 1, Narrator 2**

Blessings and Woes
Luke 6:20–26

Narrator	Looking at his disciples, Jesus said:

151

Jesus	Blessed are you who are poor—
Students	For yours is the kingdom of God.
Jesus	Blessed are you who hunger now—
Students	For you will be satisfied.
Jesus	Blessed are you who weep now—
Students	For you will laugh.
Jesus	Blessed are you when men hate you, when they exclude you and insult you and reject your name as evil, because of the Son of Man.
	Rejoice in that day and leap for joy, because great is your reward in heaven. For that is how their fathers treated the prophets.
	But woe to you who are rich—
Students	For you have already received your comfort.
Jesus	Woe to you who are well fed now—
Students	For you will go hungry.
Jesus	Woe to you who laugh now—
Students	For you will mourn and weep.
Jesus	Woe to you when all men speak well of you, for that is how their fathers treated the false prophets.

Cast: **Narrator**, **Jesus** (can be the same as Narrator), **Students** (two or more). The dramatized reading reflects the classic rabbinic way of teaching and learning this form of instruction.

Love for Enemies
Luke 6:27–36

Jesus	I tell you who hear me: Love your enemies,
Students	Do good to those who hate you.
Jesus	Bless those who curse you—
Students	Pray for those who mistreat you.
Jesus	If someone strikes you on one cheek—
Students	Turn to him the other also.
Jesus	If someone takes your cloak—
Students	Do not stop him from taking your tunic.
Jesus	Give to everyone who asks you—
Students	And if anyone takes what belongs to you, do not demand it back.

Jesus	Do to others as you would have them do to you. (PAUSE)
	If you love those who love you, what credit is that to you?
Students	Even "sinners" love those who love them.
Jesus	And if you do good to those who are good to you, what credit is that to you?
Students	Even "sinners" do that.
Jesus	And if you lend to those from whom you expect repayment, what credit is that to you?
Students	Even "sinners" lend to "sinners," expecting to be repaid in full.
Jesus	But love your enemies—
Students	Do good to them.
Jesus	And lend to them—
Students	Without expecting to get anything back.
Jesus	Then your reward will be great—
Students	And you will be sons of the Most High.
Jesus	Because he is kind to the ungrateful and wicked. Be merciful, just as your Father is merciful.

Cast: **Jesus**, **Students** (two or more). The dramatized reading reflects the classic rabbinic way of teaching and learning this form of instruction.

Judging Others
Luke 6:37–42

Jesus	Do not judge—
Students	And you will not be judged.
Jesus	Do not condemn—
Students	And you will not be condemned.
Jesus	Forgive—
Students	And you will be forgiven.
Jesus	Give—
Students	And it will be given to you.
Jesus	A good measure, pressed down, shaken together and running over, will be poured into your lap. For with the measure you use, it will be measured to you.
Narrator	He also told them this parable:

153

Jesus	Can a blind man lead a blind man? Will they not both fall into a pit? A student is not above his teacher, but everyone who is fully trained will be like his teacher. (PAUSE)

Why do you look at the speck of sawdust in your brother's eye and pay no attention to the plank in your own eye? How can you say to your brother: |
| **Voice** | Brother, let me take the speck out of your eye. |
| **Jesus** | When you yourself fail to see the plank in your own eye? You hypocrite, first take the plank out of your eye, and then you will see clearly to remove the speck from your brother's eye. |

Cast: **Jesus, Students** (two or more), **Narrator** (can be the same as one of the Students), **Voice** (can be the same as one of the Students). The dramatized reading reflects the classic rabbinic way of teaching and learning this form of instruction.

A Tree and Its Fruit
Luke 6:43–45

Reader 1	No good tree bears bad fruit.
Reader 2	Nor does a bad tree bear good fruit.
Reader 1	Each tree is recognized by its own fruit. People do not pick figs from thornbushes.
Reader 2	Or grapes from briers.
Reader 1	The good man brings good things out of the good stored up in his heart.
Reader 2	And the evil man brings evil things out of the evil stored up in his heart.
Readers 1 and 2	For out of the overflow of his heart his mouth speaks.

Cast: **Reader 1** (encouraging, happy voice), **Reader 2** (serious, warning voice)

The Wise and Foolish Builders
Luke 6:46–49

Narrator 1	[Jesus said:] Why do you call me:
Narrators 1 and 2	Lord, Lord,
Narrator 1	And do not do what I say? I will show you what he is like who comes to me and hears my words and puts them into practice. He is like a man building a house, who dug down deep and laid the foundation on rock. When a flood came, the torrent struck that house but could not shake it, because it was well built.

Narrator 2	But the one who hears my words and does not put them into practice is like a man who built a house on the ground without a foundation. The moment the torrent struck that house, it collapsed and its destruction was complete.

Cast: **Narrator 1**, **Narrator 2**

The Faith of the Centurion
Luke 7:1–10

Narrator	Jesus . . . entered Capernaum. There a centurion's servant, whom his master valued highly, was sick and about to die. The centurion heard of Jesus and sent some elders of the Jews to him, asking him to come and heal his servant. When they came to Jesus, they pleaded earnestly with him:
Elder 1	This man deserves to have you do this.
Elder 2	Because he loves our nation and has built our synagogue.
Narrator	So Jesus went with them. (PAUSE) He was not far from the house when the centurion sent friends to say to him:
Friend	Lord, don't trouble yourself, for I do not deserve to have you come under my roof. That is why I did not even consider myself worthy to come to you. But say the word, and my servant will be healed. For I myself am a man under authority, with soldiers under me. I tell this one, "Go," and he goes; and that one, "Come," and he comes. I say to my servant, "Do this," and he does it.
Narrator	When Jesus heard this, he was amazed at him, and turning to the crowd following him, he said:
Jesus	I tell you, I have not found such great faith even in Israel.
Narrator	Then the men who had been sent returned to the house and found the servant well.

Cast: **Narrator**, **Elder 1**, **Elder 2** (can be the same as Elder 1), **Friend**, **Jesus**

Jesus Raises a Widow's Son
Luke 7:11–17

Narrator	Jesus went to a town called Nain, and his disciples and a large crowd went along with him. As he approached the town gate, a dead person was being carried out—the only son of his mother, and she was a widow. And a large crowd from the town was with her. When the Lord saw her, his heart went out to her [and he said]:
Jesus	Don't cry.

155

Narrator	Then [Jesus] went up and touched the coffin, and those carrying it stood still. [He said:]
Jesus	Young man, I say to you, get up!
Narrator	The dead man sat up and began to talk, and Jesus gave him back to his mother. (PAUSE) They were all filled with awe and praised God.
Person 1	A great prophet has appeared among us.
Person 2	God has come to help his people.
Narrator	This news about Jesus spread throughout Judea and the surrounding country.

Cast: **Narrator, Jesus, Person 1, Person 2**

Jesus and John the Baptist
Luke 7:18–35

Narrator	John's disciples told him about all [Jesus was doing]. Calling two of them, he sent them to the Lord to ask, "Are you the one who was to come, or should we expect someone else?"
	When the men came to Jesus, they said:
Disciple 1	John the Baptist sent us to you to ask, "Are you the one who was to come?"
Disciple 2	"Or should we expect someone else?"
Narrator	At that very time Jesus cured many who had diseases, sicknesses and evil spirits, and gave sight to many who were blind. So he replied to the messengers:
Jesus	Go back and report to John what you have seen and heard: The blind receive sight, the lame walk, those who have leprosy are cured, the deaf hear, the dead are raised, and the good news is preached to the poor. Blessed is the man who does not fall away on account of me.
Narrator	After John's messengers left, Jesus began to speak to the crowd about John:
Jesus	What did you go out into the desert to see? A reed swayed by the wind? If not, what did you go out to see? A man dressed in fine clothes? No, those who wear expensive clothes and indulge in luxury are in palaces. But what did you go out to see? A prophet? Yes, I tell you, and more than a prophet. This is the one about whom it is written:
Malachi	I will send my messenger ahead of you, who will prepare your way before you.
Jesus	I tell you, among those born of women there is no one greater than John; yet the one who is least in the kingdom of God is greater than he.

Narrator	(All the people, even the tax collectors, when they heard Jesus' words, acknowledged that God's way was right, because they had been baptized by John. But the Pharisees and experts in the law rejected God's purpose for themselves, because they had not been baptized by John.)
Jesus	To what, then, can I compare the people of this generation? What are they like? They are like children sitting in the marketplace and calling out to each other:
Person 1	We played the flute for you, and you did not dance.
Person 2	We sang a dirge, and you did not cry.
Jesus	For John the Baptist came neither eating bread nor drinking wine, and you say:
Person 3	He has a demon.
Jesus	The Son of Man came eating and drinking, and you say:
Person 4	Here is a glutton and a drunkard, a friend of tax collectors and "sinners."
Jesus	But wisdom is proved right by all her children.

Cast: **Narrator**, **Disciple 1**, **Disciple 2** (can be the same as Disciple 1), **Jesus**, **Malachi**, **Person 1**, **Person 2** (both preferably children), **Person 3**, **Person 4**

Jesus Anointed by a Sinful Woman
Luke 7:36–50

Narrator	One of the Pharisees invited Jesus to have dinner with him, so he went to the Pharisee's house and reclined at the table. When a woman who had lived a sinful life in that town learned that Jesus was eating at the Pharisee's house, she brought an alabaster jar of perfume, and as she stood behind him at his feet weeping, she began to wet his feet with her tears. Then she wiped them with her hair, kissed them and poured perfume on them.
	When the Pharisee who had invited him saw this, he said to himself:
Simon	If this man were a prophet, he would know who is touching him and what kind of woman she is—that she is a sinner.
Narrator	Jesus answered him:
Jesus	Simon, I have something to tell you.
Simon	Tell me, teacher.
Jesus	Two men owed money to a certain moneylender. One owed him five hundred denarii, and the other fifty. Neither of them had the money to

157

pay him back, so he canceled the debts of both. Now which of them will love him more?

Simon	I suppose the one who had the bigger debt canceled.
Jesus	You have judged correctly.
Narrator	Then he turned toward the woman and said to Simon:
Jesus (to Simon)	Do you see this woman? I came into your house. You did not give me any water for my feet, but she wet my feet with her tears and wiped them with her hair. You did not give me a kiss, but this woman, from the time I entered, has not stopped kissing my feet. You did not put oil on my head, but she has poured perfume on my feet. Therefore, I tell you, her many sins have been forgiven—for she loved much. But he who has been forgiven little loves little.
Narrator	Then Jesus said to her:
Jesus	Your sins are forgiven.
Narrator	The other guests began to say among themselves:
Person 1	Who is this?
Person 2	Who even forgives sins?
Narrator	Jesus said to the woman:
Jesus	Your faith has saved you; go in peace.

Cast: **Narrator**, **Simon** (the Pharisee), **Jesus**, **Person 1**, **Person 2** (can be the same as Person 1)

The Parable of the Sower
Luke 8:4–15

Narrator	While a large crowd was gathering and people were coming to Jesus from town after town, he told this parable:
Speaker 1	A farmer went out to sow his seed.
Speaker 2	As he was scattering the seed, some fell along the path; it was trampled on, and the birds of the air ate it up.
Speaker 1	Some fell on rock, and when it came up, the plants withered because they had no moisture.
Speaker 2	Other seed fell among thorns, which grew up with it and choked the plants.
Speaker 1	Still other seed fell on good soil. It came up and yielded a crop, a hundred times more than was sown.
Narrator	When he said this, he called out—"He who has ears to hear, let him hear."

His disciples asked him what this parable meant. He said—"The knowledge of the secrets of the kingdom of God has been given to you, but to others I speak in parables, so that,

'though seeing, they may not see;
    though hearing, they may not understand.'"

This is the meaning of the parable:

Speaker 2   The seed is the word of God.

Speaker 1   Those along the path are the ones who hear, and then the devil comes and takes away the word from their hearts, so that they may not believe and be saved.

Speaker 2   Those on the rock are the ones who receive the word with joy when they hear it, but they have no root. They believe for a while, but in the time of testing they fall away.

Speaker 1   The seed that fell among thorns stands for those who hear, but as they go on their way they are choked by life's worries, riches and pleasures, and they do not mature.

Speaker 2   But the seed on good soil stands for those with a noble and good heart, who hear the word, retain it, and by persevering produce a crop.

Cast: **Narrator, Speaker 1, Speaker 2**. (See two quite different dramatizations of this parable at Matthew 13:1 and Mark 4:1.)

A Lamp on a Stand

Luke 8:16–18

Speaker 1   No one lights a lamp and hides it in a jar or puts it under a bed.

Speaker 2   Instead, he puts it on a stand, so that those who come in can see the light.

Speaker 1   For there is nothing hidden that will not be disclosed.

Speaker 2   And nothing concealed that will not be known or brought out into the open.

Speaker 1   Therefore consider carefully how you listen. Whoever has will be given more.

Speaker 2   Whoever does not have, even what he thinks he has will be taken from him.

Cast: **Speaker 1, Speaker 2**

Jesus' Mother and Brothers
Luke 8:19–21

Narrator Now Jesus' mother and brothers came to see him, but they were not able to get near him because of the crowd. Someone told him:

Person Your mother and brothers are standing outside, wanting to see you.

Narrator He replied:

Jesus My mother and brothers are those who hear God's word and put it into practice.

Cast: **Narrator, Person, Jesus**

Jesus Calms the Storm
Luke 8:22–25

Narrator One day Jesus said to his disciples:

Jesus Let's go over to the other side of the lake.

Narrator So they got into a boat and set out. As they sailed, he fell asleep. A squall came down on the lake, so that the boat was being swamped, and they were in great danger. The disciples went and woke him, saying:

Disciple 1
(calling) Master, Master.

Disciple 2 We're going to drown!

Narrator [Jesus] got up and rebuked the wind and the raging waters; the storm subsided, and all was calm. He asked his disciples:

Jesus Where is your faith?

Narrator In fear and amazement they asked one another:

Disciple 1
(amazed) Who is this?

Disciple 2 He commands even the winds and the water, and they obey him.

Cast: **Narrator, Jesus, Disciple 1, Disciple 2**

The Healing of a Demon-possessed Man
Luke 8:26–39

Narrator [Jesus and his disciples] sailed to the region of the Gerasenes, which is across the lake from Galilee. When Jesus stepped ashore, he was met by a demon-possessed man from the town. For a long time this man had not worn clothes or lived in a house, but had lived in the tombs. When he saw Jesus, he cried out and fell at his feet, shouting at the top of his voice:

Legion/Man	What do you want with me, Jesus, Son of the Most High God? I beg you, don't torture me!
Narrator	For Jesus had commanded the evil spirit to come out of the man. Many times it had seized him, and though he was chained hand and foot and kept under guard, he had broken his chains and had been driven by the demon into solitary places. Jesus asked him:
Jesus	What is your name?
Narrator	He replied, because many demons had gone into him:
Legion/Man	[My name is] Legion.
Narrator	[The demons] begged [Jesus] repeatedly not to order them to go into the Abyss. (PAUSE)
	A large herd of pigs was feeding there on the hillside. The demons begged Jesus to let them go into them, and he gave them permission. When the demons came out of the man, they went into the pigs, and the herd rushed down the steep bank into the lake and was drowned. (PAUSE)
	When those tending the pigs saw what had happened, they ran off and reported this in the town and countryside, and the people went out to see what had happened. When they came to Jesus, they found the man from whom the demons had gone out, sitting at Jesus' feet, dressed and in his right mind; and they were afraid. Those who had seen it told the people how the demon-possessed man had been cured. Then all the people of the region of the Gerasenes asked Jesus to leave them, because they were overcome with fear. So he got into the boat and left. (PAUSE) The man from whom the demons had gone out begged [Jesus]:
Legion/Man	[Let me go with you.]
Narrator	But Jesus sent him away, saying:
Jesus	Return home and tell how much God has done for you.
Narrator	So the man went away and told all over town how much Jesus had done for him.

Cast: **Narrator, Legion/Man, Jesus**

A Dead Girl and a Sick Woman
Luke 8:40–56

Narrator	Now when Jesus returned [to Galilee], a crowd welcomed him, for they were all expecting him. Then a man named Jairus, a ruler of the synagogue, came and fell at Jesus' feet, pleading with him to come to his house because his only daughter, a girl of about twelve, was dying.
	As Jesus was on his way, the crowds almost crushed him. And a woman was there who had been subject to bleeding for twelve years, but no one

161

	could heal her. She came up behind him and touched the edge of his cloak, and immediately her bleeding stopped. Jesus asked:
Jesus	Who touched me?
Narrator	When they all denied it, Peter said:
Peter	Master, the people are crowding and pressing against you.
Jesus	Someone touched me; I know that power has gone out from me.
Narrator	Then the woman, seeing that she could not go unnoticed, came trembling and fell at his feet. In the presence of all the people, she told why she had touched him and how she had been instantly healed. Then he said to her:
Jesus	Daughter, your faith has healed you. Go in peace.
Narrator	While Jesus was still speaking, someone came from the house of Jairus, the synagogue ruler. [He told Jairus:]
Messenger	Your daughter is dead. Don't bother the teacher any more.
Narrator	Hearing this, Jesus said to Jairus:
Jesus	Don't be afraid; just believe, and she will be healed. (PAUSE)
Narrator	When he arrived at the house of Jairus, he did not let anyone go in with him except Peter, John and James, and the child's father and mother. Meanwhile, all the people were wailing and mourning for her. Jesus said:
Jesus	Stop wailing. She is not dead but asleep.
Narrator	They laughed at him, knowing that she was dead. But he took her by the hand and said:
Jesus	My child, get up!
Narrator	Her spirit returned, and at once she stood up. Then Jesus told them to give her something to eat. Her parents were astonished, but he ordered them not to tell anyone what had happened.

Cast: **Narrator, Jesus, Peter, Messenger**

Jesus Sends Out the Twelve Disciples
Luke 9:1–6 [7–9], 10

Narrator	When Jesus had called the Twelve together, he gave them power and authority to drive out all demons and to cure diseases, and he sent them out to preach the kingdom of God and to heal the sick. He told them:
Jesus	Take nothing for the journey—no staff, no bag, no bread, no money, no extra tunic. Whatever house you enter, stay there until you leave that

	town. If people do not welcome you, shake the dust off your feet when you leave their town, as a testimony against them.
Narrator	So they set out and went from village to village, preaching the gospel and healing people everywhere. (PAUSE)
	[Now Herod the tetrarch heard about all that was going on. And he was perplexed, because some were saying that John had been raised from the dead, others that Elijah had appeared, and still others that one of the prophets of long ago had come back to life. But Herod said:
Herod	I beheaded John. Who, then, is this I hear such things about?
Narrator	And he tried to see him.]
Narrator	When the apostles returned, they reported to Jesus what they had done.

Cast: **Narrator, Jesus, Herod**

Jesus Feeds the Five Thousand
Luke 9:10–17

Narrator	[Jesus took his disciples] with him and they withdrew by themselves to a town called Bethsaida, but the crowds learned about it and followed him. (PAUSE) He welcomed them and spoke to them about the kingdom of God, and healed those who needed healing. (PAUSE) Late in the afternoon the Twelve came to him and said:
Disciple 1	Send the crowd away so they can go to the surrounding villages and countryside—
Disciple 2	And find food and lodging, because we are in a remote place here.
Narrator	[Jesus] replied:
Jesus	You give them something to eat.
Disciple 2	We have only five loaves of bread and two fish—
Disciple 1	Unless we go and *buy* food for all this crowd.
Narrator	(About five thousand men were there.) (PAUSE) But [Jesus] said to his disciples:
Jesus	Have them sit down in groups of about fifty each.
Narrator	The disciples did so, and everybody sat down. Taking the five loaves and the two fish and looking up to heaven, he gave thanks and broke them. Then he gave them to the disciples to set before the people. They all ate and were satisfied, and the disciples picked up twelve basketfuls of broken pieces that were left over.

Cast: **Narrator, Disciple 1, Disciple 2, Jesus**

Peter's Confession of Christ
Luke 9:18–27

Narrator	Once when Jesus was praying in private and his disciples were with him, he asked them:
Jesus	Who do the crowds say I am?
Narrator	They replied:
Disciple 1	Some say John the Baptist.
Disciple 2	Others say Elijah.
Disciple 3	And still others, that one of the prophets of long ago has come back to life.
Jesus	But what about you? Who do you say I am?
Narrator	Peter answered:
Peter	The Christ of God.
Narrator	Jesus strictly warned them not to tell this to anyone. And he said:
Jesus (to disciples)	The Son of Man must suffer many things and be rejected by the elders, chief priests and teachers of the law, and he must be killed and on the third day be raised to life.
Narrator	Then he said to them all:
Jesus (calling)	If anyone would come after me, he must deny himself and take up his cross daily and follow me. For whoever wants to save his life will lose it, but whoever loses his life for me will save it. What good is it for a man to gain the whole world, and yet lose or forfeit his very self? If anyone is ashamed of me and my words, the Son of Man will be ashamed of him when he comes in his glory and in the glory of the Father and of the holy angels. I tell you the truth, some who are standing here will not taste death before they see the kingdom of God.

Cast: **Narrator, Jesus, Disciple 1, Disciple 2, Disciple 3** (can be the same as Disciple 1), **Peter** (can be the same as Disciple 2)

The Transfiguration
Luke 9:28–36

Narrator	Jesus . . . took Peter, John and James with him and went up onto a mountain to pray. As he was praying, the appearance of his face changed, and his clothes became as bright as a flash of lightning. Two men, Moses and Elijah, appeared in glorious splendor, talking with Jesus. They spoke about his departure, which he was about to bring to fulfillment at Jerusalem. Peter and his companions were very sleepy, but

	when they became fully awake, they saw his glory and the two men standing with him. As the men were leaving Jesus, Peter said to him:
Peter	Master, it is good for us to be here. Let us put up three shelters—one for you, one for Moses and one for Elijah.
Narrator	(He did not know what he was saying.) While he was speaking, a cloud appeared and enveloped them, and they were afraid as they entered the cloud. A voice came from the cloud, saying:
Voice	This is my Son, whom I have chosen; listen to him.
Narrator	When the voice had spoken, they found that Jesus was alone. The disciples kept this to themselves, and told no one at that time what they had seen.

Cast: **Narrator, Peter, Voice**

The Healing of a Boy with an Evil Spirit
Luke 9:37–45

Narrator	The next day, when [Jesus] came down from the mountain [with Peter, John and James], a large crowd met him. A man in the crowd called out:
Man	Teacher, I beg you to look at my son, for he is my only child. A spirit seizes him and he suddenly screams; it throws him into convulsions so that he foams at the mouth. It scarcely ever leaves him and is destroying him. I begged your disciples to drive it out, but they could not.
[Narrator	Jesus replied:**]**
Jesus (to all)	O unbelieving and perverse generation, how long shall I stay with you and put up with you?
Narrator	[Then he said to the man:]
Jesus (to the man)	Bring your son here.
Narrator	Even while the boy was coming, the demon threw him to the ground in a convulsion. But Jesus rebuked the evil spirit, healed the boy and gave him back to his father. And they were all amazed at the greatness of God. (PAUSE)
	While everyone was marveling at all that Jesus did, he said to his disciples:
Jesus	Listen carefully to what I am about to tell you: The Son of Man is going to be betrayed into the hands of men.
Narrator	But they did not understand what this meant. It was hidden from them, so that they did not grasp it, and they were afraid to ask him about it.

Cast: **Narrator, Man, Jesus**

Who Will Be the Greatest?
Luke 9:46–56

Narrator   An argument started among the disciples as to which of them would be the greatest. Jesus, knowing their thoughts, took a little child and had him stand beside him. [Then he said to them:]

Jesus   Whoever welcomes this little child in my name welcomes me; and whoever welcomes me welcomes the one who sent me. For he who is least among you all—he is the greatest. (PAUSE)

Narrator   [John spoke up:]

John   Master, we saw a man driving out demons in your name and we tried to stop him, because he is not one of us.

Jesus   Do not stop him, for whoever is not against you is for you. (PAUSE)

Narrator   As the time approached for him to be taken up to heaven, Jesus resolutely set out for Jerusalem. And he sent messengers on ahead, who went into a Samaritan village to get things ready for him; but the people there did not welcome him, because he was heading for Jerusalem. When the disciples James and John saw this, they asked:

James   Lord, do you want us to call fire down from heaven . . .

John   . . . to destroy them?

Narrator   But Jesus turned and rebuked them, and they went to another village.

Cast: **Narrator, Jesus, John, James** (can be the same as John)

The Cost of Following Jesus
Luke 9:57–62

Narrator   As they were walking along the road, a man said to [Jesus]:

Man 1   I will follow you wherever you go.

Narrator   Jesus replied:

Jesus   Foxes have holes and birds of the air have nests, but the Son of Man has no place to lay his head.

Narrator   He said to another man:

Jesus   Follow me.

[Narrator   But the man replied:]

Man 2   Lord, first let me go and bury my father.

Jesus   Let the dead bury their own dead, but you go and proclaim the kingdom of God.

[Narrator   Still another said:]

Man 3   I will follow you, Lord; but first let me go back and say good-by to my family.

Jesus   No one who puts his hand to the plow and looks back is fit for service in the kingdom of God.

Cast: **Narrator, Man 1, Jesus, Man 2, Man 3**

Jesus Sends Out the Seventy-two
Luke 10:1–20

Narrator   The Lord appointed seventy-two others and sent them two by two ahead of him to every town and place where he was about to go. He told them:

Jesus   The harvest is plentiful, but the workers are few. Ask the Lord of the harvest, therefore, to send out workers into his harvest field. Go! I am sending you out like lambs among wolves. Do not take a purse or bag or sandals; and do not greet anyone on the road.

When you enter a house, first say, "Peace to this house." If a man of peace is there, your peace will rest on him; if not, it will return to you. Stay in that house, eating and drinking whatever they give you, for the worker deserves his wages. Do not move around from house to house.

When you enter a town and are welcomed, eat what is set before you. Heal the sick who are there and tell them, "The kingdom of God is near you." But when you enter a town and are not welcomed, go into its streets and say, "Even the dust of your town that sticks to our feet we wipe off against you. Yet be sure of this: The kingdom of God is near." I tell you, it will be more bearable on that day for Sodom than for that town. (PAUSE)

Narrator   [Jesus exclaimed:]

Jesus   Woe to you, Korazin! Woe to you, Bethsaida! For if the miracles that were performed in you had been performed in Tyre and Sidon, they would have repented long ago, sitting in sackcloth and ashes. But it will be more bearable for Tyre and Sidon at the judgment than for you. And you, Capernaum, will you be lifted up to the skies? No, you will go down to the depths.

Narrator   [Jesus said to his disciples:]

Jesus   He who listens to you listens to me; he who rejects you rejects me; but he who rejects me rejects him who sent me.

Narrator   The seventy-two returned with joy and said:

Man   Lord, even the demons submit to us in your name.

Jesus	I saw Satan fall like lightning from heaven. I have given you authority to trample on snakes and scorpions and to overcome all the power of the enemy; nothing will harm you. However, do not rejoice that the spirits submit to you, but rejoice that your names are written in heaven.

Cast: **Narrator, Jesus, Man**

Jesus Rejoices
Luke 10:21–24

Narrator	Jesus, full of joy through the Holy Spirit, said:
Jesus (in prayer)	I praise you, Father, Lord of heaven and earth, because you have hidden these things from the wise and learned, and revealed them to little children. Yes, Father, for this was your good pleasure. (PAUSE)
(to all)	All things have been committed to me by my Father. No one knows who the Son is except the Father, and no one knows who the Father is except the Son and those to whom the Son chooses to reveal him.
Narrator	Then he turned to his disciples [and said privately]:
Jesus (confiding)	Blessed are the eyes that see what you see. For I tell you that many prophets and kings wanted to see what you see but did not see it, and to hear what you hear but did not hear it.

Cast: **Narrator, Jesus**

The Parable of the Good Samaritan
Luke 10:25–37

Narrator	An expert in the law stood up to test Jesus.
Lawyer	Teacher, what must I do to inherit eternal life?
Narrator	[Jesus answered him:]
Jesus	What is written in the Law? How do you read it?
Lawyer	"Love the Lord your God with all your heart and with all your soul and with all your strength and with all your mind"; and, "Love your neighbor as yourself."
Jesus	You have answered correctly. Do this and you will live.
Narrator	But he wanted to justify himself, so he asked Jesus:
Lawyer (pertly)	And who is my neighbor?
Narrator	In reply Jesus said:

Jesus	A man was going down from Jerusalem to Jericho, when he fell into the hands of robbers. They stripped him of his clothes, beat him and went away, leaving him half dead. A priest happened to be going down the same road, and when he saw the man, he passed by on the other side. So too, a Levite, when he came to the place and saw him, passed by on the other side. But a Samaritan, as he traveled, came where the man was; and when he saw him, he took pity on him. He went to him and bandaged his wounds, pouring on oil and wine. Then he put the man on his own donkey, took him to an inn and took care of him. The next day he took out two silver coins and gave them to the innkeeper.
Samaritan	Look after him, and when I return, I will reimburse you for any extra expense you may have.
Narrator	[And Jesus concluded:]
Jesus	Which of these three do you think was a neighbor to the man who fell into the hands of robbers?
Narrator	The expert in the law replied:
Lawyer	The one who had mercy on him.
Jesus	Go and do likewise.

Cast: **Narrator, Lawyer, Jesus, Samaritan**

At the Home of Martha and Mary
Luke 10:38–42

Narrator	Jesus . . . came to a village where a woman named Martha opened her home to him. She had a sister called Mary, who sat at the Lord's feet listening to what he said. But Martha was distracted by all the preparations that had to be made. She came to him and asked:
Martha	Lord, don't you care that my sister has left me to do the work by myself? Tell her to help me!
[Narrator	The Lord answered:]
Jesus	Martha, Martha, you are worried and upset about many things, but only one thing is needed. Mary has chosen what is better, and it will not be taken away from her.

Cast: **Narrator, Martha, Jesus**

The Lord's Prayer
Luke 11:1–4

Narrator	One day Jesus was praying in a certain place. When he finished, one of his disciples said to him:

Disciple	Lord, teach us to pray, just as John taught his disciples.
Narrator	He said to them:
Jesus	When you pray, say:

"Father,
hallowed be your name,
your kingdom come.
Give us each day our daily bread.
Forgive us our sins,
    for we also forgive everyone who sins against us.
And lead us not into temptation."

Cast: **Narrator, Disciple, Jesus**

Jesus' Teaching on Prayer
Luke 11:5–13

Jesus	Suppose one of you has a friend, and he goes to him at midnight and says:
Disciple	Friend, lend me three loaves of bread, because a friend of mine on a journey has come to me, and I have nothing to set before him.
Jesus	Then the one inside answers:
Friend (off-stage)	Don't bother me. The door is already locked, and my children are with me in bed. I can't get up and give you anything.
Jesus	I tell you, though he will not get up and give him the bread because he is his friend, yet because of the man's boldness he will get up and give him as much as he needs.
	So I say to you: Ask and it will be given to you; seek and you will find; knock and the door will be opened to you.
Student	For everyone who asks receives; he who seeks finds; and to him who knocks, the door will be opened.
Jesus	Which of you fathers, if your son asks for a fish, will give him a snake instead?
Student	Or if he asks for an egg, will give him a scorpion?
Jesus	If you then, though you are evil, know how to give good gifts to your children, how much more will your Father in heaven give the Holy Spirit to those who ask him!

Cast: **Jesus, Disciple, Friend, Student** (can be the same as Disciple). The dramatized reading reflects the classic rabbinic way of teaching and learning this form of instruction.

Jesus and Beelzebub
Luke 11:14–22 [23]

Narrator	Jesus was driving out a demon that was mute. When the demon left, the man who had been mute spoke, and the crowd was amazed. But some of them said:
Person	By Beelzebub, the prince of demons, he is driving out demons.
Narrator	Others tested him by asking for a sign from heaven. (PAUSE) Jesus knew their thoughts and said to them:
Jesus	Any kingdom divided against itself will be ruined, and a house divided against itself will fall. If Satan is divided against himself, how can his kingdom stand? I say this because you claim that I drive out demons by Beelzebub. Now if I drive out demons by Beelzebub, by whom do your followers drive them out? So then, they will be your judges. But if I drive out demons by the finger of God, then the kingdom of God has come to you.
	When a strong man, fully armed, guards his own house, his possessions are safe. But when someone stronger attacks and overpowers him, he takes away the armor in which the man trusted and divides up the spoils.
	He who is not with me is against me, and he who does not gather with me, scatters.

Cast: **Narrator, Person, Jesus**

The Return of the Evil Spirit
Luke 11:24–28

Narrator	[Jesus said:]
Jesus	When an evil spirit comes out of a man, it goes through arid places seeking rest and does not find it. Then it says:
Evil spirit	I will return to the house I left.
Jesus	When it arrives, it finds the house swept clean and put in order. Then it goes and takes seven other spirits more wicked than itself, and they go in and live there. And the final condition of that man is worse than the first.
Narrator	As Jesus was saying these things, a woman in the crowd called out:
Woman	Blessed is the mother who gave you birth and nursed you.
[Narrator	He replied:]

Jesus	Blessed rather are those who hear the word of God and obey it.

Cast: **Narrator, Jesus, Evil spirit, Woman**

The Lamp of the Body
Luke 11:33–36

Speaker 1	No one lights a lamp and puts it in a place where it will be hidden, or under a bowl.
Speaker 2	Instead he puts it on its stand, so that those who come in may see the light. Your eye is the lamp of your body. When your eyes are good, your whole body also is full of light.
Speaker 1	But when they are bad, your body also is full of darkness.
Speaker 2	See to it, then, that the light within you is not darkness. Therefore, if your whole body is full of light, and no part of it dark, it will be completely lighted, as when the light of a lamp shines on you.

Cast: **Speaker 1** (serious voice), **Speaker 2** (cheerful voice)

Six Woes
Luke 11:37–12:3

Speaker 1	A Pharisee invited [Jesus] to eat with him; so he went in and reclined at the table. But the Pharisee, noticing that Jesus did not first wash before the meal, was surprised. (PAUSE) Then the Lord said to him:
Speaker 2	Now then, you Pharisees clean the outside of the cup and dish, but inside you are full of greed and wickedness. You foolish people! Did not the one who made the outside make the inside also? But give what is inside ⌞the dish⌟ to the poor, and everything will be clean for you.
Speaker 1	Woe to you Pharisees.
Speaker 2	Because you give God a tenth of your mint, rue and all other kinds of garden herbs, but you neglect justice and the love of God. You should have practiced the latter without leaving the former undone.
Speaker 1	Woe to you Pharisees.
Speaker 2	Because you love the most important seats in the synagogues and greetings in the marketplaces.
Speaker 1	Woe to you.
Speaker 2	Because you are like unmarked graves, which men walk over without knowing it.
Speaker 1	One of the experts in the law answered him:
Lawyer	Teacher, when you say these things, you insult us also.

Speaker 1	Jesus replied: And you experts in the law, woe to you.
Speaker 2	Because you load people down with burdens they can hardly carry, and you yourselves will not lift one finger to help them.
Speaker 1	Woe to you.
Speaker 2	Because you build tombs for the prophets, and it was your forefathers who killed them. So you testify that you approve of what your forefathers did; they killed the prophets, and you build their tombs. Because of this, God in his wisdom said:
Voice	I will send them prophets and apostles, some of whom they will kill and others they will persecute.
Speaker 2	Therefore this generation will be held responsible for the blood of all the prophets that has been shed since the beginning of the world, from the blood of Abel to the blood of Zechariah, who was killed between the altar and the sanctuary. Yes, I tell you, this generation will be held responsible for it all.
Speaker 1	Woe to you experts in the law.
Speaker 2	Because you have taken away the key to knowledge. You yourselves have not entered, and you have hindered those who were entering.
Speaker 1	When Jesus left there, the Pharisees and the teachers of the law began to oppose him fiercely and to besiege him with questions, waiting to catch him in something he might say. (PAUSE)
	Meanwhile, when a crowd of many thousands had gathered, so that they were trampling on one another, Jesus began to speak first to his disciples, saying:
Speaker 2	Be on your guard against the yeast of the Pharisees, which is hypocrisy. There is nothing concealed that will not be disclosed, or hidden that will not be made known. What you have said in the dark will be heard in the daylight, and what you have whispered in the ear in the inner rooms will be proclaimed from the roofs.

Cast: **Speaker 1, Speaker 2, Lawyer, Voice**

Warnings and Encouragements
Luke 12:4–12

Speaker 1	I tell you, my friends, do not be afraid of those who kill the body and after that can do no more.
Speaker 2	But I will show you whom you should fear: Fear him who, after the killing of the body, has power to throw you into hell. Yes, I tell you, fear him.
Speaker 1	Are not five sparrows sold for two pennies? Yet not one of them is forgotten by God.

Speaker 2	Indeed, the very hairs of your head are all numbered. Don't be afraid; you are worth more than many sparrows.
Speaker 1	I tell you, whoever acknowledges me before men, the Son of Man will also acknowledge him before the angels of God.
Speaker 2	But he who disowns me before men will be disowned before the angels of God.
Speaker 1	And everyone who speaks a word against the Son of Man will be forgiven.
Speaker 2	But anyone who blasphemes against the Holy Spirit will not be forgiven.
Speaker 1	When you are brought before synagogues, rulers and authorities, do not worry about how you will defend yourselves or what you will say.
Speaker 2	For the Holy Spirit will teach you at that time what you should say.

Cast: **Speaker 1, Speaker 2**

The Parable of the Rich Fool (longer version)
Luke 12:13–21

Narrator	Someone in the crowd said to [Jesus]:
Man (angrily)	Teacher, tell my brother to divide the inheritance with me.
[Narrator	Jesus replied:]
Jesus (to the man)	Man, who appointed me a judge or an arbiter between you?
Narrator	Then he said to them:
Jesus	Watch out! Be on your guard against all kinds of greed; a man's life does not consist in the abundance of his possessions.
Narrator	And he told them this parable:
Jesus	The ground of a certain rich man produced a good crop. He thought to himself:
Rich man	What shall I do? I have no place to store my crops. (PAUSE TO THINK)
	This is what I'll do. I will tear down my barns and build bigger ones, and there I will store all my grain and my goods. And I'll say to myself, "You have plenty of good things laid up for many years. Take life easy; eat, drink and be merry."
Jesus	But God said to him:
God	You fool! This very night your life will be demanded from you. Then who will get what you have prepared for yourself?

Narrator	[And Jesus concluded:]
Jesus	This is how it will be with anyone who stores up things for himself but is not rich toward God.

Cast: **Narrator, Man, Jesus, Rich man, God**

The Parable of the Rich Fool (shorter version)
Luke 12:16–21

Jesus	The ground of a certain rich man produced a good crop. He thought to himself:
Rich man	What shall I do? I have no place to store my crops.
Jesus	Then he said:
Rich man	This is what I'll do. I will tear down my barns and build bigger ones, and there I will store all my grain and my goods. And I'll say to myself, "You have plenty of good things laid up for many years. Take life easy; eat, drink and be merry."
Jesus	But God said to him:
God	You fool! This very night your life will be demanded from you. Then who will get what you have prepared for yourself?
Jesus	This is how it will be with anyone who stores up things for himself but is not rich toward God.

Cast: **Jesus, Rich man, God**

Jesus' Teaching about Trust in God
Luke 12:22–31

Narrator	Jesus said to his disciples:
Teacher	Therefore I tell you, do not worry about your life, what you will eat; or about your body, what you will wear. Life is more than food, and the body more than clothes.
Voice 1	Consider the ravens: They do not sow or reap, they have no storeroom or barn; yet God feeds them. And how much more valuable you are than birds!
Voice 2	Who of you by worrying can add a single hour to his life? Since you cannot do this very little thing, why do you worry about the rest?
Voice 1	Consider how the lilies grow. They do not labor or spin. Yet I tell you, not even Solomon in all his splendor was dressed like one of these.

Voice 2	If that is how God clothes the grass of the field, which is here today, and tomorrow is thrown into the fire, how much more will he clothe you, O you of little faith!
Teacher	And do not set your heart on what you will eat or drink; do not worry about it.
Narrator	For the pagan world runs after all such things, and your Father knows that you need them.
Teacher	But seek his kingdom, and these things will be given to you as well.

Cast: **Narrator, Teacher, Voice 1, Voice 2**

Watchful and Faithful Servants
Luke 12:35–48

Narrator	[Jesus said to his disciples:]
Jesus	Be dressed ready for service and keep your lamps burning, like men waiting for their master to return from a wedding banquet, so that when he comes and knocks they can immediately open the door for him. It will be good for those servants whose master finds them watching when he comes. I tell you the truth, he will dress himself to serve, will have them recline at the table and will come and wait on them. It will be good for those servants whose master finds them ready, even if he comes in the second or third watch of the night. But understand this: If the owner of the house had known at what hour the thief was coming, he would not have let his house be broken into. You also must be ready, because the Son of Man will come at an hour when you do not expect him.
Narrator	Peter asked:
Peter	Lord, are you telling this parable to us, or to everyone?
Narrator	The Lord answered:
Jesus	Who then is the faithful and wise manager, whom the master puts in charge of his servants to give them their food allowance at the proper time? It will be good for that servant whom the master finds doing so when he returns. I tell you the truth, he will put him in charge of all his possessions. But suppose the servant says to himself, "My master is taking a long time in coming," and he then begins to beat the menservants and maidservants and to eat and drink and get drunk. The master of that servant will come on a day when he does not expect him and at an hour he is not aware of. He will cut him to pieces and assign him a place with the unbelievers.
	That servant who knows his master's will and does not get ready or does not do what his master wants will be beaten with many blows. But the one who does not know and does things deserving punishment will be beaten with few blows. From everyone who has been given much,

much will be demanded; and from the one who has been entrusted with much, much more will be asked.

Cast: **Narrator, Jesus, Peter**

The Parable of the Unfruitful Fig Tree
Luke 13:6–9

Narrator [Jesus] told this parable:

Jesus A man had a fig tree, planted in his vineyard, and he went to look for fruit on it, but did not find any. So he said to the man who took care of the vineyard:

Man For three years now I've been coming to look for fruit on this fig tree and haven't found any. Cut it down! Why should it use up the soil?

Jesus [But the gardener] replied:

Gardener Sir, leave it alone for one more year, and I'll dig around it and fertilize it. If it bears fruit next year, fine! If not, then cut it down.

Cast: **Narrator, Jesus, Man, Gardener**

A Crippled Woman Healed on the Sabbath
Luke 13:10–17

Narrator On a Sabbath Jesus was teaching in one of the synagogues, and a woman was there who had been crippled by a spirit for eighteen years. She was bent over and could not straighten up at all. When Jesus saw her, he called her forward and said to her:

Jesus Woman, you are set free from your infirmity.

Narrator Then he put his hands on her, and immediately she straightened up and praised God. (PAUSE)

Indignant because Jesus had healed on the Sabbath, the synagogue ruler said to the people:

Ruler There are six days for work. So come and be healed on those days, not on the Sabbath.

[Narrator The Lord answered him:]

Jesus You hypocrites! Doesn't each of you on the Sabbath untie his ox or donkey from the stall and lead it out to give it water? Then should not this woman, a daughter of Abraham, whom Satan has kept bound for eighteen long years, be set free on the Sabbath day from what bound her?

177

| Narrator | When he said this, all his opponents were humiliated, but the people were delighted with all the wonderful things he was doing. |

Cast: **Narrator, Jesus, Ruler**

The Parables of the Mustard Seed and the Yeast
Luke 13:18–21

Speaker 1	Jesus asked, "What is the kingdom of God like? What shall I compare it to?
Speaker 2	It is like a mustard seed, which a man took and planted in his garden. It grew and became a tree, and the birds of the air perched in its branches."
Speaker 1	Again he asked, "What shall I compare the kingdom of God to?
Speaker 2	It is like yeast that a woman took and mixed into a large amount of flour until it worked all through the dough."

Cast: **Speaker 1, Speaker 2**

The Narrow Door
Luke 13:22–30

Narrator	Jesus went through the towns and villages, teaching as he made his way to Jerusalem. Someone asked him:
Person	Lord, are only a few people going to be saved?
Narrator	He said to them:
Jesus	Make every effort to enter through the narrow door, because many, I tell you, will try to enter and will not be able to. Once the owner of the house gets up and closes the door, you will stand outside knocking and pleading:
Person	Sir, open the door for us.
Jesus	But he will answer:
Master	I don't know you or where you come from.
Jesus	Then you will say:
Person	We ate and drank with you, and you taught in our streets.
Jesus	But he will reply:
Master	I don't know you or where you come from. Away from me, all you evil-doers! (PAUSE)
Jesus	There will be weeping there, and gnashing of teeth, when you see Abraham, Isaac and Jacob and all the prophets in the kingdom of God, but

178

you yourselves thrown out. People will come from east and west and north and south, and will take their places at the feast in the kingdom of God. Indeed there are those who are last who will be first, and first who will be last.

Cast: **Narrator, Person, Jesus, Master**

Jesus' Sorrow for Jerusalem
Luke 13:31–35

Narrator	Some Pharisees came to Jesus and said to him:
Pharisee 1	Leave this place and go somewhere else.
Pharisee 2	Herod wants to kill you.
[Narrator	He replied:]
Jesus (sternly)	Go tell that fox, "I will drive out demons and heal people today and tomorrow, and on the third day I will reach my goal." In any case, I must keep going today and tomorrow and the next day—for surely no prophet can die outside Jerusalem! (PAUSE)
(sadly)	O Jerusalem, Jerusalem, you who kill the prophets and stone those sent to you, how often I have longed to gather your children together, as a hen gathers her chicks under her wings, but you were not willing! Look, your house is left to you desolate. I tell you, you will not see me again until you say, "Blessed is he who comes in the name of the Lord."

Cast: **Narrator, Pharisee 1, Pharisee 2** (can be the same as Pharisee 1), **Jesus**

Jesus at a Pharisee's House
Luke 14:1–6

Narrator	One Sabbath, when Jesus went to eat in the house of a prominent Pharisee, he was being carefully watched. There in front of him was a man suffering from dropsy. Jesus asked the Pharisees and experts in the law:
Jesus	Is it lawful to heal on the Sabbath or not?
Narrator	But they remained silent. So taking hold of the man, he healed him and sent him away. Then he asked them:
Jesus	If one of you has a son or an ox that falls into a well on the Sabbath day, will you not immediately pull him out?
Narrator	And they had nothing to say.

Cast: **Narrator, Jesus**

Humility and Hospitality
Luke 14:7–14

Narrator	When [Jesus] noticed how the guests picked the places of honor at the table, he told them this parable:
Jesus	When someone invites you to a wedding feast, do not take the place of honor, for a person more distinguished than you may have been invited. If so, the host who invited both of you will come and say to you:
Host	Give this man your seat.
Jesus	Then, humiliated, you will have to take the least important place. But when you are invited, take the lowest place, so that when your host comes, he will say to you:
Host	Friend, move up to a better place. Then you will be honored in the presence of all your fellow guests.
Jesus	For everyone who exalts himself will be humbled, and he who humbles himself will be exalted.
Narrator	Then Jesus said to his host:
Jesus	When you give a luncheon or dinner, do not invite your friends, your brothers or relatives, or your rich neighbors; if you do, they may invite you back and so you will be repaid. But when you give a banquet, invite the poor, the crippled, the lame, the blind, and you will be blessed. Although they cannot repay you, you will be repaid at the resurrection of the righteous.

Cast: **Narrator, Jesus, Host**

The Parable of the Great Banquet
Luke 14:15–24

Narrator	One of those at the table [with Jesus said to him]:
Man	Blessed is the man who will eat at the feast in the kingdom of God.
[Narrator	Jesus replied:]
Jesus	A certain man was preparing a great banquet and invited many guests. At the time of the banquet he sent his servant to tell those who had been invited:
Servant	Come, for everything is now ready.
Jesus	But they all alike began to make excuses. The first said:
Guest 1	I have just bought a field, and I must go and see it. Please excuse me.
Jesus	Another said:

Guest 2	I have just bought five yoke of oxen, and I'm on my way to try them out. Please excuse me.
Jesus	Still another said:
Guest 3	I just got married, so I can't come.
Jesus	The servant came back and reported this to his master. Then the owner of the house became angry and ordered his servant:
Master	Go out quickly into the streets and alleys of the town and bring in the poor, the crippled, the blind and the lame.
Jesus	The servant said:
Servant	Sir, what you ordered has been done, but there is still room.
Jesus	Then the master told his servant:
Master	Go out to the roads and country lanes and make them come in, so that my house will be full. I tell you, not one of those men who were invited will get a taste of my banquet.

Cast: **Narrator, Man, Jesus, Servant, Guest 1, Guest 2, Guest 3, Master**

The Cost of Being a Disciple
Luke 14:25–33

Narrator	Large crowds were traveling with Jesus, and turning to them he said:
Jesus	If anyone comes to me and does not hate his father and mother, his wife and children, his brothers and sisters—yes, even his own life—he cannot be my disciple. And anyone who does not carry his cross and follow me cannot be my disciple.
	Suppose one of you wants to build a tower. Will he not first sit down and estimate the cost to see if he has enough money to complete it? For if he lays the foundation and is not able to finish it, everyone who sees it will ridicule him, saying:
Person (jeering)	This fellow began to build and was not able to finish.
Jesus	Or suppose a king is about to go to war against another king. Will he not first sit down and consider whether he is able with ten thousand men to oppose the one coming against him with twenty thousand? If he is not able, he will send a delegation while the other is still a long way off and will ask for terms of peace.
Narrator	[Jesus concluded:]
Jesus	In the same way, any of you who does not give up everything he has cannot be my disciple.

Cast: **Narrator, Jesus, Person**

The Parables of the Lost Sheep and the Lost Coin
Luke 15:1–10

Narrator   The tax collectors and "sinners" were all gathering around to hear [Jesus]. But the Pharisees and the teachers of the law muttered:

Pharisee   This man welcomes sinners—

Lawyer   And eats with them.

Narrator   Then Jesus told them this parable:

Jesus   Suppose one of you has a hundred sheep and loses one of them. Does he not leave the ninety-nine in the open country and go after the lost sheep until he finds it? And when he finds it, he joyfully puts it on his shoulders and goes home. Then he calls his friends and neighbors together and says:

Shepherd   Rejoice with me; I have found my lost sheep.

Jesus   I tell you that in the same way there will be more rejoicing in heaven over one sinner who repents than over ninety-nine righteous persons who do not need to repent. (PAUSE)

             Or suppose a woman has ten silver coins and loses one. Does she not light a lamp, sweep the house and search carefully until she finds it? And when she finds it, she calls her friends and neighbors together and says:

Woman   Rejoice with me; I have found my lost coin.

Jesus   In the same way, I tell you, there is rejoicing in the presence of the angels of God over one sinner who repents.

Cast: **Narrator, Pharisee, Lawyer** (can be the same as Pharisee), **Jesus, Shepherd, Woman**

The Parable of the Lost Son
Luke 15:11–32

Jesus   There was a man who had two sons. The younger one said to his father:

Younger son Father, give me my share of the estate.

Jesus   So he divided his property between them.

             Not long after that, the younger son got together all he had, set off for a distant country and there squandered his wealth in wild living. After he had spent everything, there was a severe famine in that whole country, and he began to be in need. So he went and hired himself out to a citizen of that country, who sent him to his fields to feed pigs. He longed to fill his stomach with the pods that the pigs were eating, but no one gave him anything. When he came to his senses, he said:

Younger son	How many of my father's hired men have food to spare, and here I am starving to death! (THEN, RESOLUTELY) I will set out and go back to my father and say to him: Father, I have sinned against heaven and against you. I am no longer worthy to be called your son; make me like one of your hired men.
Jesus	So he got up and went to his father.
	But while he was still a long way off, his father saw him and was filled with compassion for him; he ran to his son, threw his arms around him and kissed him. The son said to him:
Younger son	Father, I have sinned against heaven and against you. I am no longer worthy to be called your son.
Jesus	But the father said to his servants:
Father	Quick! Bring the best robe and put it on him. Put a ring on his finger and sandals on his feet. Bring the fattened calf and kill it. Let's have a feast and celebrate. For this son of mine was dead and is alive again; he was lost and is found.
Jesus	So they began to celebrate. (PAUSE)
	Meanwhile, the older son was in the field. When he came near the house, he heard music and dancing. So he called one of the servants and asked him what was going on.
Servant	Your brother has come, and your father has killed the fattened calf because he has him back safe and sound.
Jesus	The older brother became angry and refused to go in. So his father went out and pleaded with him. But he answered his father:
Older son	Look! All these years I've been slaving for you and never disobeyed your orders. Yet you never gave me even a young goat so I could celebrate with my friends. But when this son of yours who has squandered your property with prostitutes comes home, you kill the fattened calf for him!
[Jesus	The father said:]
Father	My son, you are always with me, and everything I have is yours. But we had to celebrate and be glad, because this brother of yours was dead and is alive again; he was lost and is found.

Cast: **Jesus, Younger son, Father, Servant, Older son**

The Parable of the Shrewd Manager
Luke 16:1–8

Jesus	There was a rich man whose manager was accused of wasting his possessions. So he called him in and asked him:

Master	What is this I hear about you? Give an account of your management, because you cannot be manager any longer.
Jesus	The manager said to himself:
Manager	What shall I do now? My master is taking away my job. I'm not strong enough to dig, and I'm ashamed to beg—I know what I'll do so that, when I lose my job here, people will welcome me into their houses.
Jesus	So he called in each one of his master's debtors. He asked the first:
Manager (to Debtor 1)	How much do you owe my master?
Debtor 1	Eight hundred gallons of olive oil.
Jesus	The manager told him:
Manager	Take your bill, sit down quickly, and make it four hundred.
[Jesus	Then he asked the second:]
Manager (to Debtor 2)	And how much do *you* owe?
Debtor 2	A thousand bushels of wheat.
Manager	Take your bill and make it eight hundred.
Jesus	The master commended the dishonest manager because he had acted shrewdly. For the people of this world are more shrewd in dealing with their own kind than are the people of the light.

Cast: **Jesus, Master, Manager, Debtor 1, Debtor 2**

More of Jesus' Teaching on Stewardship
Luke 16:9–12

Teacher	I tell you, use worldly wealth to gain friends for yourselves, so that when it is gone, you will be welcomed into eternal dwellings.
Voice 1	Whoever can be trusted with very little can also be trusted with much.
Voice 2	And whoever is dishonest with very little will also be dishonest with much.
Voice 1	So if you have not been trustworthy in handling worldly wealth, who will trust you with true riches?
Voice 2	And if you have not been trustworthy with someone else's property, who will give you property of your own?

Cast: **Teacher, Voice 1, Voice 2**

Additional Teachings
Luke 16:13–15

Narrator	[Jesus said:]
Jesus	No servant can serve two masters. Either he will hate the one and love the other, or he will be devoted to the one and despise the other. You cannot serve both God and Money.
Narrator	The Pharisees, who loved money, heard all this and were sneering at Jesus. He said to them:
Jesus	You are the ones who justify yourselves in the eyes of men, but God knows your hearts. What is highly valued among men is detestable in God's sight.

Cast: **Narrator, Jesus**

The Rich Man and Lazarus
Luke 16:19–31

Narrator 1	There was a rich man who was dressed in purple and fine linen and lived in luxury every day.
Narrator 2	At his gate was laid a beggar named Lazarus, covered with sores and longing to eat what fell from the rich man's table. Even the dogs came and licked his sores. (PAUSE) The time came when the beggar died and the angels carried him to Abraham's side.
Narrator 1	The rich man also died and was buried. In hell, where he was in torment, he looked up and saw Abraham far away, with Lazarus by his side. So he called to him:
Rich man (calling)	Father Abraham, have pity on me and send Lazarus to dip the tip of his finger in water and cool my tongue, because I am in agony in this fire.
Narrator 2	But Abraham replied:
Abraham	Son, remember that in your lifetime you received your good things, while Lazarus received bad things, but now he is comforted here and you are in agony. And besides all this, between us and you a great chasm has been fixed, so that those who want to go from here to you cannot, nor can anyone cross over from there to us.
Rich man	Then I beg you, father, send Lazarus to my father's house, for I have five brothers. Let him warn them, so that they will not also come to this place of torment.
Abraham	They have Moses and the Prophets; let them listen to them.
Rich man	No, father Abraham, but if someone from the dead goes to them, they will repent.

Abraham	If they do not listen to Moses and the Prophets, they will not be convinced even if someone rises from the dead.

Cast: **Narrator 1, Narrator 2, Rich man, Abraham**

Sin, Faith, Duty
Luke 17:1–10

Narrator	Jesus said to his disciples:
Jesus	Things that cause people to sin are bound to come, but woe to that person through whom they come. It would be better for him to be thrown into the sea with a millstone tied around his neck than for him to cause one of these little ones to sin. So watch yourselves.
	If your brother sins, rebuke him, and if he repents, forgive him. If he sins against you seven times in a day, and seven times comes back to you and says:
Voice	I repent.
Jesus	Forgive him.
Narrator	The apostles said to the Lord:
Apostle	Increase our faith!
Narrator	He replied:
Jesus	If you have faith as small as a mustard seed, you can say to this mulberry tree:
Voice	Be uprooted and planted in the sea.
Jesus	And it will obey you. (PAUSE)
	Suppose one of you had a servant plowing or looking after the sheep. Would he say to the servant when he comes in from the field, "Come along now and sit down to eat"? Would he not rather say:
Voice	Prepare my supper, get yourself ready and wait on me while I eat and drink; after that you may eat and drink?
Jesus	Would he thank the servant because he did what he was told to do? So you also, when you have done everything you were told to do, should say:
Voice	We are unworthy servants; we have only done our duty.

Cast: **Narrator, Jesus, Voice, Apostle**

Ten Healed of Leprosy
Luke 17:11–19

Narrator	On his way to Jerusalem, Jesus traveled along the border between Samaria and Galilee. As he was going into a village, ten men who had leprosy met him. They stood at a distance and called out in a loud voice:
Man 1	Jesus!
Man 2	Master!
Man 1	Have pity on us!
Narrator	When he saw them, he said:
Jesus	Go, show yourselves to the priests.
Narrator	And as they went, they were cleansed.
	One of them, when he saw he was healed, came back, praising God in a loud voice. He threw himself at Jesus' feet and thanked him—and he was a Samaritan. Jesus asked:
Jesus	Were not all ten cleansed? Where are the other nine? Was no one found to return and give praise to God except this foreigner?
[Narrator	Then he said to him:]
Jesus (to the Man)	Rise and go; your faith has made you well.

Cast: **Narrator, Man 1, Man 2, Jesus**

The Coming of the Kingdom of God
Luke 17:20–24, 31–37

Narrator	Once, having been asked by the Pharisees when the kingdom of God would come, Jesus replied:
Jesus	The kingdom of God does not come with your careful observation, nor will people say, "Here it is," or "There it is," because the kingdom of God is within you.
Narrator	Then he said to his disciples:
Jesus	The time is coming when you will long to see one of the days of the Son of Man, but you will not see it. Men will tell you:
Person 1	There he is!
Person 2	Here he is!

187

Jesus	Do not go running off after them. For the Son of Man in his day will be like the lightning, which flashes and lights up the sky from one end to the other. . . . On that day no one who is on the roof of his house, with his goods inside, should go down to get them. Likewise, no one in the field should go back for anything. Remember Lot's wife! Whoever tries to keep his life will lose it, and whoever loses his life will preserve it. I tell you, on that night two people will be in one bed; one will be taken and the other left. Two women will be grinding grain together; one will be taken and the other left.
Narrator	[The disciples asked him:]
Disciple(s)	Where, Lord?
Jesus	Where there is a dead body, there the vultures will gather.

Cast: **Narrator, Jesus, Person 1, Person 2** (Persons 1 and 2 can be the same as Jesus), **Disciple(s)**

The Parable of the Persistent Widow

Luke 18:1–8

Narrator	Jesus told his disciples a parable to show them that they should always pray and not give up.
Jesus	In a certain town there was a judge who neither feared God nor cared about men. And there was a widow in that town who kept coming to him with the plea:
Widow	Grant me justice against my adversary.
Jesus	For some time he refused. But finally he said to himself:
Judge	Even though I don't fear God or care about men, yet because this widow keeps bothering me, I will see that she gets justice, so that she won't eventually wear me out with her coming!
[Narrator	And the Lord said:]
Jesus	Listen to what the unjust judge says. And will not God bring about justice for his chosen ones, who cry out to him day and night? Will he keep putting them off? I tell you, he will see that they get justice, and quickly. However, when the Son of Man comes, will he find faith on the earth?

Cast: **Narrator, Jesus, Widow, Judge**

The Parable of the Pharisee and the Tax Collector
Luke 18:9–14

Narrator

To some who were confident of their own righteousness and looked down on everybody else, Jesus told this parable:

Jesus

Two men went up to the temple to pray, one a Pharisee and the other a tax collector. The Pharisee stood up and prayed about himself:

Pharisee
(haughtily)

God, I thank you that I am not like other men—robbers, evildoers, adulterers—or even like this tax collector. I fast twice a week and give a tenth of all I get.

Jesus

But the tax collector stood at a distance. He would not even look up to heaven, but beat his breast and said:

Tax collector
(humbly)

God, have mercy on me, a sinner.

Jesus

I tell you that this man, rather than the other, went home justified before God. For everyone who exalts himself will be humbled, and he who humbles himself will be exalted.

Cast: Narrator, Jesus, Pharisee, Tax collector

The Little Children and Jesus
Luke 18:15–17

Narrator

People were also bringing babies to Jesus to have him touch them. When the disciples saw this, they rebuked them. But Jesus called the children to him and said:

Jesus

Let the little children come to me, and do not hinder them, for the kingdom of God belongs to such as these. I tell you the truth, anyone who will not receive the kingdom of God like a little child will never enter it.

Cast: Narrator, Jesus

The Rich Ruler
Luke 18:18–30

Narrator

A certain ruler asked [Jesus]:

Ruler

Good teacher, what must I do to inherit eternal life?

[Narrator

Jesus answered:]

Jesus

Why do you call me good? No one is good—except God alone. You know the commandments: "Do not commit adultery, do not murder,

189

	do not steal, do not give false testimony, honor your father and mother."
Ruler	All these I have kept since I was a boy.
Narrator	When Jesus heard this, he said to him:
Jesus	You still lack one thing. Sell everything you have and give to the poor, and you will have treasure in heaven. Then come, follow me.
Narrator	When he heard this, he became very sad, because he was a man of great wealth. (PAUSE) Jesus looked at him and said:
Jesus	How hard it is for the rich to enter the kingdom of God! Indeed, it is easier for a camel to go through the eye of a needle than for a rich man to enter the kingdom of God.
Narrator	Those who heard this asked:
Person	Who then can be saved?
Jesus	What is impossible with men is possible with God.
Narrator	Peter said to him:
Peter	We have left all we had to follow you!
Jesus	I tell you the truth, no one who has left home or wife or brothers or parents or children for the sake of the kingdom of God will fail to receive many times as much in this age and, in the age to come, eternal life.

Cast: **Narrator, Ruler, Jesus, Person, Peter**

Jesus Again Predicts His Death
Luke 18:31–34

Narrator	Jesus took the Twelve aside [and told them:]
Jesus	We are going up to Jerusalem, and everything that is written by the prophets about the Son of Man will be fulfilled. He will be handed over to the Gentiles. They will mock him, insult him, spit on him, flog him and kill him. On the third day he will rise again.
Narrator	The disciples did not understand any of this. Its meaning was hidden from them, and they did not know what he was talking about.

Cast: **Narrator, Jesus**

A Blind Beggar Receives His Sight
Luke 18:35–43

| **Narrator** | As Jesus approached Jericho, a blind man was sitting by the roadside begging. When he heard the crowd going by, he asked what was happening. They told him: |

Person	Jesus of Nazareth is passing by.
Blind man (crying out)	Jesus, Son of David, have mercy on me!
Narrator	Those who led the way rebuked him and told him to be quiet, but he shouted all the more:
Blind man (crying out)	Son of David, have mercy on me!
Narrator	Jesus stopped and ordered the man to be brought to him. When he came near, Jesus asked him:
Jesus	What do you want me to do for you?
Blind man	Lord, I want to see.
Jesus	Receive your sight; your faith has healed you.
Narrator	Immediately he received his sight and followed Jesus, praising God. When all the people saw it, they also praised God.

Cast: **Narrator, Person, Blind man, Jesus**

Zacchaeus the Tax Collector
Luke 19:1–10

Narrator	Jesus entered Jericho and was passing through. A man was there by the name of Zacchaeus; he was a chief tax collector and was wealthy. He wanted to see who Jesus was, but being a short man he could not, because of the crowd. So he ran ahead and climbed a sycamore-fig tree to see him, since Jesus was coming that way. (PAUSE) When Jesus reached the spot, he looked up [and said to him:]
Jesus	Zacchaeus, come down immediately. I must stay at your house today.
Narrator	So he came down at once and welcomed him gladly. (PAUSE)
	All the people saw this and began to mutter:
Person (grumbling)	He has gone to be the guest of a "sinner."
Narrator	But Zacchaeus stood up and said to the Lord:
Zacchaeus (to Jesus)	Look, Lord! Here and now I give half of my possessions to the poor, and if I have cheated anybody out of anything, I will pay back four times the amount.
Jesus (to Zacchaeus)	Today salvation has come to this house, because this man, too, is a son of Abraham. For the Son of Man came to seek and to save what was lost.

Cast: **Narrator, Jesus, Person, Zacchaeus**

The Parable of the Ten Minas

Luke 19:[11], 12–26

[Narrator	[Jesus told the people] a parable, because he was near Jerusalem and [they] thought that the kingdom of God was going to appear at once. He said:]
Jesus	A man of noble birth went to a distant country to have himself appointed king and then to return. So he called ten of his servants and gave them ten minas.
King	Put this money to work, until I come back.
Jesus	But his subjects hated him and sent a delegation after him to say:
Messenger	We don't want this man to be our king.
Jesus	He was made king, however, and returned home. Then he sent for the servants to whom he had given the money, in order to find out what they had gained with it. The first one came and said:
Servant 1	Sir, your mina has earned ten more.
King (to Servant 1)	Well done, my good servant! Because you have been trustworthy in a very small matter, take charge of ten cities.
Jesus	The second came and said:
Servant 2	Sir, your mina has earned five more.
King (to Servant 2)	You take charge of five cities.
Jesus	Then another servant came and said:
Servant 3	Sir, here is your mina; I have kept it laid away in a piece of cloth. I was afraid of you, because you are a hard man. You take out what you did not put in and reap what you did not sow.
King (to Servant 3)	I will judge you by your own words, you wicked servant! You knew, did you, that I am a hard man, taking out what I did not put in, and reaping what I did not sow? Why then didn't you put my money on deposit, so that when I came back, I could have collected it with interest?
[Jesus	Then he said to those standing by:]
King	Take his mina away from him and give it to the one who has ten minas.
Person	Sir, he already has ten!

Jesus	
King	[The king] replied:
(to person)	I tell you that to everyone who has, more will be given, but as for the one who has nothing, even what he has will be taken away.

Cast: [Narrator,] **Jesus, King, Messenger, Servant 1, Servant 2, Servant 3, Person** (can be the same as Servant 2)

The Triumphal Entry
Luke 19:28–40

Narrator	Jesus . . . went on ahead, going up to Jerusalem. As he approached Beth-phage and Bethany at the hill called the Mount of Olives, he sent two of his disciples, saying to them:
Jesus	Go to the village ahead of you, and as you enter it, you will find a colt tied there, which no one has ever ridden. Untie it and bring it here. If anyone asks you, "Why are you untying it?" tell him, "The Lord needs it."
Narrator	Those who were sent ahead went and found it just as he had told them. As they were untying the colt, its owners asked them:
Owner	Why are you untying the colt?
Narrator	They replied:
Disciple	The Lord needs it.
Narrator	They brought it to Jesus, threw their cloaks on the colt and put Jesus on it. As he went along, people spread their cloaks on the road. (PAUSE)
	When he came near the place where the road goes down the Mount of Olives, the whole crowd of disciples began joyfully to praise God in loud voices for all the miracles they had seen:
Person 1 (calling)	Blessed is the king who comes in the name of the Lord!
Person 2	Peace in heaven and glory in the highest!
Narrator	Some of the Pharisees in the crowd said to Jesus:
Pharisee	Teacher, rebuke your disciples!
Jesus	I tell you, if they keep quiet, the stones will cry out.

Cast: **Narrator, Jesus, Owner, Disciple, Person 1** (can be the same as Disciple), **Person 2** (can be the same as Owner), **Pharisee**

Jesus Weeps over Jerusalem and Goes to the Temple
Luke 19:41–48

Narrator	As [Jesus] approached Jerusalem and saw the city, he wept over it and said:
Jesus	If you, even you, had only known on this day what would bring you peace—but now it is hidden from your eyes. The days will come upon you when your enemies will build an embankment against you and encircle you and hem you in on every side. They will dash you to the ground, you and the children within your walls. They will not leave one stone on another, because you did not recognize the time of God's coming to you.
Narrator	Then he entered the temple area and began driving out those who were selling. [He said to them:]
Jesus (firmly)	It is written, "My house will be a house of prayer"; but you have made it "a den of robbers."
Narrator	Every day he was teaching at the temple. But the chief priests, the teachers of the law and the leaders among the people were trying to kill him. Yet they could not find any way to do it, because all the people hung on his words.

Cast: **Narrator, Jesus**

The Authority of Jesus Questioned
Luke 20:1–8

Narrator	One day as [Jesus] was teaching the people in the temple courts and preaching the gospel, the chief priests and the teachers of the law, together with the elders, came up to him [and said:]
Priest	Tell us by what authority you are doing these things.
Teacher	Who gave you this authority?
[Narrator	He replied:]
Jesus	I will also ask you a question. Tell me, John's baptism—was it from heaven, or from men?
Narrator	They discussed it among themselves and said:
Teacher	If we say, "From heaven," he will ask, "Why didn't you believe him?"
Priest	But if we say, "From men," all the people will stone us, because they are persuaded that John was a prophet.
[Narrator	So they answered:]
Teacher	We don't know where it was from.

| Jesus | Neither will I tell you by what authority I am doing these things. |

Cast: **Narrator, Priest, Teacher, Jesus**

The Parable of the Tenants
Luke 20:9–18

Narrator	[Jesus] went on to tell the people this parable:
Jesus	A man planted a vineyard, rented it to some farmers and went away for a long time. At harvest time he sent a servant to the tenants so they would give him some of the fruit of the vineyard. But the tenants beat him and sent him away empty-handed. He sent another servant, but that one also they beat and treated shamefully and sent away empty-handed. He sent still a third, and they wounded him and threw him out. Then the owner of the vineyard said:
Owner	What shall I do? I will send my son, whom I love; perhaps they will respect him.
Jesus	But when the tenants saw him, they talked the matter over.
Tenant 1	This is the heir.
Tenant 2	Let's kill him, and the inheritance will be ours.
Jesus	So they threw him out of the vineyard and killed him.
	What then will the owner of the vineyard do to them? He will come and kill those tenants and give the vineyard to others.
Narrator	When the people heard this, they said:
Person	May this never be!
Narrator	Jesus looked directly at them and asked:
Jesus	Then what is the meaning of that which is written:
Psalmist	The stone the builders rejected has become the capstone.
Jesus	Everyone who falls on that stone will be broken to pieces, but he on whom it falls will be crushed.

Cast: **Narrator, Jesus, Owner, Tenant 1, Tenant 2, Person, Psalmist** (can be the same as Jesus)

Paying Taxes to Caesar
Luke 20:19–26

| Narrator | The teachers of the law and the chief priests looked for a way to arrest [Jesus] immediately, because they knew he had spoken this parable against them. But they were afraid of the people. |

Keeping a close watch on him, they sent spies, who pretended to be honest. They hoped to catch Jesus in something he said so that they might hand him over to the power and authority of the governor. So the spies questioned him:

Spy 1
(cunning
tone)   Teacher, we know that you speak and teach what is right.

Spy 2   And that you do not show partiality but teach the way of God in accordance with the truth.

Spy 1
(quickly)   Is it right for us to pay taxes to Caesar or not?

Narrator   He saw through their duplicity [and said to them:]

Jesus   Show me a denarius. Whose portrait and inscription are on it?

Spies 1 and 2   Caesar's.

Jesus   Then give to Caesar what is Caesar's, and to God what is God's.

Narrator   They were unable to trap him in what he had said there in public. And astonished by his answer, they became silent.

Cast: **Narrator, Spy 1, Spy 2, Jesus**

The Resurrection and Marriage
Luke 20:27–40 [41–47]

Narrator   Some of the Sadducees, who say there is no resurrection, came to Jesus with a question.

Sadducee 1   Teacher, Moses wrote for us:

[Moses]   If a man's brother dies and leaves a wife but no children, the man must marry the widow and have children for his brother.

Sadducee 1   Now there were seven brothers. The first one married a woman and died childless.

Sadducee 2   The second [one married the woman.]

Sadducee 1   And then the third married her.

Sadducee 2   And in the same way the seven died, leaving no children.

Sadducee 1   Finally, the woman died too.

Sadducee 2   Now then, at the resurrection whose wife will she be, since the seven were married to her?

[Narrator   Jesus replied:]

Jesus   The people of this age marry and are given in marriage. But those who are considered worthy of taking part in that age and in the resurrection from the dead will neither marry nor be given in marriage, and they can no longer die; for they are like the angels. They are God's children, since they are children of the resurrection. But in the account of the bush, even Moses showed that the dead rise, for he calls the Lord:

[Moses]   The God of Abraham, and the God of Isaac, and the God of Jacob.

Jesus   He is not the God of the dead, but of the living, for to him all are alive.

Narrator   Some of the teachers of the law responded:

Lawyer   Well said, teacher!

Narrator   And no one dared to ask him any more questions. (PAUSE)

[Jesus   How is it that they say the Christ is the Son of David? David himself declares in the Book of Psalms:

Psalmist   The Lord said to my Lord:
"Sit at my right hand
until I make your enemies
a footstool for your feet."

Jesus   David calls him "Lord." How then can he be his son?

Narrator   While all the people were listening, Jesus said to his disciples:

Jesus   Beware of the teachers of the law. They like to walk around in flowing robes and love to be greeted in the marketplaces and have the most important seats in the synagogues and the places of honor at banquets. They devour widows' houses and for a show make lengthy prayers. Such men will be punished most severely.]

Cast: **Narrator, Sadducee 1**, [Moses,] **Sadducee 2** (can be the same as Sadducee 1), **Jesus, Lawyer** (can be the same as Moses), **[Psalmist** (can be the same as Sadducee 1)]

The Widow's Offering
Luke 21:1–4

Narrator   As he looked up, Jesus saw the rich putting their gifts into the temple treasury. He also saw a poor widow put in two very small copper coins. [He said:]

Jesus   I tell you the truth, this poor widow has put in more than all the others. All these people gave their gifts out of their wealth; but she out of her poverty put in all she had to live on.

Cast: **Narrator, Jesus**

Jesus Speaks of the Future (i)
Luke 21:5–19

Narrator	Some of [Jesus'] disciples were remarking about how the temple was adorned with beautiful stones and with gifts dedicated to God. But Jesus said:
Jesus	As for what you see here, the time will come when not one stone will be left on another; every one of them will be thrown down.
Disciple	Teacher, when will these things happen? And what will be the sign that they are about to take place?
Jesus	Watch out that you are not deceived. For many will come in my name, claiming:
Man 1	I am he!
Man 2	The time is near!
Jesus	Do not follow them. When you hear of wars and revolutions, do not be frightened. These things must happen first, but the end will not come right away. (PAUSE)

Nation will rise against nation, and kingdom against kingdom. There will be great earthquakes, famines and pestilences in various places, and fearful events and great signs from heaven.

But before all this, they will lay hands on you and persecute you. They will deliver you to synagogues and prisons, and you will be brought before kings and governors, and all on account of my name. This will result in your being witnesses to them. But make up your mind not to worry beforehand how you will defend yourselves. For I will give you words and wisdom that none of your adversaries will be able to resist or contradict. You will be betrayed even by parents, brothers, relatives and friends, and they will put some of you to death. All men will hate you because of me. But not a hair of your head will perish. By standing firm you will gain life.

Cast: **Narrator, Jesus, Disciple, Man 1, Man 2** (Man 1 and Man 2 can be the same as Jesus)

Jesus Speaks of the Future (ii)
Luke 21:20–28

Speaker 3	When you see Jerusalem being surrounded by armies, you will know that its desolation is near.
Speaker 1	Then let those who are in Judea flee to the mountains.
Speaker 2	Let those in the city get out.
Speaker 3	And let those in the country not enter the city.

Speaker 1	For this is—
Speakers 1 and 2 (slowly)	The time of punishment.
Speaker 3	In fulfillment of all that has been written.
Speaker 1	How dreadful it will be in those days for pregnant women and nursing mothers!
Speaker 2	There will be great distress in the land and wrath against this people.
Speaker 1	They will fall by the sword—
Speaker 2	And will be taken as prisoners to all the nations.
Speaker 3	Jerusalem will be trampled on by the Gentiles until the times of the Gentiles are fulfilled.
Speaker 1	There will be signs in the sun, moon and stars.
Speaker 2	On the earth, nations will be in anguish and perplexity at the roaring and tossing of the sea.
Speaker 3	Men will faint from terror, apprehensive of what is coming on the world, for the heavenly bodies will be shaken.
Speaker 1	At that time they will see the Son of Man coming in a cloud with power and great glory.
Speaker 2	When these things begin to take place—
Speakers 1–3	Stand up and lift up your heads, because your redemption is drawing near.

Cast: **Speaker 3, Speaker 1, Speaker 2**

The Lesson of the Fig Tree
Luke 21:29–38

Narrator	[Jesus told his disciples] this parable:
Speaker 1	Look at the fig tree and all the trees.
Speaker 2	When they sprout leaves, you can see for yourselves and know that summer is near.
Speaker 3	Even so, when you see these things happening, you know that the kingdom of God is near.
Speaker 1	I tell you the truth, this generation will certainly not pass away until all these things have happened.
Speaker 2	Heaven and earth will pass away, but my words will never pass away.

199

Speakers 1–3	Be careful.
Speaker 1	Or your hearts will be weighed down with dissipation, drunkenness and the anxieties of life, and that day will close on you unexpectedly like a trap.
Speaker 2	For it will come upon all those who live on the face of the whole earth.
Speaker 3	Be always on the watch, and pray that you may be able to escape all that is about to happen, and that you may be able to stand before the Son of Man.
Narrator	Each day Jesus was teaching at the temple, and each evening he went out to spend the night on the hill called the Mount of Olives, and all the people came early in the morning to hear him at the temple.

Cast: **Narrator, Speaker 1, Speaker 2, Speaker 3**

Judas Agrees to Betray Jesus
Luke 22:1–13

Narrator	Now the Feast of Unleavened Bread, called the Passover, was approaching, and the chief priests and the teachers of the law were looking for some way to get rid of Jesus, for they were afraid of the people. (PAUSE) Then Satan entered Judas, called Iscariot, one of the Twelve. And Judas went to the chief priests and the officers of the temple guard and discussed with them how he might betray Jesus. They were delighted and agreed to give him money. He consented, and watched for an opportunity to hand Jesus over to them when no crowd was present. (PAUSE)
	Then came the day of Unleavened Bread on which the Passover lamb had to be sacrificed. Jesus sent Peter and John, saying:
Jesus	Go and make preparations for us to eat the Passover.
Peter	Where do you want us to prepare for it?
Jesus	As you enter the city, a man carrying a jar of water will meet you. Follow him to the house that he enters, and say to the owner of the house, "The Teacher asks: Where is the guest room, where I may eat the Passover with my disciples?" He will show you a large upper room, all furnished. Make preparations there.
Narrator	They left and found things just as Jesus had told them. So they prepared the Passover.

Cast: **Narrator, Jesus, Peter**

The Last Supper
Luke 22:14–20 [21–23]

Narrator	When the hour came, Jesus and his apostles reclined at the table. [And he said to them:]
Jesus	I have eagerly desired to eat this Passover with you before I suffer. For I tell you, I will not eat it again until it finds fulfillment in the kingdom of God.
Narrator	After taking the cup, he gave thanks and said:
Jesus	Take this and divide it among you. For I tell you I will not drink again of the fruit of the vine until the kingdom of God comes.
Narrator	And he took bread, gave thanks and broke it, and gave it to them, saying:
Jesus	This is my body given for you; do this in remembrance of me.
Narrator	In the same way, after the supper he took the cup, saying:
Jesus	This cup is the new covenant in my blood, which is poured out for you. (PAUSE) [But the hand of him who is going to betray me is with mine on the table. The Son of Man will go as it has been decreed, but woe to that man who betrays him.
Narrator	They began to question among themselves which of them it might be who would do this.]

Cast: **Narrator, Jesus**

The Argument about Greatness
Luke 22:24–34

Narrator	Also a dispute arose among [the apostles] as to which of them was considered to be greatest. Jesus said to them:
Jesus	The kings of the Gentiles lord it over them; and those who exercise authority over them call themselves Benefactors. But you are not to be like that. Instead, the greatest among you should be like the youngest, and the one who rules like the one who serves. For who is greater, the one who is at the table or the one who serves? Is it not the one who is at the table? But I am among you as one who serves. (PAUSE) You are those who have stood by me in my trials. And I confer on you a kingdom, just as my Father conferred one on me, so that you may eat and drink at my table in my kingdom and sit on thrones, judging the twelve tribes of Israel. (PAUSE)
(to Peter)	Simon, Simon, Satan has asked to sift you as wheat. But I have prayed for you, Simon, that your faith may not fail. And when you have turned back, strengthen your brothers.

Narrator	[But Peter replied:]
Peter	Lord, I am ready to go with you to prison and to death.
Jesus	I tell you, Peter, before the rooster crows today, you will deny three times that you know me.

Cast: **Narrator, Jesus, Peter**

Jesus Prays on the Mount of Olives
Luke 22:35–53

Narrator	Jesus asked [his disciples:]
Jesus	When I sent you without purse, bag or sandals, did you lack anything?
Disciple	Nothing.
Jesus	But now if you have a purse, take it, and also a bag; and if you don't have a sword, sell your cloak and buy one. It is written: "And he was numbered with the transgressors"; and I tell you that this must be fulfilled in me. Yes, what is written about me is reaching its fulfillment.
Disciple	See, Lord, here are two swords.
Jesus	That is enough.
Narrator	Jesus went out as usual to the Mount of Olives, and his disciples followed him. On reaching the place, he said to them:
Jesus	Pray that you will not fall into temptation.
Narrator	He withdrew about a stone's throw beyond them, knelt down and prayed.
Jesus	Father, if you are willing, take this cup from me; yet not my will, but yours be done.
Narrator	An angel from heaven appeared to him and strengthened him. And being in anguish, he prayed more earnestly, and his sweat was like drops of blood falling to the ground. (PAUSE)
	When he rose from prayer and went back to the disciples, he found them asleep, exhausted from sorrow.
Jesus	Why are you sleeping? Get up and pray so that you will not fall into temptation.
Narrator	While he was still speaking a crowd came up, and the man who was called Judas, one of the Twelve, was leading them. He approached Jesus to kiss him, but Jesus asked him:
Jesus	Judas, are you betraying the Son of Man with a kiss?
Narrator	When Jesus' followers saw what was going to happen, they said:

Disciple	Lord, should we strike with our swords?
Narrator	And one of them struck the servant of the high priest, cutting off his right ear.
Jesus	No more of this!
Narrator	And he touched the man's ear and healed him. (PAUSE) Then Jesus said to the chief priests, the officers of the temple guard, and the elders, who had come for him:
Jesus	Am I leading a rebellion, that you have come with swords and clubs? Every day I was with you in the temple courts, and you did not lay a hand on me. But this is your hour—when darkness reigns.

Cast: **Narrator, Jesus, Disciple**

Peter Disowns Jesus
Luke 22:54–62

Narrator	Then seizing [Jesus, the crowd] led him away and took him into the house of the high priest. Peter followed at a distance. But when they had kindled a fire in the middle of the courtyard and had sat down together, Peter sat down with them. A servant girl saw him seated there in the firelight. She looked closely at him and said:
Girl	This man was with him.
[Narrator	But he denied it.]
Peter	Woman, I don't know him.
Narrator	A little later someone else saw him and said:
Man 1	You also are one of them.
Peter	Man, I am not!
Narrator	About an hour later another asserted:
Man 2	Certainly this fellow was with him, for he is a Galilean.
[Narrator	Peter replied:]
Peter	Man, I don't know what you're talking about!
Narrator	Just as he was speaking, the rooster crowed. The Lord turned and looked straight at Peter. Then Peter remembered the word the Lord had spoken to him:
Jesus	Before the rooster crows today, you will disown me three times.
Narrator	And he went outside and wept bitterly.

Cast: **Narrator, Girl, Peter, Man 1, Man 2, Jesus** (can be the same as Narrator)

Jesus before the Sanhedrin
Luke 22:63–71

Narrator	The men who were guarding Jesus began mocking and beating him. They blindfolded him and demanded:
Guard 1	Prophesy!
Guard 2	Who hit you?
Narrator	And they said many other insulting things to him. (PAUSE)
	At daybreak the council of the elders of the people, both the chief priests and teachers of the law, met together, and Jesus was led before them.
Lawyer	If you are the Christ, tell us.
[Narrator	Jesus answered:]
Jesus	If I tell you, you will not believe me, and if I asked you, you would not answer. But from now on, the Son of Man will be seated at the right hand of the mighty God.
Lawyer	Are you then the Son of God?
Jesus	You are right in saying I am.
Lawyer	Why do we need any more testimony? We have heard it from his own lips.

Cast: **Narrator, Guard 1, Guard 2, Lawyer, Jesus**

Jesus before Pilate
Luke 23:1–11 [12]

Narrator	The whole assembly rose and led [Jesus] off to Pilate. And they began to accuse him, saying:
Leader 1	We have found this man subverting our nation.
Leader 2	He opposes payment of taxes to Caesar.
Leader 1	And claims to be Christ, a king.
[Narrator	So Pilate asked Jesus:]
Pilate (to Jesus)	Are you the king of the Jews?
[Narrator	Jesus replied:]
Jesus	Yes, it is as you say.
Narrator	Then Pilate announced to the chief priests and the crowd:
Pilate	I find no basis for a charge against this man.

Narrator	But they insisted:
Leader 1	He stirs up the people all over Judea by his teaching.
Leader 2	He started in Galilee and has come all the way here.
Narrator	On hearing this, Pilate asked if the man was a Galilean. When he learned that Jesus was under Herod's jurisdiction, he sent him to Herod, who was also in Jerusalem at that time.
	When Herod saw Jesus, he was greatly pleased, because for a long time he had been wanting to see him. From what he had heard about him, he hoped to see him perform some miracle. He plied him with many questions, but Jesus gave him no answer. (PAUSE) The chief priests and the teachers of the law were standing there, vehemently accusing him. Then Herod and his soldiers ridiculed and mocked him. Dressing him in an elegant robe, they sent him back to Pilate. [That day Herod and Pilate became friends—before this they had been enemies.]

Cast: **Narrator, Leader 1, Leader 2** (can be the same as Leader 1), **Pilate, Jesus**

Jesus Sentenced to Death
Luke 23:13–25

Narrator	Pilate called together the chief priests, the rulers and the people, and said to them:
Pilate	You brought me this man as one who was inciting the people to rebellion. I have examined him in your presence and have found no basis for your charges against him. Neither has Herod, for he sent him back to us; as you can see, he has done nothing to deserve death. Therefore, I will punish him and then release him.
Narrator	[At every Passover Pilate had to set free one prisoner for them.]
	With one voice they cried out:
Persons 1 and 2	Away with this man!
Person 2	Release Barabbas to us!
Narrator	(Barabbas had been thrown into prison for an insurrection in the city, and for murder.)
	Wanting to release Jesus, Pilate appealed to them again. But they kept shouting:
Person 1	Crucify him!
Persons 1 and 2	Crucify him!
Narrator	For the third time he spoke to them:

Pilate	Why? What crime has this man committed? I have found in him no grounds for the death penalty. Therefore I will have him punished and then release him.
Narrator	But with loud shouts they insistently demanded that he be crucified, and their shouts prevailed. So Pilate decided to grant their demand. He released the man who had been thrown into prison for insurrection and murder, the one they asked for, and surrendered Jesus to their will.

Cast: **Narrator, Pilate, Person 1, Person 2**

The Crucifixion (i)
Luke 23:26–32

Narrator	As [the soldiers led Jesus] away, they seized Simon from Cyrene, who was on his way in from the country, and put the cross on him and made him carry it behind Jesus. A large number of people followed him, including women who mourned and wailed for him. Jesus turned and said to them:
Jesus	Daughters of Jerusalem, do not weep for me; weep for yourselves and for your children. For the time will come when you will say, "Blessed are the barren women, the wombs that never bore and the breasts that never nursed!" Then
	"they will say to the mountains, 'Fall on us!' and to the hills, 'Cover us!'"
	For if men do these things when the tree is green, what will happen when it is dry?
Narrator	Two other men, both criminals, were also led out with him to be executed.

Cast: **Narrator, Jesus**

The Crucifixion (ii)
Luke 23:33–43

Narrator	When they came to the place called the Skull, there they crucified [Jesus,] along with the criminals—one on his right, the other on his left. Jesus said:
Jesus	Father, forgive them, for they do not know what they are doing.
Narrator	And they divided up his clothes by casting lots.
	The people stood watching, and the rulers even sneered at him. [They said:]
Ruler 1	He saved others; let him save himself—
Ruler 2	If he is the Christ of God, the Chosen One.

Narrator	The soldiers also came up and mocked him. They offered him wine vinegar and said:
Soldier	If you are the king of the Jews, save yourself.
Narrator	There was a written notice above him, which read:
Pilate	THIS IS THE KING OF THE JEWS.
Narrator	One of the criminals who hung there hurled insults at him:
Criminal 1	Aren't you the Christ? Save yourself and us!
Narrator	But the other criminal rebuked him.
Criminal 2	Don't you fear God, since you are under the same sentence? We are punished justly, for we are getting what our deeds deserve. But this man has done nothing wrong.
Narrator	Then he said:
Criminal 2	Jesus, remember me when you come into your kingdom.
Narrator	Jesus answered him:
Jesus	I tell you the truth, today you will be with me in paradise.

Cast: **Narrator, Jesus, Ruler 1, Ruler 2** (can be the same as Ruler 1), **Soldier, Pilate, Criminal 1, Criminal 2**

Jesus' Death
Luke 23:44–49

Narrator	It was now about the sixth hour, and darkness came over the whole land until the ninth hour, for the sun stopped shining. And the curtain of the temple was torn in two. Jesus called out with a loud voice:
Jesus	Father, into your hands I commit my spirit.
Narrator	When he had said this, he breathed his last. (PAUSE)
	The centurion, seeing what had happened, praised God and said:
Centurion	Surely this was a righteous man.
Narrator	When all the people who had gathered to witness this sight saw what took place, they beat their breasts and went away. But all those who knew him, including the women who had followed him from Galilee, stood at a distance, watching these things.

Cast: **Narrator, Jesus, Centurion**

Jesus' Burial
Luke 23:50–56

Narrator 1　There was a man named Joseph, a member of the Council, a good and upright man, who had not consented to their decision and action. He came from the Judean town of Arimathea and he was waiting for the kingdom of God. Going to Pilate, he asked for Jesus' body. Then he took it down, wrapped it in linen cloth and placed it in a tomb cut in the rock, one in which no one had yet been laid. It was Preparation Day, and the Sabbath was about to begin.

Narrator 2　The women who had come with Jesus from Galilee followed Joseph and saw the tomb and how his body was laid in it. Then they went home and prepared spices and perfumes.

Narrator 1　But they rested on the Sabbath in obedience to the commandment.

Cast: **Narrator 1, Narrator 2**

The Resurrection
Luke 24:1–12

Narrator　On the first day of the week, very early in the morning, the women took the spices they had prepared and went to the tomb. They found the stone rolled away from the tomb, but when they entered, they did not find the body of the Lord Jesus. While they were wondering about this, suddenly two men in clothes that gleamed like lightning stood beside them. In their fright the women bowed down with their faces to the ground, but the men said to them:

Man 1　Why do you look for the living among the dead?

Man 2　He is not here; he has risen!

Man 1　Remember how he told you, while he was still with you in Galilee:

Man 2　"The Son of Man must be delivered into the hands of sinful men, be crucified—

Man 1　And on the third day be raised again."

Narrator　Then they remembered his words. (PAUSE) When they came back from the tomb, they told all these things to the Eleven and to all the others. It was Mary Magdalene, Joanna, Mary the mother of James, and the others with them who told this to the apostles. But they did not believe the women, because their words seemed to them like nonsense. Peter, however, got up and ran to the tomb. Bending over, he saw the strips of linen lying by themselves, and he went away, wondering to himself what had happened.

Cast: **Narrator, Man 1, Man 2**

On the Road to Emmaus
Luke 24:13–35

Narrator	Now that same day two of [the disciples] were going to a village called Emmaus, about seven miles from Jerusalem. They were talking with each other about everything that had happened. As they talked and discussed these things with each other, Jesus himself came up and walked along with them; but they were kept from recognizing him. He asked them:
Jesus	What are you discussing together as you walk along?
Narrator	They stood still, their faces downcast. One of them, named Cleopas, asked him:
Cleopas	Are you only a visitor to Jerusalem and do not know the things that have happened there in these days?
Jesus	What things?
Cleopas	About Jesus of Nazareth.
Companion	He was a prophet, powerful in word and deed before God and all the people.
Cleopas	The chief priests and our rulers handed him over to be sentenced to death, and they crucified him.
Companion	But we had hoped that he was the one who was going to redeem Israel.
Cleopas	And what is more, it is the third day since all this took place.
Companion	In addition, some of our women amazed us. They went to the tomb early this morning but didn't find his body.
Cleopas	They came and told us that they had seen a vision of angels, who said he was alive.
Companion	Then some of our companions went to the tomb and found it just as the women had said.
Cleopas	But him they did not see.
Jesus	How foolish you are, and how slow of heart to believe all that the prophets have spoken! Did not the Christ have to suffer these things and then enter his glory?
Narrator	And beginning with Moses and all the Prophets, he explained to them what was said in all the Scriptures concerning himself. (PAUSE) As they approached the village to which they were going, Jesus acted as if he were going farther. But they urged him strongly:
Companion	Stay with us, for it is nearly evening.
Cleopas	The day is almost over.

209

Narrator	So he went in to stay with them. (PAUSE) When he was at the table with them, he took bread, gave thanks, broke it and began to give it to them. Then their eyes were opened and they recognized him, and he disappeared from their sight. (PAUSE) They asked each other:
Cleopas	Were not our hearts burning within us while he talked with us on the road . . .
Companion	. . . and opened the Scriptures to us?
Narrator	They got up and returned at once to Jerusalem. There they found the Eleven and those with them, assembled together and saying:
Disciple 1	It is true!
Disciple 2	The Lord has risen—
Disciple 1	And has appeared to Simon.
Narrator	Then the two told what had happened on the way, and how Jesus was recognized by them when he broke the bread.

Cast: **Narrator, Jesus, Cleopas, Companion, Disciple 1, Disciple 2**

Jesus Appears to His Disciples and Is Taken up to Heaven
Luke 24:36–53

Narrator	While [the disciples] were talking, Jesus himself stood among them [and said to them:]
Jesus	Peace be with you.
Narrator	They were startled and frightened, thinking they saw a ghost.
Jesus	Why are you troubled, and why do doubts rise in your minds? Look at my hands and my feet. It is I myself! Touch me and see; a ghost does not have flesh and bones, as you see I have.
Narrator	When he had said this, he showed them his hands and feet. And while they still did not believe it because of joy and amazement, he asked them:
Jesus	Do you have anything here to eat?
Narrator	They gave him a piece of broiled fish, and he took it and ate it in their presence. (PAUSE)
Jesus	This is what I told you while I was still with you: Everything must be fulfilled that is written about me in the Law of Moses, the Prophets and the Psalms.
Narrator	Then he opened their minds so they could understand the Scriptures:

Jesus	This is what is written: The Christ will suffer and rise from the dead on the third day, and repentance and forgiveness of sins will be preached in his name to all nations, beginning at Jerusalem. You are witnesses of these things. I am going to send you what my Father has promised; but stay in the city until you have been clothed with power from on high.
Narrator	When he had led them out to the vicinity of Bethany, he lifted up his hands and blessed them. While he was blessing them, he left them and was taken up into heaven. Then they worshiped him and returned to Jerusalem with great joy. And they stayed continually at the temple, praising God.

Cast: **Narrator, Jesus**

See also the Passion Readings, beginning on page 423, and the Easter Readings, beginning on page 466.

The Gospel of John

The Word Became Flesh
John 1:1–14 [15–18]

Voice 1   In the beginning was the Word, and the Word was with God, and the Word was God. He was with God in the beginning.

Voice 2   Through him all things were made; without him nothing was made that has been made.

Voice 1   In him was life, and that life was the light of men. The light shines in the darkness, but the darkness has not understood it.

Voice 3   There came a man who was sent from God; his name was John. He came as a witness to testify concerning that light, so that through him all men might believe.

Voice 4   He himself was not the light; he came only as a witness to the light.

Voice 2   The true light that gives light to every man was coming into the world.

Voice 1   He was in the world, and though the world was made through him, the world did not recognize him.

Voice 2   He came to that which was his own, but his own did not receive him. Yet to all who received him, to those who believed in his name, he gave the right to become children of God—

Voice 4   Children born not of natural descent, nor of human decision or a husband's will, but born of God.

Voice 1   The Word became flesh and made his dwelling among us. We have seen his glory, the glory of the One and Only, who came from the Father, full of grace and truth.

[Voice 3   John testifies concerning him. He cries out, saying:

John the
   Baptist   This was he of whom I said, "He who comes after me has surpassed me because he was before me."

Voice 2   From the fullness of his grace we have all received one blessing after another.

Voice 3   For the law was given through Moses; grace and truth came through Jesus Christ.

Voice 1   No one has ever seen God, but God the One and Only, who is at the Father's side, has made him known.]

Cast: **Voice 1, Voice 2, Voice 3, Voice 4, [John the Baptist].** (See also Appendix: Christmas Readings, page 422.)

John—the Messenger
From John 1:6–36

Narrator	There came a man who was sent from God; his name was John. He came as a witness to testify concerning that light, so that through him all men might believe. He himself was not the light; he came only as a witness to the light. The true light that gives light to every man was coming into the world. . . .
	John testifies concerning him. He cries out, saying:
John	This was he of whom I said, "He who comes after me has surpassed me because he was before me."
Narrator	. . . The Jews of Jerusalem sent priests and Levites to ask [John] who he was. He did not fail to confess, but confessed freely:
John	I am not the Christ.
Lawyer	Then who are you?
Priest	Are you Elijah?
John	I am not.
Lawyer	Are you the Prophet?
John	No.
Lawyer	Who are you?
Priest	Give us an answer to take back to those who sent us.
Lawyer	What do you say about yourself?
Narrator	John replied in the words of Isaiah the prophet:
John	I am the voice of one calling in the desert, "Make straight the way for the Lord."
Narrator	Now some Pharisees who had been sent questioned him:
Pharisee	Why then do you baptize if you are not the Christ, nor Elijah, nor the Prophet?
John	I baptize with water, but among you stands one you do not know. He is the one who comes after me, the thongs of whose sandals I am not worthy to untie.
Narrator	This all happened at Bethany on the other side of the Jordan, where John was baptizing. (PAUSE)
	The next day John saw Jesus coming toward him and said:
John	Look, the Lamb of God, who takes away the sin of the world! This is the one I meant when I said, "A man who comes after me has surpassed me

because he was before me." I myself did not know him, but the reason I came baptizing with water was that he might be revealed to Israel.

Narrator	Then John gave this testimony:
John	I saw the Spirit come down from heaven as a dove and remain on him. I would not have known him, except that the one who sent me to baptize with water told me, "The man on whom you see the Spirit come down and remain is he who will baptize with the Holy Spirit." I have seen and I testify that this is the Son of God.
Narrator	The next day John was there again with two of his disciples. When he saw Jesus passing by, he said:
John	Look, the Lamb of God!

Cast: **Narrator**, **John**, **Lawyer**, **Priest** (can be the same as Lawyer), **Pharisee** (can be the same as Priest). (See also Appendix: Christmas Readings, page 419.)

Jesus' First Disciples
John 1:38–51

Narrator	Turning around, Jesus saw [two of John's disciples] following and asked:
Jesus	What do you want?
Disciple and **Andrew**	Rabbi!
Narrator	(Which means Teacher.)
Disciple	Where are you staying?
Jesus	Come, and you will see.
Narrator	So they went and saw where he was staying, and spent that day with him. It was about the tenth hour. (PAUSE)
	Andrew, Simon Peter's brother, was one of the two who heard what John had said and who had followed Jesus. The first thing Andrew did was to find his brother Simon [and tell him:]
Andrew	We have found the Messiah.
Narrator	(That is, the Christ.) And he brought [Simon] to Jesus. Jesus looked at him [and said:]
Jesus	You are Simon son of John. You will be called Cephas.
Narrator	(Which, when translated, is Peter.) (PAUSE) The next day Jesus decided to leave for Galilee. Finding Philip, he said to him:
Jesus	Follow me.
Narrator	Philip, like Andrew and Peter, was from the town of Bethsaida. Philip found Nathanael [and told him:]

Philip	We have found the one Moses wrote about in the Law, and about whom the prophets also wrote—Jesus of Nazareth, the son of Joseph.
[Narrator	Nathanael asked:]
Nathanael	Nazareth! Can anything good come from there?
Philip	Come and see.
Narrator	When Jesus saw Nathanael approaching, he said of him,
Jesus	Here is a true Israelite, in whom there is nothing false.
Nathanael	How do you know me?
Jesus	I saw you while you were still under the fig tree before Philip called you.
Nathanael	Rabbi, you are the Son of God; you are the King of Israel.
Jesus	You believe because I told you I saw you under the fig tree. You shall see greater things than that.
(to the disciples)	I tell you the truth, you shall see heaven open, and the angels of God ascending and descending on the Son of Man.

Cast: **Narrator**, **Jesus**, **Disciple**, **Andrew** (can be the same as Disciple), **Philip**, **Nathanael**. (See also composite reading below.)

Jesus Makes Up His Team
From John 1 and Matthew 4 and 9

Narrator	Jesus decided to leave for Galilee. Finding Philip, he said to him:
Jesus	Follow me.
Narrator	Philip found Nathanael [and told him:]
Philip	We have found the one Moses wrote about in the Law, and about whom the prophets also wrote—Jesus of Nazareth, the son of Joseph.
[Narrator	Nathanael asked:]
Nathanael	Nazareth! Can anything good come from there?
Philip	Come and see.
Narrator	When Jesus saw Nathanael approaching, he said of him:
Jesus	Here is a true Israelite, in whom there is nothing false.
Nathanael	How do you know me?
Jesus	I saw you while you were still under the fig tree before Philip called you.
Nathanael	Rabbi, you are the Son of God; you are the King of Israel. (PAUSE)

215

Narrator	As Jesus was walking beside the Sea of Galilee, he saw two brothers, Simon called Peter and his brother Andrew. They were casting a net into the lake, for they were fishermen. [Jesus said:]
Jesus	Come, follow me, and I will make you fishers of men.
Narrator	At once they left their nets and followed him. (PAUSE)
	Going on from there, he saw two other brothers, James son of Zebedee and his brother John. They were in a boat with their father Zebedee, preparing their nets. Jesus called them, and immediately they left the boat and their father and followed him.
	[Later, Jesus] saw a man named Matthew sitting at the tax collector's booth. [He told him:]
Jesus	Follow me.
Narrator	Matthew got up and followed him. (PAUSE)
	While Jesus was having dinner at Matthew's house, many tax collectors and "sinners" came and ate with him and his disciples. When the Pharisees saw this, they asked his disciples:
Pharisee	Why does your teacher eat with tax collectors and "sinners"?
Narrator	On hearing this, Jesus said:
Jesus	It is not the healthy who need a doctor, but the sick. But go and learn what this means: "I desire mercy, not sacrifice." For I have not come to call the righteous, but sinners.

Cast: **Narrator, Jesus, Philip, Nathanael, Pharisee.** (See pages 214–15 for Johannine version only.)

Jesus Changes Water to Wine
John 2:1–11

Narrator	A wedding took place at Cana in Galilee. Jesus' mother was there, and Jesus and his disciples had also been invited to the wedding. When the wine was gone, Jesus' mother said to him:
Mary	They have no more wine.
Jesus	Dear woman, why do you involve me? My time has not yet come.
Narrator	His mother said to the servants:
Mary	Do whatever he tells you.
Narrator	Nearby stood six stone water jars, the kind used by the Jews for ceremonial washing, each holding from twenty to thirty gallons. Jesus said to the servants:
Jesus	Fill the jars with water.

Narrator	So they filled them to the brim.
Jesus	Now draw some out and take it to the master of the banquet.
Narrator	They did so, and the master of the banquet tasted the water that had been turned into wine. He did not realize where it had come from, though the servants who had drawn the water knew. Then he called the bridegroom aside and said:
Master	Everyone brings out the choice wine first and then the cheaper wine after the guests have had too much to drink; but you have saved the best till now.
Narrator	This, the first of his miraculous signs, Jesus performed in Cana in Galilee. He thus revealed his glory, and his disciples put their faith in him.

Cast: **Narrator, Mary, Jesus, Master**

Jesus Clears the Temple
John 2:13–22 [23–25]

Narrator	When it was almost time for the Jewish Passover, Jesus went up to Jerusalem. In the temple courts he found men selling cattle, sheep and doves, and others sitting at tables exchanging money. So he made a whip out of cords, and drove all from the temple area, both sheep and cattle; he scattered the coins of the money changers and overturned their tables. To those who sold doves he said:
Jesus	Get these out of here! How dare you turn my Father's house into a market!
Narrator	His disciples remembered that it is written:
Psalmist	Zeal for your house will consume me.
Narrator	Then the Jews demanded of him:
Lawyer	What miraculous sign can you show us to prove your authority to do all this?
Jesus	Destroy this temple, and I will raise it again in three days.
Lawyer	It has taken forty-six years to build this temple, and you are going to raise it in three days?
Narrator	But the temple he had spoken of was his body. After he was raised from the dead, his disciples recalled what he had said. Then they believed the Scripture and the words that Jesus had spoken.
	[Now while he was in Jerusalem at the Passover Feast, many people saw the miraculous signs he was doing and believed in his name. But Jesus

would not entrust himself to them, for he knew all men. He did not need man's testimony about man, for he knew what was in a man.]

Cast: **Narrator, Jesus, Psalmist** (can be the same as Narrator), **Lawyer**

Jesus Teaches Nicodemus
John 3:1–17 [18–21]

Narrator   There was a man of the Pharisees named Nicodemus, a member of the Jewish ruling council. He came to Jesus at night and said:

Nicodemus   Rabbi, we know you are a teacher who has come from God. For no one could perform the miraculous signs you are doing if God were not with him.

Narrator   In reply Jesus declared:

Jesus   I tell you the truth, no one can see the kingdom of God unless he is born again.

Nicodemus   How can a man be born when he is old? Surely he cannot enter a second time into his mother's womb to be born!

Jesus   I tell you the truth, no one can enter the kingdom of God unless he is born of water and the Spirit. Flesh gives birth to flesh, but the Spirit gives birth to spirit. You should not be surprised at my saying, "You must be born again." The wind blows wherever it pleases. You hear its sound, but you cannot tell where it comes from or where it is going. So it is with everyone born of the Spirit.

Nicodemus   How can this be?

Jesus   You are Israel's teacher, and do you not understand these things? I tell you the truth, we speak of what we know, and we testify to what we have seen, but still you people do not accept our testimony. I have spoken to you of earthly things and you do not believe; how then will you believe if I speak of heavenly things? No one has ever gone into heaven except the one who came from heaven—the Son of Man. Just as Moses lifted up the snake in the desert, so the Son of Man must be lifted up, that everyone who believes in him may have eternal life.

For God so loved the world that he gave his one and only Son, that whoever believes in him shall not perish but have eternal life. For God did not send his Son into the world to condemn the world, but to save the world through him. [Whoever believes in him is not condemned, but whoever does not believe stands condemned already because he has not believed in the name of God's one and only Son. This is the verdict: Light has come into the world, but men loved darkness instead of light because their deeds were evil. Everyone who does evil hates the light, and will not come into the light for fear that his deeds will be exposed.

But whoever lives by the truth comes into the light, so that it may be seen plainly that what he has done has been done through God.]

Cast: **Narrator, Nicodemus, Jesus**

John the Baptist's Testimony about Jesus
John 3:22–30 [31–36]

Narrator
Jesus and his disciples went out into the Judean countryside, where he spent some time with them, and baptized. Now John also was baptizing at Aenon near Salim, because there was plenty of water, and people were constantly coming to be baptized.

[Commen-
tator
This was before John was put in prison.]

Narrator
An argument developed between some of John's disciples and a certain Jew over the matter of ceremonial washing. They came to John and said to him:

Disciple 1
Rabbi, that man who was with you on the other side of the Jordan—

Disciple 2
The one you testified about—

Disciple 1
Well, *he* is baptizing.

Disciple 2
And everyone is going to him.

Narrator
To this John replied:

John
A man can receive only what is given him from heaven. You yourselves can testify that I said, "I am not the Christ but am sent ahead of him." The bride belongs to the bridegroom. The friend who attends the bridegroom waits and listens for him, and is full of joy when he hears the bridegroom's voice. That joy is mine, and it is now complete. He must become greater; I must become less.

[The one who comes from above is above all; the one who is from the earth belongs to the earth, and speaks as one from the earth. The one who comes from heaven is above all. He testifies to what he has seen and heard, but no one accepts his testimony. The man who has accepted it has certified that God is truthful. For the one whom God has sent speaks the words of God, for God gives the Spirit without limit. The Father loves the Son and has placed everything in his hands. Whoever believes in the Son has eternal life, but whoever rejects the Son will not see life, for God's wrath remains on him.]

Cast: **Narrator, [Commentator,] Disciple 1, Disciple 2, John**

Jesus Talks with a Samaritan Woman
John 4:5–18 [19–27], 28–29, 39–42

Narrator	[Jesus] came to a town in Samaria called Sychar, near the plot of ground Jacob had given to his son Joseph. Jacob's well was there, and Jesus, tired as he was from the journey, sat down by the well. It was about the sixth hour. When a Samaritan woman came to draw water, Jesus said to her:
Jesus	Will you give me a drink?
Narrator	(His disciples had gone into the town to buy food.) [The Samaritan woman said to him:]
Woman	You are a Jew and I am a Samaritan woman. How can you ask me for a drink?
Narrator	(For Jews do not associate with Samaritans.)
Jesus	If you knew the gift of God and who it is that asks you for a drink, you would have asked him and he would have given you living water.
Woman	Sir, you have nothing to draw with and the well is deep. Where can you get this living water? Are you greater than our father Jacob, who gave us the well and drank from it himself, as did also his sons and his flocks and herds?
Jesus	Everyone who drinks this water will be thirsty again, but whoever drinks the water I give him will never thirst. Indeed, the water I give him will become in him a spring of water welling up to eternal life.
Woman	Sir, give me this water so that I won't get thirsty and have to keep coming here to draw water.
Jesus	Go, call your husband and come back.
Woman	I have no husband.
Jesus	You are right when you say you have no husband. The fact is, you have had five husbands, and the man you now have is not your husband. What you have just said is quite true.
[Woman	Sir, I can see that you are a prophet. Our fathers worshiped on this mountain, but you Jews claim that the place where we must worship is in Jerusalem.
Jesus	Believe me, woman, a time is coming when you will worship the Father neither on this mountain nor in Jerusalem. You Samaritans worship what you do not know; we worship what we do know, for salvation is from the Jews. Yet a time is coming and has now come when the true worshipers will worship the Father in spirit and truth, for they are the kind of worshipers the Father seeks. God is spirit, and his worshipers must worship in spirit and in truth.

Woman	I know that Messiah is coming. When he comes, he will explain everything to us. (PAUSE)
Jesus (slowly)	I who speak to you am he.
Narrator	Just then his disciples returned and were surprised to find him talking with a woman. But no one asked, "What do you want?" or "Why are you talking with her?" (PAUSE)]
	Then, leaving her water jar, the woman went back to the town and said to the people:
Woman	Come, see a man who told me everything I ever did. Could this be the Christ? . . .
Narrator	Many of the Samaritans from that town believed in him because of the woman's testimony:
[Woman]	He told me everything I ever did.
Narrator	So when the Samaritans came to him, they urged him to stay with them, and he stayed two days. And because of his words many more became believers. They said to the woman:
Person 1	We no longer believe just because of what you said; now we have heard for ourselves.
Person 2	And we know that this man really is the Savior of the world.

Cast: **Narrator, Jesus, Woman, Person 1, Person 2** (can be the same as Person 1)

Jesus Heals the Official's Son
John 4:43–54

Narrator	After two days [Jesus] left for Galilee. (Now [he] himself had pointed out:
[Jesus]	A prophet has no honor in his own country.)
Narrator	When he arrived in Galilee, the Galileans welcomed him. They had seen all that he had done in Jerusalem at the Passover Feast, for they also had been there. (PAUSE)
	Once more he visited Cana in Galilee, where he had turned the water into wine. And there was a certain royal official whose son lay sick at Capernaum. When this man heard that Jesus had arrived in Galilee from Judea, he went to him and begged him to come and heal his son, who was close to death. Jesus told him:
Jesus	Unless you people see miraculous signs and wonders, you will never believe.
[Narrator	The royal official said:]
Official	Sir, come down before my child dies.

Jesus	You may go. Your son will live.
Narrator	The man took Jesus at his word and departed. While he was still on the way, his servants met him with the news that his boy was living. When he inquired as to the time when his son got better, they said to him:
Servant 1	The fever left him yesterday.
Servant 2	At the seventh hour.
Narrator	Then the father realized that this was the exact time at which Jesus had said to him, "Your son will live." So he and all his household believed.
	This was the second miraculous sign that Jesus performed, having come from Judea to Galilee.

Cast: **Narrator, Jesus, Official, Servant 1, Servant 2** (can be the same as Servant 1)

The Healing at the Pool
John 5:1–18

Narrator	Jesus went up to Jerusalem for a feast of the Jews. Now there is in Jerusalem near the Sheep Gate a pool, which in Aramaic is called Bethesda and which is surrounded by five covered colonnades. Here a great number of disabled people used to lie—the blind, the lame, the paralyzed. One who was there had been an invalid for thirty-eight years. When Jesus saw him lying there and learned that he had been in this condition for a long time, he asked him:
Jesus	Do you want to get well?
[Narrator	The invalid replied:]
Man	Sir, I have no one to help me into the pool when the water is stirred. While I am trying to get in, someone else goes down ahead of me.
Jesus	Get up! Pick up your mat and walk.
Narrator	At once the man was cured; he picked up his mat and walked. (PAUSE)
	The day on which this took place was a Sabbath, and so the Jews said to the man who had been healed:
Lawyer 1	It is the Sabbath.
Lawyer 2	The law forbids you to carry your mat.
Man	The man who made me well said to me, "Pick up your mat and walk."
Lawyer 1	Who is this fellow who told you to pick it up and walk?
Narrator	The man who was healed had no idea who it was, for Jesus had slipped away into the crowd that was there. (PAUSE)
	Later Jesus found him at the temple and said to him:

222

Jesus	See, you are well again. Stop sinning or something worse may happen to you.
Narrator	The man went away and told the Jews that it was Jesus who had made him well.
	So, because Jesus was doing these things on the Sabbath, the Jews persecuted him. Jesus said to them:
Jesus (to lawyers)	My Father is always at his work to this very day, and I, too, am working.
Narrator	For this reason the Jews tried all the harder to kill him; not only was he breaking the Sabbath, but he was even calling God his own Father, making himself equal with God.

Cast: **Narrator, Jesus, Man, Lawyer 1, Lawyer 2** (can be the same as Lawyer 1)

Jesus Feeds the Five Thousand
John 6:1–15

Narrator	Jesus crossed to the far shore of the Sea of Galilee (that is, the Sea of Tiberias), and a great crowd of people followed him because they saw the miraculous signs he had performed on the sick. Then Jesus went up on a mountainside and sat down with his disciples. The Jewish Passover Feast was near.
	When Jesus looked up and saw a great crowd coming toward him, he said to Philip:
Jesus	Where shall we buy bread for these people to eat?
Narrator	He asked this only to test him, for he already had in mind what he was going to do. [Philip answered him:]
Philip	Eight months' wages would not buy enough bread for each one to have a bite!
Narrator	Another of his disciples, Andrew, Simon Peter's brother, spoke up:
Andrew	Here is a boy with five small barley loaves and two small fish, but how far will they go among so many?
Jesus	Have the people sit down.
Narrator	There was plenty of grass in that place, and the men sat down, about five thousand of them. Jesus then took the loaves, gave thanks, and distributed to those who were seated as much as they wanted. He did the same with the fish. When they had all had enough to eat, he said to his disciples:
Jesus	Gather the pieces that are left over. Let nothing be wasted.
Narrator	So they gathered them and filled twelve baskets with the pieces of the five barley loaves left over by those who had eaten. (PAUSE)

After the people saw the miraculous sign that Jesus did, they began to say:

**Persons 1
and 2**   Surely this is the Prophet who is to come into the world.

Narrator   Jesus, knowing that they intended to come and make him king by force, withdrew again to a mountain by himself.

Cast: **Narrator, Jesus, Philip, Andrew, Person 1, Person 2** (Persons 1 and 2 can be the same as Philip and Andrew)

Jesus Walks on the Water
John 6:16–24

Narrator 1   When evening came, [Jesus'] disciples went down to the lake, where they got into a boat and set off across the lake for Capernaum.

Narrator 2   By now it was dark, and Jesus had not yet joined them. A strong wind was blowing and the waters grew rough.

Narrator 1   When they had rowed three or three and a half miles, they saw Jesus approaching the boat, walking on the water; and they were terrified. But he said to them:

Jesus   It is I; don't be afraid.

Narrator 1   Then they were willing to take him into the boat, and immediately the boat reached the shore where they were heading.

Narrator 2   The next day the crowd that had stayed on the opposite shore of the lake realized that only one boat had been there, and that Jesus had not entered it with his disciples, but that they had gone away alone.

Narrator 1   Then some boats from Tiberias landed near the place where the people had eaten the bread after the Lord had given thanks. Once the crowd realized that neither Jesus nor his disciples were there, they got into the boats and went to Capernaum in search of Jesus.

Cast: **Narrator 1, Narrator 2, Jesus**

Jesus the Bread of Life
John 6:25–35

Narrator   When [the crowd] found [Jesus] on the other side of the lake, they asked him:

Person 1   Rabbi!

Person 2   When did you get here?

Jesus   I tell you the truth, you are looking for me, not because you saw miraculous signs but because you ate the loaves and had your fill. Do not work for food that spoils, but for food that endures to eternal life, which the Son of Man will give you. On him God the Father has placed his seal of approval.

Person 1	What must we do to do the works God requires?
Jesus	The work of God is this: to believe in the one he has sent.
Person 2	What miraculous sign then will you give that we may see it and believe you?
Person 1	What will you do? Our forefathers ate the manna in the desert; as it is written: "He gave them bread from heaven to eat."
Jesus	I tell you the truth, it is not Moses who has given you the bread from heaven, but it is my Father who gives you the true bread from heaven. For the bread of God is he who comes down from heaven and gives life to the world.
Persons 1 and 2	Sir, from now on give us this bread.
Jesus	I am the bread of life. He who comes to me will never go hungry, and he who believes in me will never be thirsty.

Cast: **Narrator, Person 1, Person 2, Jesus**

Life-giving Bread
John 6:41–51 [52–55]

Narrator	The Jews began to grumble about [Jesus] because he said:
Jesus	I am the bread that came down from heaven.
Narrator	They said:
Person 1	Is this not Jesus, the son of Joseph?
Person 2	Whose father and mother we know?
Person 1	How can he now say, "I came down from heaven"?
[Narrator	Jesus answered:]
Jesus	Stop grumbling among yourselves. No one can come to me unless the Father who sent me draws him, and I will raise him up at the last day. It is written in the Prophets: "They will all be taught by God." Everyone who listens to the Father and learns from him comes to me. No one has seen the Father except the one who is from God; only he has seen the Father. I tell you the truth, he who believes has everlasting life. I am the bread of life. Your forefathers ate the manna in the desert, yet they died. But here is the bread that comes down from heaven, which a man may eat and not die. I am the living bread that came down from heaven. If anyone eats of this bread, he will live forever. This bread is my flesh, which I will give for the life of the world.

225

[Narrator	Then the Jews began to argue sharply among themselves:
Person 2	How can this man give us his flesh to eat?
Narrator	Jesus said to them:
Jesus	I tell you the truth, unless you eat the flesh of the Son of Man and drink his blood, you have no life in you. Whoever eats my flesh and drinks my blood has eternal life, and I will raise him up at the last day. For my flesh is real food and my blood is real drink.]

Cast: **Narrator, Jesus, Person 1, Person 2**

Many Disciples Desert Jesus
John 6:56–69 [70–71]

Narrator	[Jesus] said this while teaching in the synagogue in Capernaum:
Jesus	Whoever eats my flesh and drinks my blood remains in me, and I in him. Just as the living Father sent me and I live because of the Father, so the one who feeds on me will live because of me. This is the bread that came down from heaven. Your forefathers ate manna and died, but he who feeds on this bread will live forever.
Narrator	On hearing it, many of his disciples said:
Follower 1	This is a hard teaching.
Follower 2	Who can accept it?
Narrator	Aware that his disciples were grumbling about this, Jesus said to them:
Jesus	Does this offend you? What if you see the Son of Man ascend to where he was before! The Spirit gives life; the flesh counts for nothing. The words I have spoken to you are spirit and they are life. Yet there are some of you who do not believe.
[Narrator	For Jesus had known from the beginning which of them did not believe and who would betray him. He went on to say:]
Jesus	This is why I told you that no one can come to me unless the Father has enabled him.
Narrator	From this time many of his disciples turned back and no longer followed him. Jesus asked the Twelve:
Jesus	You do not want to leave too, do you?
Narrator	Simon Peter answered him:
Peter	Lord, to whom shall we go? You have the words of eternal life. We believe and know that you are the Holy One of God.
[Narrator	Then Jesus replied:
Jesus	Have I not chosen you, the Twelve? Yet one of you is a devil!

Narrator	(He meant Judas, the son of Simon Iscariot, who, though one of the Twelve, was later to betray him.)**]**

Cast: **Narrator, Jesus, Follower 1, Follower 2, Peter** (can be the same as Follower 1)

Jesus Goes to the Feast of Tabernacles
John 7:1–10 [11–13]

Narrator	Jesus went around in Galilee, purposely staying away from Judea because the Jews there were waiting to take his life. But when the Jewish Feast of Tabernacles was near, Jesus' brothers said to him:
Brother 1	You ought to leave here and go to Judea, so that your disciples may see the miracles you do.
Brother 2	No one who wants to become a public figure acts in secret. Since you are doing these things, show yourself to the world.
Narrator	For even his own brothers did not believe in him. Therefore Jesus told them:
Jesus	The right time for me has not yet come; for you any time is right. The world cannot hate you, but it hates me because I testify that what it does is evil. You go to the Feast. I am not yet going up to this Feast, because for me the right time has not yet come.
Narrator	Having said this, he stayed in Galilee. (PAUSE) However, after his brothers had left for the Feast, he went also, not publicly, but in secret. **[**Now at the Feast the Jews were watching for him and asking:
Person 1	Where is that man?
Narrator	Among the crowds there was widespread whispering about him. Some said:
Person 2	He is a good man.
Narrator	Others replied:
Person 1	No, he deceives the people.
Narrator	But no one would say anything publicly about him for fear of the Jews.**]**

Cast: **Narrator, Brother 1, Brother 2, Jesus, [Person 1** (harsh voice), **Person 2** (appreciative voice)**]**. (The bracketed section should be omitted if the next reading is also to be used.)

Jesus Teaches at the Feast
John 7:11–18, 25–31

Narrator	At the Feast the Jews were watching for [Jesus] and asking:
Ruler	Where is that man?

Narrator	Among the crowds there was widespread whispering about him. Some said:
Person 1 (positive voice)	He is a good man.
Narrator	Others replied:
Person 2 (critical voice)	No, he deceives the people.
Narrator	But no one would say anything publicly about him for fear of the Jews. (PAUSE)
	Not until halfway through the Feast did Jesus go up to the temple courts and begin to teach. The Jews were amazed and asked:
Ruler	How did this man get such learning without having studied?
[Narrator	Jesus answered:]
Jesus	My teaching is not my own. It comes from him who sent me. If anyone chooses to do God's will, he will find out whether my teaching comes from God or whether I speak on my own. He who speaks on his own does so to gain honor for himself, but he who works for the honor of the one who sent him is a man of truth; there is nothing false about him. . . . (PAUSE)
Person 1	Isn't this the man they are trying to kill?
Person 2	Here he is, speaking publicly, and they are not saying a word to him.
Person 1	Have the authorities really concluded that he is the Christ?
Person 2	But we know where this man is from; when the Christ comes, no one will know where he is from.
Narrator	Then Jesus, still teaching in the temple courts, cried out:
Jesus (loudly)	Yes, you know me, and you know where I am from. I am not here on my own, but he who sent me is true. You do not know him, but I know him because I am from him and he sent me.
Narrator	At this they tried to seize him, but no one laid a hand on him, because his time had not yet come. Still, many in the crowd put their faith in him. They said:
Person 1	When the Christ comes, will he do more miraculous signs than this man?

Cast: **Narrator, Ruler, Person 1, Person 2** (can be the same as Ruler), **Jesus**

Guards Are Sent to Arrest Jesus
John 7:32–36, 45–52

Narrator	The Pharisees heard the crowd whispering . . . about [Jesus.] Then the chief priests and the Pharisees sent temple guards to arrest him. Jesus said:
Jesus	I am with you for only a short time, and then I go to the one who sent me. You will look for me, but you will not find me; and where I am, you cannot come.
Narrator	The Jews said to one another:
Leader 1	Where does this man intend to go that we cannot find him?
Leader 2	Will he go where our people live scattered among the Greeks, and teach the Greeks?
Leader 1	What did he mean when he said, "You will look for me, but you will not find me," and "Where I am, you cannot come"? . . .
Narrator	Finally the temple guards went back to the chief priests and Pharisees, who asked them:
Pharisee 1	Why didn't you bring him in?
Narrator	The guards declared:
Guard	No one ever spoke the way this man does!
Pharisee 1	You mean he has deceived you also?
Pharisee 2	Has any of the rulers or of the Pharisees believed in him?
Pharisee 1	No! But this mob that knows nothing of the law—there is a curse on them.
Narrator	Nicodemus, who had gone to Jesus earlier and who was one of their own number, asked:
Nicodemus	Does our law condemn anyone without first hearing him to find out what he is doing?
Pharisee 1	Are you from Galilee, too?
Pharisee 2	Look into it, and you will find that a prophet does not come out of Galilee.

Cast: Narrator, Jesus, Leader 1, Leader 2, Pharisee 1, Guard, Pharisee 2, Nicodemus

Streams of Life-giving Water
John 7:37–44

Narrator	On the last and greatest day of the Feast, Jesus stood and said in a loud voice:

Jesus	If anyone is thirsty, let him come to me and drink. Whoever believes in me, as the Scripture has said:
[Scripture]	Streams of living water will flow from within him.
Narrator	By this he meant the Spirit, whom those who believed in him were later to receive. Up to that time the Spirit had not been given, since Jesus had not yet been glorified. On hearing his words, some of the people said:
Person 1	Surely this man is the Prophet.
[Narrator	Others said:]
Person 2	He is the *Christ*.
[Narrator	Still others asked:]
Person 3	How can the Christ come from Galilee? Does not the Scripture say that the Christ will come from David's family and from Bethlehem, the town where David lived?
Narrator	Thus the people were divided because of Jesus. Some wanted to seize him, but no one laid a hand on him.

Cast: **Narrator, Jesus, [Scripture,] Person 1, Person 2, Person 3**

The Woman Caught in Adultery
John 8:2–11

Narrator	At dawn [Jesus] appeared again in the temple courts, where all the people gathered around him, and he sat down to teach them. (PAUSE) The teachers of the law and the Pharisees brought in a woman caught in adultery. They made her stand before the group and said to Jesus:
Pharisee	Teacher, this woman was caught in the act of adultery.
Lawyer	In the Law Moses commanded us to stone such women.
Pharisee	Now what do you say?
Narrator	They were using this question as a trap, in order to have a basis for accusing him.
	But Jesus bent down and started to write on the ground with his finger. When they kept on questioning him, he straightened up and said to them:
Jesus	If any one of you is without sin, let him be the first to throw a stone at her.
Narrator	Again he stooped down and wrote on the ground.

At this, those who heard began to go away one at a time, the older ones first, until only Jesus was left, with the woman still standing there. Jesus straightened up and asked her:

Jesus (to the woman)   Woman, where are they? Has no one condemned you?

Woman   No one, sir.

Jesus   Then neither do I condemn you. Go now and leave your life of sin.

Cast: **Narrator, Pharisee, Lawyer** (can be the same as Pharisee), **Jesus, Woman**

The Validity of Jesus' Testimony
John 8:12–20

Narrator   Jesus spoke again to the people [and] said:

Jesus   I am the light of the world. Whoever follows me will never walk in darkness, but will have the light of life.

Narrator   The Pharisees challenged him:

Pharisee 1   Here you are, appearing as your own witness.

Pharisee 2   Your testimony is not valid.

Jesus   Even if I testify on my own behalf, my testimony is valid, for I know where I came from and where I am going. But you have no idea where I come from or where I am going. You judge by human standards; I pass judgment on no one. But if I do judge, my decisions are right, because I am not alone. I stand with the Father, who sent me. In your own Law it is written that the testimony of two men is valid. I am one who testifies for myself; my other witness is the Father, who sent me.

Pharisee 2   Where *is* your father?

Jesus   You do not know me *or* my Father. If you knew me, you would know my Father also.

Narrator   He spoke these words while teaching in the temple area near the place where the offerings were put. Yet no one seized him, because his time had not yet come.

Cast: **Narrator, Jesus, Pharisee 1, Pharisee 2**

You Cannot Go Where I Am Going
John 8:21–30

Narrator   [In the temple courts Jesus said:]

Jesus   I am going away, and you will look for me, and you will die in your sin. Where I go, you cannot come.

Narrator	This made the Jews ask:
Person 1	Will he kill himself?
Person 2	Is that why he says, "Where I go, you cannot come"?
Jesus	You are from below; I am from above. You are of this world; I am not of this world. I told you that you would die in your sins; if you do not believe that I am ˌthe one I claim to beˌ, you will indeed die in your sins.
Person 1	Who are you?
Jesus	Just what I have been claiming all along. I have much to say in judgment of you. But he who sent me is reliable, and what I have heard from him I tell the world.
Narrator	They did not understand that he was telling them about his Father. So Jesus said:
Jesus	When you have lifted up the Son of Man, then you will know that I am ˌthe one I claim to beˌ and that I do nothing on my own but speak just what the Father has taught me. The one who sent me is with me; he has not left me alone, for I always do what pleases him.
Narrator	Even as he spoke, many put their faith in him.

Cast: **Narrator, Jesus, Person 1, Person 2** (can be the same as Person 1)

The Children of Abraham
John 8:31–36

Narrator	To the Jews who had believed him, Jesus said:
Jesus	If you hold to my teaching, you are really my disciples. Then you will know the truth, and the truth will set you free.
[Narrator	They answered him:]
Believer 1	We are Abraham's descendants and have never been slaves of anyone.
Believer 2	How can you say that we shall be set *free*?
Jesus	I tell you the truth, everyone who sins is a slave to sin. Now a slave has no permanent place in the family, but a son belongs to it forever. So if the Son sets you free, you will be free indeed.

Cast: **Narrator, Jesus, Believer 1, Believer 2** (can be the same as Believer 1)

Jesus and Abraham
John 8:37–59

Narrator	[Jesus said to the Jews:]

232

Jesus	I know you are Abraham's descendants. Yet you are ready to kill me, because you have no room for my word. I am telling you what I have seen in the Father's presence, and you do what you have heard from your father.
[Narrator	They answered:]
Person 1	Abraham is our father.
Jesus	If you were Abraham's children, then you would do the things Abraham did. As it is, you are determined to kill me, a man who has told you the truth that I heard from God. Abraham did not do such things. You are doing the things your own father does.
Person 2	We are not illegitimate children.
Person 1	The only Father we have is God himself.
Jesus	If God were your Father, you would love me, for I came from God and now am here. I have not come on my own; but he sent me. Why is my language not clear to you? Because you are unable to hear what I say. You belong to your father, the devil, and you want to carry out your father's desire. He was a murderer from the beginning, not holding to the truth, for there is no truth in him. When he lies, he speaks his native language, for he is a liar and the father of lies. Yet because I tell the truth, you do not believe me! Can any of you prove me guilty of sin? If I am telling the truth, why don't you believe me? He who belongs to God hears what God says. The reason you do not hear is that you do not belong to God.
[Narrator	The Jews answered him:]
Person 1	Aren't we right in saying that you are a Samaritan—
Person 2	And demon-possessed?
Jesus	I am not possessed by a demon, but I honor my Father and you dishonor me. I am not seeking glory for myself; but there is one who seeks it, and he is the judge. I tell you the truth, if anyone keeps my word, he will never see death.
Person 2	Now we *know* that you are demon-possessed!
Person 1	Abraham died and so did the prophets, yet you say that if anyone keeps your word, he will never taste death.
Person 2	Are you greater than our father Abraham? He died, and so did the prophets. Who do you think you are?
Jesus	If I glorify myself, my glory means nothing. My Father, whom you claim as your God, is the one who glorifies me. Though you do not know him, I know him. If I said I did not, I would be a liar like you, but I do know him and keep his word. Your father Abraham rejoiced at the thought of seeing my day; he saw it and was glad.

233

Person 1	You are not yet fifty years old, and you have seen Abraham?
Jesus (slowly)	I tell you the truth, before Abraham was born, I am!
Narrator	At this, they picked up stones to stone him, but Jesus hid himself, slipping away from the temple grounds.

Cast: **Narrator, Jesus, Person 1, Person 2**

Jesus Heals a Man Born Blind (i)
John 9:1–12

Narrator	As [Jesus] went along, he saw a man blind from birth. His disciples asked him:
Disciple 1	Rabbi, who sinned, that he was born blind?
Disciple 2	This man or his parents?
Jesus	Neither this man nor his parents sinned, but this happened so that the work of God might be displayed in his life. As long as it is day, we must do the work of him who sent me. Night is coming, when no one can work. While I am in the world, I am the light of the world.
Narrator	Having said this, he spit on the ground, made some mud with the saliva, and put it on the man's eyes. [He told him:]
Jesus	Go, wash in the Pool of Siloam.
Narrator	(This word means Sent.) (PAUSE) So the man went and washed, and came home seeing. (PAUSE) His neighbors and those who had formerly seen him begging asked:
Person 1	Isn't this the same man who used to sit and beg?
[Narrator	Some claimed that he was. Others said:]
Person 2	No, he only looks like him.
Narrator	But he himself insisted:
Man	I *am* the man.
[Narrator	They demanded:]
Person 1	How then were your eyes opened?
Man	The man they call Jesus made some mud and put it on my eyes. He told me to go to Siloam and wash. So I went and washed, and then I could see.
Person 2	Where is this man?
Man	I don't know.

Cast: **Narrator, Disciple 1, Disciple 2, Jesus, Person 1, Person 2, Man**

Jesus Heals a Man Born Blind (ii)
John 9:13–25

Narrator	They brought to the Pharisees the man who had been blind. Now the day on which Jesus had made the mud and opened the man's eyes was a Sabbath. Therefore the Pharisees also asked him how he had received his sight.
Man	He put mud on my eyes, and I washed, and now I see.
[Narrator	Some of the Pharisees said:]
Pharisee 1	This man is not from God, for he does not keep the Sabbath.
[Narrator	But others asked:]
Pharisee 2	How can a sinner do such miraculous signs?
Narrator	So they were divided. (PAUSE) Finally they turned again to the blind man:
Pharisee 1	What have you to say about him? It was *your* eyes he opened.
Man	He is a prophet.
Narrator	The Jews still did not believe that he had been blind and had received his sight until they sent for the man's parents.
Pharisee 1 (to Father)	Is this your son?
Pharisee 2	Is this the one you say was born blind? How is it that now he can see?
Father	We know he is our son, and we know he was born blind.
Mother	But how he can see now, or who opened his eyes, we don't know.
Father	Ask him. He is of age; he will speak for himself.
[Narrator	His parents said this because they were afraid of the Jews, for already the Jews had decided that anyone who acknowledged that Jesus was the Christ would be put out of the synagogue. That was why his parents said, "He is of age; ask him."]
	A second time they summoned the man who had been blind.
Pharisee 2	Give glory to God.
Pharisee 1	We know this man is a sinner.
Man (with conviction)	Whether he is a sinner or not, I don't know. One thing I do know. I was blind but now I see!

Cast: **Narrator, Man, Pharisee 1, Pharisee 2, Father, Mother**

Jesus Heals a Man Born Blind (iii)
John 9:26–34

Narrator	[The Pharisees asked the man born blind, whom Jesus had made to see:]
Pharisee 1	What did he do to you?
Pharisee 2	How did he open your eyes?
Narrator	He answered:
Man	I have told you already and you did not listen. Why do you want to hear it again? Do you want to become his disciples, too?
Narrator	Then they hurled insults at him and said:
Pharisee 1	You are this fellow's disciple!
Pharisee 2	We are disciples of Moses!
Pharisee 1	We know that God spoke to Moses, but as for this fellow, we don't even know where he comes from.
Man	Now that is remarkable! You don't know where he comes from, yet he opened my eyes. We know that God does not listen to sinners. He listens to the godly man who does his will. Nobody has ever heard of opening the eyes of a man born blind. If this man were not from God, he could do nothing.
Pharisee 1	You were steeped in sin at birth; how dare you lecture us!
Narrator	And they threw him out.

Cast: **Narrator, Pharisee 1, Pharisee 2, Man**

Spiritual Blindness
John 9:35–41

Narrator	Jesus heard that they had thrown out [the man born blind, whom he had made to see.] When he found him, he said:
Jesus	Do you believe in the Son of Man?
Man	Who is he, sir? Tell me so that I may believe in him.
Jesus	You have now seen him; in fact, he is the one speaking with you.
Man	Lord, I believe.
Narrator	And he worshiped him. Jesus said:
Jesus	For judgment I have come into this world, so that the blind will see and those who see will become blind.
Narrator	Some Pharisees who were with him heard him say this [and asked:]

Pharisee	What? Are we blind too?
Jesus (to Pharisee)	If you were blind, you would not be guilty of sin; but now that you claim you can see, your guilt remains.

Cast: **Narrator, Jesus, Man, Pharisee**

The Shepherd and His Flock
John 10:1–10

Narrator	[Jesus said:]
Jesus	I tell you the truth, the man who does not enter the sheep pen by the gate, but climbs in by some other way, is a thief and a robber. The man who enters by the gate is the shepherd of his sheep. The watchman opens the gate for him, and the sheep listen to his voice. He calls his own sheep by name and leads them out. When he has brought out all his own, he goes on ahead of them, and his sheep follow him because they know his voice. But they will never follow a stranger; in fact, they will run away from him because they do not recognize a stranger's voice.
Narrator	Jesus used this figure of speech, but they did not understand what he was telling them.
	Therefore Jesus said again:
Jesus	I tell you the truth, I am the gate for the sheep. All who ever came before me were thieves and robbers, but the sheep did not listen to them. I am the gate; whoever enters through me will be saved. He will come in and go out, and find pasture. The thief comes only to steal and kill and destroy; I have come that they may have life, and have it to the full.

Cast: **Narrator, Jesus**

Jesus the Good Shepherd
John 10:[11–13], 14–21

Narrator	[Jesus said:]
Jesus	[I am the good shepherd. The good shepherd lays down his life for the sheep. The hired hand is not the shepherd who owns the sheep. So when he sees the wolf coming, he abandons the sheep and runs away. Then the wolf attacks the flock and scatters it. The man runs away because he is a hired hand and cares nothing for the sheep.]
	I am the good shepherd; I know my sheep and my sheep know me— just as the Father knows me and I know the Father—and I lay down my life for the sheep. I have other sheep that are not of this sheep pen. I must bring them also. They too will listen to my voice, and there shall

be one flock and one shepherd. (PAUSE) The reason my Father loves me is that I lay down my life—only to take it up again. No one takes it from me, but I lay it down of my own accord. I have authority to lay it down and authority to take it up again. This command I received from my Father.

Narrator   At these words the Jews were again divided. [Many of them said:]

Person 1   He is demon-possessed.

Person 2   And raving mad.

Person 1   Why listen to him?

[Narrator   But others said:]

Person 3   These are not the sayings of a man possessed by a demon.

Person 4   Can a demon open the eyes of the blind?

Cast: **Narrator, Jesus, Person 1, Person 2, Person 3, Person 4**

The Unbelief of the Jews
John 10:22–42

Narrator   Then came the Feast of Dedication at Jerusalem. It was winter, and Jesus was in the temple area walking in Solomon's Colonnade. The Jews gathered around him, saying:

Person 1   How long will you keep us in suspense?

Person 2   If you are the Christ, tell us plainly.

Jesus   I did tell you, but you do not believe. The miracles I do in my Father's name speak for me, but you do not believe because you are not my sheep. My sheep listen to my voice; I know them, and they follow me. I give them eternal life, and they shall never perish; no one can snatch them out of my hand. My Father, who has given them to me, is greater than all; no one can snatch them out of my Father's hand. I and the Father are one.

Narrator   Again the Jews picked up stones to stone him, [but Jesus said to them:]

Jesus   I have shown you many great miracles from the Father. For which of these do you stone me?

Person 1   We are not stoning you for any of these, but for blasphemy.

Person 2   Because you, a mere man, claim to be God.

Jesus   Is it not written in your Law, "I have said you are gods"? If he called them "gods," to whom the word of God came—and the Scripture cannot be broken—what about the one whom the Father set apart as his very own and sent into the world? Why then do you accuse me of blasphemy because I said, "I am God's Son"? Do not believe me unless I do what my Father does. But if I do it, even though you do not believe me, believe the miracles, that you may know and understand that the Father is in me, and I in the Father.

Narrator   Again they tried to seize him, but he escaped their grasp. (PAUSE)

Then Jesus went back across the Jordan to the place where John had been baptizing in the early days. Here he stayed and many people came to him. They said:

Person 3   Though John never performed a miraculous sign, all that John said about this man was true.

Narrator   And in that place many believed in Jesus.

Cast: **Narrator, Person 1, Person 2, Jesus, Person 3**

The Death of Lazarus
From John 11:1–44

Narrator   Now a man named Lazarus was sick. He was from Bethany, the village of Mary and her sister Martha. This Mary, whose brother Lazarus now lay sick, was the same one who poured perfume on the Lord and wiped his feet with her hair. So the sisters sent word to Jesus:

Mary   Lord, the one you love is sick.

Narrator   When he heard this, Jesus said:

Jesus   This sickness will not end in death. No, it is for God's glory so that God's Son may be glorified through it.

Narrator   Jesus loved Martha and her sister and Lazarus. Yet when he heard that Lazarus was sick, he stayed where he was two more days. Then he said to his disciples:

Jesus   Let us go back to Judea. . . . Our friend Lazarus has fallen asleep; but I am going there to wake him up. (PAUSE)

Narrator   . . . On his arrival, Jesus found that Lazarus had already been in the tomb for four days. . . . When Martha heard that Jesus was coming, she went out to meet him, but Mary stayed at home. Martha said to Jesus:

Martha   Lord, if you had been here, my brother would not have died. But I know that even now God will give you whatever you ask.

Jesus   Your brother will rise again.

Martha   I know he will rise again—in the resurrection at the last day.

Jesus	I am the resurrection and the life. He who believes in me will live, even though he dies; and whoever lives and believes in me will never die. Do you believe this?
Martha	Yes, Lord. I believe that you are the Christ, the Son of God, who was to come into the world.
Narrator	And after she had said this, she went back and called her sister Mary aside.
Martha (to Mary)	The Teacher is here and is asking for you.
Narrator	When Mary heard this, she got up quickly and went to him. Now Jesus had not yet entered the village, but was still at the place where Martha had met him. When the Jews who had been with Mary in the house, comforting her, noticed how quickly she got up and went out, they followed her, supposing she was going to the tomb to mourn there. (PAUSE)
	When Mary reached the place where Jesus was and saw him, she fell at his feet and said:
Mary	Lord, if you had been here, my brother would not have died.
Narrator	When Jesus saw her weeping, and the Jews who had come along with her also weeping, he was deeply moved in spirit and troubled.
Jesus	Where have you laid him?
Mary and **Martha**	Come and see, Lord.
Narrator (slowly)	Jesus wept.
	Then the Jews said:
Person 1	See how he loved him!
Narrator	But some of them said:
Person 2	Could not he who opened the eyes of the blind man have kept this man from dying?
Narrator	Jesus, once more deeply moved, came to the tomb. It was a cave with a stone laid across the entrance.
Jesus	Take away the stone.
Martha	But, Lord, by this time there is a bad odor, for he has been there four days.
Jesus	Did I not tell you that if you believed, you would see the glory of God?
Narrator	So they took away the stone. Then Jesus looked up and said:

Jesus	Father, I thank you that you have heard me. I knew that you always hear me, but I said this for the benefit of the people standing here, that they may believe that you sent me. (PAUSE)
Narrator	When he had said this, Jesus called in a loud voice:
Jesus (loudly)	Lazarus, come out!
Narrator	The dead man came out, his hands and feet wrapped with strips of linen, and a cloth around his face. Jesus said to them:
Jesus	Take off the grave clothes and let him go.

Cast: **Narrator, Mary, Jesus, Martha, Person 1, Person 2**

The Plot to Kill Jesus
John 11:45–57

Narrator	Many of the Jews who had come to visit Mary, and had seen what Jesus did, put their faith in him. But some of them went to the Pharisees and told them what Jesus had done. Then the chief priests and the Pharisees called a meeting of the Sanhedrin.
Chief priest	What are we accomplishing?
Pharisee	Here is this man performing many miraculous signs. If we let him go on like this, everyone will believe in him—
Chief priest	And then the Romans will come and take away both our place and our nation.
Narrator	Then one of them, named Caiaphas, who was high priest that year, spoke up:
Caiaphas	You know nothing at all! You do not realize that it is better for you that one man die for the people than that the whole nation perish.
Narrator	He did not say this on his own, but as high priest that year he prophesied that Jesus would die for the Jewish nation, and not only for that nation but also for the scattered children of God, to bring them together and make them one. So from that day on they plotted to take his life.
	Therefore Jesus no longer moved about publicly among the Jews. Instead he withdrew to a region near the desert, to a village called Ephraim, where he stayed with his disciples.
	When it was almost time for the Jewish Passover, many went up from the country to Jerusalem for their ceremonial cleansing before the Passover. They kept looking for Jesus, and as they stood in the temple area they asked one another:
Person	What do you think? Isn't he coming to the Feast at all?

| Narrator | But the chief priests and Pharisees had given orders that if anyone found out where Jesus was, he should report it so that they might arrest him. |

Cast: **Narrator, Chief priest, Pharisee, Caiaphas, Person**

Jesus Anointed at Bethany
John 12:1–8 [9–11]

Narrator	Six days before the Passover, Jesus arrived at Bethany, where Lazarus lived, whom Jesus had raised from the dead. Here a dinner was given in Jesus' honor. Martha served, while Lazarus was among those reclining at the table with him. Then Mary took about a pint of pure nard, an expensive perfume; she poured it on Jesus' feet and wiped his feet with her hair. And the house was filled with the fragrance of the perfume.
	But one of his disciples, Judas Iscariot, who was later to betray him, objected:
Judas	Why wasn't this perfume sold and the money given to the poor? It was worth a year's wages.
Narrator	He did not say this because he cared about the poor but because he was a thief; as keeper of the money bag, he used to help himself to what was put into it. [But Jesus said:]
Jesus	Leave her alone. ˌIt was intendedˌ that she should save this perfume for the day of my burial. You will always have the poor among you, but you will not always have me.
[Narrator	Meanwhile a large crowd of Jews found out that Jesus was there and came, not only because of him but also to see Lazarus, whom he had raised from the dead. So the chief priests made plans to kill Lazarus as well, for on account of him many of the Jews were going over to Jesus and putting their faith in him.]

Cast: **Narrator, Judas, Jesus**

The Triumphal Entry
John 12:12–19

Narrator	The great crowd that had come for the Feast heard that Jesus was on his way to Jerusalem. They took palm branches and went out to meet him, shouting:
Persons 1 and 2	Hosanna!
Person 1	Blessed is he who comes in the name of the Lord!
Person 2	Blessed is the King of Israel!

Narrator	Jesus found a young donkey and sat upon it, as it is written:

Zechariah
Do not be afraid, Daughter of Zion;
   see, your king is coming,
    seated on a donkey's colt.

Narrator
At first his disciples did not understand all this. Only after Jesus was glorified did they realize that these things had been written about him and that they had done these things to him.

Now the crowd that was with him when he called Lazarus from the tomb and raised him from the dead continued to spread the word. Many people, because they had heard that he had given this miraculous sign, went out to meet him. So the Pharisees said to one another:

Pharisee 1
See, this is getting us nowhere.

Pharisee 2
Look how the whole world has gone after him!

Cast: **Narrator, Person 1, Person 2, Zechariah** (can be the same as Narrator), **Pharisee 1, Pharisee 2** (can be the same as Pharisee 1)

Jesus Predicts His Death

John 12:20–26

Narrator
Now there were some Greeks among those who went up to worship at the Feast. They came to Philip, who was from Bethsaida in Galilee, with a request.

Greeks 1
and 2
Sir—

Greek 2
We would like to see Jesus.

Narrator
Philip went to tell Andrew; Andrew and Philip in turn told Jesus. Jesus replied:

Jesus
The hour has come for the Son of Man to be glorified. I tell you the truth, unless a kernel of wheat falls to the ground and dies, it remains only a single seed. But if it dies, it produces many seeds. The man who loves his life will lose it, while the man who hates his life in this world will keep it for eternal life. Whoever serves me must follow me; and where I am, my servant also will be. My Father will honor the one who serves me.

Cast: **Narrator, Greek 1, Greek 2** (can be the same as Greek 1), **Jesus**

Jesus Speaks about His Death
John 12:27–36

Jesus   Now my heart is troubled, and what shall I say? "Father, save me from this hour"? No, it was for this very reason I came to this hour. Father, glorify your name!

Narrator   Then a voice came from heaven:

Voice   I have glorified it, and will glorify it again.

Narrator   The crowd that was there and heard it said it had thundered; others said an angel had spoken to him. Jesus said:

Jesus   This voice was for your benefit, not mine. Now is the time for judgment on this world; now the prince of this world will be driven out. But I, when I am lifted up from the earth, will draw all men to myself.

Narrator   He said this to show the kind of death he was going to die. The crowd spoke up:

Person 1   We have heard from the Law that the Christ will remain forever.

Person 2   So how can you say, "The Son of Man must be lifted up"?

Person 1   Who is this "Son of Man"?

Jesus   You are going to have the light just a little while longer. Walk while you have the light, before darkness overtakes you. The man who walks in the dark does not know where he is going. Put your trust in the light while you have it, so that you may become sons of light.

Cast: **Jesus, Narrator, Voice, Person 1, Person 2**

The Jews Continue in Their Unbelief
John 12:36–43

Narrator   When he had finished speaking, Jesus left and hid himself from [the crowd.]

Even after [he] had done all these miraculous signs in their presence, they still would not believe in him. This was to fulfill the word of Isaiah the prophet:

Isaiah   Lord, who has believed our message
    and to whom has the arm of the Lord been revealed?

Narrator   For this reason they could not believe, because, as Isaiah says elsewhere:

Isaiah   He has blinded their eyes
    and deadened their hearts,
so they can neither see with their eyes,
    nor understand with their hearts,
    nor turn—and I would heal them.

Narrator	Isaiah said this because he saw Jesus' glory and spoke about him.
	Yet at the same time many even among the leaders believed in him. But because of the Pharisees they would not confess their faith for fear they would be put out of the synagogue; for they loved praise from men more than praise from God.

Cast: **Narrator, Isaiah**

Jesus Washes His Disciples' Feet
John 13:1–15 [16–20]

Narrator	It was just before the Passover Feast. Jesus knew that the time had come for him to leave this world and go to the Father. Having loved his own who were in the world, he now showed them the full extent of his love.
	The evening meal was being served, and the devil had already prompted Judas Iscariot, son of Simon, to betray Jesus. Jesus knew that the Father had put all things under his power, and that he had come from God and was returning to God; so he got up from the meal, took off his outer clothing, and wrapped a towel around his waist. After that, he poured water into a basin and began to wash his disciples' feet, drying them with the towel that was wrapped around him. He came to Simon Peter, who said to him:
Peter	Lord, are *you* going to wash *my* feet?
[Narrator	Jesus replied:]
Jesus	You do not realize now what I am doing, but later you will understand.
Peter	No, *you* shall never wash my feet.
Narrator	Jesus answered:
Jesus	Unless I *wash* you, you have no part with me.
Peter	Then, Lord, not just my feet but my hands and my head as well!
Jesus	A person who has had a bath needs only to wash his feet; his whole body is clean. And you are clean, though not every one of you.
Narrator	For he knew who was going to betray him, and that was why he said not every one was clean. (PAUSE)
	When he had finished washing their feet, he put on his clothes and returned to his place.
Jesus	Do you understand what I have done for you? You call me "Teacher" and "Lord," and rightly so, for that is what I am. Now that I, your Lord and Teacher, have washed your feet, you also should wash one another's feet. I have set you an example that you should do as I have done for you. (PAUSE) **[I tell you the truth, no servant is greater than his**

245

master, nor is a messenger greater than the one who sent him. Now that you know these things, you will be blessed if you do them.

I am not referring to all of you; I know those I have chosen. But this is to fulfill the scripture: "He who shares my bread has lifted up his heel against me."

I am telling you now before it happens, so that when it does happen you will believe that I am He. I tell you the truth, whoever accepts anyone I send accepts me; and whoever accepts me accepts the one who sent me.]

Cast: **Narrator, Peter, Jesus**

Jesus Predicts His Betrayal
John 13:21–30

Narrator   Jesus was troubled in spirit and testified:

Jesus   I tell you the truth, one of you is going to betray me.

Narrator   His disciples stared at one another, at a loss to know which of them he meant. One of them, the disciple whom Jesus loved, was reclining next to him. Simon Peter motioned to this disciple and said:

Peter (to John)   Ask him which one he means.

Narrator   Leaning back against Jesus, he asked him:

John (to Jesus)   Lord, who is it?

Jesus   It is the one to whom I will give this piece of bread when I have dipped it in the dish.

Narrator   Then, dipping the piece of bread, he gave it to Judas Iscariot, son of Simon. As soon as Judas took the bread, Satan entered into him. Jesus told him:

Jesus   What you are about to do, do quickly.

Narrator   But no one at the meal understood why Jesus said this to him. Since Judas had charge of the money, some thought Jesus was telling him to buy what was needed for the Feast, or to give something to the poor. As soon as Judas had taken the bread, he went out. (PAUSE) And it was night.

Cast: **Narrator, Jesus, Peter, John**

Jesus Predicts Peter's Denial
John 13:31–38

Narrator   When [Judas] was gone, Jesus said:

Jesus	Now is the Son of Man glorified and God is glorified in him. If God is glorified in him, God will glorify the Son in himself, and will glorify him at once.
	My children, I will be with you only a little longer. You will look for me, and just as I told the Jews, so I tell you now: Where I am going, you cannot come.
	A new command I give you: Love one another. As I have loved you, so you must love one another. By this all men will know that you are my disciples, if you love one another.
[Narrator	Simon Peter asked him:]
Peter	Lord, where are you going?
Jesus	Where I am going, you cannot follow now, but you will follow later.
Peter	Lord, why can't I follow you now? I will lay down my life for you.
Jesus	Will you really lay down your life for me? I tell you the truth, before the rooster crows, you will disown me three times!

Cast: **Narrator, Jesus, Peter**

Jesus the Way to the Father
John 14:1–11

Narrator	[Jesus told his disciples:]
Jesus	Do not let your hearts be troubled. Trust in God; trust also in me. In my Father's house are many rooms; if it were not so, I would have told you. I am going there to prepare a place for you. And if I go and prepare a place for you, I will come back and take you to be with me that you also may be where I am. You know the way to the place where I am going.
Narrator	Thomas said to him:
Thomas	Lord, we don't know where you are going, so how can we know the way?
Jesus	I am the way and the truth and the life. No one comes to the Father except through me. If you really knew me, you would know my Father as well. From now on, you do know him and have seen him.
Narrator	Philip said:
Philip	Lord, show us the Father and that will be enough for us.
Jesus	Don't you know me, Philip, even after I have been among you such a long time? Anyone who has seen me has seen the Father. How can you say, "Show us the Father"? Don't you believe that I am in the Father, and that the Father is in me? The words I say to you are not just my own. Rather, it is the Father, living in me, who is doing his work. Believe

247

me when I say that I am in the Father and the Father is in me; or at least believe on the evidence of the miracles themselves.

Cast: **Narrator, Jesus, Thomas, Philip.** (This reading is included in the next.)

Jesus Comforts His Disciples
From John 14:1–26 [27–31]

Jesus	Do not let your hearts be troubled. Trust in God; trust also in me. In my Father's house are many rooms; if it were not so, I would have told you. I am going there to prepare a place for you. And if I go and prepare a place for you, I will come back and take you to be with me that you also may be where I am. You know the way to the place where I am going.
Thomas	Lord, we don't know where you are going, so how can we know the way?
Jesus	I am the way and the truth and the life. No one comes to the Father except through me. If you really knew me, you would know my Father as well. From now on, you do know him and have seen him.
Philip	Lord, show us the Father and that will be enough for us.
Jesus	Don't you know me, Philip, even after I have been among you such a long time? Anyone who has seen me has seen the Father. How can you say, "Show us the Father"? Don't you believe that I am in the Father, and that the Father is in me? The words I say to you are not just my own. Rather, it is the Father, living in me, who is doing his work. Believe me when I say that I am in the Father and the Father is in me; or at least believe on the evidence of the miracles themselves. I tell you the truth, anyone who has faith in me will do what I have been doing. He will do even greater things than these, because I am going to the Father. And I will do whatever you ask in my name, so that the Son may bring glory to the Father. You may ask me for anything in my name, and I will do it.
	If you love me, you will obey what I command. And I will ask the Father, and he will give you another Counselor to be with you forever—the Spirit of truth. . . . I will not leave you as orphans; I will come to you. . . . On that day you will realize that I am in my Father, and you are in me, and I am in you. . . . He who loves me will be loved by my Father, and I too will love him and show myself to him.
Judas	But, Lord, why do you intend to show yourself to us and not to the world?
Jesus	If anyone loves me, he will obey my teaching. My Father will love him, and we will come to him and make our home with him. (PAUSE) He who does not love me will not obey my teaching. These words you hear are not my own; they belong to the Father who sent me.
	All this I have spoken while still with you. But the Counselor, the Holy Spirit, whom the Father will send in my name, will teach you all things

and will remind you of everything I have said to you. [Peace I leave with you; my peace I give you. I do not give to you as the world gives. Do not let your hearts be troubled and do not be afraid.

You heard me say, "I am going away and I am coming back to you." If you loved me, you would be glad that I am going to the Father, for the Father is greater than I. I have told you now before it happens, so that when it does happen you will believe. I will not speak with you much longer, for the prince of this world is coming. He has no hold on me, but the world must learn that I love the Father and that I do exactly what my Father has commanded me. (PAUSE) Come now; let us leave.]

Cast: **Jesus, Thomas, Philip, Judas** (not Judas Iscariot), (Thomas, Philip, and Judas can all be the same person.) A shortened version of this reading is on pages 247–48.

The Disciples' Grief Will Turn to Joy
John 16:16–24

Narrator   [Jesus was talking to his disciples:]

Jesus   In a little while you will see me no more, and then after a little while you will see me.

Narrator   Some of his disciples said to one another:

Disciple 1   What does he mean?

Disciple 2   [He says,] "In a little while you will see me no more, and then after a little while you will see me."

Disciple 1   And, "Because I am going to the Father."

Disciple 2   What does he mean by "a little while"?

Disciple 1   We don't understand what he is saying.

Narrator   Jesus saw that they wanted to ask him about this, so he said to them:

Jesus   Are you asking one another what I meant when I said, "In a little while you will see me no more, and then after a little while you will see me"? I tell you the truth, you will weep and mourn while the world rejoices. You will grieve, but your grief will turn to joy. A woman giving birth to a child has pain because her time has come; but when her baby is born she forgets the anguish because of her joy that a child is born into the world. So with you: Now is your time of grief, but I will see you again and you will rejoice, and no one will take away your joy. In that day you will no longer ask me anything. I tell you the truth, my Father will give you whatever you ask in my name. Until now you have not asked for anything in my name. Ask and you will receive, and your joy will be complete.

Cast: **Narrator, Jesus, Disciple 1, Disciple 2**

Jesus Speaks of Victory over the World
John 16:25–33

[Narrator   Jesus said to his disciples:]

Jesus   Though I have been speaking figuratively, a time is coming when I will no longer use this kind of language but will tell you plainly about my Father. In that day you will ask in my name. I am not saying that I will ask the Father on your behalf. No, the Father himself loves you because you have loved me and have believed that I came from God. I came from the Father and entered the world; now I am leaving the world and going back to the Father.

[Narrator   Then Jesus' disciples said:]

Disciple 1   Now you are speaking clearly and without figures of speech.

Disciple 2   Now we can see that you know all things and that you do not even need to have anyone ask you questions.

Disciple 1   This makes us believe that you came from God.

Jesus   You believe at last! But a time is coming, and has come, when you will be scattered, each to his own home. You will leave me all alone. Yet I am not alone, for my Father is with me

I have told you these things, so that in me you may have peace. In this world you will have trouble. But take heart! I have overcome the world.

Cast: **Narrator, Jesus, Disciple 1, Disciple 2**

Jesus Arrested
John 18:1–13

Narrator   When he had finished praying, Jesus left with his disciples and crossed the Kidron Valley. On the other side there was an olive grove, and he and his disciples went into it.

Now Judas, who betrayed him, knew the place, because Jesus had often met there with his disciples. So Judas came to the grove, guiding a detachment of soldiers and some officials from the chief priests and Pharisees. They were carrying torches, lanterns and weapons. Jesus, knowing all that was going to happen to him, went out [and asked them:]

Jesus   Who is it you want?

Soldier 1   Jesus of Nazareth.

Jesus   I am he.

Narrator   (Judas the traitor was standing there with them.) When Jesus said, "I am he," they drew back and fell to the ground. Again he asked them:

Jesus   Who is it you want?

Soldier 2	Jesus of Nazareth.
Jesus	I told you that I am he. If you are looking for me, then let these men go.
Narrator	This happened so that the words he had spoken would be fulfilled: "I have not lost one of those you gave me."
	Then Simon Peter, who had a sword, drew it and struck the high priest's servant, cutting off his right ear. (The servant's name was Malchus.) [Jesus commanded Peter:]
Jesus	Put your sword away! Shall I not drink the cup the Father has given me?
Narrator	Then the detachment of soldiers with its commander and the Jewish officials arrested Jesus. They bound him and brought him first to Annas, who was the father-in-law of Caiaphas, the high priest that year.

Cast: **Narrator, Jesus, Soldier 1, Soldier 2** (can be the same as Soldier 1)

Peter Disowns Jesus
John 18:[12–14], 15–27

Narrator	[The detachment of soldiers with its commander and the Jewish officials arrested Jesus. They bound him and brought him first to Annas, who was the father-in-law of Caiaphas, the high priest that year. Caiaphas was the one who had advised the Jews that it would be good if one man died for the people.]
	Simon Peter and another disciple were following Jesus. Because this disciple was known to the high priest, he went with Jesus into the high priest's courtyard, but Peter had to wait outside at the door. The other disciple, who was known to the high priest, came back, spoke to the girl on duty there and brought Peter in. The girl at the door asked Peter:
Girl (to Peter)	You are not one of his disciples, are you?
Peter	I am not.
Narrator	It was cold, and the servants and officials stood around a fire they had made to keep warm. Peter also was standing with them, warming himself. (PAUSE)
	Meanwhile, the high priest questioned Jesus about his disciples and his teaching. Jesus replied:
Jesus	I have spoken openly to the world. I always taught in synagogues or at the temple, where all the Jews come together. I said nothing in secret. Why question me? Ask those who heard me. Surely they know what I said.
Narrator	When Jesus said this, one of the officials nearby struck him in the face.
Guard	Is this the way you answer the high priest?

251

Jesus	If I said something wrong, testify as to what is wrong. But if I spoke the truth, why did you strike me?
Narrator	Then Annas sent him, still bound, to Caiaphas the high priest. (PAUSE)
	As Simon Peter stood warming himself, he was asked:
Person 1 (to Peter)	You are not one of his disciples, are you?
Narrator	[Peter] denied it, saying:
Peter	I am not.
Narrator	One of the high priest's servants, a relative of the man whose ear Peter had cut off, challenged him:
Person 2 (to Peter)	Didn't I see you with him in the olive grove?
Peter	[No]!
Narrator (slowly)	And at that moment a rooster began to crow.

Cast: **Narrator, Girl, Peter, Jesus, Guard, Person 1, Person 2**

Jesus before Pilate
John 18:28–19:16

Narrator	The Jews led Jesus from Caiaphas to the palace of the Roman governor. By now it was early morning, and to avoid ceremonial uncleanness the Jews did not enter the palace; they wanted to be able to eat the Passover. So Pilate came out to them and asked:
Pilate	What charges are you bringing against this man?
Priest	If he were not a criminal, we would not have handed him over to you.
Pilate	Take him yourselves and judge him by your own law.
Person 1	But we have no right to execute anyone. (PAUSE)
Narrator	This happened so that the words Jesus had spoken indicating the kind of death he was going to die would be fulfilled.
	Pilate then went back inside the palace, summoned Jesus and asked him:
Pilate	Are you the king of the Jews?
[Narrator	Jesus asked:]
Jesus	Is that your own idea, or did others talk to you about me?
Pilate	Am I a Jew? It was your people and your chief priests who handed you over to me. What is it you have done?

Jesus	My kingdom is not of this world. If it were, my servants would fight to prevent my arrest by the Jews. But now my kingdom is from another place.
Pilate	You are a king, then! (PAUSE)
Jesus	You are right in saying I am a king. In fact, for this reason I was born, and for this I came into the world, to testify to the truth. Everyone on the side of truth listens to me.
Pilate (slowly)	What is truth? (PAUSE)
Narrator	With this [Pilate] went out again to the Jews and said:
Pilate	I find no basis for a charge against him. But it is your custom for me to release to you one prisoner at the time of the Passover. Do you want me to release "the king of the Jews"?
Person 1	No, not him!
Person 2	Give us Barabbas!
Narrator (slowly)	Now Barabbas had taken part in a rebellion. (PAUSE)
	Then Pilate took Jesus and had him flogged. The soldiers twisted together a crown of thorns and put it on his head. They clothed him in a purple robe and went up to him again and again, saying:
Soldiers 1 and 2	Hail, king of the Jews!
Narrator	And they struck him in the face.
	Once more Pilate came out and said to the Jews:
Pilate	Look, I am bringing him out to you to let you know that I find no basis for a charge against him.
Narrator	When Jesus came out wearing the crown of thorns and the purple robe, Pilate said to them:
Pilate	Here is the man!
Narrator	As soon as the chief priests and their officials saw him, they shouted:
Priest	Crucify!
Soldiers 1 and 2	Crucify!
Pilate	You take him and crucify him. As for me, I find no basis for a charge against him.
Person 1	We have a law, and according to that law he must die, because he claimed to be the Son of God.

253

Narrator	When Pilate heard this, he was even more afraid, and he went back inside the palace.
Pilate	Where do you come from?
Narrator	But Jesus gave him no answer. (PAUSE)
Pilate	Do you refuse to speak to me? Don't you realize I have power either to free you or to crucify you?
Jesus	You would have no power over me if it were not given to you from above. Therefore the one who handed me over to you is guilty of a greater sin.
Narrator	From then on, Pilate tried to set Jesus free, but the Jews kept shouting:
Person 2	If you let this man go, you are no friend of Caesar.
Person 1	Anyone who claims to be a king opposes Caesar.
Narrator	When Pilate heard this, he brought Jesus out and sat down on the judge's seat at a place known as the Stone Pavement (which in Aramaic is Gabbatha). It was the day of Preparation of Passover Week, about the sixth hour.
Pilate (to all)	Here is your king.
Persons 1 and 2	Take him away!
Soldiers 1 and 2	Take him away!
Priest	Crucify him!
Pilate	Shall I crucify your king?
Priest	We have no king but Caesar.
Narrator	Finally Pilate handed him over to them to be crucified. (PAUSE) So the soldiers took charge of Jesus.

Cast: **Narrator, Pilate, Priest, Person 1, Jesus, Person 2** (can be the same as Person 1), **Soldier 1, Soldier 2** (Soldiers 1 and 2 can also be Persons 1 and 2)

The Crucifixion
John 19:17–30

Narrator	Carrying his own cross, [Jesus] went out to the place of the Skull (which in Aramaic is called Golgotha). Here they crucified him, and with him two others—one on each side and Jesus in the middle.
	Pilate had a notice prepared and fastened to the cross. It read:
Pilate	JESUS OF NAZARETH, THE KING OF THE JEWS.

Narrator	Many of the Jews read this sign, for the place where Jesus was crucified was near the city, and the sign was written in Aramaic, Latin and Greek. The chief priests of the Jews protested to Pilate:
Priest	Do not write "The King of the Jews," but that this man claimed to be king of the Jews.
Pilate	What I have written, I have written.
Narrator	When the soldiers crucified Jesus, they took his clothes, dividing them into four shares, one for each of them, with the undergarment remaining. This garment was seamless, woven in one piece from top to bottom. [They said to one another:]
Soldier 1 (to Soldier 2)	Let's not tear it.
Soldier 2 (to Soldier 1)	Let's decide by lot who will get it.
Narrator	This happened that the scripture might be fulfilled which said:
Psalmist	They divided my garments among them and cast lots for my clothing.
Narrator	So this is what the soldiers did. (PAUSE) Near the cross of Jesus stood his mother, his mother's sister, Mary the wife of Clopas, and Mary Magdalene. When Jesus saw his mother there, and the disciple whom he loved standing nearby, he said to his mother:
Jesus	Dear woman, here is your son.
Narrator	And to the disciple:
Jesus	Here is your mother.
Narrator	From that time on, this disciple took her into his home. (PAUSE) Later, knowing that all was now completed, and so that the Scripture would be fulfilled, Jesus said:
Jesus	I am thirsty.
Narrator	A jar of wine vinegar was there, so they soaked a sponge in it, put the sponge on a stalk of the hyssop plant, and lifted it to Jesus' lips. When he had received the drink, Jesus said:
Jesus	It is finished. (PAUSE)
Narrator	With that, he bowed his head and gave up his spirit.

Cast: **Narrator**, **Pilate**, **Priest**, **Soldier 1**, **Soldier 2**, **Psalmist** (can be the same as Priest), **Jesus**

The Burial of Jesus
John 19:31–42

Narrator   It was the day of Preparation, and the next day was to be a special Sabbath. Because the Jews did not want the bodies left on the crosses during the Sabbath, they asked Pilate to have the legs broken and the bodies taken down. The soldiers therefore came and broke the legs of the first man who had been crucified with Jesus, and then those of the other. But when they came to Jesus and found that he was already dead, they did not break his legs. Instead, one of the soldiers pierced Jesus' side with a spear, bringing a sudden flow of blood and water.

Witness   The man who saw it has given testimony, and his testimony is true. He knows that he tells the truth, and he testifies so that you also may believe.

Narrator   These things happened so that the scripture would be fulfilled:

Scripture 1   Not one of his bones will be broken.

Narrator   And, as another scripture says:

Scripture 2   They will look on the one they have pierced.

Narrator   Later, Joseph of Arimathea asked Pilate for the body of Jesus.

Witness   Now Joseph was a disciple of Jesus, but secretly because he feared the Jews.

Narrator   With Pilate's permission, he came and took the body away. He was accompanied by Nicodemus, the man who earlier had visited Jesus at night. Nicodemus brought a mixture of myrrh and aloes, about seventy-five pounds. Taking Jesus' body, the two of them wrapped it, with the spices, in strips of linen. This was in accordance with Jewish burial customs. At the place where Jesus was crucified, there was a garden, and in the garden a new tomb, in which no one had ever been laid. Because it was the Jewish day of Preparation and since the tomb was nearby, they laid Jesus there.

Cast: **Narrator, Witness, Scripture 1, Scripture 2** (can be the same as Scripture 1)

The Empty Tomb
John 20:1–18

Narrator   Early on the first day of the week, while it was still dark, Mary Magdalene went to the tomb and saw that the stone had been removed from the entrance. So she came running to Simon Peter and the other disciple, the one Jesus loved, and said:

Mary   They have taken the Lord out of the tomb, and we don't know where they have put him!

Narrator	So Peter and the other disciple started for the tomb. Both were running, but the other disciple outran Peter and reached the tomb first. He bent over and looked in at the strips of linen lying there but did not go in. Then Simon Peter, who was behind him, arrived and went into the tomb. He saw the strips of linen lying there, as well as the burial cloth that had been around Jesus' head. The cloth was folded up by itself, separate from the linen. Finally the other disciple, who had reached the tomb first, also went inside. He saw and believed.
Commentator	(They still did not understand from Scripture that Jesus had to rise from the dead.)
Narrator	Then the disciples went back to their homes. (PAUSE) But Mary stood outside the tomb crying. As she wept, she bent over to look into the tomb and saw two angels in white, seated where Jesus' body had been, one at the head and the other at the foot. They asked her:
Angel(s)	Woman, why are you crying?
Mary	They have taken my Lord away, and I don't know where they have put him.
Narrator	At this, she turned around and saw Jesus standing there, but she did not realize that it was Jesus.
Jesus	Woman, why are you crying? Who is it you are looking for?
Narrator	Thinking he was the gardener, she said:
Mary	Sir, if you have carried him away, tell me where you have put him, and I will get him.
Jesus	Mary.
Mary	Rabboni! Teacher!
Jesus	Do not hold on to me, for I have not yet returned to the Father. Go instead to my brothers and tell them, "I am returning to my Father and your Father, to my God and your God."
Narrator	Mary Magdalene went to the disciples with the news, "I have seen the Lord!" And she told them that he had said these things to her.

Cast: **Narrator, Mary, Commentator, Angel(s), Jesus**

Jesus Appears to His Disciples
John 20:19–23

Narrator	On the evening of that first day of the week, when the disciples were together, with the doors locked for fear of the Jews, Jesus came and stood among them and said:
Jesus	Peace be with you!

Narrator	After he said this, he showed them his hands and side. The disciples were overjoyed when they saw the Lord. [Again Jesus said:]
Jesus	Peace be with you! As the Father has sent me, I am sending you.
Narrator	And with that he breathed on them [and said:]
Jesus	Receive the Holy Spirit. If you forgive anyone his sins, they are forgiven; if you do not forgive them, they are not forgiven.

Cast: **Narrator, Jesus**

Jesus Appears to Thomas
John 20:24–29

Narrator	Thomas (called Didymus), one of the Twelve, was not with the disciples when Jesus came. So the other disciples told him:
Disciple(s)	We have seen the Lord!
[Narrator	But he said to them:]
Thomas	Unless I see the nail marks in his hands and put my finger where the nails were, and put my hand into his side, I will not believe it.
Narrator	A week later his disciples were in the house again, and Thomas was with them. Though the doors were locked, Jesus came and stood among them and said:
Jesus	Peace be with you!
[Narrator	Then he said to Thomas:]
Jesus (to Thomas)	Put your finger here; see my hands. Reach out your hand and put it into my side. Stop doubting and believe.
Thomas	My Lord and my God!
Jesus	Because you have seen me, you have believed; blessed are those who have not seen and yet have believed.

Cast: **Narrator, Disciple(s), Thomas, Jesus**

Jesus and the Miraculous Catch of Fish
John 21:1–14

Narrator	Jesus appeared again to his disciples, by the Sea of Tiberias. It happened this way: Simon Peter, Thomas—
Commentator	Called Didymus—
Narrator	Nathanael from Cana in Galilee, the sons of Zebedee, and two other disciples were together. Simon Peter [said to the others:]

Peter	I'm going out to fish.
Disciple	We'll go with you.
Narrator	So they went out and got into the boat, but that night they caught nothing.
	Early in the morning, Jesus stood on the shore, but the disciples did not realize that it was Jesus. He called out to them:
Jesus (calling)	Friends, haven't you any fish?
Disciple	No.
Jesus (calling)	Throw your net on the right side of the boat and you will find some.
Narrator	When they did, they were unable to haul the net in because of the large number of fish. Then the disciple whom Jesus loved said to Peter:
John	It is the Lord!
Narrator	As soon as Simon Peter heard him say, "It is the Lord," he wrapped his outer garment around him—
Commentator	(For he had taken it off)—
Narrator	And jumped into the water. The other disciples followed in the boat, towing the net full of fish, for they were not far from shore, about a hundred yards. When they landed, they saw a fire of burning coals there with fish on it, and some bread. [Jesus said to them:]
Jesus	Bring some of the fish you have just caught.
Narrator	Simon Peter climbed aboard and dragged the net ashore. It was full of large fish—
Commentator	153.
Narrator	But even with so many the net was not torn. [Jesus said to them:]
Jesus	Come and have breakfast.
Narrator	None of the disciples dared ask him, "Who are you?" They knew it was the Lord. Jesus came, took the bread and gave it to them, and did the same with the fish. (PAUSE) This was now the third time Jesus appeared to his disciples after he was raised from the dead.

Cast: **Narrator, Commentator, Peter, Disciple, Jesus, John** (can be the same as Disciple)

Jesus Reinstates Peter
John 21:15–22

Narrator	When they had finished eating, Jesus said to Simon Peter:
Jesus	Simon son of John, do you truly love me more than these?
Peter	Yes, Lord, you know that I love you.

Jesus	Feed my lambs. (PAUSE) Simon son of John, do you truly love me?
Peter	Yes, Lord, you know that I love you.
Jesus	Take care of my sheep. (PAUSE) Simon son of John, do you love me?
Narrator	Peter was hurt because Jesus asked him the third time, "Do you love me?"
Peter	Lord, you know all things; you know that I love you.
Jesus	Feed my sheep. (PAUSE) I tell you the truth, when you were younger you dressed yourself and went where you wanted; but when you are old you will stretch out your hands, and someone else will dress you and lead you where you do not want to go.
Narrator	Jesus said this to indicate the kind of death by which Peter would glorify God. (PAUSE) Then he said to him:
Jesus	Follow me!
Narrator	Peter turned and saw that the disciple whom Jesus loved was following them. (This was the one who had leaned back against Jesus at the supper and had said, "Lord, who is going to betray you?") When Peter saw him, he asked:
Peter	Lord, what about him?
Jesus	If I want him to remain alive until I return, what is that to you? You must follow me.

Cast: **Narrator, Jesus, Peter**

Conclusion to the Gospel of John
John 20:30–31; 21:24–25

Voice 1	Jesus did many other miraculous signs in the presence of his disciples, which are not recorded in this book. But these are written that you may believe that Jesus is the Christ, the Son of God, and that by believing you may have life in his name. . . .
Voice 2	This is the disciple who testifies to these things and who wrote them down. We know that his testimony is true.
Voice 1	Jesus did many other things as well. If every one of them were written down, I suppose that even the whole world would not have room for the books that would be written.

Cast: **Voice 1, Voice 2**

See also the Passion Readings, beginning on page 423, and the Easter Readings, beginning on page 466.

Acts

Jesus Taken Up into Heaven
Acts 1:4–11

Narrator	On one occasion, while [Jesus] was eating with [his apostles,] he gave them this command:
Jesus	Do not leave Jerusalem, but wait for the gift my Father promised, which you have heard me speak about. For John baptized with water, but in a few days you will be baptized with the Holy Spirit.
Narrator	So when they met together, they asked him:
Apostle	Lord, are you at this time going to restore the kingdom to Israel?
Jesus	It is not for you to know the times or dates the Father has set by his own authority. But you will receive power when the Holy Spirit comes on you; and you will be my witnesses in Jerusalem, and in all Judea and Samaria, and to the ends of the earth.
Narrator	After he said this, he was taken up before their very eyes, and a cloud hid him from their sight.
	They were looking intently up into the sky as he was going, when suddenly two men dressed in white stood beside them.
Angel	Men of Galilee, why do you stand here looking into the sky? This same Jesus, who has been taken from you into heaven, will come back in the same way you have seen him go into heaven.

Cast: **Narrator, Jesus, Apostle, Angel**

Matthias Chosen to Replace Judas
Acts 1:12–26

Narrator	[The apostles] returned to Jerusalem from the hill called the Mount of Olives, a Sabbath day's walk from the city. When they arrived, they went upstairs to the room where they were staying. Those present were Peter, John, James and Andrew; Philip and Thomas, Bartholomew and Matthew; James son of Alphaeus and Simon the Zealot, and Judas son of James. They all joined together constantly in prayer, along with the women and Mary the mother of Jesus, and with his brothers.
	In those days Peter stood up among the believers (a group numbering about a hundred and twenty) and said:
Peter	Brothers, the Scripture had to be fulfilled which the Holy Spirit spoke long ago through the mouth of David concerning Judas, who served as

guide for those who arrested Jesus—he was one of our number and shared in this ministry.

Narrator   (With the reward he got for his wickedness, Judas bought a field; there he fell headlong, his body burst open and all his intestines spilled out. Everyone in Jerusalem heard about this, so they called that field in their language Akeldama, that is, Field of Blood.)

Peter   For, it is written in the book of Psalms:

Voice   May his place be deserted;
let there be no one to dwell in it.

Peter   [It is also written:]

Voice   May another take his place of leadership.

Peter   Therefore it is necessary to choose one of the men who have been with us the whole time the Lord Jesus went in and out among us, beginning from John's baptism to the time when Jesus was taken up from us. For one of these must become a witness with us of his resurrection.

Narrator   So they proposed two men: Joseph called Barsabbas (also known as Justus) and Matthias. Then they prayed:

Peter   Lord, you know everyone's heart. Show us which of these two you have chosen to take over this apostolic ministry, which Judas left to go where he belongs.

Narrator   Then they cast lots, and the lot fell to Matthias; so he was added to the eleven apostles.

Cast: **Narrator, Peter, Voice** (can be the same as Peter)

The Holy Spirit Comes at Pentecost
From Acts 2:1–21

Narrator   When the day of Pentecost came, [the disciples] were all together in one place. Suddenly a sound like the blowing of a violent wind came from heaven and filled the whole house where they were sitting. They saw what seemed to be tongues of fire that separated and came to rest on each of them. All of them were filled with the Holy Spirit and began to speak in other tongues as the Spirit enabled them.

Now there were staying in Jerusalem God-fearing Jews from every nation under heaven. When they heard this sound, a crowd came together in bewilderment, because each one heard them speaking in his own language. [Utterly amazed, they asked:]

Person 1
(amazed)   Are not all these men who are speaking Galileans? Then how is it that each of us hears them . . . declaring the wonders of God in our own tongues!

Narrator	Amazed and perplexed, they asked one another:
Persons 1 and 2	What does this mean?
Narrator	Some, however, made fun of them and said:
Person 2	They have had too much wine.
Narrator	Then Peter stood up with the Eleven, raised his voice and addressed the crowd:
Peter	Fellow Jews and all of you who live in Jerusalem, let me explain this to you; listen carefully to what I say. These men are not drunk, as you suppose. It's only nine in the morning! No, this is what was spoken by the prophet Joel:

Joel	In the last days, God says,
	    I will pour out my Spirit on all people.
	Your sons and daughters will prophesy,
	    your young men will see visions,
	    your old men will dream dreams.
	Even on my servants, both men and women,
	    I will pour out my Spirit in those days,
	    and they will prophesy.
	I will show wonders in the heaven above
	    and signs on the earth below,
	    blood and fire and billows of smoke.
	The sun will be turned to darkness
	    and the moon to blood
	    before the coming of the great and glorious day of the Lord.
	And everyone who calls
	    on the name of the Lord will be saved.

Cast: **Narrator, Person 1, Person 2, Peter, Joel** (can be the same as Peter)

Peter Addresses the Crowd
Acts 2:22–35

Peter	Men of Israel, listen to this: Jesus of Nazareth was a man accredited by God to you by miracles, wonders and signs, which God did among you through him, as you yourselves know. This man was handed over to you by God's set purpose and foreknowledge; and you, with the help of wicked men, put him to death by nailing him to the cross. But God raised him from the dead, freeing him from the agony of death, because it was impossible for death to keep its hold on him. David said about him:

David	I saw the Lord always before me.
	    Because he is at my right hand,
	    I will not be shaken.

> Therefore my heart is glad and my tongue rejoices;
>> my body also will live in hope,
> because you will not abandon me to the grave,
>> nor will you let your Holy One see decay.
> You have made known to me the paths of life;
>> you will fill me with joy in your presence.

Peter Brothers, I can tell you confidently that the patriarch David died and was buried, and his tomb is here to this day. But he was a prophet and knew that God had promised him on oath that he would place one of his descendants on his throne. Seeing what was ahead, he spoke of the resurrection of the Christ [when he said]:

David He was not abandoned to the grave, or did his body see decay.

Peter God has raised this Jesus to life, and we are all witnesses of the fact. Exalted to the right hand of God, he has received from the Father the promised Holy Spirit and has poured out what you now see and hear. For David did not ascend to heaven, and yet he said:

David The Lord said to my Lord:
> Sit at my right hand
until I make your enemies
> a footstool for your feet.

Cast: **Peter, David**

The Fellowship of the Believers
Acts 2:36–47

Narrator [Peter said:]

Peter Therefore let all Israel be assured of this: God has made this Jesus, whom you crucified, both Lord and Christ.

Narrator When the people heard this, they were cut to the heart and said to Peter and the other apostles:

Person Brothers, what shall we do?

Peter Repent and be baptized, every one of you, in the name of Jesus Christ for the forgiveness of your sins. And you will receive the gift of the Holy Spirit. The promise is for you and your children and for all who are far off—for all whom the Lord our God will call.

Narrator With many other words [Peter] warned them; and he pleaded with them:

Peter Save yourselves from this corrupt generation.

Narrator Those who accepted his message were baptized, and about three thousand were added to their number that day.

They devoted themselves to the apostles' teaching and to the fellowship, to the breaking of bread and to prayer. (PAUSE) Everyone was filled with awe, and many wonders and miraculous signs were done by the apostles. All the believers were together and had everything in common. Selling their possessions and goods, they gave to anyone as he had need. Every day they continued to meet together in the temple courts. They broke bread in their homes and ate together with glad and sincere hearts, praising God and enjoying the favor of all the people. And the Lord added to their number daily those who were being saved.

Cast: **Narrator, Peter, Person**

Peter Heals the Crippled Beggar
Acts 3:1–10 [11–16]

Narrator	One day Peter and John were going up to the temple at the time of prayer—at three in the afternoon. Now a man crippled from birth was being carried to the temple gate called Beautiful, where he was put every day to beg from those going into the temple courts. When he saw Peter and John about to enter, he asked them for money. Peter looked straight at him, as did John. Then Peter said:
Peter	Look at us!
Narrator	So the man gave them his attention, expecting to get something from them. Then Peter said:
Peter	Silver or gold I do not have, but what I have I give you. In the name of Jesus Christ of Nazareth, walk.
Narrator	Taking him by the right hand, he helped him up, and instantly the man's feet and ankles became strong. He jumped to his feet and began to walk. Then he went with them into the temple courts, walking and jumping, and praising God. When all the people saw him walking and praising God, they recognized him as the same man who used to sit begging at the temple gate called Beautiful, and they were filled with wonder and amazement at what had happened to him.
	[While the beggar held on to Peter and John, all the people were astonished and came running to them in the place called Solomon's Colonnade. When Peter saw this, he said to them:
Peter	Men of Israel, why does this surprise you? Why do you stare at us as if by our own power or godliness we had made this man walk? The God of Abraham, Isaac and Jacob, the God of our fathers, has glorified his servant Jesus. You handed him over to be killed, and you disowned him before Pilate, though he had decided to let him go. You disowned the Holy and Righteous One and asked that a murderer be released to you. You killed the author of life, but God raised him from the dead. We are witnesses of this. By faith in the name of Jesus, this man whom you see and know was made strong. It is Jesus' name and the faith that comes

through him that has given this complete healing to him, as you can all see.]

Cast: **Narrator, Peter**

Peter Speaks to the Onlookers
Acts 3:17–26

Peter   Now, brothers, I know that you acted in ignorance [when you demanded Jesus' death], as did your leaders. But this is how God fulfilled what he had foretold through all the prophets, saying that his Christ would suffer. Repent, then, and turn to God, so that your sins may be wiped out, that times of refreshing may come from the Lord, and that he may send the Christ, who has been appointed for you—even Jesus. He must remain in heaven until the time comes for God to restore everything, as he promised long ago through his holy prophets. For Moses said:

Moses   The Lord your God will raise up for you a prophet like me from among your own people; you must listen to everything he tells you. Anyone who does not listen to him will be completely cut off from among his people.

Peter   Indeed, all the prophets from Samuel on, as many as have spoken, have foretold these days. And you are heirs of the prophets and of the covenant God made with your fathers. He said to Abraham:

God   Through your offspring all peoples on earth will be blessed.

Peter   When God raised up his servant, he sent him first to you to bless you by turning each of you from your wicked ways.

Cast: **Peter, Moses, God**

Peter and John before the Sanhedrin
Acts 4:1–22

Narrator   The priests and the captain of the temple guard and the Sadducees came up to Peter and John while they were speaking to the people. They were greatly disturbed because the apostles were teaching the people and proclaiming in Jesus the resurrection of the dead. They seized Peter and John, and because it was evening, they put them in jail until the next day. But many who heard the message believed, and the number of men grew to about five thousand.

The next day the rulers, elders and teachers of the law met in Jerusalem. Annas the high priest was there, and so were Caiaphas, John, Alexander and the other men of the high priest's family. They had Peter and John brought before them and began to question them:

Elder 1   By what power did you do this?

Elder 2	By what name did you do this?
Narrator	Then Peter, filled with the Holy Spirit, said to them:
Peter	Rulers and elders of the people! If we are being called to account today for an act of kindness shown to a cripple and are asked how he was healed, then know this, you and all the people of Israel: It is by the name of Jesus Christ of Nazareth, whom you crucified but whom God raised from the dead, that this man stands before you healed. He is
Psalmist	The stone you builders rejected, which has become the capstone.
Peter	Salvation is found in no one else, for there is no other name under heaven given to men by which we must be saved.
Narrator	When they saw the courage of Peter and John and realized that they were unschooled, ordinary men, they were astonished and they took note that these men had been with Jesus. But since they could see the man who had been healed standing there with them, there was nothing they could say. So they ordered them to withdraw from the Sanhedrin and then conferred together.
Elder 1	What are we going to do with these men?
Elder 2	Everybody living in Jerusalem knows they have done an outstanding miracle, and we cannot deny it. But to stop this thing from spreading any further among the people, we must warn these men to speak no longer to anyone in this name.
Narrator	Then they called them in again and commanded them not to speak or teach at all in the name of Jesus. But Peter and John replied:
Peter	Judge for yourselves whether it is right in God's sight to obey you rather than God. For we cannot help speaking about what we have seen and heard.
Narrator	After further threats they let them go. They could not decide how to punish them, because all the people were praising God for what had happened. For the man who was miraculously healed was over forty years old.

Cast: **Narrator, Elder 1, Elder 2, Peter, Psalmist** (can be the same as Peter)

The Believers' Prayer
Acts 4:23–31

Narrator	On their release, Peter and John went back to their own people and reported all that the chief priests and elders had said to them. When they heard this, they raised their voices together in prayer to God.

Believer 1   Sovereign Lord, you made the heaven and the earth and the sea, and everything in them. You spoke by the Holy Spirit through the mouth of your servant, our father David:

David   Why do the nations rage
      and the peoples plot in vain?
The kings of the earth take their stand
      and the rulers gather together
against the Lord
      and against his Anointed One.

Believer 1   Indeed Herod and Pontius Pilate met together with the Gentiles and the people of Israel in this city to conspire against your holy servant Jesus, whom you anointed. They did what your power and will had decided beforehand should happen.

Believer 2   Now, Lord, consider their threats and enable your servants to speak your word with great boldness. Stretch out your hand to heal and perform miraculous signs and wonders through the name of your holy servant Jesus.

Narrator   After they prayed, the place where they were meeting was shaken. And they were all filled with the Holy Spirit and spoke the word of God boldly.

Cast: **Narrator, Believer 1, David, Believer 2** (can be the same as Believer 1)

The Believers Share Their Possessions
Acts 4:32–37

Voice 1   All the believers were one in heart and mind.

Voice 2   No one claimed that any of his possessions was his own, but they shared everything they had.

Voice 1   With great power the apostles continued to testify to the resurrection of the Lord Jesus, and much grace was upon them all.

Voice 2   There were no needy persons among them. For from time to time those who owned lands or houses sold them, brought the money from the sales and put it at the apostles' feet, and it was distributed to anyone as he had need.

Voice 1   Joseph, a Levite from Cyprus, whom the apostles called Barnabas (which means Son of Encouragement), sold a field he owned and brought the money and put it at the apostles' feet.

Cast: **Voice 1, Voice 2**

Ananias and Sapphira
Acts 5:1–11

Narrator
Now a man named Ananias, together with his wife Sapphira, also sold a piece of property. With his wife's full knowledge he kept back part of the money for himself, but brought the rest and put it at the apostles' feet. Then Peter said:

Peter
Ananias, how is it that Satan has so filled your heart that you have lied to the Holy Spirit and have kept for yourself some of the money you received for the land? Didn't it belong to you before it was sold? And after it was sold, wasn't the money at your disposal? What made you think of doing such a thing? You have not lied to men but to God.

Narrator
When Ananias heard this, he fell down and died. And great fear seized all who heard what had happened. Then the young men came forward, wrapped up his body, and carried him out and buried him. (PAUSE)

About three hours later his wife came in, not knowing what had happened. Peter asked her:

Peter
Tell me, is this the price you and Ananias got for the land?

[Narrator
She answered:]

Sapphira
Yes, that is the price.

Peter
How could you agree to test the Spirit of the Lord? Look! The feet of the men who buried your husband are at the door, and they will carry you out also.

Narrator
At that moment she fell down at his feet and died. Then the young men came in and, finding her dead, carried her out and buried her beside her husband. Great fear seized the whole church and all who heard about these events.

Cast: **Narrator, Peter, Sapphira**

The Apostles Persecuted
Acts 5:12–26

Narrator
The apostles performed many miraculous signs and wonders among the people. And all the believers used to meet together in Solomon's Colonnade. No one else dared join them, even though they were highly regarded by the people. Nevertheless, more and more men and women believed in the Lord and were added to their number. As a result, people brought the sick into the streets and laid them on beds and mats so that at least Peter's shadow might fall on some of them as he passed by. Crowds gathered also from the towns around Jerusalem, bringing their sick and those tormented by evil spirits, and all of them were healed.

Then the high priest and all his associates, who were members of the party of the Sadducees, were filled with jealousy. They arrested the apostles and put them in the public jail. But during the night an angel of the Lord opened the doors of the jail and brought them out. [He said to them:]

Angel Go, stand in the temple courts, and tell the people the full message of this new life.

Narrator At daybreak they entered the temple courts, as they had been told, and began to teach the people.

When the high priest and his associates arrived, they called together the Sanhedrin—the full assembly of the elders of Israel—and sent to the jail for the apostles. But on arriving at the jail, the officers did not find them there. So they went back [and reported:]

Official We found the jail securely locked, with the guards standing at the doors; but when we opened them, we found no one inside.

Narrator On hearing this report, the captain of the temple guard and the chief priests were puzzled, wondering what would come of this. Then someone came and said:

Man Look! The men you put in jail are standing in the temple courts teaching the people.

Narrator At that, the captain went with his officers and brought the apostles. They did not use force, because they feared that the people would stone them.

Cast: **Narrator, Angel, Official, Man**

The Apostles before the Sanhedrin
Acts 5:27–42

Narrator [The captain and his officers made the apostles] appear before the Sanhedrin to be questioned by the high priest.

High priest We gave you strict orders not to teach in this name. Yet you have filled Jerusalem with your teaching and are determined to make us guilty of this man's blood.

[Narrator Peter and the other apostles replied:]

Peter We must obey God rather than men! The God of our fathers raised Jesus from the dead—whom you had killed by hanging him on a tree. God exalted him to his own right hand as Prince and Savior that he might give repentance and forgiveness of sins to Israel. We are witnesses of these things, and so is the Holy Spirit, whom God has given to those who obey him.

Narrator	When they heard this, [the men of the Sanhedrin] were furious and wanted to put them to death. But a Pharisee named Gamaliel, a teacher of the law, who was honored by all the people, stood up in the Sanhedrin and ordered that the men be put outside for a little while. Then he addressed them:
Gamaliel	Men of Israel, consider carefully what you intend to do to these men. Some time ago Theudas appeared, claiming to be somebody, and about four hundred men rallied to him. He was killed, all his followers were dispersed, and it all came to nothing. After him, Judas the Galilean appeared in the days of the census and led a band of people in revolt. He too was killed, and all his followers were scattered. Therefore, in the present case I advise you: Leave these men alone! Let them go! For if their purpose or activity is of human origin, it will fail. But if it is from God, you will not be able to stop these men; you will only find yourselves fighting against God.
Narrator	His speech persuaded them. They called the apostles in and had them flogged. Then they ordered them not to speak in the name of Jesus, and let them go. The apostles left the Sanhedrin, rejoicing because they had been counted worthy of suffering disgrace for the Name. Day after day, in the temple courts and from house to house, they never stopped teaching and proclaiming the good news that Jesus is the Christ.

Cast: **Narrator, High priest, Peter, Gamaliel**

The Choosing of the Seven

Acts 6:1–7

Narrator	In those days when the number of disciples was increasing, the Grecian Jews among them complained against the Hebraic Jews because their widows were being overlooked in the daily distribution of food. So the Twelve gathered all the disciples together and said:
Apostle	It would not be right for us to neglect the ministry of the word of God in order to wait on tables. Brothers, choose seven men from among you who are known to be full of the Spirit and wisdom. We will turn this responsibility over to them and will give our attention to prayer and the ministry of the word.
Narrator	This proposal pleased the whole group. They chose Stephen, a man full of faith and of the Holy Spirit; also Philip, Procorus, Nicanor, Timon, Parmenas, and Nicolas from Antioch, a convert to Judaism. They presented these men to the apostles, who prayed and laid their hands on them.

So the word of God spread. The number of disciples in Jerusalem increased rapidly, and a large number of priests became obedient to the faith.

Cast: **Narrator, Apostle**

The Arrest and Martyrdom of Stephen
Acts 6:8–7:2; 7:48–8:1

Narrator Stephen, a man full of God's grace and power, did great wonders and miraculous signs among the people. Opposition arose, however, from members of the Synagogue of the Freedmen (as it was called)—Jews of Cyrene and Alexandria as well as the provinces of Cilicia and Asia. These men began to argue with Stephen, but they could not stand up against his wisdom or the Spirit by whom he spoke. Then they secretly persuaded some men to say:

Man 1 We have heard Stephen speak words of blasphemy against Moses.

Man 2 And against God.

Narrator So they stirred up the people and the elders and the teachers of the law. They seized Stephen and brought him before the Sanhedrin. They produced false witnesses, who testified:

Man 3 This fellow never stops speaking against this holy place and against the law.

Man 4 For we have heard him say that this Jesus of Nazareth will destroy this place and change the customs Moses handed down to us.

Narrator All who were sitting in the Sanhedrin looked intently at Stephen, and they saw that his face was like the face of an angel. (PAUSE)

Then the high priest asked [Stephen]:

High priest Are these charges true?

Narrator To this he replied:

Stephen Brothers and fathers, listen to me! . . . The Most High does not live in houses made by men. As the prophet says:

Isaiah Heaven is my throne,
  and the earth is my footstool.
What kind of house will you build for me?

says the Lord.

  Or where will my resting place be?
Has not my hand made all these things?

Stephen You stiff-necked people, with uncircumcised hearts and ears! You are just like your fathers: You always resist the Holy Spirit! Was there ever a prophet your fathers did not persecute? They even killed those who predicted the coming of the Righteous One. And now you have betrayed and murdered him—you who have received the law that was put into effect through angels but have not obeyed it.

Narrator   When they heard this, they were furious and gnashed their teeth at him. But Stephen, full of the Holy Spirit, looked up to heaven and saw the glory of God, and Jesus standing at the right hand of God.

Stephen   Look, I see heaven open and the Son of Man standing at the right hand of God.

Narrator   At this they covered their ears and, yelling at the top of their voices, they all rushed at him, dragged him out of the city and began to stone him. Meanwhile, the witnesses laid their clothes at the feet of a young man named Saul. While they were stoning him, Stephen prayed:

Stephen   Lord Jesus, receive my spirit.

Narrator   Then he fell on his knees and cried out:

Stephen   Lord, do not hold this sin against them.

Narrator   When he had said this, he fell asleep. (PAUSE) And Saul was there, giving approval to his death.

Cast: **Narrator, Man 1, Man 2, Man 3** (can be the same as Man 1), **Man 4** (can be the same as Man 2), **High priest, Stephen, Isaiah**

The Church Persecuted and Scattered
Acts 8:1–25

Narrator   [On the day that Stephen was killed] a great persecution broke out against the church at Jerusalem, and all except the apostles were scattered throughout Judea and Samaria. Godly men buried Stephen and mourned deeply for him. But Saul began to destroy the church. Going from house to house, he dragged off men and women and put them in prison.

Those who had been scattered preached the word wherever they went. Philip went down to a city in Samaria and proclaimed the Christ there. When the crowds heard Philip and saw the miraculous signs he did, they all paid close attention to what he said. With shrieks, evil spirits came out of many, and many paralytics and cripples were healed. So there was great joy in that city.

Now for some time a man named Simon had practiced sorcery in the city and amazed all the people of Samaria. He boasted that he was someone great, and all the people, both high and low, gave him their attention and exclaimed:

Person   This man is the divine power known as the Great Power.

Narrator   They followed him because he had amazed them for a long time with his magic. But when they believed Philip as he preached the good news of the kingdom of God and the name of Jesus Christ, they were baptized, both men and women. Simon himself believed and was baptized. And he followed Philip everywhere, astonished by the great signs and miracles he saw. (PAUSE)

When the apostles in Jerusalem heard that Samaria had accepted the word of God, they sent Peter and John to them. When they arrived, they prayed for them that they might receive the Holy Spirit, because the Holy Spirit had not yet come upon any of them; they had simply been baptized into the name of the Lord Jesus. Then Peter and John placed their hands on them, and they received the Holy Spirit.

When Simon saw that the Spirit was given at the laying on of the apostles' hands, he offered them money and said:

Simon   Give me also this ability so that everyone on whom I lay my hands may receive the Holy Spirit.

Peter   May your money perish with you, because you thought you could buy the gift of God with money! You have no part or share in this ministry, because your heart is not right before God. Repent of this wickedness and pray to the Lord. Perhaps he will forgive you for having such a thought in your heart. For I see that you are full of bitterness and captive to sin.

Simon   Pray to the Lord for me so that nothing you have said may happen to me.

Narrator   When they had testified and proclaimed the word of the Lord, Peter and John returned to Jerusalem, preaching the gospel in many Samaritan villages.

Cast: **Narrator, Person, Simon, Peter**

Philip and the Ethiopian
Acts 8:26–40

Narrator   An angel of the Lord said to Philip:

Angel   Go south to the road—the desert road—that goes down from Jerusalem to Gaza.

Narrator   So he started out, and on his way he met an Ethiopian eunuch, an important official in charge of all the treasury of Candace, queen of the Ethiopians. This man had gone to Jerusalem to worship, and on his way home was sitting in his chariot reading the book of Isaiah the prophet. The Spirit told Philip:

Holy Spirit   Go to that chariot and stay near it.

Narrator   Then Philip ran up to the chariot and heard the man reading Isaiah the prophet. [He asked him:]

Philip	Do you understand what you are reading?
Ethiopian	How can I, unless someone explains it to me?
Narrator	So he invited Philip to come up and sit with him. (PAUSE) The eunuch was reading this passage of Scripture:

Isaiah	He was led like a sheep to the slaughter,
	    and as a lamb before the shearer is silent,
	    so he did not open his mouth.
	In his humiliation he was deprived of justice.
	    Who can speak of his descendants?
	    For his life was taken from the earth.

[Narrator	The eunuch asked Philip:]
Ethiopian	Tell me, please, who is the prophet talking about, himself or someone else?
Narrator	Then Philip began with that very passage of Scripture and told him the good news about Jesus. As they traveled along the road, they came to some water and the eunuch said:
Ethiopian	Look, here is water. Why shouldn't I be baptized?
Narrator	And he gave orders to stop the chariot. Then both Philip and the eunuch went down into the water and Philip baptized him. When they came up out of the water, the Spirit of the Lord suddenly took Philip away, and the eunuch did not see him again, but went on his way rejoicing. Philip, however, appeared at Azotus and traveled about, preaching the gospel in all the towns until he reached Caesarea.

Cast: **Narrator, Angel, Holy Spirit, Philip, Ethiopian, Isaiah**

Saul's Conversion
Acts 9:1–8

Narrator	Saul was still breathing out murderous threats against the Lord's disciples. He went to the high priest and asked him for letters to the synagogues in Damascus, so that if he found any there who belonged to the Way, whether men or women, he might take them as prisoners to Jerusalem.(PAUSE) As he neared Damascus on his journey, suddenly a light from heaven flashed around him. He fell to the ground and heard a voice [say to him:]
The Lord	Saul, Saul, why do you persecute me?
[Narrator	Saul asked:]
Saul	Who are you, Lord?
The Lord	I am Jesus, whom you are persecuting. Now get up and go into the city, and you will be told what you must do.

Narrator	The men traveling with Saul stood there speechless; they heard the sound but did not see anyone. Saul got up from the ground, but when he opened his eyes he could see nothing. So they led him by the hand into Damascus.

Cast: **Narrator, the Lord, Saul**

Saul Meets Ananias
Acts 9:9–19

Narrator	For three days [Saul] was blind, and did not eat or drink anything. (PAUSE) In Damascus there was a disciple named Ananias. The Lord called to him in a vision:
The Lord	Ananias!
[Narrator	He answered:]
Ananias	Yes, Lord.
The Lord	Go to the house of Judas on Straight Street and ask for a man from Tarsus named Saul, for he is praying. In a vision he has seen a man named Ananias come and place his hands on him to restore his sight.
Ananias	Lord, I have heard many reports about this man and all the harm he has done to your saints in Jerusalem. And he has come here with authority from the chief priests to arrest all who call on your name.
The Lord	Go! This man is my chosen instrument to carry my name before the Gentiles and their kings and before the people of Israel. I will show him how much he must suffer for my name.
Narrator	Then Ananias went to the house and entered it. Placing his hands on Saul, he said:
Ananias	Brother Saul, the Lord—Jesus, who appeared to you on the road as you were coming here—has sent me so that you may see again and be filled with the Holy Spirit.
Narrator	Immediately, something like scales fell from Saul's eyes, and he could see again. He got up and was baptized, and after taking some food, he regained his strength.

Cast: **Narrator, the Lord, Ananias**

Saul in Damascus
Acts 9:19–25

Narrator	Saul spent several days with the disciples in Damascus. At once he began to preach in the synagogues that Jesus is the Son of God. All those who heard him were astonished and asked:

Hearer 1	Isn't he the man who raised havoc in Jerusalem among those who call on this name?
Hearer 2	And hasn't he come here to take them as prisoners to the chief priests?
Narrator	Yet Saul grew more and more powerful and baffled the Jews living in Damascus by proving that Jesus is the Christ. (PAUSE)
	After many days had gone by, the Jews conspired to kill him, but Saul learned of their plan. Day and night they kept close watch on the city gates in order to kill him. But his followers took him by night and lowered him in a basket through an opening in the wall.

Cast: **Narrator, Hearer 1, Hearer 2**

Saul in Jerusalem
Acts 9:26–31

Narrator 1	When [Saul] came to Jerusalem, he tried to join the disciples.
Narrator 2	But they were all afraid of him, not believing that he really was a disciple.
Narrator 1	But Barnabas took him and brought him to the apostles. He told them how Saul on his journey had seen the Lord and that the Lord had spoken to him.
Narrator 2	And how in Damascus he had preached fearlessly in the name of Jesus.
Narrator 1	So Saul stayed with them and moved about freely in Jerusalem, speaking boldly in the name of the Lord. He talked and debated with the Grecian Jews, but they tried to kill him.
Narrator 2	When the brothers learned of this, they took him down to Caesarea and sent him off to Tarsus.
Narrator 1	Then the church throughout Judea, Galilee and Samaria enjoyed a time of peace. It was strengthened; and encouraged by the Holy Spirit, it grew in numbers, living in the fear of the Lord.

Cast: **Narrator 1, Narrator 2**

Aeneas and Dorcas
Acts 9:32–43

Narrator	As Peter traveled about the country, he went to visit the saints in Lydda. There he found a man named Aeneas, a paralytic who had been bedridden for eight years. Peter said to him:
Peter	Aeneas, Jesus Christ heals you. Get up and take care of your mat.
Narrator	Immediately Aeneas got up. All those who lived in Lydda and Sharon saw him and turned to the Lord. (PAUSE)

In Joppa there was a disciple named Tabitha (which, when translated, is Dorcas), who was always doing good and helping the poor. About that time she became sick and died, and her body was washed and placed in an upstairs room. Lydda was near Joppa; so when the disciples heard that Peter was in Lydda, they sent two men to him and urged him:

Man   Please come at once!

Narrator   Peter went with them, and when he arrived he was taken upstairs to the room. All the widows stood around him, crying and showing him the robes and other clothing that Dorcas had made while she was still with them.

Peter sent them all out of the room; then he got down on his knees and prayed. Turning toward the dead woman, he said:

Peter   Tabitha, get up.

Narrator   She opened her eyes, and seeing Peter she sat up. He took her by the hand and helped her to her feet. Then he called the believers and the widows and presented her to them alive. This became known all over Joppa, and many people believed in the Lord. Peter stayed in Joppa for some time with a tanner named Simon.

Cast: **Narrator, Peter, Man**

Cornelius Calls for Peter
Acts 10:1–48

Narrator   At Caesarea there was a man named Cornelius, a centurion in what was known as the Italian Regiment. He and all his family were devout and God-fearing; he gave generously to those in need and prayed to God regularly. One day at about three in the afternoon he had a vision. He distinctly saw an angel of God, who came to him and said:

Angel   Cornelius!

Narrator   Cornelius stared at him in fear. He asked:

Cornelius   What is it, Lord?

Angel   Your prayers and gifts to the poor have come up as a memorial offering before God. Now send men to Joppa to bring back a man named Simon who is called Peter. He is staying with Simon the tanner, whose house is by the sea.

Narrator   When the angel who spoke to him had gone, Cornelius called two of his servants and a devout soldier who was one of his attendants. He told them everything that had happened and sent them to Joppa.

About noon the following day as they were on their journey and approaching the city, Peter went up on the roof to pray. He became hungry and wanted something to eat, and while the meal was being prepared, he fell into a trance. He saw heaven opened and something like a large sheet being let down to earth by its four corners. It contained all kinds of four-footed animals, as well as reptiles of the earth and birds of the air. Then a voice told him:

The Lord   Get up, Peter. Kill and eat.

[Narrator   Peter replied:]

Peter   Surely not, Lord! I have never eaten anything impure or unclean.

Narrator   The voice spoke to him a second time:

The Lord   Do not call anything impure that God has made clean.

Narrator   This happened three times, and immediately the sheet was taken back to heaven.

While Peter was wondering about the meaning of the vision, the men sent by Cornelius found out where Simon's house was and stopped at the gate. They called out, asking:

Man 1   [Is Simon who is known as Peter staying there?]

Narrator   While Peter was still thinking about the vision, the Spirit said to him:

Holy Spirit   Simon, three men are looking for you. So get up and go downstairs. Do not hesitate to go with them, for I have sent them.

Narrator   Peter went down and said to the men:

Peter   I'm the one you're looking for. Why have you come?

[Narrator   The men replied:]

Man 1   We have come from Cornelius the centurion. He is a righteous and God-fearing man, who is respected by all the Jewish people.

Man 2   A holy angel told him to have you come to his house so that he could hear what you have to say.

Narrator   Then Peter invited the men into the house to be his guests. (PAUSE)

The next day Peter started out with them, and some of the brothers from Joppa went along. The following day he arrived in Caesarea. Cornelius was expecting them and had called together his relatives and close friends. As Peter entered the house, Cornelius met him and fell at his feet in reverence. But Peter made him get up.

Peter   Stand up, I am only a man myself.

Narrator	Talking with him, Peter went inside and found a large gathering of people. He said to them:
Peter (to the people)	You are well aware that it is against our law for a Jew to associate with a Gentile or visit him. But God has shown me that I should not call any man impure or unclean.
(to Cornelius)	So when I was sent for, I came without raising any objection. May I ask why you sent for me?
[Narrator	Cornelius answered:]
Cornelius	Four days ago I was in my house praying at this hour, at three in the afternoon. Suddenly a man in shining clothes stood before me and said:
Angel	Cornelius, God has heard your prayer and remembered your gifts to the poor. Send to Joppa for Simon who is called Peter. He is a guest in the home of Simon the tanner, who lives by the sea.
Cornelius	So I sent for you immediately, and it was good of you to come. Now we are all here in the presence of God to listen to everything the Lord has commanded you to tell us.
[Narrator	Then Peter began to speak:]
Peter	I now realize how true it is that God does not show favoritism but accepts men from every nation who fear him and do what is right. You know the message God sent to the people of Israel, telling the good news of peace through Jesus Christ, who is Lord of all. You know what has happened throughout Judea, beginning in Galilee after the baptism that John preached—how God anointed Jesus of Nazareth with the Holy Spirit and power, and how he went around doing good and healing all who were under the power of the devil, because God was with him.
	We are witnesses of everything he did in the country of the Jews and in Jerusalem. They killed him by hanging him on a tree, but God raised him from the dead on the third day and caused him to be seen. He was not seen by all the people, but by witnesses whom God had already chosen—by us who ate and drank with him after he rose from the dead. He commanded us to preach to the people and to testify that he is the one whom God appointed as judge of the living and the dead. All the prophets testify about him that everyone who believes in him receives forgiveness of sins through his name.
Narrator	While Peter was still speaking these words, the Holy Spirit came on all who heard the message. The circumcised believers who had come with Peter were astonished that the gift of the Holy Spirit had been poured out even on the Gentiles. For they heard them speaking in tongues and praising God. Then Peter said:

Peter	Can anyone keep these people from being baptized with water? They have received the Holy Spirit just as we have.
Narrator	So he ordered that they be baptized in the name of Jesus Christ.

Cast: **Narrator**, **Angel** (male voice), **Cornelius**, **the Lord**, **Peter**, **Man 1**, **Holy Spirit** (can be the same as the Lord), **Man 2** (can be the same as Man 1)

Peter Explains His Actions
Acts 11:1–18

Narrator	The apostles and the brothers throughout Judea heard that the Gentiles also had received the word of God. So when Peter went up to Jerusalem, the circumcised believers criticized him and said:
Apostle 1	You went into the house of uncircumcised men.
Apostle 2	And ate with them.
Narrator	Peter began and explained everything to them precisely as it had happened:
Peter	I was in the city of Joppa praying, and in a trance I saw a vision. I saw something like a large sheet being let down from heaven by its four corners, and it came down to where I was. I looked into it and saw four-footed animals of the earth, wild beasts, reptiles, and birds of the air. Then I heard a voice [telling me:]
The Lord	Get up, Peter. Kill and eat.
Peter	I replied, "Surely not, Lord! Nothing impure or unclean has ever entered my mouth." The voice spoke from heaven a second time:
The Lord	Do not call anything impure that God has made clean.
Peter	This happened three times, and then it was all pulled up to heaven again. Right then three men who had been sent to me from Caesarea stopped at the house where I was staying. The Spirit told me to have no hesitation about going with them. These six brothers also went with me, and we entered the man's house. He told us how he had seen an angel appear in his house and say:
Angel	Send to Joppa for Simon who is called Peter. He will bring you a message through which you and all your household will be saved.
Peter	As I began to speak, the Holy Spirit came on them as he had come on us at the beginning. Then I remembered what the Lord had said:
The Lord	John baptized with water, but you will be baptized with the Holy Spirit.
Peter	So if God gave them the same gift as he gave us, who believed in the Lord Jesus Christ, who was I to think that I could oppose God?

281

Narrator	When they heard this, they had no further objections and praised God [saying:]
Apostle 1	So then, God has granted even the Gentiles repentance unto life.

Cast: **Narrator, Apostle 1, Apostle 2** (can be the same as Apostle 1), **Peter, the Lord** (preferably unseen), **Angel**

The Church in Antioch
Acts 11:19–30

Narrator 1	[The believers] who had been scattered by the persecution in connection with Stephen traveled as far as Phoenicia, Cyprus and Antioch, telling the message only to Jews.
Narrator 2	Some of them, however, men from Cyprus and Cyrene, went to Antioch and began to speak to Greeks also, telling them the good news about the Lord Jesus. The Lord's hand was with them, and a great number of people believed and turned to the Lord.
	News of this reached the ears of the church at Jerusalem, and they sent Barnabas to Antioch.
Narrator 1	When he arrived and saw the evidence of the grace of God, he was glad and encouraged them all to remain true to the Lord with all their hearts.
Narrator 3	[Barnabas] was a good man, full of the Holy Spirit and faith, and a great number of people were brought to the Lord.
Narrator 1	Then Barnabas went to Tarsus to look for Saul, and when he found him, he brought him to Antioch. So for a whole year Barnabas and Saul met with the church and taught great numbers of people. The disciples were called Christians first at Antioch.
Narrator 2	During this time some prophets came down from Jerusalem to Antioch. One of them, named Agabus, stood up and through the Spirit predicted that a severe famine would spread over the entire Roman world.
Narrator 3	(This happened during the reign of Claudius.)
Narrator 2	The disciples, each according to his ability, decided to provide help for the brothers living in Judea. This they did, sending their gift to the elders by Barnabas and Saul.

Cast: **Narrator 1, Narrator 2, Narrator 3**

Peter's Miraculous Escape from Prison
Acts 12:1–19

Narrator	King Herod arrested some who belonged to the church, intending to persecute them. He had James, the brother of John, put to death with the sword. When he saw that this pleased the Jews, he proceeded to

seize Peter also. This happened during the Feast of Unleavened Bread. After arresting him, he put him in prison, handing him over to be guarded by four squads of four soldiers each. Herod intended to bring him out for public trial after the Passover.

So Peter was kept in prison, but the church was earnestly praying to God for him.

The night before Herod was to bring him to trial, Peter was sleeping between two soldiers, bound with two chains, and sentries stood guard at the entrance. Suddenly an angel of the Lord appeared and a light shone in the cell. He struck Peter on the side and woke him up:

Angel	Quick, get up!
Narrator	And the chains fell off Peter's wrists. Then the angel said to him:
Angel	Put on your clothes and sandals.
[Narrator	And Peter did so. (PAUSE) The angel told him:]
Angel	Wrap your cloak around you and follow me.
Narrator	Peter followed him out of the prison, but he had no idea that what the angel was doing was really happening; he thought he was seeing a vision. They passed the first and second guards and came to the iron gate leading to the city. It opened for them by itself, and they went through it. When they had walked the length of one street, suddenly the angel left him. Then Peter came to himself and said:
Peter	Now I know without a doubt that the Lord sent his angel and rescued me from Herod's clutches and from everything the Jewish people were anticipating.
Narrator	When this had dawned on him, he went to the house of Mary the mother of John, also called Mark, where many people had gathered and were praying. Peter knocked at the outer entrance, and a servant girl named Rhoda came to answer the door. When she recognized Peter's voice, she was so overjoyed she ran back without opening it and exclaimed:
Rhoda	Peter is at the door!
Person	You're out of your mind.
Narrator	When she kept insisting that it was so, they said:
Person	It must be his angel.
Narrator	But Peter kept on knocking, and when they opened the door and saw him, they were astonished. Peter motioned with his hand for them to be quiet and described how the Lord had brought him out of prison.
Peter	Tell James and the brothers about this.
Narrator	Then he left for another place.

In the morning, there was no small commotion among the soldiers as to what had become of Peter. After Herod had a thorough search made for him and did not find him, he cross-examined the guards and ordered that they be executed. (PAUSE) Then Herod went from Judea to Caesarea and stayed there a while.

Cast: **Narrator, Angel, Peter, Rhoda, Person**

Herod's Death
Acts 12:20–25

Narrator   [Herod] had been quarreling with the people of Tyre and Sidon; they now joined together and sought an audience with him. Having secured the support of Blastus, a trusted personal servant of the king, they asked for peace, because they depended on the king's country for their food supply.

On the appointed day Herod, wearing his royal robes, sat on his throne and delivered a public address to the people. They shouted:

Person 1   This is the voice of a god.

Persons 1 and 2   Not of a man.

Narrator   Immediately, because Herod did not give praise to God, an angel of the Lord struck him down, and he was eaten by worms and died.

But the word of God continued to increase and spread.

When Barnabas and Saul had finished their mission, they returned from Jerusalem, taking with them John, also called Mark.

Cast: **Narrator, Person 1, Person 2** (can be the same as Person 1)

Barnabas and Saul Sent Off
Acts 13:1–3

Narrator   In the church at Antioch there were prophets and teachers: Barnabas, Simeon—

Commentator   Called Niger.

Narrator   Lucius—

Commentator   Of Cyrene.

Narrator   Manaen—

Commentator   Who had been brought up with Herod the tetrarch.

Narrator   And Saul. While they were worshiping the Lord and fasting, the Holy Spirit said:

Holy Spirit	Set apart for me Barnabas and Saul for the work to which I have called them.
Narrator	So after they had fasted and prayed, they placed their hands on them and sent them off.

Cast: **Narrator, Commentator, Holy Spirit**

Barnabas and Saul on Cyprus
Acts 13:4–12

Narrator	[Barnabas and Saul,] sent on their way by the Holy Spirit, went down to Seleucia and sailed from there to Cyprus. When they arrived at Salamis, they proclaimed the word of God in the Jewish synagogues. John was with them as their helper.
	They traveled through the whole island until they came to Paphos. There they met a Jewish sorcerer and false prophet named Bar-Jesus, who was an attendant of the proconsul, Sergius Paulus. The proconsul, an intelligent man, sent for Barnabas and Saul because he wanted to hear the word of God. But Elymas the sorcerer (for that is what his name means) opposed them and tried to turn the proconsul from the faith. Then Saul, who was also called Paul, filled with the Holy Spirit, looked straight at Elymas and said:
Paul	You are a child of the devil and an enemy of everything that is right! You are full of all kinds of deceit and trickery. Will you never stop perverting the right ways of the Lord? Now the hand of the Lord is against you. You are going to be blind, and for a time you will be unable to see the light of the sun.
Narrator	Immediately mist and darkness came over him, and he groped about, seeking someone to lead him by the hand. When the proconsul saw what had happened, he believed, for he was amazed at the teaching about the Lord.

Cast: **Narrator, Paul**

Paul Preaches in Pisidian Antioch (i)
From Acts 13:13–28

Narrator	From Paphos, Paul and his companions sailed to Perga in Pamphylia, where John left them to return to Jerusalem. From Perga they went on to Pisidian Antioch. On the Sabbath they entered the synagogue and sat down. After the reading from the Law and the Prophets, the synagogue rulers sent word to them, saying:
Official	Brothers, if you have a message of encouragement for the people, please speak.
Narrator	Standing up, Paul motioned with his hand and said:

Paul	Men of Israel and you Gentiles who worship God, listen to me! The God of the people of Israel chose our fathers; he made the people prosper during their stay in Egypt. . . . He made David their king. He testified concerning him:
Voice	I have found David son of Jesse a man after my own heart; he will do everything I want him to do.
Paul	From this man's descendants God has brought to Israel the Savior Jesus, as he promised. Before the coming of Jesus, John preached repentance and baptism to all the people of Israel. As John was completing his work, he said:
John	Who do you think I am? I am not that one. No, but he is coming after me, whose sandals I am not worthy to untie.
Paul	Brothers, children of Abraham, and you God-fearing Gentiles, it is to us that this message of salvation has been sent. The people of Jerusalem and their rulers did not recognize Jesus, yet in condemning him they fulfilled the words of the prophets that are read every Sabbath. Though they found no proper ground for a death sentence, they asked Pilate to have him executed.

Cast: **Narrator, Official, Paul, Voice, John**

Paul Preaches in Pisidian Antioch (ii)
Acts 13:29–52

Paul	When [the people of Jerusalem and their leaders] had carried out all that was written about [Jesus,] they took him down from the tree and laid him in a tomb. But God raised him from the dead, and for many days he was seen by those who had traveled with him from Galilee to Jeru–salem. They are now his witnesses to our people.
	We tell you the good news: What God promised our fathers he has ful-filled for us, their children, by raising up Jesus. As it is written in the second Psalm:
Voice	You are my Son; today I have become your Father.
Paul	The fact that God raised him from the dead, never to decay, is stated in these words:
Voice	I will give you the holy and sure blessings promised to David.
Paul	So it is stated elsewhere:
Voice	You will not let your Holy One see decay.
Paul	For when David had served God's purpose in his own generation, he fell asleep; he was buried with his fathers and his body decayed. But the one whom God raised from the dead did not see decay.

Therefore, my brothers, I want you to know that through Jesus the forgiveness of sins is proclaimed to you. Through him everyone who believes is justified from everything you could not be justified from by the law of Moses. Take care that what the prophets have said does not happen to you:

Voice
Look, you scoffers,
  wonder and perish,
for I am going to do something in your days
  that you would never believe,
  even if someone told you.

Narrator
As Paul and Barnabas were leaving the synagogue, the people invited them to speak further about these things on the next Sabbath. When the congregation was dismissed, many of the Jews and devout converts to Judaism followed Paul and Barnabas, who talked with them and urged them to continue in the grace of God. (PAUSE)

On the next Sabbath almost the whole city gathered to hear the word of the Lord. When the Jews saw the crowds, they were filled with jealousy and talked abusively against what Paul was saying. Then Paul and Barnabas answered them boldly:

Paul
We had to speak the word of God to you first. Since you reject it and do not consider yourselves worthy of eternal life, we now turn to the Gentiles. For this is what the Lord has commanded us:

Voice
I have made you a light for the Gentiles,
  that you may bring salvation to the ends of the earth.

Narrator
When the Gentiles heard this, they were glad and honored the word of the Lord; and all who were appointed for eternal life believed. (PAUSE)

The word of the Lord spread through the whole region. But the Jews incited the God-fearing women of high standing and the leading men of the city. They stirred up persecution against Paul and Barnabas, and expelled them from their region. So they shook the dust from their feet in protest against them and went to Iconium. And the disciples were filled with joy and with the Holy Spirit.

Cast: **Paul, Voice, Narrator**

Paul and Barnabas in Iconium
Acts 14:1–7

Narrator 1
At Iconium Paul and Barnabas went as usual into the Jewish synagogue. There they spoke so effectively that a great number of Jews and Gentiles believed.

Narrator 2
But the Jews who refused to believe stirred up the Gentiles and poisoned their minds against the brothers.

Narrator 1	So Paul and Barnabas spent considerable time there, speaking boldly for the Lord, who confirmed the message of his grace by enabling them to do miraculous signs and wonders.
Narrator 2	The people of the city were divided; some sided with the Jews, others with the apostles. There was a plot afoot among the Gentiles and Jews, together with their leaders, to mistreat them and stone them. But they found out about it and fled to the Lycaonian cities of Lystra and Derbe and to the surrounding country.
Narrators 1 and 2	[There] they continued to preach the good news.

Cast: **Narrator 1** (excited voice), **Narrator 2** (serious voice)

Paul and Barnabas in Lystra and Derbe
Acts 14:8–20

Narrator	In Lystra there sat a man crippled in his feet, who was lame from birth and had never walked. He listened to Paul as he was speaking. Paul looked directly at him, saw that he had faith to be healed and called out:
Paul (loudly)	Stand up on your feet!
Narrator	At that, the man jumped up and began to walk. When the crowd saw what Paul had done, they shouted in the Lycaonian language:
Person 1	The gods have come down to us.
Person 2	In human form!
Narrator	Barnabas they called Zeus, and Paul they called Hermes because he was the chief speaker. The priest of Zeus, whose temple was just outside the city, brought bulls and wreaths to the city gates because he and the crowd wanted to offer sacrifices to them.
	But when the apostles Barnabas and Paul heard of this, they tore their clothes and rushed out into the crowd [shouting:]
Barnabas	Men, why are you doing this? We too are only men, human like you.
Paul	We are bringing you good news.
Barnabas	Telling you to turn from these worthless things to the living God, who made heaven and earth and sea and everything in them.
Paul	In the past, he let all nations go their own way. Yet he has not left himself without testimony: He has shown kindness by giving you rain from heaven and crops in their seasons; he provides you with plenty of food and fills your hearts with joy.
Narrator	Even with these words, they had difficulty keeping the crowd from sacrificing to them. (PAUSE)

Then some Jews came from Antioch and Iconium and won the crowd over. They stoned Paul and dragged him outside the city, thinking he was dead. But after the disciples had gathered around him, he got up and went back into the city. The next day he and Barnabas left for Derbe.

Cast: **Narrator, Paul, Person 1, Person 2** (can be the same as Person 1), **Barnabas**

Paul and Barnabas Return to Antioch in Syria
Acts 14:21–26

Narrator   [Paul and Barnabas] preached the good news in [Derbe] and won a large number of disciples. Then they returned to Lystra, Iconium and Antioch, strengthening the disciples and encouraging them to remain true to the faith.

Paul   We must go through many hardships to enter the kingdom of God.

Narrator   Paul and Barnabas appointed elders for them in each church and, with prayer and fasting, committed them to the Lord, in whom they had put their trust. (PAUSE) After going through Pisidia, they came into Pamphylia, and when they had preached the word in Perga, they went down to Attalia.

From Attalia they sailed back to Antioch, where they had been committed to the grace of God for the work they had now completed.

Cast: **Narrator, Paul**

The Council at Jerusalem
Acts 14:27–15:21

Narrator   On arriving [in Antioch,] Paul and Barnabas gathered the church together and reported all that God had done through them and how he had opened the door of faith to the Gentiles. And they stayed there a long time with the disciples. Some men came down from Judea to Antioch and were teaching the brothers:

Man   Unless you are circumcised, according to the custom taught by Moses, you cannot be saved.

Narrator   This brought Paul and Barnabas into sharp dispute and debate with them. So Paul and Barnabas were appointed, along with some other believers, to go up to Jerusalem to see the apostles and elders about this question. The church sent them on their way, and as they traveled through Phoenicia and Samaria, they told how the Gentiles had been converted. This news made all the brothers very glad. (PAUSE) When they came to Jerusalem, they were welcomed by the church and the apostles and elders, to whom they reported everything God had done through them. Then some of the believers who belonged to the party of the Pharisees stood up and said:

Believer 1   The Gentiles must be circumcised.

Believer 2   And required to obey the law of Moses.

Narrator   The apostles and elders met to consider this question. After much discussion, Peter got up and addressed them:

Peter   Brothers, you know that some time ago God made a choice among you that the Gentiles might hear from my lips the message of the gospel and believe. God, who knows the heart, showed that he accepted them by giving the Holy Spirit to them, just as he did to us. He made no distinction between us and them, for he purified their hearts by faith. Now then, why do you try to test God by putting on the necks of the disciples a yoke that neither we nor our fathers have been able to bear? No! We believe it is through the grace of our Lord Jesus that we are saved, just as they are.

Narrator   The whole assembly became silent as they listened to Barnabas and Paul telling about the miraculous signs and wonders God had done among the Gentiles through them. When they finished, James spoke up:

James   Brothers, listen to me. Simon has described to us how God at first showed his concern by taking from the Gentiles a people for himself. The words of the prophets are in agreement with this, as it is written:

Amos   After this I will return
    and rebuild David's fallen tent.
Its ruins I will rebuild,
    and I will restore it,
that the remnant of men may seek the Lord,
    and all the Gentiles who bear my name,
says the Lord, who does these things
that have been known for ages.

James   It is my judgment, therefore, that we should not make it difficult for the Gentiles who are turning to God. Instead we should write to them, telling them to abstain from food polluted by idols, from sexual immorality, from the meat of strangled animals and from blood. For Moses has been preached in every city from the earliest times and is read in the synagogues on every Sabbath.

Cast: **Narrator, Man, Believer 1, Believer 2** (can be the same as Believer 1), **Peter, James, Amos.**
The phrase "that have been known for ages" is the commentary of James and does not appear in Amos 9:11–12. It is included here with the words of Amos for clarity.

The Council's Letter to Gentile Believers
Acts 15:22–33

Narrator | The apostles and elders, with the whole church, decided to choose some of their own men and send them to Antioch with Paul and Barnabas. They chose Judas (called Barsabbas) and Silas, two men who were leaders among the brothers. With them they sent the following letter:

Apostle | The apostles and elders, your brothers, To the Gentile believers in Antioch, Syria and Cilicia: Greetings.

We have heard that some went out from us without our authorization and disturbed you, troubling your minds by what they said. So we all agreed to choose some men and send them to you with our dear friends Barnabas and Paul—men who have risked their lives for the name of our Lord Jesus Christ. Therefore we are sending Judas and Silas to confirm by word of mouth what we are writing. It seemed good to the Holy Spirit and to us not to burden you with anything beyond the following requirements: You are to abstain from food sacrificed to idols, from blood, from the meat of strangled animals and from sexual immorality. You will do well to avoid these things. Farewell.

Narrator | The men were sent off and went down to Antioch, where they gathered the church together and delivered the letter. The people read it and were glad for its encouraging message. Judas and Silas, who themselves were prophets, said much to encourage and strengthen the brothers. After spending some time there, they were sent off by the brothers with the blessing of peace to return to those who had sent them.

Cast: **Narrator, Apostle**

Disagreement between Paul and Barnabas
Acts 15:35–41

Narrator | Paul and Barnabas remained in Antioch, where they and many others taught and preached the word of the Lord. (PAUSE)

Some time later Paul said to Barnabas:

Paul | Let us go back and visit the brothers in all the towns where we preached the word of the Lord and see how they are doing.

Narrator | Barnabas wanted to take John, also called Mark, with them, but Paul did not think it wise to take him, because he had deserted them in Pamphylia and had not continued with them in the work. They had such a sharp disagreement that they parted company. Barnabas took Mark and sailed for Cyprus, but Paul chose Silas and left, commended by the brothers to the grace of the Lord. He went through Syria and Cilicia, strengthening the churches.

Cast: **Narrator, Paul**

Paul and Silas in Troas and in Philippi
Acts 16:6–15

Narrator   Paul and his companions traveled throughout the region of Phrygia and Galatia, having been kept by the Holy Spirit from preaching the word in the province of Asia. When they came to the border of Mysia, they tried to enter Bithynia, but the Spirit of Jesus would not allow them to. So they passed by Mysia and went down to Troas. During the night Paul had a vision of a man of Macedonia standing and begging him:

Macedonian   Come over to Macedonia and help us.

Luke   After Paul had seen the vision, we got ready at once to leave for Macedonia, concluding that God had called us to preach the gospel to them.

From Troas we put out to sea and sailed straight for Samothrace, and the next day on to Neapolis. From there we traveled to Philippi, a Roman colony and the leading city of that district of Macedonia. And we stayed there several days.

On the Sabbath we went outside the city gate to the river, where we expected to find a place of prayer. We sat down and began to speak to the women who had gathered there. One of those listening was a woman named Lydia, a dealer in purple cloth from the city of Thyatira, who was a worshiper of God. The Lord opened her heart to respond to Paul's message. When she and the members of her household were baptized, she invited us to her home.

Lydia   If you consider me a believer in the Lord, come and stay at my house.

Luke   And she persuaded us.

Cast: **Narrator, Macedonian, Luke** (can be the same as Narrator), **Lydia**

Paul and Silas in Prison
Acts 16:16–24

Luke   Once when we were going to the place of prayer, we were met by a slave girl who had a spirit by which she predicted the future. She earned a great deal of money for her owners by fortune-telling. This girl followed Paul and the rest of us, shouting:

Slave girl   These men are servants of the Most High God, who are telling you the way to be saved.

Luke   She kept this up for many days. Finally Paul became so troubled that he turned around and said to the spirit:

Paul   In the name of Jesus Christ I command you to come out of her!

Luke   At that moment the spirit left her. (PAUSE)

When the owners of the slave girl realized that their hope of making money was gone, they seized Paul and Silas and dragged them into the marketplace to face the authorities. They brought them before the magistrates and said:

Owner   These men are Jews, and are throwing our city into an uproar by advocating customs unlawful for us Romans to accept or practice.

Luke   The crowd joined in the attack against Paul and Silas, and the magistrates ordered them to be stripped and beaten. After they had been severely flogged, they were thrown into prison, and the jailer was commanded to guard them carefully. Upon receiving such orders, he put them in the inner cell and fastened their feet in the stocks.

Cast: **Luke, Slave girl, Paul, Owner**

A Baptism in Philippi
Acts 16:25–34

Narrator   About midnight Paul and Silas were praying and singing hymns to God, and the other prisoners were listening to them. Suddenly there was such a violent earthquake that the foundations of the prison were shaken. At once all the prison doors flew open, and everybody's chains came loose. The jailer woke up, and when he saw the prison doors open, he drew his sword and was about to kill himself because he thought the prisoners had escaped. But Paul shouted:

Paul (loudly) Don't harm yourself! We are all here!

Narrator   The jailer called for lights, rushed in and fell trembling before Paul and Silas. He then brought them out and asked:

Jailer   Sirs, what must I do to be saved?

Paul   Believe in the Lord Jesus, and you will be saved—you and your household.

Narrator   Then they spoke the word of the Lord to him and to all the others in his house. At that hour of the night the jailer took them and washed their wounds; then immediately he and all his family were baptized. The jailer brought them into his house and set a meal before them; he was filled with joy because he had come to believe in God—he and his whole family.

Cast: **Narrator, Paul, Jailer**

After the Earthquake
Acts 16:35–40

Narrator   When it was daylight, the magistrates sent their officers to the jailer with the order:

Officer	Release those men.
Narrator	The jailer told Paul:
Jailer	The magistrates have ordered that you and Silas be released. Now you can leave. Go in peace.
Narrator	But Paul said to the officers:
Paul	They beat us publicly without a trial, even though we are Roman citizens, and threw us into prison. And now do they want to get rid of us quietly? No! Let them come themselves and escort us out.
Narrator	The officers reported this to the magistrates, and when they heard that Paul and Silas were Roman citizens, they were alarmed. They came to appease them and escorted them from the prison, requesting them to leave the city. After Paul and Silas came out of the prison, they went to Lydia's house, where they met with the brothers and encouraged them. Then they left.

Cast: **Narrator, Officer, Jailer, Paul**

Paul and Silas in Thessalonica
Acts 17:1–10

Narrator	When they had passed through Amphipolis and Apollonia, they came to Thessalonica, where there was a Jewish synagogue. As his custom was, Paul went into the synagogue, and on three Sabbath days he reasoned with them from the Scriptures, explaining and proving that the Christ had to suffer and rise from the dead.
Paul	This Jesus I am proclaiming to you is the Christ.
Narrator	Some of the Jews were persuaded and joined Paul and Silas, as did a large number of God-fearing Greeks and not a few prominent women.
	But the Jews were jealous; so they rounded up some bad characters from the marketplace, formed a mob and started a riot in the city. They rushed to Jason's house in search of Paul and Silas in order to bring them out to the crowd. But when they did not find them, they dragged Jason and some other brothers before the city officials, [shouting:]
Person (loudly)	These men who have caused trouble all over the world have now come here, and Jason has welcomed them into his house. They are all defying Caesar's decrees, saying that there is another king, one called Jesus.
Narrator	When they heard this, the crowd and the city officials were thrown into turmoil. Then they made Jason and the others post bond and let them go.

As soon as it was night, the brothers sent Paul and Silas away to Berea.

Cast: **Narrator, Paul, Person**

Paul and Silas in Berea
Acts 17:10–15

Narrator 1	As soon as it was night, the brothers sent Paul and Silas away to Berea. On arriving there, they went to the Jewish synagogue.
Narrator 2	Now the Bereans were of more noble character than the Thessalonians, for they received the message with great eagerness and examined the Scriptures every day to see if what Paul said was true.
Narrator 1	Many of the Jews believed, as did also a number of prominent Greek women and many Greek men.
Narrator 2	When the Jews in Thessalonica learned that Paul was preaching the word of God at Berea, they went there too, agitating the crowds and stirring them up.
Narrator 1	The brothers immediately sent Paul to the coast.
Narrator 2	But Silas and Timothy stayed at Berea.
Narrator 1	The men who escorted Paul brought him to Athens and then left with instructions for Silas and Timothy to join him as soon as possible.

Cast: **Narrator 1, Narrator 2**

Paul in Athens
Acts 17:16–34

Narrator	While Paul was waiting for [Silas and Timothy] in Athens, he was greatly distressed to see that the city was full of idols. So he reasoned in the synagogue with the Jews and the God-fearing Greeks, as well as in the marketplace day by day with those who happened to be there. A group of Epicurean and Stoic philosophers began to dispute with him. Some of them asked:
Teacher 1	What is this babbler trying to say?
Narrator	Others remarked:
Teacher 2	He seems to be advocating foreign gods.
Narrator	They said this because Paul was preaching the good news about Jesus and the resurrection. Then they took him and brought him to a meeting of the Areopagus, where they said to him:
Teacher 1	May we know what this new teaching is that you are presenting?

Teacher 2	You are bringing some strange ideas to our ears, and we want to know what they mean.
Narrator	(All the Athenians and the foreigners who lived there spent their time doing nothing but talking about and listening to the latest ideas.)
	Paul then stood up in the meeting of the Areopagus and said:
Paul	Men of Athens! I see that in every way you are very religious. For as I walked around and looked carefully at your objects of worship, I even found an altar with this inscription:
Voice 1 (slowly)	TO AN UNKNOWN GOD.
Paul	Now what you worship as something unknown I am going to proclaim to you.
	The God who made the world and everything in it is the Lord of heaven and earth and does not live in temples built by hands. And he is not served by human hands, as if he needed anything, because he himself gives all men life and breath and everything else. From one man he made every nation of men, that they should inhabit the whole earth; and he determined the times set for them and the exact places where they should live. God did this so that men would seek him and perhaps reach out for him and find him, though he is not far from each one of us.
Voice 2	For in him we live and move and have our being.
Paul	As some of your own poets have said:
Voice 1	We are his offspring.
Paul	Therefore since we are God's offspring, we should not think that the divine being is like gold or silver or stone—an image made by man's design and skill. In the past God overlooked such ignorance, but now he commands all people everywhere to repent. For he has set a day when he will judge the world with justice by the man he has appointed. He has given proof of this to all men by raising him from the dead.
Narrator	When they heard about the resurrection of the dead, some of them sneered, but others said:
Teacher 2	We want to hear you again on this subject.
Narrator	At that, Paul left the Council. A few men became followers of Paul and believed. Among them was Dionysius, a member of the Areopagus, also a woman named Damaris, and a number of others.

Cast: **Narrator, Teacher 1, Teacher 2, Paul, Voice 1** (can be the same as Teacher 1), **Voice 2** (can be the same as Teacher 2)

Paul in Corinth

Acts 18:1–17

Narrator   Paul left Athens and went to Corinth. There he met a Jew named Aquila, a native of Pontus, who had recently come from Italy with his wife Priscilla, because Claudius had ordered all the Jews to leave Rome. Paul went to see them, and because he was a tentmaker as they were, he stayed and worked with them. Every Sabbath he reasoned in the synagogue, trying to persuade Jews and Greeks.

When Silas and Timothy came from Macedonia, Paul devoted himself exclusively to preaching, testifying to the Jews that Jesus was the Christ. But when the Jews opposed Paul and became abusive, he shook out his clothes in protest and said to them:

Paul (firmly)   Your blood be on your own heads! I am clear of my responsibility. From now on I will go to the Gentiles.

Narrator   Then Paul left the synagogue and went next door to the house of Titius Justus, a worshiper of God. Crispus, the synagogue ruler, and his entire household believed in the Lord; and many of the Corinthians who heard him believed and were baptized. (PAUSE) One night the Lord spoke to Paul in a vision:

The Lord   Do not be afraid; keep on speaking, do not be silent. For I am with you, and no one is going to attack and harm you, because I have many people in this city.

Narrator   So Paul stayed for a year and a half, teaching them the word of God. (PAUSE)

While Gallio was proconsul of Achaia, the Jews made a united attack on Paul and brought him into court. They charged:

Jew   This man is persuading the people to worship God in ways contrary to the law.

Narrator   Just as Paul was about to speak, Gallio said to the Jews:

Gallio   If you Jews were making a complaint about some misdemeanor or serious crime, it would be reasonable for me to listen to you. But since it involves questions about words and names and your own law—settle the matter yourselves. I will not be a judge of such things.

Narrator   So he had them ejected from the court. Then they all turned on Sosthenes the synagogue ruler and beat him in front of the court. But Gallio showed no concern whatever.

Cast: **Narrator, Paul, the Lord, Jew, Gallio**

Paul Returns to Antioch
Acts 18:18–23

Narrator | Paul stayed on in Corinth for some time. Then he left the brothers and sailed for Syria, accompanied by Priscilla and Aquila. Before he sailed, he had his hair cut off at Cenchrea because of a vow he had taken. They arrived at Ephesus, where Paul left Priscilla and Aquila. He himself went into the synagogue and reasoned with the Jews. When they asked him to spend more time with them, he declined. But as he left, he promised:

Paul | I will come back if it is God's will.

Narrator | Then he set sail from Ephesus. (PAUSE) When he landed at Caesarea, he went up and greeted the church and then went down to Antioch.

After spending some time in Antioch, Paul set out from there and traveled from place to place throughout the region of Galatia and Phrygia, strengthening all the disciples.

Cast: **Narrator, Paul**

Apollos
Acts 18:24–28

Narrator 1 | A Jew named Apollos, a native of Alexandria, came to Ephesus.

Narrator 2 | He was a learned man, with a thorough knowledge of the Scriptures. He had been instructed in the way of the Lord, and he spoke with great fervor and taught about Jesus accurately, though he knew only the baptism of John. He began to speak boldly in the synagogue.

Narrator 1 | When Priscilla and Aquila heard him, they invited him to their home and explained to him the way of God more adequately.

Narrator 2 | When Apollos wanted to go to Achaia, the brothers encouraged him and wrote to the disciples there to welcome him. On arriving, he was a great help to those who by grace had believed. For he vigorously refuted the Jews in public debate, proving from the Scriptures that Jesus was the Christ.

Cast: **Narrator 1, Narrator 2**

Paul in Ephesus
Acts 19:1–10

Narrator | While Apollos was at Corinth, Paul took the road through the interior and arrived at Ephesus. There he found some disciples and asked them:

Paul | Did you receive the Holy Spirit when you believed?

[Narrator | They answered:]

Believer 1	No, we have not even heard that there is a Holy Spirit.
[Narrator	So Paul asked:]
Paul	Then what baptism did you receive?
Believer 2	John's baptism.
Paul	John's baptism was a baptism of repentance. He told the people to believe in the one coming after him, that is, in Jesus.
Narrator	On hearing this, they were baptized into the name of the Lord Jesus. When Paul placed his hands on them, the Holy Spirit came on them, and they spoke in tongues and prophesied. There were about twelve men in all.
	Paul entered the synagogue and spoke boldly there for three months, arguing persuasively about the kingdom of God. But some of them became obstinate; they refused to believe and publicly maligned the Way. So Paul left them. He took the disciples with him and had discussions daily in the lecture hall of Tyrannus. This went on for two years, so that all the Jews and Greeks who lived in the province of Asia heard the word of the Lord.

Cast: **Narrator, Paul, Believer 1, Believer 2**

The Sons of Sceva
Acts 19:11–20

Narrator	God did extraordinary miracles through Paul, so that even handkerchiefs and aprons that had touched him were taken to the sick, and their illnesses were cured and the evil spirits left them.
	Some Jews who went around driving out evil spirits tried to invoke the name of the Lord Jesus over those who were demon-possessed. They would say:
Jew	In the name of Jesus, whom Paul preaches, I command you to come out.
Narrator	Seven sons of Sceva, a Jewish chief priest, were doing this. The evil spirit answered them:
Evil spirit	Jesus I know, and I know about Paul, but who are you?
Narrator	Then the man who had the evil spirit jumped on them and overpowered them all. He gave them such a beating that they ran out of the house naked and bleeding.
	When this became known to the Jews and Greeks living in Ephesus, they were all seized with fear, and the name of the Lord Jesus was held in high honor. Many of those who believed now came and openly confessed their evil deeds. A number who had practiced sorcery brought their scrolls together and burned them publicly. When they calculated

the value of the scrolls, the total came to fifty thousand drachmas. In this way the word of the Lord spread widely and grew in power.

Cast: **Narrator, Jew, Evil spirit**

The Riot in Ephesus
Acts 19:21–41

Narrator   Paul decided to go to Jerusalem, passing through Macedonia and Achaia. He said:

Paul   After I have been there, I must visit Rome also.

Narrator   He sent two of his helpers, Timothy and Erastus, to Macedonia, while he stayed in the province of Asia a little longer.

About that time there arose a great disturbance about the Way. A silversmith named Demetrius, who made silver shrines of Artemis, brought in no little business for the craftsmen. He called them together, along with the workmen in related trades, and said:

Demetrius   Men, you know we receive a good income from this business. And you see and hear how this fellow Paul has convinced and led astray large numbers of people here in Ephesus and in practically the whole province of Asia. He says that man-made gods are no gods at all. There is danger not only that our trade will lose its good name, but also that the temple of the great goddess Artemis will be discredited, and the goddess herself, who is worshiped throughout the province of Asia and the world, will be robbed of her divine majesty.

Narrator   When they heard this, they were furious [and began shouting:]

Person(s)
(shouting)   Great is Artemis of the Ephesians!

Narrator   Soon the whole city was in an uproar. The people seized Gaius and Aristarchus, Paul's traveling companions from Macedonia, and rushed as one man into the theater. Paul wanted to appear before the crowd, but the disciples would not let him. Even some of the officials of the province, friends of Paul, sent him a message begging him not to venture into the theater.

The assembly was in confusion: Some were shouting one thing, some another. Most of the people did not even know why they were there. The Jews pushed Alexander to the front, and some of the crowd shouted instructions to him. He motioned for silence in order to make a defense before the people. But when they realized he was a Jew, they all shouted in unison for about two hours:

Person(s)   Great is Artemis of the Ephesians!

Narrator   The city clerk quieted the crowd and said:

300

City clerk	Men of Ephesus, doesn't all the world know that the city of Ephesus is the guardian of the temple of the great Artemis and of her image, which fell from heaven? Therefore, since these facts are undeniable, you ought to be quiet and not do anything rash. You have brought these men here, though they have neither robbed temples nor blasphemed our goddess. If, then, Demetrius and his fellow craftsmen have a grievance against anybody, the courts are open and there are proconsuls. They can press charges. If there is anything further you want to bring up, it must be settled in a legal assembly. As it is, we are in danger of being charged with rioting because of today's events. In that case we would not be able to account for this commotion, since there is no reason for it.
Narrator	After he had said this, he dismissed the assembly.

Cast: **Narrator, Paul, Demetrius, Person(s), City clerk**

Paul's Last Visit to Troas

Acts 20:7–13 [14–16]

Luke	On the first day of the week we came together to break bread. Paul spoke to the people and, because he intended to leave the next day, kept on talking until midnight. There were many lamps in the upstairs room where we were meeting. Seated in a window was a young man named Eutychus, who was sinking into a deep sleep as Paul talked on and on. When he was sound asleep, he fell to the ground from the third story and was picked up dead. Paul went down, threw himself on the young man and put his arms around him. [He said:]
Paul	Don't be alarmed. He's alive!
Luke	Then he went upstairs again and broke bread and ate. After talking until daylight, he left. The people took the young man home alive and were greatly comforted.
	We went on ahead to the ship and sailed for Assos, where we were going to take Paul aboard. He had made this arrangement because he was going there on foot. [When he met us at Assos, we took him aboard and went on to Mitylene. The next day we set sail from there and arrived off Kios. The day after that we crossed over to Samos, and on the following day arrived at Miletus. Paul had decided to sail past Ephesus to avoid spending time in the province of Asia, for he was in a hurry to reach Jerusalem, if possible, by the day of Pentecost.]

Cast: **Luke, Paul**

Paul's Farewell to the Ephesian Elders

Acts 20:17–24 [25–31], 32–38

Narrator   From Miletus, Paul sent to Ephesus for the elders of the church. When they arrived, he said to them:

Paul   You know how I lived the whole time I was with you, from the first day I came into the province of Asia. I served the Lord with great humility and with tears, although I was severely tested by the plots of the Jews. You know that I have not hesitated to preach anything that would be helpful to you but have taught you publicly and from house to house. I have declared to both Jews and Greeks that they must turn to God in repentance and have faith in our Lord Jesus.

And now, compelled by the Spirit, I am going to Jerusalem, not knowing what will happen to me there. I only know that in every city the Holy Spirit warns me that prison and hardships are facing me. However, I consider my life worth nothing to me, if only I may finish the race and complete the task the Lord Jesus has given me—the task of testifying to the gospel of God's grace.

[Now I know that none of you among whom I have gone about preaching the kingdom will ever see me again. Therefore, I declare to you today that I am innocent of the blood of all men. For I have not hesitated to proclaim to you the whole will of God. Keep watch over yourselves and all the flock of which the Holy Spirit has made you overseers. Be shepherds of the church of God, which he bought with his own blood. I know that after I leave, savage wolves will come in among you and will not spare the flock. Even from your own number men will arise and distort the truth in order to draw away disciples after them. So be on your guard! Remember that for three years I never stopped warning each of you night and day with tears.]

Now I commit you to God and to the word of his grace, which can build you up and give you an inheritance among all those who are sanctified. I have not coveted anyone's silver or gold or clothing. You yourselves know that these hands of mine have supplied my own needs and the needs of my companions. In everything I did, I showed you that by this kind of hard work we must help the weak, remembering the words the Lord Jesus himself said: "It is more blessed to give than to receive."

Narrator   When he had said this, he knelt down with all of them and prayed. They all wept as they embraced him and kissed him. What grieved them most was his statement that they would never see his face again. Then they accompanied him to the ship.

Cast: **Narrator, Paul**

Paul Goes On to Jerusalem
Acts 21:3b–16

Luke   We landed at Tyre, where our ship was to unload its cargo. Finding the disciples there, we stayed with them seven days. Through the Spirit they urged Paul not to go on to Jerusalem. But when our time was up, we left and continued on our way. All the disciples and their wives and children accompanied us out of the city, and there on the beach we knelt to pray. After saying good-by to each other, we went aboard the ship, and they returned home.

We continued our voyage from Tyre and landed at Ptolemais, where we greeted the brothers and stayed with them for a day. Leaving the next day, we reached Caesarea and stayed at the house of Philip the evangelist, one of the Seven. He had four unmarried daughters who prophesied.

After we had been there a number of days, a prophet named Agabus came down from Judea. Coming over to us, he took Paul's belt, tied his own hands and feet with it and said:

Agabus   The Holy Spirit says, "In this way the Jews of Jerusalem will bind the owner of this belt and will hand him over to the Gentiles."

Luke   When we heard this, we and the people there pleaded with Paul not to go up to Jerusalem. [But he] answered:

Paul   Why are you weeping and breaking my heart? I am ready not only to be bound, but also to die in Jerusalem for the name of the Lord Jesus.

Luke   When he would not be dissuaded, we gave up [and said:]

Younger Luke The Lord's will be done.

Luke   After this, we got ready and went up to Jerusalem. Some of the disciples from Caesarea accompanied us and brought us to the home of Mnason, where we were to stay. He was a man from Cyprus and one of the early disciples.

Cast: **Luke**, **Agabus**, **Paul**, **younger Luke** (can be the same as Luke)

Paul's Arrival at Jerusalem
Acts 21:17–24, 26

Luke   When we arrived at Jerusalem, the brothers received us warmly. The next day Paul and the rest of us went to see James, and all the elders were present. Paul greeted them and reported in detail what God had done among the Gentiles through his ministry.

When they heard this, they praised God. [Then they said to Paul:]

303

Elder 1	You see, brother, how many thousands of Jews have believed, and all of them are zealous for the law.
Elder 2	They have been informed that you teach all the Jews who live among the Gentiles to turn away from Moses, telling them not to circumcise their children or live according to our customs.
Elder 1	What shall we do? (PAUSE) They will certainly hear that you have come, so do what we tell you.
Elder 2	There are four men with us who have made a vow. Take these men, join in their purification rites and pay their expenses, so that they can have their heads shaved.
Elder 1	Then everybody will know there is no truth in these reports about you, but that you yourself are living in obedience to the law. . . .
Luke	The next day Paul took the men and purified himself along with them. Then he went to the temple to give notice of the date when the days of purification would end and the offering would be made for each of them.

Cast: **Luke, Elder 1, Elder 2**

Paul Arrested
Acts 21:27–22:2

Narrator	When the seven days [of purification for Paul and four others] were nearly over, some Jews from the province of Asia saw Paul at the temple. They stirred up the whole crowd and seized him, [shouting:]
Jew 1 (loudly)	Men of Israel!
Jews 1 and 2	Help us!
Jew 2	This is the man who teaches all men everywhere against our people and our law and this place.
Jew 1	And besides, he has brought Greeks into the temple area and defiled this holy place.
Narrator	(They had previously seen Trophimus the Ephesian in the city with Paul and assumed that Paul had brought him into the temple area.)
	The whole city was aroused, and the people came running from all directions. Seizing Paul, they dragged him from the temple, and immediately the gates were shut. While they were trying to kill him, news reached the commander of the Roman troops that the whole city of Jerusalem was in an uproar. He at once took some officers and soldiers and ran down to the crowd. When the rioters saw the commander and his soldiers, they stopped beating Paul.
	The commander came up and arrested him and ordered him to be bound with two chains. [Then he asked:]

Commander	[Who is he, and what has he done?]
Narrator	Some in the crowd shouted one thing and some another, and since the commander could not get at the truth because of the uproar, he ordered that Paul be taken into the barracks. When Paul reached the steps, the violence of the mob was so great he had to be carried by the soldiers. The crowd that followed kept shouting:
Jews 1 and 2	Away with him!
Narrator	As the soldiers were about to take Paul into the barracks, he asked the commander:
Paul	May I say something to you?
Commander	Do you speak Greek? (PAUSE) Aren't you the Egyptian who started a revolt and led four thousand terrorists out into the desert some time ago?
Paul	I am a Jew, from Tarsus in Cilicia, a citizen of no ordinary city. Please let me speak to the people.
Narrator	Having received the commander's permission, Paul stood on the steps and motioned to the crowd. When they were all silent, he said to them in Aramaic:
Paul	Brothers and fathers, listen now to my defense.
Narrator	When they heard him speak to them in Aramaic, they became very quiet. [Then Paul said . . .]

Cast: **Narrator, Jew 1, Jew 2, Commander, Paul**

Paul Speaks to the Crowd
Acts 22:3–16

Paul	I am a Jew, born in Tarsus of Cilicia, but brought up in this city. Under Gamaliel I was thoroughly trained in the law of our fathers and was just as zealous for God as any of you are today. I persecuted the followers of this Way to their death, arresting both men and women and throwing them into prison, as also the high priest and all the Council can testify. I even obtained letters from them to their brothers in Damascus, and went there to bring these people as prisoners to Jerusalem to be punished.
	About noon as I came near Damascus, suddenly a bright light from heaven flashed around me. I fell to the ground and heard a voice say to me:
Voice	Saul! Saul! Why do you persecute me?
Paul	I asked:
Younger Paul	Who are you, Lord?

Voice	I am Jesus of Nazareth, whom you are persecuting.
Paul	My companions saw the light, but they did not understand the voice of him who was speaking to me.
Younger Paul	What shall I do, Lord?
Voice	Get up, and go into Damascus. There you will be told all that you have been assigned to do.
Paul	My companions led me by the hand into Damascus, because the brilliance of the light had blinded me.
	A man named Ananias came to see me. He was a devout observer of the law and highly respected by all the Jews living there. He stood beside me and said:
Ananias	Brother Saul, receive your sight!
Paul	And at that very moment I was able to see him.
Ananias	The God of our fathers has chosen you to know his will and to see the Righteous One and to hear words from his mouth. You will be his witness to all men of what you have seen and heard. And now what are you waiting for? Get up, be baptized and wash your sins away, calling on his name.

Cast: **Paul**, **Voice**, **younger Paul** (can be the same as Paul), **Ananias**

Paul Tells of His Call to Preach to the Gentiles
Acts 22:17–29

Paul	When I returned to Jerusalem and was praying at the temple, I fell into a trance and saw the Lord speaking.
The Lord	Quick! Leave Jerusalem immediately, because they will not accept your testimony about me.
Paul	Lord, these men know that I went from one synagogue to another to imprison and beat those who believe in you. And when the blood of your martyr Stephen was shed, I stood there giving my approval and guarding the clothes of those who were killing him. [Then the Lord said to me:]
The Lord	Go; I will send you far away to the Gentiles.
Narrator	The crowd listened to Paul until he said this. Then they raised their voices and shouted:
Person 1	Rid the earth of him!
Person 2	He's not fit to live!
Narrator	As they were shouting and throwing off their cloaks and flinging dust into the air, the commander ordered Paul to be taken into the barracks.

He directed that he be flogged and questioned in order to find out why the people were shouting at him like this. As they stretched him out to flog him, Paul said to the centurion standing there:

Paul
Is it legal for you to flog a Roman citizen who hasn't even been found guilty?

Narrator
When the centurion heard this, he went to the commander and reported it.

Centurion
(alarmed) What are you going to do? This man is a Roman citizen.

Narrator
The commander went to Paul and asked:

Commander
Tell me, are you a Roman citizen?

Paul
Yes, I am.

Commander
(ruefully) I had to pay a big price for my citizenship.

Paul
But I was born a citizen.

Narrator
Those who were about to question him withdrew immediately. The commander himself was alarmed when he realized that he had put Paul, a Roman citizen, in chains.

Cast: **Paul, the Lord, Narrator, Person 1, Person 2** (can be the same as Person 1), **Centurion, Commander**

Paul before the Sanhedrin
Acts 22:30–23:11

Narrator
Since the commander wanted to find out exactly why Paul was being accused by the Jews, he released him and ordered the chief priests and all the Sanhedrin to assemble. Then he brought Paul and had him stand before them. Paul looked straight at the Sanhedrin and said:

Paul
My brothers, I have fulfilled my duty to God in all good conscience to this day.

Narrator
At this the high priest Ananias ordered those standing near Paul to strike him on the mouth.

Paul
God will strike you, you whitewashed wall! You sit there to judge me according to the law, yet you yourself violate the law by commanding that I be struck!

[Narrator
Those who were standing near Paul said:]

Man
You dare to insult God's high priest?

Paul
Brothers, I did not realize that he was the high priest; for it is written: "Do not speak evil about the ruler of your people."

Narrator	Then Paul, knowing that some of them were Sadducees and the others Pharisees, called out in the Sanhedrin:
Paul	My brothers, I am a Pharisee, the son of a Pharisee. I stand on trial because of my hope in the resurrection of the dead.
Narrator	When he said this, a dispute broke out between the Pharisees and the Sadducees, and the assembly was divided. (The Sadducees say that there is no resurrection, and that there are neither angels nor spirits, but the Pharisees acknowledge them all.)
	There was a great uproar, and some of the teachers of the law who were Pharisees stood up and argued vigorously.
Pharisee 1	We find nothing wrong with this man.
Pharisee 2	What if a spirit or an angel has spoken to him?
Narrator	The dispute became so violent that the commander was afraid Paul would be torn to pieces by them. He ordered the troops to go down and take him away from them by force and bring him into the barracks. (PAUSE)
	The following night the Lord stood near Paul and said:
The Lord	Take courage! As you have testified about me in Jerusalem, so you must also testify (PAUSE) in Rome.

Cast: **Narrator, Paul, Man, Pharisee 1, Pharisee 2** (can be the same as Pharisee 1), **the Lord**

The Plot to Kill Paul
Acts 23:12–22

Narrator	The Jews formed a conspiracy and bound themselves with an oath not to eat or drink until they had killed Paul. More than forty men were involved in this plot. They went to the chief priests and elders and said:
Conspirator	We have taken a solemn oath not to eat anything until we have killed Paul. Now then, you and the Sanhedrin petition the commander to bring him before you on the pretext of wanting more accurate information about his case. We are ready to kill him before he gets here.
Narrator	But when the son of Paul's sister heard of this plot, he went into the barracks and told Paul. Then Paul called one of the centurions and said:
Paul	Take this young man to the commander; he has something to tell him.
Narrator	So he took him to the commander. The centurion said:
Centurion (to Commander)	Paul, the prisoner, sent for me and asked me to bring this young man to you because he has something to tell you.

Narrator	The commander took the young man by the hand, drew him aside and asked:
Commander	What is it you want to tell me?
Narrator	He said:
Paul's nephew	The Jews have agreed to ask you to bring Paul before the Sanhedrin tomorrow on the pretext of wanting more accurate information about him. Don't give in to them, because more than forty of them are waiting in ambush for him. They have taken an oath not to eat or drink until they have killed him. They are ready now, waiting for your consent to their request.
Narrator	The commander dismissed the young man and cautioned him:
Commander	Don't tell anyone that you have reported this to me.

Cast: **Narrator**, **Conspirator**, **Paul**, **Centurion**, **Commander**, **Paul's nephew**

Paul Transferred to Caesarea
Acts 23:23–35

Narrator	[The commander] called two of his centurions and ordered them:
Commander	Get ready a detachment of two hundred soldiers, seventy horsemen and two hundred spearmen to go to Caesarea at nine tonight. Provide mounts for Paul so that he may be taken safely to Governor Felix.
Narrator	He wrote a letter as follows:
Commander	Claudius Lysias, To His Excellency, Governor Felix: Greetings.
	This man was seized by the Jews and they were about to kill him, but I came with my troops and rescued him, for I had learned that he is a Roman citizen. I wanted to know why they were accusing him, so I brought him to their Sanhedrin. I found that the accusation had to do with questions about their law, but there was no charge against him that deserved death or imprisonment. When I was informed of a plot to be carried out against the man, I sent him to you at once. I also ordered his accusers to present to you their case against him.
Narrator	So the soldiers, carrying out their orders, took Paul with them during the night and brought him as far as Antipatris. The next day they let the cavalry go on with him, while they returned to the barracks. When the cavalry arrived in Caesarea, they delivered the letter to the governor and handed Paul over to him. The governor read the letter and asked what province he was from. Learning that he was from Cilicia, he said:
Governor	I will hear your case when your accusers get here.

Narrator   Then he ordered that Paul be kept under guard in Herod's palace.

Cast: **Narrator, Commander, Governor**

Paul Accused by the Jews
Acts 24:1–23

Narrator   [Five days later] the high priest Ananias went down to Caesarea with some of the elders and a lawyer named Tertullus, and they brought their charges against Paul before the governor. When Paul was called in, Tertullus presented his case before Felix [as follows:]

Tertullus   We have enjoyed a long period of peace under you, and your foresight has brought about reforms in this nation. Everywhere and in every way, most excellent Felix, we acknowledge this with profound gratitude. But in order not to weary you further, I would request that you be kind enough to hear us briefly.

We have found this man to be a troublemaker, stirring up riots among the Jews all over the world. He is a ringleader of the Nazarene sect and even tried to desecrate the temple; so we seized him. By examining him yourself you will be able to learn the truth about all these charges we are bringing against him.

Narrator   The Jews joined in the accusation, asserting that these things were true. (PAUSE) When the governor motioned for him to speak, Paul replied:

Paul   I know that for a number of years you have been a judge over this nation; so I gladly make my defense. You can easily verify that no more than twelve days ago I went up to Jerusalem to worship. My accusers did not find me arguing with anyone at the temple, or stirring up a crowd in the synagogues or anywhere else in the city. And they cannot prove to you the charges they are now making against me. However, I admit that I worship the God of our fathers as a follower of the Way, which they call a sect. I believe everything that agrees with the Law and that is written in the Prophets, and I have the same hope in God as these men, that there will be a resurrection of both the righteous and the wicked. So I strive always to keep my conscience clear before God and man.

After an absence of several years, I came to Jerusalem to bring my people gifts for the poor and to present offerings. I was ceremonially clean when they found me in the temple courts doing this. There was no crowd with me, nor was I involved in any disturbance. But there are some Jews from the province of Asia, who ought to be here before you and bring charges if they have anything against me. Or these who are here should state what crime they found in me when I stood before the Sanhedrin—unless it was this one thing I shouted as I stood in their presence: "It is concerning the resurrection of the dead that I am on trial before you today."

Narrator	Then Felix, who was well acquainted with the Way, adjourned the proceedings [saying:]
Felix	When Lysias the commander comes, I will decide your case.
Narrator	He ordered the centurion to keep Paul under guard but to give him some freedom and permit his friends to take care of his needs.

Cast: **Narrator, Tertullus, Paul, Felix**

Paul before Felix and Drusilla
Acts 24:24–27

Narrator	Felix came with his wife Drusilla, who was a Jewess. He sent for Paul and listened to him as he spoke about faith in Christ Jesus. As Paul discoursed on righteousness, self-control and the judgment to come, Felix was afraid and said:
Felix (nervously)	That's enough for now! You may leave. When I find it convenient, I will send for you.
Narrator	At the same time he was hoping that Paul would offer him a bribe, so he sent for him frequently and talked with him.
	When two years had passed, Felix was succeeded by Porcius Festus, but because Felix wanted to grant a favor to the Jews, he left Paul in prison.

Cast: **Narrator, Felix**

The Trial before Festus
Acts 25:1–12

Narrator	Three days after arriving in the province, Festus went up from Caesarea to Jerusalem, where the chief priests and Jewish leaders appeared before him and presented the charges against Paul. They urgently requested Festus, as a favor to them, to have Paul transferred to Jerusalem, for they were preparing an ambush to kill him along the way. Festus answered:
Festus	Paul is being held at Caesarea, and I myself am going there soon. Let some of your leaders come with me and press charges against the man there, if he has done anything wrong.
Narrator	After spending eight or ten days with them, [Festus] went down to Caesarea, and the next day he convened the court and ordered that Paul be brought before him. When Paul appeared, the Jews who had come down from Jerusalem stood around him, bringing many serious charges against him, which they could not prove. Then Paul made his defense:
Paul	I have done nothing wrong against the law of the Jews or against the temple or against Caesar.

Narrator	Festus, wishing to do the Jews a favor, said to Paul:
Festus	Are you willing to go up to Jerusalem and stand trial before me there on these charges?
Paul	I am now standing before Caesar's court, where I ought to be tried. I have not done any wrong to the Jews, as you yourself know very well. If, however, I am guilty of doing anything deserving death, I do not refuse to die. But if the charges brought against me by these Jews are not true, no one has the right to hand me over to them. I appeal to Caesar!
Narrator	After Festus had conferred with his council, he declared:
Festus	You have appealed to Caesar. To Caesar you will go!

Cast: **Narrator, Festus, Paul**

Paul before Agrippa
Acts 25:13–27

Narrator	King Agrippa and Bernice arrived at Caesarea to pay their respects to Festus. Since they were spending many days there, Festus discussed Paul's case with the king. He said:
Festus	There is a man here whom Felix left as a prisoner. When I went to Jerusalem, the chief priests and elders of the Jews brought charges against him and asked that he be condemned.
	I told them that it is not the Roman custom to hand over any man before he has faced his accusers and has had an opportunity to defend himself against their charges. When they came here with me, I did not delay the case, but convened the court the next day and ordered the man to be brought in. When his accusers got up to speak, they did not charge him with any of the crimes I had expected. Instead, they had some points of dispute with him about their own religion and about a dead man named Jesus who Paul claimed was alive. I was at a loss how to investigate such matters; so I asked if he would be willing to go to Jerusalem and stand trial there on these charges. When Paul made his appeal to be held over for the Emperor's decision, I ordered him held until I could send him to Caesar.
Narrator	Then Agrippa said to Festus:
Agrippa	I would like to hear this man myself.
Festus	Tomorrow you will hear him.
Narrator	The next day Agrippa and Bernice came with great pomp and entered the audience room with the high ranking officers and the leading men of the city. At the command of Festus, Paul was brought in. Festus said:
Festus	King Agrippa, and all who are present with us, you see this man! The whole Jewish community has petitioned me about him in Jerusalem

and here in Caesarea, shouting that he ought not to live any longer. I found he had done nothing deserving of death, but because he made his appeal to the Emperor I decided to send him to Rome. But I have nothing definite to write to His Majesty about him. Therefore I have brought him before all of you, and especially before you, King Agrippa, so that as a result of this investigation I may have something to write. For I think it is unreasonable to send on a prisoner without specifying the charges against him.

Cast: **Narrator, Festus, Agrippa**

Paul Defends Himself before Agrippa
Acts 26:1–18

Narrator   Agrippa said to Paul:

Agrippa   You have permission to speak for yourself.

Narrator   So Paul motioned with his hand and began his defense:

Paul   King Agrippa, I consider myself fortunate to stand before you today as I make my defense against all the accusations of the Jews, and especially so because you are well acquainted with all the Jewish customs and controversies. Therefore, I beg you to listen to me patiently. (PAUSE)

The Jews all know the way I have lived ever since I was a child, from the beginning of my life in my own country, and also in Jerusalem. They have known me for a long time and can testify, if they are willing, that according to the strictest sect of our religion, I lived as a Pharisee. And now it is because of my hope in what God has promised our fathers that I am on trial today. This is the promise our twelve tribes are hoping to see fulfilled as they earnestly serve God day and night. O king, it is because of this hope that the Jews are accusing me. Why should any of you consider it incredible that God raises the dead

I too was convinced that I ought to do all that was possible to oppose the name of Jesus of Nazareth. And that is just what I did in Jerusalem. On the authority of the chief priests I put many of the saints in prison, and when they were put to death, I cast my vote against them. Many a time I went from one synagogue to another to have them punished, and I tried to force them to blaspheme. In my obsession against them, I even went to foreign cities to persecute them.

On one of these journeys I was going to Damascus with the authority and commission of the chief priests. About noon, O king, as I was on the road, I saw a light from heaven, brighter than the sun, blazing around me and my companions. We all fell to the ground, and I heard a voice saying to me in Aramaic:

Voice   Saul, Saul, why do you persecute me? It is hard for you to kick against the goads.

313

Paul	Then I asked, "Who are you, Lord?"
Voice	I am Jesus, whom you are persecuting. Now get up and stand on your feet. I have appeared to you to appoint you as a servant and as a witness of what you have seen of me and what I will show you. I will rescue you from your own people and from the Gentiles. I am sending you to them to open their eyes and turn them from darkness to light, and from the power of Satan to God, so that they may receive forgiveness of sins and a place among those who are sanctified by faith in me.

Cast: **Narrator, Agrippa, Paul, Voice**

Paul Tells of His Work
Acts 26:19–32

Paul	King Agrippa, I was not disobedient to the vision from heaven. First to those in Damascus, then to those in Jerusalem and in all Judea, and to the Gentiles also, I preached that they should repent and turn to God and prove their repentance by their deeds. That is why the Jews seized me in the temple courts and tried to kill me. But I have had God's help to this very day, and so I stand here and testify to small and great alike. I am saying nothing beyond what the prophets and Moses said would happen—that the Christ would suffer and, as the first to rise from the dead, would proclaim light to his own people and to the Gentiles.
Narrator	At this point Festus interrupted Paul's defense.
Festus	You are out of your mind, Paul! Your great learning is driving you insane.
Paul	I am not insane, most excellent Festus. What I am saying is true and reasonable. The king is familiar with these things, and I can speak freely to him. I am convinced that none of this has escaped his notice, because it was not done in a corner. King Agrippa, do you believe the prophets? I know you do.
[Narrator	Then Agrippa said to Paul:]
Agrippa	Do you think that in such a short time you can persuade me to be a Christian?
Paul	Short time or long—I pray God that not only you but all who are listening to me today may become what I am, except for these chains.
Narrator	The king rose, and with him the governor and Bernice and those sitting with them. They left the room, and while talking with one another, they said:
Agrippa (to Companion)	This man is not doing anything that deserves death—
Companion	Or imprisonment.

314

Narrator	Agrippa said to Festus:
Agrippa	This man could have been set free if he had not appealed to Caesar.

Cast: **Paul, Narrator, Festus, Agrippa, Companion** (can be the same as Agrippa)

Paul Sails for Rome
Acts 27:1–12

Luke	When it was decided that we would sail for Italy, Paul and some other prisoners were handed over to a centurion named Julius, who belonged to the Imperial Regiment. We boarded a ship from Adramyttium about to sail for ports along the coast of the province of Asia, and we put out to sea. Aristarchus, a Macedonian from Thessalonica, was with us.
	The next day we landed at Sidon; and Julius, in kindness to Paul, allowed him to go to his friends so they might provide for his needs. From there we put out to sea again and passed to the lee of Cyprus because the winds were against us. When we had sailed across the open sea off the coast of Cilicia and Pamphylia, we landed at Myra in Lycia. There the centurion found an Alexandrian ship sailing for Italy and put us on board. We made slow headway for many days and had difficulty arriving off Cnidus. When the wind did not allow us to hold our course, we sailed to the lee of Crete, opposite Salmone. We moved along the coast with difficulty and came to a place called Fair Havens, near the town of Lasea.
	Much time had been lost, and sailing had already become dangerous because by now it was after the Fast. So Paul warned them:
Paul	Men, I can see that our voyage is going to be disastrous and bring great loss to ship and cargo, and to our own lives also.
Luke	But the centurion, instead of listening to what Paul said, followed the advice of the pilot and of the owner of the ship. Since the harbor was unsuitable to winter in, the majority decided that we should sail on, hoping to reach Phoenix and winter there. This was a harbor in Crete, facing both southwest and northwest.

Cast: **Luke, Paul.** (Please note overlap with the reading from Acts 27:9–38.)

The Storm
Acts 27:9–38

Luke	Much time had been lost, and sailing had already become dangerous because by now it was after the Fast. So Paul warned them:
Paul	Men, I can see that our voyage is going to be disastrous and bring great loss to ship and cargo, and to our own lives also.

Luke But the centurion, instead of listening to what Paul said, followed the advice of the pilot and of the owner of the ship. Since the harbor was unsuitable to winter in, the majority decided that we should sail on, hoping to reach Phoenix and winter there. This was a harbor in Crete, facing both southwest and northwest.

When a gentle south wind began to blow, they thought they had obtained what they wanted; so they weighed anchor and sailed along the shore of Crete. Before very long, a wind of hurricane force, called the "northeaster," swept down from the island. The ship was caught by the storm and could not head into the wind; so we gave way to it and were driven along. As we passed to the lee of a small island called Cauda, we were hardly able to make the lifeboat secure. When the men had hoisted it aboard, they passed ropes under the ship itself to hold it together. Fearing that they would run aground on the sandbars of Syrtis, they lowered the sea anchor and let the ship be driven along. We took such a violent battering from the storm that the next day they began to throw the cargo overboard. On the third day, they threw the ship's tackle overboard with their own hands. When neither sun nor stars appeared for many days and the storm continued raging, we finally gave up all hope of being saved.

After the men had gone a long time without food, Paul stood up before them and said:

Paul Men, you should have taken my advice not to sail from Crete; then you would have spared yourselves this damage and loss. But now I urge you to keep up your courage, because not one of you will be lost; only the ship will be destroyed. Last night an angel of the God whose I am and whom I serve stood beside me and said, "Do not be afraid, Paul. You must stand trial before Caesar; and God has graciously given you the lives of all who sail with you." So keep up your courage, men, for I have faith in God that it will happen just as he told me. Nevertheless, we must run aground on some island.

Luke On the fourteenth night we were still being driven across the Adriatic Sea, when about midnight the sailors sensed they were approaching land. They took soundings and found that the water was a hundred and twenty feet deep. A short time later they took soundings again and found it was ninety feet deep. Fearing that we would be dashed against the rocks, they dropped four anchors from the stern and prayed for daylight. In an attempt to escape from the ship, the sailors let the lifeboat down into the sea, pretending they were going to lower some anchors from the bow. Then Paul said to the centurion and the soldiers:

Paul Unless these men stay with the ship, you cannot be saved.

Luke So the soldiers cut the ropes that held the lifeboat and let it fall away.

Just before dawn Paul urged them all to eat.

Paul	For the last fourteen days, you have been in constant suspense and have gone without food—you haven't eaten anything. Now I urge you to take some food. You need it to survive. Not one of you will lose a single hair from his head.
Luke	After he said this, he took some bread and gave thanks to God in front of them all. Then he broke it and began to eat. They were all encouraged and ate some food themselves. Altogether there were 276 of us on board. When they had eaten as much as they wanted, they lightened the ship by throwing the grain into the sea.

Cast: **Luke, Paul.** (Please note overlap with the reading from Acts 27:1–12.)

The Shipwreck
Acts 27:39–44

Narrator 1	When daylight came, [the sailors] did not recognize the land, but they saw a bay with a sandy beach, where they decided to run the ship aground if they could.
Narrator 2	Cutting loose the anchors, they left them in the sea and at the same time untied the ropes that held the rudders.
Narrator 1	Then they hoisted the foresail to the wind and made for the beach.
Narrator 2	But the ship struck a sandbar and ran aground. The bow stuck fast and would not move, and the stern was broken to pieces by the pounding of the surf.
Narrator 1	The soldiers planned to kill the prisoners to prevent any of them from swimming away and escaping.
Narrator 2	But the centurion wanted to spare Paul's life and kept them from carrying out their plan.
Narrator 1	He ordered those who could swim to jump overboard first and get to land.
Narrator 2	The rest were to get there on planks or on pieces of the ship.
Narrator 1	In this way everyone reached land in safety.

Cast: **Narrator 1, Narrator 2.** (If used with previous and/or subsequent readings, both Narrators are the same as Luke.)

Paul Ashore on Malta—and on to Rome
Acts 28:1–10 [11–15]

Luke	Once safely on shore, we found out that the island was called Malta. The islanders showed us unusual kindness. They built a fire and welcomed us all because it was raining and cold. Paul gathered a pile of brushwood and, as he put it on the fire, a viper, driven out by the heat,

	fastened itself on his hand. When the islanders saw the snake hanging from his hand, they said to each other:
Person 1	This man must be a murderer.
Person 2	For though he escaped from the sea, Justice has not allowed him to live.
Luke	But Paul shook the snake off into the fire and suffered no ill effects. The people expected him to swell up or suddenly fall dead, but after waiting a long time and seeing nothing unusual happen to him, they changed their minds and said:
Persons 1 and 2	He [is] a god.
Luke	There was an estate nearby that belonged to Publius, the chief official of the island. He welcomed us to his home and for three days entertained us hospitably. His father was sick in bed, suffering from fever and dysentery. Paul went in to see him and, after prayer, placed his hands on him and healed him. When this had happened, the rest of the sick on the island came and were cured. They honored us in many ways and when we were ready to sail, they furnished us with the supplies we needed. (PAUSE)

[After three months we put out to sea in a ship that had wintered in the island. It was an Alexandrian ship with the figurehead of the twin gods Castor and Pollux. We put in at Syracuse and stayed there three days. From there we set sail and arrived at Rhegium. The next day the south wind came up, and on the following day we reached Puteoli. There we found some brothers who invited us to spend a week with them. And so we came to Rome. The brothers there had heard that we were coming, and they traveled as far as the Forum of Appius and the Three Taverns to meet us. At the sight of these men Paul thanked God and was encouraged.]

Cast: **Luke, Person 1, Person 2**

Paul Preaches at Rome under Guard
Acts 28:16–31

Luke	When we got to Rome, Paul was allowed to live by himself, with a soldier to guard him.
	Three days later he called together the leaders of the Jews. [When they had assembled, Paul said to them:]
Paul	My brothers, although I have done nothing against our people or against the customs of our ancestors, I was arrested in Jerusalem and handed over to the Romans. They examined me and wanted to release me, because I was not guilty of any crime deserving death. But when the Jews objected, I was compelled to appeal to Caesar—not that I had any charge to bring against my own people. For this reason I have asked to

see you and talk with you. It is because of the hope of Israel that I am bound with this chain.

[Luke　　　　They replied:]

Jewish leader　We have not received any letters from Judea concerning you, and none of the brothers who have come from there has reported or said anything bad about you. But we want to hear what your views are, for we know that people everywhere are talking against this sect.

Luke　　　　They arranged to meet Paul on a certain day, and came in even larger numbers to the place where he was staying. From morning till evening he explained and declared to them the kingdom of God and tried to convince them about Jesus from the Law of Moses and from the Prophets. Some were convinced by what he said, but others would not believe. They disagreed among themselves and began to leave after Paul had made this final statement:

Paul　　　　The Holy Spirit spoke the truth to your forefathers when he said through Isaiah the prophet:

Isaiah　　　　Go to this people and say:
"You will be ever hearing but never understanding;
　you will be ever seeing but never perceiving."
For this people's heart has become calloused;
　they hardly hear with their ears,
　and they have closed their eyes.
Otherwise they might see with their eyes,
　hear with their ears,
　understand with their hearts
　and turn, and I would heal them.

Paul　　　　Therefore I want you to know that God's salvation has been sent to the Gentiles, and they will listen!

Luke　　　　For two whole years Paul stayed there in his own rented house and welcomed all who came to see him. Boldly and without hindrance he preached the kingdom of God and taught about the Lord Jesus Christ.

Cast: **Luke, Paul, Jewish leader, Isaiah**

Romans

Is God Being Just?
Romans 2:28–3:8

Answer   A man is not a Jew if he is only one outwardly, nor is circumcision merely outward and physical. No, a man is a Jew if he is one inwardly; and circumcision is circumcision of the heart, by the Spirit, not by the written code. Such a man's praise is not from men, but from God.

Question   What advantage, then, is there in being a Jew, or what value is there in circumcision?

Answer   Much in every way! First of all, they have been entrusted with the very words of God.

Question   What if some did not have faith? Will their lack of faith nullify God's faithfulness?

Answer   Not at all! Let God be true, and every man a liar. As it is written:

Psalmist   So that you may be proved right when you speak
    and prevail when you judge.

Question   But if our unrighteousness brings out God's righteousness more clearly, what shall we say? That God is unjust in bringing his wrath on us? (I am using a human argument.)

Answer   Certainly not! If that were so, how could God judge the world?

Question   If my falsehood enhances God's truthfulness and so increases his glory, why am I still condemned as a sinner? Why not say—as we are being slanderously reported as saying and as some claim that we say—"Let us do evil that good may result"?

Answer   Their condemnation is deserved.

Cast: **Answer**, **Question**, **Psalmist** (can be the same as Answer)

Righteousness through Faith
Romans 3:9–26

Paul   What shall we conclude then? Are we any better? Not at all! We have already made the charge that Jews and Gentiles alike are all under sin. As it is written:

Psalmist   There is no one righteous, not even one;
    there is no one who understands,
    no one who seeks God.
All have turned away,
    they have together become worthless;

320

there is no one who does good,
not even one.
Their throats are open graves;
their tongues practice deceit.
The poison of vipers is on their lips.
Their mouths are full of cursing and bitterness.

Isaiah

Their feet are swift to shed blood;
ruin and misery mark their ways,
and the way of peace they do not know.

Psalmist

There is no fear of God before their eyes.

Paul

Now we know that whatever the law says, it says to those who are under the law, so that every mouth may be silenced and the whole world held accountable to God. Therefore no one will be declared righteous in his sight by observing the law; rather, through the law we become conscious of sin.

But now a righteousness from God, apart from law, has been made known, to which the Law and the Prophets testify. This righteousness from God comes through faith in Jesus Christ to all who believe. There is no difference, for all have sinned and fall short of the glory of God, and are justified freely by his grace through the redemption that came by Christ Jesus. God presented him as a sacrifice of atonement, through faith in his blood. He did this to demonstrate his justice, because in his forbearance he had left the sins committed beforehand unpunished—he did it to demonstrate his justice at the present time, so as to be just and the one who justifies those who have faith in Jesus.

Cast: **Paul, Psalmist, Isaiah**

Faith and Law
Romans 3:[25–26], 27–31

Question

[God . . . in his forbearance . . . left the sins committed beforehand unpunished—he did it to demonstrate his justice at the present time, so as to be just and the one who justifies those who have faith in Jesus.]* (PAUSE) Where, then, is boasting?

Answer

It is excluded.

Question

On what principle? On that of observing the law?

Answer

No, but on that of faith. For we maintain that a man is justified by faith apart from observing the law.

Question

Is God the God of Jews only? Is he not the God of Gentiles too?

Answer

Yes, of Gentiles too, since there is only one God, who will justify the circumcised by faith and the uncircumcised through that same faith.

Question

Do we, then, nullify the law by this faith?

Answer	Not at all! Rather, we uphold the law.

Cast: **Question, Answer.** (*The words in brackets must be omitted if this passage is read in sequence with the last.)

Abraham Justified by Faith
Romans 4:1–12

Question	What then shall we say that Abraham, our forefather, discovered in this matter?
Answer	If, in fact, Abraham was justified by works, he had something to boast about—but not before God. What does the Scripture say?
Reader	Abraham believed God, and it was credited to him as righteousness.
Answer	Now when a man works, his wages are not credited to him as a gift, but as an obligation. However, to the man who does not work but trusts God who justifies the wicked, his faith is credited as righteousness. David says the same thing when he speaks of the blessedness of the man to whom God credits righteousness apart from works:

Reader	"Blessed are they
	    whose transgressions are forgiven,
	    whose sins are covered.
	Blessed is the man
	    whose sin the Lord will never count against him."

Question	Is this blessedness only for the circumcised, or also for the uncircumcised?
Reader	We have been saying that Abraham's faith was credited to him as righteousness.
Question	Under what circumstances was it credited? Was it after he was circumcised, or before?
Answer	It was not after, but before! And he received the sign of circumcision, a seal of the righteousness that he had by faith while he was still uncircumcised. So then, he is the father of all who believe but have not been circumcised, in order that righteousness might be credited to them. And he is also the father of the circumcised who not only are circumcised but who also walk in the footsteps of the faith that our father Abraham had before he was circumcised.

Cast: **Question, Answer, Reader**

God's Promise Received through Faith
Romans 4:13–25

Paul	It was not through law that Abraham and his offspring received the promise that he would be heir of the world, but through the righteous-

ness that comes by faith. For if those who live by law are heirs, faith has no value and the promise is worthless, because law brings wrath. And where there is no law there is no transgression.

Therefore, the promise comes by faith, so that it may be by grace and may be guaranteed to all Abraham's offspring—not only to those who are of the law but also to those who are of the faith of Abraham. He is the father of us all. As it is written:

Genesis   I have made you a father of many nations.

Paul   He is our father in the sight of God, in whom he believed—the God who gives life to the dead and calls things that are not as though they were.

Against all hope, Abraham in hope believed and so became the father of many nations, just as it had been said to him:

Genesis   So shall your offspring be.

Paul   Without weakening in his faith, he faced the fact that his body was as good as dead—since he was about a hundred years old—and that Sarah's womb was also dead. Yet he did not waver through unbelief regarding the promise of God, but was strengthened in his faith and gave glory to God, being fully persuaded that God had power to do what he had promised. This is why:

Genesis   It was credited to him as righteousness.

Paul   The words:

Genesis   It was credited to him—

Paul   were written not for him alone, but also for us, to whom God will credit righteousness—for us who believe in him who raised Jesus our Lord from the dead. He was delivered over to death for our sins and was raised to life for our justification.

Cast: **Paul, Genesis**

Peace and Joy
Romans 5:1–11

Voice 1   Since we have been justified through faith, we have peace with God through our Lord Jesus Christ, through whom we have gained access by faith into this grace in which we now stand. And we rejoice in the hope of the glory of God.

Voice 2   Not only so, but we also rejoice in our sufferings, because we know that suffering produces perseverance; perseverance, character; and character, hope.

Voice 1   And hope does not disappoint us, because God has poured out his love into our hearts by the Holy Spirit, whom he has given us.

You see, at just the right time, when we were still powerless, Christ died for the ungodly.

Voice 2   Very rarely will anyone die for a righteous man, though for a good man someone might possibly dare to die. But God demonstrates his own love for us in this: While we were still sinners, Christ died for us.

Voice 1   Since we have now been justified by his blood, how much more shall we be saved from God's wrath through him!

Voice 2   For if, when we were God's enemies, we were reconciled to him through the death of his Son, how much more, having been reconciled, shall we be saved through his life!

Voice 1   Not only is this so, but we also rejoice in God through our Lord Jesus Christ, through whom we have now received reconciliation.

Cast: **Voice 1** (enthusiastic), **Voice 2** (serious)

Dead to Sin, Alive in Christ
From Romans 6:1–23

Question   What shall we say, then? Shall we go on sinning so that grace may increase?

Answer   By no means! We died to sin; how can we live in it any longer? . . . Therefore do not let sin reign in your mortal body so that you obey its evil desires. Do not offer the parts of your body to sin, as instruments of wickedness, but rather offer yourselves to God, as those who have been brought from death to life; and offer the parts of your body to him as instruments of righteousness. For sin shall not be your master, because you are not under law, but under grace.

Question   What then? Shall we sin because we are not under law but under grace?

Answer   By no means! Don't you know that when you offer yourselves to someone to obey him as slaves, you are slaves to the one whom you obey—whether you are slaves to sin, which leads to death, or to obedience, which leads to righteousness? But thanks be to God that, though you used to be slaves to sin, you wholeheartedly obeyed the form of teaching to which you were entrusted. You have been set free from sin and have become slaves to righteousness. . . . What benefit did you reap at that time from the things you are now ashamed of?

Question   Those things result in death!

Answer   But now that you have been set free from sin and have become slaves to God, the benefit you reap leads to holiness, and the result is eternal life. For the wages of sin is death, but the gift of God is eternal life in Christ Jesus our Lord.

Cast: **Question, Answer**

Struggling with Sin
Romans 7:6–13

Answer   Now, by dying to what once bound us, we have been released from the law so that we serve in the new way of the Spirit, and not in the old way of the written code.

Question   What shall we say, then? Is the law sin?

Answer   Certainly not! Indeed I would not have known what sin was except through the law. For I would not have known what coveting really was if the law had not said, "Do not covet." But sin, seizing the opportunity afforded by the commandment, produced in me every kind of covetous desire. For apart from law, sin is dead. Once I was alive apart from law; but when the commandment came, sin sprang to life and I died. I found that the very commandment that was intended to bring life actually brought death. For sin, seizing the opportunity afforded by the commandment, deceived me, and through the commandment put me to death. So then, the law is holy, and the commandment is holy, righteous and good.

Question   Did that which is good, then, become death to me?

Answer   By no means! But in order that sin might be recognized as sin, it produced death in me through what was good, so that through the commandment sin might become utterly sinful.

Cast: **Answer, Question**

Life through the Spirit
Romans 8:1–11

Voice 1   There is now no condemnation for those who are in Christ Jesus, because through Christ Jesus the law of the Spirit of life set me free from the law of sin and death. For what the law was powerless to do in that it was weakened by the sinful nature, God did by sending his own Son in the likeness of sinful man to be a sin offering. And so he condemned sin in sinful man, in order that the righteous requirements of the law might be fully met in us, who do not live according to the sinful nature but according to the Spirit.

Voice 2   Those who live according to the sinful nature have their minds set on what that nature desires.

Voice 1   But those who live in accordance with the Spirit have their minds set on what the Spirit desires.

Voice 2   The mind of sinful man is death.

Voice 1   But the mind controlled by the Spirit is life and peace.

Voice 2	The sinful mind is hostile to God. It does not submit to God's law, nor can it do so. Those controlled by the sinful nature cannot please God.
Voice 1	You, however, are controlled not by the sinful nature but by the Spirit, if the Spirit of God lives in you.
Voice 2	And if anyone does not have the Spirit of Christ, he does not belong to Christ.
Voice 1	But if Christ is in you, your body is dead because of sin, yet your spirit is alive because of righteousness. And if the Spirit of him who raised Jesus from the dead is living in you, he who raised Christ from the dead will also give life to your mortal bodies through his Spirit, who lives in you.

Cast: **Voice 1** (triumphant), **Voice 2** (serious)

Led by God's Spirit
Romans 8:14–17

Reader	Those who are led by the Spirit of God are sons of God. For you did not receive a spirit that makes you a slave again to fear, but you received the Spirit of sonship. And by him we cry:
Person 1	*Abba*, Father.
Reader	The Spirit himself testifies with our spirit that we are God's children.
Person 2	Now if we are children, then we are heirs—heirs of God.
Persons 1 and 2	And co-heirs with Christ.
Person 1	If indeed we share in his sufferings in order that we may also share in his glory.

Cast: **Reader, Person 1, Person 2**

More Than Conquerors
Romans 8:28–39

Answer	We know that in all things God works for the good of those who love him, who have been called according to his purpose. For those God foreknew he also predestined to be conformed to the likeness of his Son, that he might be the firstborn among many brothers. And those he predestined, he also called; those he called, he also justified; those he justified, he also glorified.
Question	What, then, shall we say in response to this? If God is for us, who can be against us?
Answer	He who did not spare his own Son, but gave him up for us all—how will he not also, along with him, graciously give us all things?

Question	Who will bring any charge against those whom God has chosen?
Answer	It is God who justifies.
Question	Who is he that condemns?
Answer	Christ Jesus, who died—more than that, who was raised to life—is at the right hand of God and is also interceding for us.
Question	Who shall separate us from the love of Christ? Shall trouble or hardship or persecution or famine or nakedness or danger or sword? As it is written:
Psalmist	For your sake we face death all day long; we are considered as sheep to be slaughtered.
Answer	No, in all these things we are more than conquerors through him who loved us. For I am convinced that neither death nor life, neither angels nor demons, neither the present nor the future, nor any powers, neither height nor depth, nor anything else in all creation, will be able to separate us from the love of God that is in Christ Jesus our Lord.

Cast: **Answer, Question, Psalmist** (can be the same as Question)

God and His People
Romans 9:6–18

Paul	It is not as though God's word had failed. For not all who are descended from Israel are Israel. Nor because they are his descendants are they all Abraham's children. On the contrary:
God	It is through Isaac that your offspring will be reckoned.
Paul	In other words, it is not the *natural children* who are God's children, but it is the *children of the promise* who are regarded as Abraham's offspring. For this was how the promise was stated:
God	At the appointed time I will return, and Sarah will have a son.
Paul	Not only that, but Rebekah's children had one and the same father, our father Isaac. Yet, before the twins were born or had done anything good or bad—in order that God's purpose in election might stand: not by works but by him who calls—she was told:
God	The older will serve the younger.
Paul	Just as it is written:
God	Jacob I loved, but Esau I hated.
Questioner	What then shall we say? Is God unjust?
Paul	Not at all! For he says to Moses:

God	I will have mercy on whom I have mercy, and I will have compassion on whom I have compassion.
Paul	It does not, therefore, depend on man's desire or effort, but on God's mercy. For the Scripture says to Pharaoh:
God	I raised you up for this very purpose, that I might display my power in you and that my name might be proclaimed in all the earth.
Paul	Therefore God has mercy on whom he wants to have mercy, and he hardens whom he wants to harden.

Cast: **Paul, God, Questioner** (can be the same as Paul)

God's Anger and Mercy

Romans 9:19–29

Paul	One of you will say to me:
Questioner	Then why does God still blame us? For who resists his will?
Paul	But who are you, O man, to talk back to God? Shall what is formed say to him who formed it, "Why did you make me like this?" Does not the potter have the right to make out of the same lump of clay some pottery for noble purposes and some for common use?
	What if God, choosing to show his wrath and make his power known, bore with great patience the objects of his wrath—prepared for destruction? What if he did this to make the riches of his glory known to the objects of his mercy, whom he prepared in advance for glory—even us, whom he also called, not only from the Jews but also from the Gentiles? As he says in Hosea:
God	I will call them "my people" who are not my people; and I will call her "my loved one" who is not my loved one.
	It will happen that in the very place where it was said to them, "You are not my people," they will be called "sons of the living God."
Paul	Isaiah cries out concerning Israel:

Isaiah	Though the number of the Israelites be like the sand by the sea,
	    only the remnant will be saved.
	For the Lord will carry out
	    his sentence on earth with speed and finality.

Paul	It is just as Isaiah said previously:

328

Isaiah	Unless the Lord Almighty
	    had left us descendants,
	we would have become like Sodom,
	    we would have been like Gomorrah.

Cast: **Paul, Questioner, God, Isaiah**

Salvation Is for All
Romans 10:5-21

Paul	Moses describes in this way the righteousness that is by the law:
Reader	The man who does these things will live by them.
Paul	But the righteousness that is by faith says:
Reader	Do not say in your heart, "Who will ascend into heaven?"
Paul	(That is, to bring Christ down.)
Reader	Or "Who will descend into the deep?"
Paul	(That is, to bring Christ up from the dead.)
Reader	The word is near you; it is in your mouth and in your heart.
Paul	That is, the word of faith we are proclaiming: (PAUSE) That if you confess with your mouth, "Jesus is Lord," and believe in your heart that God raised him from the dead, you will be saved. For it is with your heart that you believe and are justified, and it is with your mouth that you confess and are saved. As the Scripture says:
Reader	Anyone who trusts in him will never be put to shame.
Paul	For there is no difference between Jew and Gentile—the same Lord is Lord of all and richly blesses all who call on him, for:
Reader	Everyone who calls on the name of the Lord will be saved.
Paul	How, then, can they call on the one they have not believed in? And how can they believe in the one of whom they have not heard? And how can they hear without someone preaching to them? And how can they preach unless they are sent? As it is written:
Reader	How beautiful are the feet of those who bring good news!
Paul	But not all the Israelites accepted the good news. For Isaiah says:
Reader	Lord, who has believed our message?
Paul	Consequently, faith comes from hearing the message, and the message is heard through the word of Christ. But I ask: Did they not hear? Of course they did:
Reader	Their voice has gone out into all the earth, their words to the ends of the world.

Paul	Again I ask: Did Israel not understand? First, Moses says:
Reader	I will make you envious by those who are not a nation; I will make you angry by a nation that has no understanding.
Paul	And Isaiah boldly says:
Reader	I was found by those who did not seek me; I revealed myself to those who did not ask for me.
Paul	But concerning Israel he says:
Reader	All day long I have held out my hands to a disobedient and obstinate people.

Cast: **Paul, Reader.** (A shorter version of this dramatized reading follows.)

The Message of Salvation
Romans 10:8–17

Deuteronomy	The word is near you; it is in your mouth and in your heart.
Paul	That is, the word of faith we are proclaiming: That if you confess with your mouth, "Jesus is Lord," and believe in your heart that God raised him from the dead, you will be saved. For it is with your heart that you believe and are justified, and it is with your mouth that you confess and are saved. As the Scripture says:
Isaiah	Anyone who trusts in him will never be put to shame.
Paul	For there is no difference between Jew and Gentile—the same Lord is Lord of all and richly blesses all who call on him, for,
Joel	*Everyone* who calls on the name of the Lord will be saved.
Paul	How, then, can they call on the one they have not believed in? And how can they believe in the one of whom they have not heard? And how can they hear without someone preaching to them? And how can they preach unless they are sent? [As it is written:]
Isaiah	How beautiful are the feet of those who bring good news!
Paul	But not all the Israelites accepted the good news. For Isaiah says:
Isaiah	Lord, who has believed our message?
Paul	Consequently, faith comes from hearing the message, and the message is heard through the word of Christ.

Cast: **Deuteronomy, Paul, Isaiah, Joel** (Deuteronomy, Isaiah, and Joel can be the same). (For a fuller version of this reading see pages 329–30.)

The Remnant of Israel
Romans 11:1–12

Question   I ask then: Did God reject his people?

Answer   By no means! I am an Israelite myself, a descendant of Abraham, from the tribe of Benjamin. God did not reject his people, whom he foreknew. Don't you know what the Scripture says in the passage about Elijah—how he appealed to God against Israel:

Reader   Lord, they have killed your prophets and torn down your altars; I am the only one left, and they are trying to kill me.

Question   And what was God's answer to him?

Reader   I have reserved for myself seven thousand who have not bowed the knee to Baal.

Answer   So too, at the present time there is a remnant chosen by grace. And if by grace, then it is no longer by works; if it were, grace would no longer be grace.

Question   What then?

Answer   What Israel sought so earnestly it did not obtain, but the elect did. The others were hardened, as it is written:

Reader   God gave them a spirit of stupor,
eyes so that they could not see
and ears so that they could not hear,
to this very day.

Answer   And David says:

Reader   May their table become a snare and a trap,
a stumbling block and a retribution for them.
May their eyes be darkened so they cannot see,
and their backs be bent forever.

Question   Again I ask: Did they stumble so as to fall beyond recovery?

Answer   Not at all! Rather, because of their transgression, salvation has come to the Gentiles to make Israel envious. But if their transgression means riches for the world, and their loss means riches for the Gentiles, how much greater riches will their fullness bring!

Cast: **Question, Answer, Reader**

All Israel Will Be Saved
Romans 11:25–36

Paul   I do not want you to be ignorant of this mystery, brothers, so that you may not be conceited: Israel has experienced a hardening in part until

	the full number of the Gentiles has come in. And so all Israel will be saved, as it is written:
Isaiah	The deliverer will come from Zion; he will turn godlessness away from Jacob.
Jeremiah	And this is my covenant with them when I take away their sins.
Paul	As far as the gospel is concerned, they are enemies on your account; but as far as election is concerned, they are loved on account of the patriarchs, for God's gifts and his call are irrevocable. Just as you who were at one time disobedient to God have now received mercy as a result of their disobedience, so they too have now become disobedient in order that they too may now receive mercy as a result of God's mercy to you. For God has bound all men over to disobedience so that he may have mercy on them all.
Isaiah	Oh, the depth of the riches of the wisdom and knowledge of God! How unsearchable his judgments, and his paths beyond tracing out!
Paul	[As the Scripture says:]
Isaiah	Who has known the mind of the Lord? Or who has been his counselor?
Job	Who has ever given to God, that God should repay him?
Paul	For from him and through him and to him are all things. To him be the glory forever! Amen.

Cast: **Paul, Isaiah, Jeremiah, Job.** (Please note: this reading overlaps with the next.)

Living Sacrifices
Romans 11:33–12:2

Paul	Oh, the depth of the riches of the wisdom and knowledge of God! How unsearchable his judgments, and his paths beyond tracing out!
Reader	Who has known the mind of the Lord? Or who has been his counselor? Who has ever given to God, that God should repay him?
Paul	For from him and through him and to him are all things. To him be the glory forever!
Paul and **Reader**	Amen.

| Paul | Therefore, I urge you, brothers, in view of God's mercy, to offer your bodies as living sacrifices, holy and pleasing to God—this is your spiritual act of worship. Do not conform any longer to the pattern of this world, but be transformed by the renewing of your mind. Then you will be able to test and approve what God's will is—his good, pleasing and perfect will. |

Cast: **Paul, Reader.** (Note that this reading overlaps with the previous one.)

One Body
Romans 12:4–13

Person 1	Just as each of us has one body with many members, and these members do not all have the same function.
Person 2	So in Christ we who are many form one body, and each member belongs to all the others.
Person 3	We have different gifts, according to the grace given us.
Person 1	If a man's gift is prophesying, let him use it in proportion to his faith.
Person 2	If it is serving, let him serve.
Person 3	If it is teaching, let him teach.
Person 1	If it is encouraging, let him encourage.
Person 2	If it is contributing to the needs of others, let him give generously.
Person 3	If it is leadership, let him govern diligently.
Person 1	If it is showing mercy, let him do it cheerfully.
Teacher	Love must be sincere. Hate what is evil; cling to what is good. Be devoted to one another in brotherly love. Honor one another above yourselves. Never be lacking in zeal, but keep your spiritual fervor, serving the Lord. Be joyful in hope, patient in affliction, faithful in prayer. Share with God's people who are in need. Practice hospitality.

Cast: **Person 1, Person 2, Person 3, Teacher** (may be divided among Persons 1–3)

About Revenge
Romans 12:14–21

| Paul | Bless those who persecute you; bless and do not curse. Rejoice with those who rejoice; mourn with those who mourn. Live in harmony with one another. Do not be proud, but be willing to associate with people of low position. Do not be conceited. |
| | Do not repay anyone evil for evil. Be careful to do what is right in the eyes of everybody. If it is possible, as far as it depends on you, live at |

	peace with everyone. Do not take revenge, my friends, but leave room for God's wrath, for it is written:

Reader "It is mine to avenge; I will repay," says the Lord.

Paul On the contrary:

Reader If your enemy is hungry, feed him;
  if he is thirsty, give him something to drink.
In doing this, you will heap burning coals on his head.

Paul Do not be overcome by evil, but overcome evil with good.

Cast: **Paul, Reader**

Duties toward One Another
Romans 13:8–10 [11–14]

Paul Let no debt remain outstanding, except the continuing debt to love one another, for he who loves his fellowman has fulfilled the law. The commandments:

Reader Do not commit adultery; do not murder; do not steal; do not covet.

Paul And whatever other commandment there may be, are summed up in this one rule:

Reader Love your neighbor as yourself.

Paul Love does no harm to its neighbor. Therefore love is the fulfillment of the law.

[And do this, understanding the present time. The hour has come for you to wake up from your slumber, because our salvation is nearer now than when we first believed. The night is nearly over; the day is almost here. So let us put aside the deeds of darkness and put on the armor of light. Let us behave decently, as in the daytime, not in orgies and drunkenness, not in sexual immorality and debauchery, not in dissension and jealousy. Rather, clothe yourselves with the Lord Jesus Christ, and do not think about how to gratify the desires of the sinful nature.]

Cast: **Paul, Reader**

Good News for the Gentiles
Romans 15:7–13

Paul Accept one another, then, just as Christ accepted you, in order to bring praise to God. For I tell you that Christ has become a servant of the Jews on behalf of God's truth, to confirm the promises made to the patriarchs so that the Gentiles may glorify God for his mercy, as it is written:

Reader Therefore I will praise you among the Gentiles;
  I will sing hymns to your name.

Paul	Again, it says:
Reader	Rejoice, O Gentiles, with his people.
Paul	And again:
Reader	Praise the Lord, all you Gentiles, and sing praises to him, all you peoples.
Paul	And again, Isaiah says:
Reader	The Root of Jesse will spring up, one who will arise to rule over the nations; the Gentiles will hope in him.
Paul	May the God of hope fill you with all joy and peace as you trust in him, so that you may overflow with hope by the power of the Holy Spirit.

Cast: **Paul, Reader**

1 Corinthians

Divisions in the Church
1 Corinthians 1:10–17

Paul	I appeal to you, brothers, in the name of our Lord Jesus Christ, that all of you agree with one another so that there may be no divisions among you and that you may be perfectly united in mind and thought. My brothers, some from Chloe's household have informed me that there are quarrels among you. What I mean is this: One of you says:
Person 1	I follow Paul.
Person 2	I follow Apollos.
Person 3	I follow Cephas. (PAUSE)
Person 4 (emphatically)	I follow Christ.
Paul	Is Christ divided? Was Paul crucified for you? Were you baptized into the name of Paul? I am thankful that I did not baptize any of you except Crispus and Gaius, so no one can say that you were baptized into my name.
(as an afterthought)	(Yes, I also baptized the household of Stephanas; beyond that, I don't remember if I baptized anyone else.)
	For Christ did not send me to baptize, but to preach the gospel—not with words of human wisdom, lest the cross of Christ be emptied of its power.

Cast: **Paul, Person 1, Person 2, Person 3** (can be the same as Person 1), **Person 4** (can be the same as Person 2)

Sexual Immorality
1 Corinthians 6:12–20

Person 1	Everything is permissible for me.
Paul	But not everything is beneficial.
Person 2	Everything is permissible for me.
Paul	But I will not be mastered by anything.
Person 1	Food for the stomach and the stomach for food.
Paul	But God will destroy them both. The body is not meant for sexual immorality, but for the Lord, and the Lord for the body. By his power God

raised the Lord from the dead, and he will raise us also. Do you not know that your bodies are members of Christ himself? Shall I then take the members of Christ and unite them with a prostitute? Never! Do you not know that he who unites himself with a prostitute is one with her in body? For it is said:

Scripture The two will become one flesh.

Paul But he who unites himself with the Lord is one with him in spirit.

Flee from sexual immorality. All other sins a man commits are outside his body, but he who sins sexually sins against his own body. Do you not know that your body is a temple of the Holy Spirit, who is in you, whom you have received from God? You are not your own; you were bought at a price. Therefore honor God with your body.

Cast: **Person 1**, **Paul**, **Person 2**, **Scripture** (can be the same as Paul)

The Lord's Supper
1 Corinthians 11:23–26

Paul I received from the Lord what I also passed on to you: The Lord Jesus, on the night he was betrayed, took bread, and when he had given thanks, he broke it [and said:]

Jesus This is my body, which is for you; do this in remembrance of me.

Paul In the same way, after supper he took the cup, [saying:]

Jesus This cup is the new covenant in my blood; do this, whenever you drink it, in remembrance of me.

Paul For whenever you eat this bread and drink this cup, you proclaim the Lord's death until he comes.

Cast: **Paul**, **Jesus**

One Body, Many Parts
From 1 Corinthians 12:12–27

Paul The body is a unit, though it is made up of many parts; and though all its parts are many, they form one body. So it is with Christ. For we were all baptized by one Spirit into one body—whether Jews or Greeks, slave or free—and we were all given the one Spirit to drink.

Now the body is not made up of one part but of many. If the foot should say:

Foot Because I am not a hand, I do not belong to the body.

Paul It would not for that reason cease to be part of the body. And if the ear should say:

Ear	Because I am not an eye, I do not belong to the body.
Paul	It would not for that reason cease to be part of the body. If the whole body were an eye, where would the sense of hearing be? If the whole body were an ear, where would the sense of smell be? But in fact God has arranged the parts in the body, every one of them, just as he wanted them to be. If they were all one part, where would the body be? As it is, there are many parts, but one body.
	The eye cannot say to the hand:
Eye	I don't need you!
Paul	And the head cannot say to the feet:
Head	I don't need *you!*
Paul	On the contrary, those parts of the body that seem to be weaker are indispensable, and the parts that we think are less honorable we treat with special honor. . . .
Cast	Now you are the body of Christ, and each one of you is a part of it.

Cast: **Paul, Foot, Ear, Eye, Head**

Love
1 Corinthians 12:31b–13:13

Reader 1	I will show you the most excellent way.
Reader 2	If I speak in the tongues of men and of angels, but have not love, I am only a resounding gong or a clanging cymbal.
Reader 3	If I have the gift of prophecy and can fathom all mysteries and all knowledge, and if I have a faith that can move mountains, but have not love, I am nothing.
Reader 4	If I give all I possess to the poor and surrender my body to the flames, but have not love, I gain nothing. (PAUSE)
Reader 1	Love is patient, love is kind. It does not envy, it does not boast, it is not proud.
Reader 2	It is not rude, it is not self-seeking, it is not easily angered, it keeps no record of wrongs.
Reader 3	Love does not delight in evil but rejoices with the truth. It always protects, always trusts, always hopes, always perseveres.
Reader 4	Love never fails.
Reader 1	But where there are prophecies, they will cease.
Reader 2	Where there are tongues, they will be stilled.
Reader 3	Where there is knowledge, it will pass away.

Reader 4	For we know in part and we prophesy in part, but when perfection comes, the imperfect disappears.
Reader 1	When I was a child, I talked like a child, I thought like a child, I reasoned like a child. When I became a man, I put childish ways behind me.
Reader 2	Now we see but a poor reflection as in a mirror; then we shall see face to face.
Reader 3	Now I know in part; then I shall know fully, even as I am fully known. (PAUSE)
Reader 4	And now these three remain:
Reader 1 (slowly)	Faith. (PAUSE)
Reader 2	Hope. (PAUSE)
Reader 3	And love.
Reader 4	But the greatest of these is love.

Cast: **Reader 1, Reader 2, Reader 3, Reader 4**

Tongues
1 Corinthians 14:18–25

Paul	I thank God that I speak in tongues more than all of you. But in the church I would rather speak five intelligible words to instruct others than ten thousand words in a tongue.
	Brothers, stop thinking like children. In regard to evil be infants, but in your thinking be adults. In the Law it is written:

Scripture	Through men of strange tongues
	  and through the lips of foreigners
	I will speak to this people,
	  but even then they will not listen to me.

Paul	Tongues, then, are a sign, not for believers but for unbelievers; prophecy, however, is for believers, not for unbelievers. (PAUSE) So if the whole church comes together and everyone speaks in tongues, and some who do not understand or some unbelievers come in, will they not say that you are out of your mind? But if an unbeliever or someone who does not understand comes in while everybody is prophesying, he will be convinced by all that he is a sinner and will be judged by all, and the secrets of his heart will be laid bare. So he will fall down and worship God, exclaiming:
Person	God is really among you!

Cast: **Paul, Scripture, Person**

The Resurrection of Christ
1 Corinthians 15:1–11

Paul   I want to remind you of the gospel I preached to you, which you received and on which you have taken your stand. By this gospel you are saved, if you hold firmly to the word I preached to you. Otherwise, you have believed in vain.

For what I received I passed on to you as of first importance:

Younger Paul   That Christ died for our sins according to the Scriptures, that he was buried, that he was raised on the third day according to the Scriptures, and that he appeared to Peter, and then to the Twelve. After that, he appeared to more than five hundred of the brothers at the same time, most of whom are still living, though some have fallen asleep. Then he appeared to James, then to all the apostles.

Paul   And last of all he appeared to me also, as to one abnormally born. (PAUSE) For I am the least of the apostles and do not even deserve to be called an apostle, because I persecuted the church of God. But by the grace of God I am what I am, and his grace to me was not without effect. No, I worked harder than all of them—yet not I, but the grace of God that was with me. Whether, then, it was I or they, this is what we preach, and this is what you believed.

Cast: **Paul, younger Paul** (or, perhaps, Peter—see Galatians 1:18). It Peter speaks here, change his name in text to "me.")

The Resurrection Body
From 1 Corinthians 15:35–57

Paul   Someone may ask:

Person   How are the dead raised? With what kind of body will they come?

Paul   How foolish! What you sow does not come to life unless it dies. When you sow, you do not plant the body that will be, but just a seed, perhaps of wheat or of something else. But God gives it a body as he has determined, and to each kind of seed he gives its own body. All flesh is not the same. . . . (PAUSE) If there is a natural body, there is also a spiritual body. So it is written:

Scripture   The first man Adam became a living being.

Paul   The last Adam, a life-giving spirit. The spiritual did not come first, but the natural, and after that the spiritual. The first man was of the dust of the earth, the second man from heaven. As was the earthly man, so are those who are of the earth; and as is the man from heaven, so also are those who are of heaven. And just as we have borne the likeness of the earthly man, so shall we bear the likeness of the man from heaven.

I declare to you, brothers, that flesh and blood cannot inherit the kingdom of God, nor does the perishable inherit the imperishable. (PAUSE) Listen, I tell you a mystery: We will not all sleep, but we will all be changed—in a flash, in the twinkling of an eye, at the last trumpet. For the trumpet will sound, the dead will be raised imperishable, and we will be changed. For the perishable must clothe itself with the imperishable, and the mortal with immortality. When the perishable has been clothed with the imperishable, and the mortal with immortality, then the saying that is written will come true:

Scripture   Death has been swallowed up in victory.

Where, O death, is your victory?
　Where, O death, is your sting?

Paul   The sting of death is sin, and the power of sin is the law. But thanks be to God! He gives us the victory through our Lord Jesus Christ.

Cast: **Paul, Person, Scripture**

2 Corinthians

Do Not Be Yoked with Unbelievers
2 Corinthians 6:14–7:1

Paul
Do not be yoked together with unbelievers. For what do righteousness and wickedness have in common? Or what fellowship can light have with darkness? What harmony is there between Christ and Belial? What does a believer have in common with an unbeliever? What agreement is there between the temple of God and idols? For we are the temple of the living God. As God has said:

Scripture
I will live with them and walk among them, and I will be their God, and they will be my people.

Paul
[And so the Lord says:]

Scripture
Therefore come out from them
   and be separate.
Touch no unclean thing,
   and I will receive you.

I will be a Father to you,
   and you will be my sons and daughters,
   says the Lord Almighty.

Paul
Since we have these promises, dear friends, let us purify ourselves from everything that contaminates body and spirit, perfecting holiness out of reverence for God.

Cast: **Paul, Scripture**

Christian Giving
From 2 Corinthians 8:7–15; 9:6–15

Reader 1
Just as you excel in everything—in faith, in speech, in knowledge, in complete earnestness and in your love for us—see that you also excel in this grace of giving.

Reader 2
I am not commanding you, but I want to test the sincerity of your love by comparing it with the earnestness of others.

Reader 3
For you know the grace of our Lord Jesus Christ, that though he was rich, yet for your sakes he became poor, so that you through his poverty might become rich. . . .

Reader 1
If the willingness is there, the gift is acceptable according to what one has, not according to what he does not have.

Reader 2	Our desire is not that others might be relieved while you are hard pressed, but that there might be equality. At the present time your plenty will supply what they need, so that in turn their plenty will supply what you need. Then there will be equality, as it is written:
Reader 3	He who gathered much did not have too much, and he who gathered little did not have too little. . . .
Reader 2	Remember this: Whoever sows sparingly will also reap sparingly, and whoever sows generously will also reap generously.
Reader 1	Each man should give what he has decided in his heart to give, not reluctantly or under compulsion, for God loves a cheerful giver.
Reader 2	And God is able to make all grace abound to you, so that in all things at all times, having all that you need, you will abound in every good work. As it is written:
Reader 3	He has scattered abroad his gifts to the poor; his righteousness endures forever. . . .
Readers 1–3	Thanks be to God for his indescribable gift!

Cast: **Reader 1, Reader 2, Reader 3**

Paul's Authority
2 Corinthians 10:7–13, 17–18

Paul	You are looking only on the surface of things. If anyone is confident that he belongs to Christ, he should consider again that we belong to Christ just as much as he. For even if I boast somewhat freely about the authority the Lord gave us for building you up rather than pulling you down, I will not be ashamed of it. I do not want to seem to be trying to frighten you with my letters. For some say:
Corinthian	His letters are weighty and forceful, but in person he is unimpressive and his speaking amounts to nothing.
Paul	Such people should realize that what we are in our letters when we are absent, we will be in our actions when we are present.
	We do not dare to classify or compare ourselves with some who commend themselves. When they measure themselves by themselves and compare themselves with themselves, they are not wise. We, however, will not boast beyond proper limits, but will confine our boasting to the field God has assigned to us, a field that reaches even to you. . . .
Scripture	Let him who boasts boast in the Lord.
Paul	For it is not the one who commends himself who is approved, but the one whom the Lord commends.

Cast: **Paul, Corinthian, Scripture**

Paul's Vision and His Thorn
2 Corinthians 12:1, 6–10

Paul

I *must* go on boasting. Although there is nothing to be gained, I will go on to visions and revelations from the Lord. . . . Even if I should choose to boast, I would not be a fool, because I would be speaking the truth. But I refrain, so no one will think more of me than is warranted by what I do or say.

To keep me from becoming conceited because of these surpassingly great revelations, there was given me a thorn in my flesh, a messenger of Satan, to torment me. Three times I pleaded with the Lord to take it away from me. But he said to me:

The Lord
(slowly)

My grace is sufficient for you, for my power is made perfect in weakness.

Paul

Therefore I will boast all the more gladly about my weaknesses, so that Christ's power may rest on me. That is why, for Christ's sake, I delight in weaknesses, in insults, in hardships, in persecutions, in difficulties. For when I am weak, then I am strong.

Cast: **Paul, the Lord**

Galatians

Faith or Observance of the Law
Galatians 3:1–14

Paul   You foolish Galatians! Who has bewitched you? Before your very eyes Jesus Christ was clearly portrayed as crucified. I would like to learn just one thing from you: Did you receive the Spirit by observing the law, or by believing what you heard? Are you so foolish? After beginning with the Spirit, are you now trying to attain your goal by human effort? Have you suffered so much for nothing—if it really was for nothing? Does God give you his Spirit and work miracles among you because you observe the law, or because you believe what you heard?

Consider Abraham:

Reader   He believed God, and it was credited to him as righteousness.

Paul   Understand, then, that those who believe are children of Abraham. The Scripture foresaw that God would justify the Gentiles by faith, and announced the gospel in advance to Abraham:

Reader   All nations will be blessed through you.

Paul   So those who have faith are blessed along with Abraham, the man of faith.

All who rely on observing the law are under a curse, for it is written:

Reader   Cursed is everyone who does not continue to do everything written in the Book of the Law.

Paul   Clearly no one is justified before God by the law, because:

Reader   The righteous will live by faith.

Paul   The law is not based on faith; on the contrary:

Reader   The man who does these things will live by them.

Paul   Christ redeemed us from the curse of the law by becoming a curse for us, for it is written:

Reader   Cursed is everyone who is hung on a tree.

Paul   He redeemed us in order that the blessing given to Abraham might come to the Gentiles through Christ Jesus, so that by faith we might receive the promise of the Spirit.

Cast: **Paul, Reader**

God's Law and His Promises
Galatians 3:17–22 [23–29]

Paul	The law . . . does not set aside the covenant previously established by God and thus do away with the promise. For if the inheritance depends on the law, then it no longer depends on a promise; but God in his grace gave it to Abraham through a promise.
Questioner	What, then, was the purpose of the law?
Paul	It was added because of transgressions until the Seed to whom the promise referred had come. The law was put into effect through angels by a mediator. A mediator, however, does not represent just one party; but God is one.
Questioner	Is the law, therefore, opposed to the promises of God?
Paul	Absolutely not! For if a law had been given that could impart life, then righteousness would certainly have come by the law. But the Scripture declares that the whole world is a prisoner of sin, so that what was promised, being given through faith in Jesus Christ, might be given to those who believe.
	[Before this faith came, we were held prisoners by the law, locked up until faith should be revealed. So the law was put in charge to lead us to Christ that we might be justified by faith. Now that faith has come, we are no longer under the supervision of the law.
	You are all sons of God through faith in Christ Jesus, for all of you who were baptized into Christ have clothed yourselves with Christ. There is neither Jew nor Greek, slave nor free, male nor female, for you are all one in Christ Jesus. If you belong to Christ, then you are Abraham's seed, and heirs according to the promise.]

Cast: **Paul, Questioner**

Hagar and Sarah
Galatians 4:21–31

Paul	Tell me, you who want to be under the law, are you not aware of what the law says? For it is written that Abraham had two sons, one by the slave woman and the other by the free woman. His son by the slave woman was born in the ordinary way; but his son by the free woman was born as the result of a promise.
	These things may be taken figuratively, for the women represent two covenants. One covenant is from Mount Sinai and bears children who are to be slaves: This is Hagar. Now Hagar stands for Mount Sinai in Arabia and corresponds to the present city of Jerusalem, because she is in slavery with her children. But the Jerusalem that is above is free, and she is our mother. For it is written:

Reader	Be glad, O barren woman,
	    who bears no children;
	break forth and cry aloud,
	    you who have no labor pains;
	because more are the children of the desolate woman
	    than of her who has a husband.

Paul	Now you, brothers, like Isaac, are children of promise. At that time the son born in the ordinary way persecuted the son born by the power of the Spirit. It is the same now. But what does the Scripture say?
Reader	Get rid of the slave woman and her son, for the slave woman's son will never share in the inheritance with the free woman's son.
Paul	Therefore, brothers, we are not children of the slave woman, but of the free woman.

Cast: **Paul**, **Reader**

347

Ephesians

Spiritual Blessings in Christ
Ephesians 1:2–14

Voices 1 and 2 Grace and peace to you from God our Father and the Lord Jesus Christ.

Voice 1 Praise be to the God and Father of our Lord Jesus Christ, who has blessed us in the heavenly realms with every spiritual blessing in Christ.

Voice 2 For he chose us in him before the creation of the world to be holy and blameless in his sight.

Voice 1 In love he predestined us to be adopted as his sons through Jesus Christ, in accordance with his pleasure and will—

Voices 1 and 2 To the praise of his glorious grace.

Voice 2 Which he has freely given us in the One he loves.

Voice 1 In him we have redemption through his blood.

Voice 2 The forgiveness of sins, in accordance with the riches of God's grace.

Voice 1 That he lavished on us with all wisdom and understanding. And he made known to us the mystery of his will according to his good pleasure, which he purposed in Christ, to be put into effect when the times will have reached their fulfillment—to bring all things in heaven and on earth together under one head, even Christ.

Voice 2 In him we were also chosen, having been predestined according to the plan of him who works out everything in conformity with the purpose of his will.

Voices 1 and 2 In order that we, who were the first to hope in Christ, might be for the praise of his glory.

Voice 1 And you also were included in Christ when you heard the word of truth, the gospel of your salvation. Having believed, you were marked in him with a seal, the promised Holy Spirit—

Voice 2 Who is a deposit guaranteeing our inheritance until the redemption of those who are God's possession.

Voices 1 and 2 To the praise of his glory.

Cast: **Voice 1, Voice 2**

God's Power and the Church
Ephesians 1:19–23; 3:20–21

Voice 1	[God's] incomparably great power for us who believe . . . is like the working of his mighty strength, which he exerted in Christ when he raised him from the dead and seated him at his right hand in the heavenly realms.
Voice 2	Far above all rule and authority, power and dominion, and every title that can be given, not only in the present age but also in the one to come.
Voice 3	And God placed all things under his feet and appointed him to be head over everything for the church.
Voice 1	Which is his body, the fullness of him who fills everything in every way. . . .
Voice 2	Now to him who is able to do immeasurably more than all we ask or imagine, according to his power that is at work within us:
Voice 3	To him be glory in the church and in Christ Jesus throughout all generations, for ever and ever!
Voices 1–3	Amen.

Cast: **Voice 1, Voice 2, Voice 3**

Made Alive in Christ
Ephesians 2:1–10

Voice 1	As for *you,* you were dead in your transgressions and sins, in which you used to live when you followed the ways of this world and of the ruler of the kingdom of the air, the spirit who is now at work in those who are disobedient.
Voice 2	All of *us* also lived among them at one time, gratifying the cravings of our sinful nature and following its desires and thoughts. Like the rest, we were by nature objects of wrath. But because of his great love for us, God, who is rich in mercy, made us alive with Christ even when we were dead in transgressions—
Voices 1 and 2	It is by grace you have been saved.
Voice 2	And God raised us up with Christ and seated us with him in the heavenly realms in Christ Jesus, in order that in the coming ages he might show the incomparable riches of his grace, expressed in his kindness to us in Christ Jesus.
Voice 1	For it is by grace you have been saved, through faith—and this not from yourselves, it is the gift of God—not by works, so that no one can boast.

Voice 2	For we are God's workmanship, created in Christ Jesus to do good works, which God prepared in advance for us to do.

Cast: **Voice 1** (authoritative), **Voice 2** (grateful)

Unity in the Body of Christ
Ephesians 4:1–16

Voice 1	As a prisoner for the Lord, then, I urge you to live a life worthy of the calling you have received.
Voice 2	Be completely humble and gentle; be patient, bearing with one another in love.
Voice 3	Make every effort to keep the unity of the Spirit through the bond of peace.
Voice 1	There is one body and one Spirit—just as you were called to one hope when you were called—
Voice 2	One Lord, one faith, one baptism;
Voice 3	One God and Father of all, who is over all and through all and in all.
Voice 1	But to each one of us grace has been given as Christ apportioned it. This is why it says:
Psalmist	When he ascended on high, he led captives in his train and gave gifts to men.
Voice 2	(What does "he ascended" mean except that he also descended to the lower, earthly regions?
Voice 3	He who descended is the very one who ascended higher than all the heavens, in order to fill the whole universe.)
Voice 1	It was he who gave some to be apostles, some to be prophets, some to be evangelists, and some to be pastors and teachers, to prepare God's people for works of service, so that the body of Christ may be built up—
Voice 2	Until we all reach unity in the faith and in the knowledge of the Son of God and become mature, attaining to the whole measure of the fullness of Christ.
Voice 3	Then we will no longer be infants, tossed back and forth by the waves, and blown here and there by every wind of teaching and by the cunning and craftiness of men in their deceitful scheming.
Voice 1	Instead, speaking the truth in love, we will in all things grow up into him who is the Head, that is, Christ.
Voice 2	From him the whole body, joined and held together by every supporting ligament—

Voice 3	Grows and builds itself up in love, as each part does its work.

Cast: **Voice 1**, **Voice 2**, **Voice 3**, **Psalmist** (can be the same as Voice 3)

Christian Dos and Don'ts (i)
Ephesians 4:22b–32

Don't	Put off your old self, which is being corrupted by its deceitful desires—
Do	Be made new in the attitude of your minds. Put on the new self, created to be like God in true righteousness and holiness.
Don't	Therefore each of you must put off falsehood—
Do	Speak truthfully to [your] neighbor, for we are all members of one body.
Don't	"In your anger do not sin": Do not let the sun go down while you are still angry, and do not give the devil a foothold. He who has been stealing must steal no longer.
Do	[He] must work, doing something useful with his own hands, that he may have something to share with those in need.
Don't	Do not let any unwholesome talk come out of your mouths.
Do	But only what is helpful for building others up according to their needs, that it may benefit those who listen.
Don't	And do not grieve the Holy Spirit of God—
Do	With whom you were sealed for the day of redemption.
Don't	Get rid of all bitterness, rage and anger, brawling and slander, along with every form of malice.
Do	Be kind and compassionate to one another, forgiving each other, just as in Christ God forgave you.

Cast: **Don't** (a negative voice), **Do** (a positive voice)

Christian Dos and Don'ts (ii)
From Ephesians 5:3–20

Don't	Among you there must not be even a hint of sexual immorality, or of any kind of impurity, or of greed—
Do	Because these are improper for God's holy people.
Don't	Nor should there be obscenity, foolish talk or coarse joking, which are out of place—
Do	But rather thanksgiving.
Don't	For of this you can be sure: No immoral, impure or greedy person—such a man is an idolater—has any inheritance in the kingdom of Christ and

	of God. (PAUSE) Let no one deceive you with empty words, for because of such things God's wrath comes on those who are disobedient. Therefore do not be partners with them.
Do	You were once darkness, but now you are light in the Lord. Live as children of light (for the fruit of the light consists in all goodness, righteousness and truth) and find out what pleases the Lord.
Don't	Have nothing to do with the fruitless deeds of darkness—
Do	But rather expose them. . . . Everything exposed by the light becomes visible, for it is light that makes everything visible. . . .
Don't	Be very careful, then, how you live—not as unwise but as wise—
Do	Making the most of every opportunity, because the days are evil.
Don't	Therefore do not be foolish—
Do	But understand what the Lord's will is.
Don't	Do not get drunk on wine, which leads to debauchery.
Do	Instead, be filled with the Spirit. (PAUSE) Speak to one another with psalms, hymns and spiritual songs. Sing and make music in your heart to the Lord, always giving thanks to God the Father for everything, in the name of our Lord Jesus Christ.

Cast: **Don't** (a negative voice), **Do** (a positive voice)

The Christian Family
From Ephesians 5:1–6:12

Minister/ Leader	Be imitators of God . . . as dearly loved children and live a life of love, just as Christ loved us and gave himself up for us as a fragrant offering and sacrifice to God. . . . Speak to one another with psalms, hymns and spiritual songs. Sing and make music in your heart to the Lord, always giving thanks to God the Father for everything, in the name of our Lord Jesus Christ. (PAUSE) Submit to one another out of reverence for Christ.
Wife	Wives, submit to your husbands as to the Lord. For the husband is the head of the wife as Christ is the head of the church, his body, of which he is the Savior. Now as the church submits to Christ, so also wives should submit to their husbands in everything.
Husband	Husbands, love your wives, just as Christ loved the church and gave himself up for her to make her holy, cleansing her by the washing with water through the word, and to present her to himself as a radiant church, without stain or wrinkle or any other blemish, but holy and blameless. In this same way, husbands ought to love their wives as their own bodies. He who loves his wife loves himself. After all, no one ever

	hated his own body, but he feeds and cares for it, just as Christ does the church. . . .
Minister/ Leader	For this reason a man will leave his father and mother and be united to his wife, and the two will become one flesh. This is a profound mystery—but I am talking about Christ and the church. However, each one of you also must love his wife as he loves himself, and the wife must respect her husband.
Child	Children, obey your parents in the Lord, for this is right. "Honor your father and mother"—which is the first commandment with a promise—"that it may go well with you and that you may enjoy long life on the earth."
Father	Fathers, do not exasperate your children; instead, bring them up in the training and instruction of the Lord. . . .
Minister/ Leader	Finally, be strong in the Lord and in his mighty power. Put on the full armor of God so that you can take your stand against the devil's schemes. For our struggle is not against flesh and blood, but against the rulers, against the authorities, against the powers of this dark world and against the spiritual forces of evil in the heavenly realms.

Cast: **Minister/Leader, Wife, Husband, Child, Father**

The Armor of God
Ephesians 6:10–18

Voice 1	Be strong in the Lord and in his mighty power.
Voice 2	Put on the full armor of God so that you can take your stand against the devil's schemes.
Voice 1	For our struggle is not against flesh and blood, but against the rulers, against the authorities, against the powers of this dark world and against the spiritual forces of evil in the heavenly realms.
Voice 2	Therefore put on the full armor of God—
Voice 1	So that when the day of evil comes, you may be able to stand your ground, and after you have done everything, to stand.
Voice 2	Stand firm then—
Voice 3	With the belt of truth buckled around your waist.
Voice 2	With the breastplate of righteousness in place.
Voice 3	And with your feet fitted with the readiness that comes from the gospel of peace.
Voice 2	In addition to all this, take up the shield of faith, with which you can extinguish all the flaming arrows of the evil one.
Voice 3	Take the helmet of salvation and the sword of the Spirit—

Voice 2   Which is the word of God.

Voice 1   And pray in the Spirit on all occasions with all kinds of prayers and requests. With this in mind, be alert and always keep on praying for all the saints.

Cast: **Voice 1**, **Voice 2** (urgent), **Voice 3** (can be the same as Voice 1)

Philippians

Imitating Christ's Humility

Philippians 2:1–11

Paul   If you have any encouragement from being united with Christ, if any comfort from his love, if any fellowship with the Spirit, if any tenderness and compassion, then make my joy complete by being like-minded, having the same love, being one in spirit and purpose. Do nothing out of selfish ambition or vain conceit, but in humility consider others better than yourselves. Each of you should look not only to your own interests, but also to the interests of others.

Your attitude should be the same as that of Christ Jesus:

Singer 1   Who, being in very nature God—

Singer 2   Did not consider equality with God omething to be grasped,
but made himself nothing,
    taking the very nature of a servant,
    being made in human likeness.

Singer 1   And being found in appearance as a man—

Singer 2   He humbled himself
    and became obedient to death—
    even death on a cross!

Singer 3   Therefore God exalted him to the highest place—

Singer 4   And gave him the name that is above every name—

Singer 3   That at the name of Jesus every knee should bow,
    in heaven and on earth and under the earth,

Singer 4   And every tongue confess—

Singers 1–4   That Jesus Christ is Lord—

Singer 4   To the glory of God the Father.

Cast: **Paul, Singer 1, Singer 2, Singer 3, Singer 4.** (See also appendix: Christmas Readings, page 420.)

Colossians

The Supremacy of Christ
Colossians 1:15–20

Voice 1   [Christ] is the image of the invisible God, the firstborn over all creation.

Voice 2   For by him all things were created—

Voice 3   Things in heaven and on earth, visible and invisible, whether thrones or powers or rulers or authorities.

Voice 1   All things were created by him and for him.

Voice 2   He is before all things, and in him all things hold together.

Voice 3   And he is the head of the body, the church—

Voice 1   He is the beginning and the firstborn from among the dead, so that in everything he might have the supremacy.

Voice 2   For God was pleased to have all his fullness dwell in him, and through him to reconcile to himself all things—

Voice 3   Whether things on earth or things in heaven—

Voice 1   By making peace through his blood, shed on the cross.

Cast: **Voice 1, Voice 2, Voice 3.** (See also Appendix: Christmas Readings, page 422.)

God's Chosen People
Colossians 3:12–17 [18–4:1]

Voice 1   As God's chosen people, holy and dearly loved, clothe yourselves with compassion, kindness, humility, gentleness and patience.

Voice 2   Bear with each other and forgive whatever grievances you may have against one another.

Voice 1   Forgive as the Lord forgave you.

Voice 2   And over all these virtues put on love, which binds them all together in perfect unity.

Voice 1   Let the peace of Christ rule in your hearts, since as members of one body you were called to peace.

Voices 1 and **2**
(slowly)   And be thankful. (PAUSE)

Voice 1   Let the word of Christ dwell in you richly as you teach and admonish one another with all wisdom, and as you sing psalms, hymns and spiritual songs with gratitude in your hearts to God.

Voice 2	And whatever you do, whether in word or deed, do it all in the name of the Lord Jesus, giving thanks to God the Father through him.
[Voice 3	Wives, submit to your husbands, as is fitting in the Lord.
Voice 1	Husbands, love your wives and do not be harsh with them.
Voice 2	Children, obey your parents in everything, for this pleases the Lord.
Voice 3	Fathers, do not embitter your children, or they will become discouraged.
Voice 1	Slaves, obey your earthly masters in everything; and do it, not only when their eye is on you and to win their favor, but with sincerity of heart and reverence for the Lord.
Voice 2	Whatever you do, work at it with all your heart, as working for the Lord, not for men, since you know that you will receive an inheritance from the Lord as a reward. It is the Lord Christ you are serving.
Voice 1	Anyone who does wrong will be repaid for his wrong, and there is no favoritism.
Voice 3	Masters, provide your slaves with what is right and fair, because you know that you also have a Master in heaven.]

Cast: **Voice 1**, **Voice 2** [**Voice 3** (preferably female)]

1 Thessalonians

The Coming of the Lord
1 Thessalonians 4:13–18

Voice 1   [Brothers,] we do not want you to be ignorant about those who fall asleep, or to grieve like the rest of men, who have no hope.

Voice 2   We believe that Jesus died and rose again (PAUSE) and so we believe that God will bring with Jesus those who have fallen asleep in him.

Voice 1   According to the Lord's own word, we tell you that we who are still alive, who are left till the coming of the Lord, will certainly not precede those who have fallen asleep.

Voice 2   For the Lord himself will come down from heaven, with a loud command, with the voice of the archangel and with the trumpet call of God—

Voice 1   And the dead in Christ will rise first.

Voice 2   After that, we who are still alive and are left will be caught up together with them in the clouds to meet the Lord in the air.

Voice 1   And so we will be with the Lord forever.

Voices 1 and 2   Therefore encourage each other with these words.

Cast: **Voice 1, Voice 2**

Instructions to the Church
From 1 Thessalonians 5:12–28

Voice 1   [Now we ask you, brothers, to] respect those who work hard among you, who are over you in the Lord and who admonish you.

Voice 2   Hold them in the highest regard in love because of their work.

Voice 3   Live in peace with each other.

Voice 1   And we urge you—

Voice 2   Warn those who are idle.

Voice 3   Encourage the timid.

Voice 1   Help the weak.

Voice 2   Be patient with everyone.

Voice 3   Make sure that nobody pays back wrong for wrong, but always try to be kind to each other and to everyone else.

Voice 1	Be joyful always—
Voice 2	Pray continually; give thanks in all circumstances—
Voice 3	For this is God's will for you in Christ Jesus.
Voice 1	Do not put out the Spirit's fire; do not treat prophecies with contempt.
Voice 2	Test everything.
Voice 3	Hold on to the good.
Voice 1	Avoid every kind of evil.
Voice 2	May God himself, the God of peace, sanctify you through and through.
Voice 3	May your whole spirit, soul and body be kept blameless at the coming of our Lord Jesus Christ.
Voice 1	The one who calls you is faithful and he will do it. . . .
Voices 1–3	The grace of our Lord Jesus Christ be with you.

Cast: **Voice 1, Voice 2, Voice 3**

2 Thessalonians

Blessings
2 Thessalonians 1:2, 11; 2:16–17; 3:5, 16, 18

Voice 1   Grace and peace to you from God the Father and the Lord Jesus Christ.

Voice 2   We constantly pray for you, that our God may count you worthy of his calling, and that by his power he may fulfill every good purpose of yours and every act prompted by your faith.

Voice 3   May our Lord Jesus Christ himself and God our Father, who loved us and by his grace gave us eternal encouragement and good hope, encourage your hearts and strengthen you in every good deed and word.

Voice 2   May the Lord direct your hearts into God's love and Christ's perseverance.

Voice 1   May the Lord of peace himself give you peace at all times and in every way. The Lord be with all of you.

Voices 1–3   The grace of our Lord Jesus Christ be with you all.

Cast: **Voice 1, Voice 2, Voice 3**

1 Timothy

Overseers and Deacons
1 Timothy 3:1–13

Voice 1	Here is a trustworthy saying:
Voice 2	If anyone sets his heart on being an overseer, he desires a noble task.
Voice 1	Now the overseer must be above reproach.
Voice 2	The husband of but one wife, temperate, self-controlled.
Voice 1	Respectable, hospitable—
Voice 2	Able to teach—
Voice 1	Not given to drunkenness, not violent but gentle, not quarrelsome.
Voice 2	Not a lover of money.
Voice 1	He must manage his own family well and see that his children obey him with proper respect.
Voice 3	(If anyone does not know how to manage his own family, how can he take care of God's church?)
Voice 1	He must not be a recent convert, or he may become conceited and fall under the same judgment as the devil.
Voice 2	He must also have a good reputation with outsiders, so that he will not fall into disgrace and into the devil's trap.
Voice 1	Deacons, likewise, are to be men worthy of respect, sincere.
Voice 2	Not indulging in much wine, and not pursuing dishonest gain.
Voice 1	They must keep hold of the deep truths of the faith with a clear conscience.
Voice 2	They must first be tested; and then if there is nothing against them, let them serve as deacons.
Voice 3	In the same way, their wives are to be women worthy of respect, not malicious talkers but temperate and trustworthy in everything.
Voice 1	A deacon must be the husband of but one wife and must manage his children and his household well.
Voice 2	Those who have served well gain an excellent standing and great assurance in their faith in Christ Jesus.

Cast: **Voice 1, Voice 2, Voice 3**

The Great Secret
1 Timothy 3:14–16

Paul   Although I hope to come to you soon, I am writing you these instructions so that, if I am delayed, you will know how people ought to conduct themselves in God's household, which is the church of the living God, the pillar and foundation of the truth. Beyond all question, the mystery of godliness is great:

Voice 1   He appeared in a body—

Voice 2   [He] was vindicated by the Spirit—

Voice 3   [He] was seen by angels—

Voice 1   [He] was preached among the nations—

Voice 2   [He] was believed on in the world—

Voice 3   [He] was taken up in glory.

Cast: **Paul, Voice 1, Voice 2, Voice 3**

A Good Servant of Christ Jesus
From 1 Timothy 4:7–5:21

Voice 1   Have nothing to do with godless myths and old wives' tales; rather, train yourself to be godly. For physical training is of some value, but godliness has value for all things, holding promise for both the present life and the life to come.

Voice 2   This is a trustworthy saying that deserves full acceptance (and for this we labor and strive), that we have put our hope in the living God, who is the Savior of all men, and especially of those who believe. . . .

Voice 3   Don't let anyone look down on you because you are young, but set an example for the believers in speech, in life, in love, in faith and in purity.

Voice 1   Until I come, devote yourself to the public reading of Scripture, to preaching and to teaching. Do not neglect your gift, which was given you through a prophetic message when the body of elders laid their hands on you.

Be diligent in these matters; give yourself wholly to them, so that everyone may see your progress. Watch your life and doctrine closely. Persevere in them, because if you do, you will save both yourself and your hearers.

Voice 2   Do not rebuke an older man harshly, but exhort him as if he were your father. Treat younger men as brothers, older women as mothers, and younger women as sisters, with absolute purity.

Voice 3 Give proper recognition to those widows who are really in need. . . . (PAUSE) No widow may be put on the list of widows unless she is over sixty, has been faithful to her husband, and is well known for her good deeds, such as bringing up children, showing hospitality, washing the feet of the saints, helping those in trouble and devoting herself to all kinds of good deeds. . . .

Voice 1 Do not entertain an accusation against an elder unless it is brought by two or three witnesses.

Voice 2 Those who sin are to be rebuked publicly, so that the others may take warning.

Voice 3 I charge you, in the sight of God and Christ Jesus and the elect angels, to keep these instructions without partiality, and to do nothing out of favoritism.

Cast: **Voice 1, Voice 2, Voice 3**

2 Timothy

Encouragement to Be Faithful

From 2 Timothy 1:2–2:13

Voices 1–3 Grace, mercy and peace from God the Father and Christ Jesus our Lord. . . . Fan into flame the gift of God, which is in you through the laying on of my hands. For God did not give us a spirit of timidity, but a spirit of power, of love and of self-discipline. . . . Be strong in the grace that is in Christ Jesus. . . . Endure hardship with us like a good soldier of Christ Jesus.

Voice 1 No one serving as a soldier gets involved in civilian affairs—he wants to please his commanding officer.

Voice 2 Similarly, if anyone competes as an athlete, he does not receive the victor's crown unless he competes according to the rules. . . .

Paul This is my gospel, for which I am suffering even to the point of being chained like a criminal. But God's word is not chained. Therefore I endure everything for the sake of the elect, that they too may obtain the salvation that is in Christ Jesus, with eternal glory. Here is a trustworthy saying:

Voice 1 If we died with him—

Voice 2 We will also live with him.

Voice 1 If we endure—

Voices 2 and 3 We will also reign with him.

Voice 1 If we disown him—

Voices 2 and 3 He will also disown us.

Voice 1 If we are faithless—

Voices 2 and 3 He will remain faithful—

Voice 3 For he cannot disown himself.

Cast: **Voice 1, Voice 2, Voice 3, Paul** (can be the same as Voice 3)

Titus

The Grace of Christ
From Titus 2:11–3:7

Voice 1   The grace of God that brings salvation has appeared to all men. It teaches us to say:

Voices 1–3   No!

Voice 1   . . . to ungodliness and worldly passions, and to live self-controlled, upright and godly lives in this present age, while we wait for the blessed hope—

Voice 2   The glorious appearing of our great God and Savior, Jesus Christ, who gave himself for us to redeem us from all wickedness—

Voice 3   And to purify for himself a people that are his very own, eager to do what is good. . . .

Voice 1   At one time we too were foolish—

Voice 2   Disobedient—

Voice 3   Deceived and enslaved by all kinds of passions and pleasures.

Voice 1   We lived in malice and envy, being hated and hating one another.

Voice 2   But when the kindness and love of God our Savior appeared, he saved us—

Voice 3   Not because of righteous things we had done, but because of his mercy.

Voice 2   He saved us through the washing of rebirth and renewal by the Holy Spirit, whom he poured out on us generously through Jesus Christ our Savior.

Voice 1   So that, having been justified by his grace, we might become heirs having the hope of eternal life.

Cast: **Voice 1, Voice 2, Voice 3**

Philemon

Thanksgiving and Prayer
Philemon 3–7, 25

Voices 1–3   Grace to you and peace from God our Father and the Lord Jesus Christ.

Voice 1   I always thank my God as I remember you in my prayers, because I hear about your faith in the Lord Jesus and your love for all the saints.

Voice 2   I pray that you may be active in sharing your faith, so that you will have a full understanding of every good thing we have in Christ.

Voice 3   Your love has given me great joy and encouragement, because you, brother, have refreshed the hearts of the saints. . . .

Voices 1–3   The grace of the Lord Jesus Christ be with your spirit.

Cast: **Voice 1, Voice 2, Voice 3**

Hebrews

The Son Superior to Angels
Hebrews 1:1–14

Narrator   In the past God spoke to our forefathers through the prophets at many times and in various ways, but in these last days he has spoken to us by his Son, whom he appointed heir of all things, and through whom he made the universe. The Son is the radiance of God's glory and the exact representation of his being, sustaining all things by his powerful word. After he had provided purification for sins, he sat down at the right hand of the Majesty in heaven.

So he became as much superior to the angels as the name he has inherited is superior to theirs. For to which of the angels did God ever say:

God   You are my Son;
　　today I have become your Father.

Narrator   Or again:

God   I will be his Father,
　　and he will be my Son.

Narrator   And again, when God brings his firstborn into the world, he says:

God   Let all God's *angels* worship him.

Narrator   In speaking of the angels he says:

God   He makes his angels winds,
　　his servants flames of fire.

Narrator   But about the *Son* he says:

God   Your throne, O God, will last for ever and ever,
　　and righteousness will be the scepter of your kingdom.
You have loved righteousness and hated wickedness;
　　therefore God, your God, has set you above your companions
　　by anointing you with the oil of joy.

Narrator   He also says:

God   In the beginning, O Lord, you laid the foundations of the earth,
　　and the heavens are the work of your hands.
They will perish, but you remain;
　　they will all wear out like a garment.
You will roll them up like a robe;
　　like a garment they will be changed.
But you remain the same,
　　and your years will never end.

Narrator	To which of the angels did God ever say:
God	Sit at my right hand until I make your enemies a footstool for your feet.
Narrator	Are not all angels ministering spirits sent to serve those who will inherit salvation?

Cast: **Narrator, God.** (See also Appendix: Christmas Readings, page 420.)

Jesus Made Like His Brothers
Hebrews 2:5–18

Narrator	It is not to angels that [God] has subjected the world to come, about which we are speaking. But there is a place where someone has testified:
Psalmist	What is man that you are mindful of him, the son of man that you care for him? You made him a little lower than the angels; you crowned him with glory and honor and put everything under his feet.
Narrator	In putting everything under him, God left nothing that is not subject to him. Yet at present we do not see everything subject to him. But we see Jesus, who was made a little lower than the angels, now crowned with glory and honor because he suffered death, so that by the grace of God he might taste death for everyone. In bringing many sons to glory, it was fitting that God, for whom and through whom everything exists, should make the author of their salvation perfect through suffering. Both the one who makes men holy and those who are made holy are of the same family. So Jesus is not ashamed to call them brothers. He says:
Psalmist	I will declare your name to my brothers; in the presence of the congregation I will sing your praises.
Narrator	And again:
Isaiah	I will put my trust in him.
Narrator	And again he says:
Isaiah	Here am I, and the children God has given me.
Narrator	Since the children have flesh and blood, he too shared in their humanity so that by his death he might destroy him who holds the power of death—that is, the devil—and free those who all their lives were held in slavery by their fear of death. For surely it is not angels he helps, but Abraham's descendants. For this reason he had to be made like his brothers in every way, in order that he might become a merciful and faithful high priest in service to God, and that he might make atone-

ment for the sins of the people. Because he himself suffered when he was tempted, he is able to help those who are being tempted.

Cast: **Narrator, Psalmist, Isaiah**

Warnings against Unbelief
Hebrews 3:7–4:2, 12–13

Narrator   As the Holy Spirit says:

Psalmist   Today, if you hear his voice,
              do not harden your hearts
          as you did in the rebellion,
              during the time of testing in the desert,
          where your fathers tested and tried me
              and for forty years saw what I did.
          That is why I was angry with that generation,
              and I said, "Their hearts are always going astray,
              and they have not known my ways."
          So I declared on oath in my anger,
              "They shall never enter my rest."

Narrator   See to it, brothers, that none of you has a sinful, unbelieving heart that turns away from the living God. But encourage one another daily, as long as it is called Today, so that none of you may be hardened by sin's deceitfulness. We have come to share in Christ if we hold firmly till the end the confidence we had at first. As has just been said:

Psalmist   Today, if you hear his voice,
              do not harden your hearts
          as you did in the rebellion.

Narrator   Who were they who heard and rebelled? Were they not all those Moses led out of Egypt? And with whom was he angry for forty years? Was it not with those who sinned, whose bodies fell in the desert? And to whom did God swear:

Psalmist   [They shall never enter my rest]

Narrator   . . . if not to those who disobeyed? (PAUSE) So we see that they were not able to enter, because of their unbelief.

Therefore, since the promise of entering his rest still stands, let us be careful that none of you be found to have fallen short of it. For we also have had the gospel preached to us, just as they did; but the message they heard was of no value to them, because those who heard did not combine it with faith. . . .

For the word of God is living and active. Sharper than any double-edged sword, it penetrates even to dividing soul and spirit, joints and marrow; it judges the thoughts and attitudes of the heart. Nothing in all creation

369

is hidden from God's sight. Everything is uncovered and laid bare before the eyes of him to whom we must give account.

Cast: **Narrator, Psalmist**

Jesus the Great High Priest
Hebrews 4:14–5:10

Voice 1   Since we have a great high priest who has gone through the heavens, Jesus the Son of God, let us hold firmly to the faith we profess. For we do not have a high priest who is unable to sympathize with our weaknesses.

Voice 2   But we have one who has been tempted in every way, just as we are—yet was without sin.

Voice 1   Let us then approach the throne of grace with confidence, so that we may receive mercy—

Voice 2   And find grace to help us in our time of need.

Voice 1   Every high priest is selected from among men and is appointed to represent them in matters related to God, to offer gifts and sacrifices for sins. He is able to deal gently with those who are ignorant and are going astray, since he himself is subject to weakness. This is why he has to offer sacrifices for his own sins, as well as for the sins of the people.

Voice 2   No one takes this honor upon himself; he must be called by God, just as Aaron was.

Voice 1   So Christ also did not take upon himself the glory of becoming a high priest. But God said to him:

God   You are my Son;
    today I have become your Father.

Voice 2   And he says in another place:

God   You are a priest forever,
    in the order of Melchizedek.

Voice 1   During the days of Jesus' life on earth, he offered up prayers and petitions with loud cries and tears to the one who could save him from death, and he was heard because of his reverent submission.

Voice 2   Although he was a son, he learned obedience from what he suffered.

Voice 1   And, once made perfect, he became the source of eternal salvation for all who obey him.

Voice 2   And was designated by God to be high priest in the order of Melchizedek.

Cast: **Voice 1, Voice 2, God**

The Certainty of God's Promise
Hebrews 6:13–19

Narrator 1   When God made his promise to Abraham, since there was no one greater for him to swear by, he swore by himself, saying:

God   I will surely bless you and give you many descendants. (PAUSE)

Narrator 2   And so after waiting patiently, Abraham received what was promised.

Narrator 1   Men swear by someone greater than themselves, and the oath confirms what is said and puts an end to all argument. Because God wanted to make the unchanging nature of his purpose very clear to the heirs of what was promised, he confirmed it with an oath. (PAUSE)

Narrator 2   God did this so that, by two unchangeable things in which it is impossible for God to lie, we who have fled to take hold of the hope offered to us may be greatly encouraged.

Narrator 1   We have this hope as an anchor for the soul, firm and secure.

Cast: **Narrator 1, God, Narrator 2**

Jesus Like Melchizedek
Hebrews 7:15–28

Narrator   What we have said is even more clear if another priest like Melchizedek appears, one who has become a priest not on the basis of a regulation as to his ancestry but on the basis of the power of an indestructible life. For it is declared:

Psalmist   You are a priest forever,
  in the order of Melchizedek.

Narrator   The former regulation is set aside because it was weak and useless (for the law made nothing perfect), and a better hope is introduced, by which we draw near to God.

And it was not without an oath! Others became priests without any oath, but he became a priest with an oath when God said to him:

Psalmist   The Lord has sworn
  and will not change his mind:
"You are a priest forever."

Narrator   Because of this oath, Jesus has become the guarantee of a better covenant.

Now there have been many of those priests, since death prevented them from continuing in office; but because Jesus lives forever, he has a permanent priesthood. Therefore he is able to save completely those who come to God through him, because he always lives to intercede for them.

371

Such a high priest meets our need—one who is holy, blameless, pure, set apart from sinners, exalted above the heavens. Unlike the other high priests, he does not need to offer sacrifices day after day, first for his own sins, and then for the sins of the people. He sacrificed for their sins once for all when he offered himself. For the law appoints as high priests men who are weak; but the oath, which came after the law, appointed the Son, who has been made perfect forever.

Cast: **Narrator, Psalmist**

The High Priest of a New Covenant
Hebrews 8:3–13

Narrator Every high priest is appointed to offer both gifts and sacrifices, and so it was necessary for this one also to have something to offer. If he were on earth, he would not be a priest, for there are already men who offer the gifts prescribed by the law. They serve at a sanctuary that is a copy and shadow of what is in heaven. This is why Moses was warned when he was about to build the tabernacle:

Voice of God See to it that you make everything according to the pattern shown you on the mountain.

Narrator But the ministry Jesus has received is as superior to theirs as the covenant of which he is mediator is superior to the old one, and it is founded on better promises.

For if there had been nothing wrong with that first covenant, no place would have been sought for another. But God found fault with the people and said:

Jeremiah The time is coming, declares the Lord,
    when I will make a new covenant
with the house of Israel
    and with the house of Judah.
It will not be like the covenant
    I made with their forefathers
when I took them by the hand
    to lead them out of Egypt,
because they did not remain faithful to my covenant,
    and I turned away from them, declares the Lord.
This is the covenant I will make with the house of Israel
    after that time, declares the Lord.
I will put my laws in their minds
    and write them on their hearts.
I will be their God,
    and they will be my people.
No longer will a man teach his neighbor,
    or a man his brother, saying, "Know the Lord,"

because they will all know me,
>from the least of them to the greatest.
For I will forgive their wickedness
>and will remember their sins no more.

Narrator By calling this covenant "new," he has made the first one obsolete; and what is obsolete and aging will soon disappear.

Cast: **Narrator, Voice of God, Jeremiah**

Christ's Sacrifice Once for All
Hebrews 10:1–18

Narrator The law is only a shadow of the good things that are coming—not the realities themselves. For this reason it can never, by the same sacrifices repeated endlessly year after year, make perfect those who draw near to worship. If it could, would they not have stopped being offered? For the worshipers would have been cleansed once for all, and would no longer have felt guilty for their sins. But those sacrifices are an annual reminder of sins, because it is impossible for the blood of bulls and goats to take away sins.

Therefore, when Christ came into the world, he said:

Christ Sacrifice and offering you did not desire,
>but a body you prepared for me;
with burnt offerings and sin offerings
>you were not pleased.
Then I said, "Here I am—it is written about me in the scroll—
>I have come to do your will, O God."

Narrator First he said:

Christ Sacrifices and offerings, burnt offerings and sin offerings you did not desire, nor were you pleased with them.

Narrator (Although the law required them to be made.) Then he said:

Christ Here I am, I have come to do your will.

Narrator He sets aside the first to establish the second. And by that will, we have been made holy through the sacrifice of the body of Jesus Christ once for all.

Day after day every priest stands and performs his religious duties; again and again he offers the same sacrifices, which can never take away sins. But when this priest had offered for all time one sacrifice for sins, he sat down at the right hand of God. Since that time he waits for his enemies to be made his footstool, because by one sacrifice he has made perfect forever those who are being made holy.

The Holy Spirit also testifies to us about this. First he says:

Holy Spirit	This is the covenant I will make with them
	after that time, says the Lord.
	I will put my laws in their hearts,
	and I will write them on their minds.

Narrator	Then he adds:

Holy Spirit	Their sins and lawless acts
	I will remember no more.

Narrator	And where these have been forgiven, there is no longer any sacrifice for sin.

Cast: **Narrator, Christ, Holy Spirit**

A Call to Persevere
From Hebrews 10:19–39

Voice 1	Since we have confidence to enter the Most Holy Place by the blood of Jesus, by a new and living way opened for us through the curtain, that is, his body—
Voice 2	And since we have a great priest over the house of God, let us draw near to God with a sincere heart in full assurance of faith, having our hearts sprinkled to cleanse us from a guilty conscience and having our bodies washed with pure water.
Voice 1	Let us hold unswervingly to the hope we profess, for he who promised is faithful.
Voice 2	And let us consider how we may spur one another on toward love and good deeds.
Voice 1	Let us not give up meeting together, as some are in the habit of doing, but let us encourage one another—and all the more as you see the Day approaching.
	[If we deliberately keep on sinning after we have received the knowledge of the truth—
Voice 2	No sacrifice for sins is left, but only a fearful expectation of judgment and of raging fire that will consume the enemies of God. . . . For we know him who said:
Voice 3	It is mine to avenge; I will repay.
Voice 2	And again:
Voice 3	The Lord will judge his people.
Voice 1	It is a dreadful thing to fall into the hands of the living God.]
Voice 2	Remember those earlier days after you had received the light, when you stood your ground in a great contest in the face of suffering. . . .

So do not throw away your confidence; it will be richly rewarded. You need to persevere so that when you have done the will of God, you will receive what he has promised. For in just a very little while:

Voice 3   He who is coming will come and will not delay.
         But my righteous one will live by faith.
     And if he shrinks back,
         I will not be pleased with him.

Voice 1   But we are not of those who shrink back and are destroyed, but of those who believe and are saved.

Cast: **Voice 1, Voice 2, Voice 3**

Faith (i)
Hebrews 11:1–16

Voice 1   Faith is being sure of what we hope for and certain of what we do not see.

Voice 2   This is what the ancients were commended for.

Voice 3   By faith we understand that the universe was formed at God's command, so that what is seen was not made out of what was visible.

Voice 1   By faith Abel offered God a better sacrifice than Cain did. By faith he was commended as a righteous man, when God spoke well of his offerings. And by faith he still speaks, even though he is dead.

Voice 2   By faith Enoch was taken from this life, so that he did not experience death; he could not be found, because God had taken him away. For before he was taken, he was commended as one who pleased God. And without faith it is impossible to please God, because anyone who comes to him must believe that he exists and that he rewards those who earnestly seek him.

Voice 3   By faith Noah, when warned about things not yet seen, in holy fear built an ark to save his family. By his faith he condemned the world and became heir of the righteousness that comes by faith.

Voice 1   By faith Abraham, when called to go to a place he would later receive as his inheritance, obeyed and went, even though he did not know where he was going.

Voice 2   By faith he made his home in the promised land like a stranger in a foreign country; he lived in tents, as did Isaac and Jacob, who were heirs with him of the same promise. For he was looking forward to the city with foundations, whose architect and builder is God.

Voice 3   By faith Abraham, even though he was past age—and Sarah herself was barren—was enabled to become a father because he considered him faithful who had made the promise. And so from this one man, and he as good as dead, came descendants as numerous as the stars in the sky and as countless as the sand on the seashore.

Voice 1   All these people were still living by faith when they died. They did not receive the things promised; they only saw them and welcomed them from a distance. And they admitted that they were aliens and strangers on earth. People who say such things show that they are looking for a country of their own. If they had been thinking of the country they had left, they would have had opportunity to return. Instead, they were longing for a better country—a heavenly one. Therefore God is not ashamed to be called their God, for he has prepared a city for them.

Cast: **Voice 1, Voice 2, Voice 3**

Faith (ii)
Hebrews 11:17–33

Voice 1   By faith Abraham, when God tested him, offered Isaac as a sacrifice. He who had received the promises was about to sacrifice his one and only son, even though God had said to him, "It is through Isaac that your offspring will be reckoned." Abraham reasoned that God could raise the dead, and figuratively speaking, he did receive Isaac back from death.

Voice 2   By faith Isaac blessed Jacob and Esau in regard to their future.

By faith Jacob, when he was dying, blessed each of Joseph's sons, and worshiped as he leaned on the top of his staff.

Voice 3   By faith Joseph, when his end was near, spoke about the exodus of the Israelites from Egypt and gave instructions about his bones.

Voice 1   By faith Moses' parents hid him for three months after he was born, because they saw he was no ordinary child, and they were not afraid of the king's edict.

Voice 2   By faith Moses, when he had grown up, refused to be known as the son of Pharaoh's daughter. He chose to be mistreated along with the people of God rather than to enjoy the pleasures of sin for a short time. He regarded disgrace for the sake of Christ as of greater value than the treasures of Egypt, because he was looking ahead to his reward.

Voice 3   By faith he left Egypt, not fearing the king's anger; he persevered because he saw him who is invisible. By faith he kept the Passover and the sprinkling of blood, so that the destroyer of the firstborn would not touch the firstborn of Israel.

Voice 1   By faith the people passed through the Red Sea as on dry land; but when the Egyptians tried to do so, they were drowned.

Voice 2   By faith the walls of Jericho fell, after the people had marched around them for seven days.

By faith the prostitute Rahab, because she welcomed the spies, was not killed with those who were disobedient.

Voice 3   And what more shall I say? I do not have time to tell about Gideon, Barak, Samson, Jephthah, David, Samuel and the prophets, who through faith conquered kingdoms, administered justice, and gained what was promised.

Cast: **Voice 1**, **Voice 2**, **Voice 3**. (Please note that this reading overlaps with the reading from Hebrews 11:32–12:2.)

Faith (iii)
Hebrews 11:32–12:2

Voice 1   And what more shall I say? I do not have time to tell about Gideon, Barak, Samson, Jephthah, David, Samuel and the prophets, who through faith conquered kingdoms, administered justice, and gained what was promised; who shut the mouths of lions, quenched the fury of the flames, and escaped the edge of the sword; whose weakness was turned to strength; and who became powerful in battle and routed foreign armies.

Voice 2   Women received back their dead, raised to life again. Others were tortured and refused to be released, so that they might gain a better resurrection. Some faced jeers and flogging, while still others were chained and put in prison. They were stoned; they were sawed in two; they were put to death by the sword. They went about in sheepskins and goatskins, destitute, persecuted and mistreated—the world was not worthy of them. They wandered in deserts and mountains, and in caves and holes in the ground.

Voice 3   These were all commended for their faith, yet none of them received what had been promised. God had planned something better for us so that only together with us would they be made perfect.

Voice 1   Therefore, since we are surrounded by such a great cloud of witnesses, let us throw off everything that hinders and the sin that so easily entangles, and let us run with perseverance the race marked out for us. Let us fix our eyes on Jesus, the author and perfecter of our faith, who for the joy set before him endured the cross, scorning its shame, and sat down at the right hand of the throne of God.

Cast: **Voice 1**, **Voice 2**, **Voice 3**. (Please note that this reading overlaps with the reading from Hebrews 11:17–33.)

God Disciplines His Children
Hebrews 12:3–11

Voice 1   Consider him who endured such opposition from sinful men, so that you will not grow weary and lose heart.

377

Voice 2	In your struggle against sin, you have not yet resisted to the point of shedding your blood.
Voice 3	And you have forgotten that word of encouragement that addresses you as sons:

Scripture	My son, do not make light of the Lord's discipline,
	    and do not lose heart when he rebukes you,
	because the Lord disciplines those he loves,
	    and he punishes everyone he accepts as a son.

Voice 3	Endure hardship as discipline; God is treating you as sons. For what son is not disciplined by his father?
Voice 2	If you are not disciplined (and everyone undergoes discipline), then you are illegitimate children and not true sons.
Voice 1	Moreover, we have all had human fathers who disciplined us and we respected them for it. How much more should we submit to the Father of our spirits and live!
Voice 3	Our fathers disciplined us for a little while as they thought best; but God disciplines us for our good, that we may share in his holiness.
Voice 1	No discipline seems pleasant at the time, but painful. Later on, however, it produces a harvest of righteousness and peace for those who have been trained by it.

Cast: **Voice 1, Voice 2, Voice 3, Scripture**

Warning against Refusing God
From Hebrews 12:14–29

Voice 1	Make every effort to live in peace with all men and to be holy; without holiness no one will see the Lord.
Voice 2	See to it that no one misses the grace of God. . . .
Voice 3	You have not come to a mountain that can be touched and that is burning with fire; to darkness, gloom and storm; to a trumpet blast or to such a voice speaking words that those who heard it begged that no further word be spoken to them, because they could not bear what was commanded:
Exodus	If even an animal touches the mountain, it must be stoned.
Voice 3	The sight was so terrifying that Moses said:
Moses	I am trembling with fear.
Voice 1	But you have come to Mount Zion, to the heavenly Jerusalem, the city of the living God.

Voice 2	You have come to thousands upon thousands of angels in joyful assembly, to the church of the firstborn, whose names are written in heaven.
Voice 3	You have come to God, the judge of all men, to the spirits of righteous men made perfect—
Voice 1	To Jesus the mediator of a new covenant, and to the sprinkled blood that speaks a better word than the blood of Abel.
Voice 2	See to it that you do not refuse him who speaks.
Voice 3	If they did not escape when they refused him who warned them on earth, how much less will we, if we turn away from him who warns us from heaven?
Voice 1	At that time his voice shook the earth, but now he has promised:
Haggai	Once more I will shake not only the earth but also the heavens.
Voice 1	The words "once more" indicate the removing of what can be shaken— that is, created things—so that what cannot be shaken may remain.
Voice 2	Therefore, since we are receiving a kingdom that cannot be shaken—
Voice 3	Let us be thankful, and so worship God acceptably with reverence and awe, for:
Voices 1–3	Our God is a consuming fire.

Cast: **Voice 1**, **Voice 2**, **Voice 3**, **Exodus**, **Moses** (can be the same as Exodus), **Haggai** (can be the same as Exodus)

How to Please God
From Hebrews 13:1–21

Voice 1	Keep on loving each other as brothers.
Voice 2	Do not forget to entertain strangers, for by so doing some people have entertained angels without knowing it.
Voice 3	Remember those in prison as if you were their fellow prisoners—
Voice 1	And those who are mistreated as if you yourselves were suffering.
Voice 2	Marriage should be honored by all, and the marriage bed kept pure, for God will judge the adulterer and all the sexually immoral.
Voice 3	Keep your lives free from the love of money and be content with what you have, because God has said:
God	Never will I leave you; never will I forsake you.

379

Voice 2	So we say with confidence:
Voices 1 and 2	The Lord is my helper; I will not be afraid. What can man do to me?
Voice 1	Remember your leaders, who spoke the word of God to you. Consider the outcome of their way of life and imitate their faith. Jesus Christ is the same yesterday and today and forever. . . .
Voice 2	For here we do not have an enduring city, but we are looking for the city that is to come.
	Through Jesus, therefore, let us continually offer to God a sacrifice of praise—the fruit of lips that confess his name.
Voice 3	And do not forget to do good and to share with others, for with such sacrifices God is pleased.
Voice 1	Obey your leaders and submit to their authority. They keep watch over you as men who must give an account. Obey them so that their work will be a joy, not a burden, for that would be of no advantage to you. . . .
Voice 2	May the God of peace . . . equip you with everything good for doing his will, and may he work in us what is pleasing to him, through Jesus Christ.
Voice 3	To whom be glory for ever and ever.
Voices 1 and 2	Amen.

Cast: **Voice 1, Voice 2, Voice 3, God** (can be the same as Voice 1)

James

Favoritism Forbidden
James 2:1–13

James   As believers in our glorious Lord Jesus Christ, don't show favoritism. Suppose a man comes into your meeting wearing a gold ring and fine clothes, and a poor man in shabby clothes also comes in. If you show special attention to the man wearing fine clothes and say:

Person   Here's a good seat for you.

James   But say to the poor man:

Person   You stand there, or sit on the floor by my feet.

James   Have you not discriminated among yourselves and become judges with evil thoughts? (PAUSE)

Listen, my dear brothers: Has not God chosen those who are poor in the eyes of the world to be rich in faith and to inherit the kingdom he promised those who love him? But you have insulted the poor. Is it not the rich who are exploiting you? Are they not the ones who are dragging you into court? Are they not the ones who are slandering the noble name of him to whom you belong? (PAUSE)

You are doing right if you really keep the royal law found in Scripture:

Scripture   Love your neighbor as yourself.

James   But if you show favoritism, you sin and are convicted by the law as lawbreakers. For whoever keeps the whole law and yet stumbles at just one point is guilty of breaking all of it. For he who said:

Scripture   Do not commit adultery.

James   Also said:

Scripture   Do not murder.

James   If you do not commit adultery but do commit murder, you have become a lawbreaker.

Speak and act as those who are going to be judged by the law that gives freedom, because judgment without mercy will be shown to anyone who has not been merciful. Mercy triumphs over judgment!

Cast: **James, Person, Scripture**

Faith and Deeds
James 2:14–26

James   What good is it, my brothers, if a man claims to have faith but has no deeds? Can such faith save him? Suppose a brother or sister is without clothes and daily food. If one of you says to him:

Person 1   Go, I wish you well.

Person 2   Keep warm and well fed.

James   But does nothing about his physical needs, what good is it? In the same way, faith by itself, if it is not accompanied by action, is dead. But someone will say:

Person 1   You have faith; I have deeds.

James   Show me your faith without deeds, and I will show you my faith by what I do. You believe that there is one God. Good! Even the demons believe that—and shudder.

You foolish man, do you want evidence that faith without deeds is useless? Was not our ancestor Abraham considered righteous for what he did when he offered his son Isaac on the altar? You see that his faith and his actions were working together, and his faith was made complete by what he did. And the scripture was fulfilled that says:

Scripture   Abraham believed God, and it was credited to him as righteousness.

James   And he was called God's friend. You see that a person is justified by what he does and not by faith alone.

In the same way, was not even Rahab the prostitute considered righteous for what she did when she gave lodging to the spies and sent them off in a different direction? As the body without the spirit is dead, so faith without deeds is dead.

Cast: **James, Person 1, Person 2** (can be the same as Person 1), **Scripture**

Submit Yourselves to God
James 4:1–10

James   What causes fights and quarrels among you? Don't they come from your desires that battle within you? You want something but don't get it. You kill and covet, but you cannot have what you want. You quarrel and fight. You do not have, because you do not ask God. When you ask, you do not receive, because you ask with wrong motives, that you may spend what you get on your pleasures.

You adulterous people, don't you know that friendship with the world is hatred toward God? Anyone who chooses to be a friend of the world

	becomes an enemy of God. Or do you think Scripture says without reason:
Scripture	The spirit he caused to live in us envies intensely.
James	But he gives us more grace. That is why Scripture says:
Scripture	God opposes the proud but gives grace to the humble.
James	Submit yourselves, then, to God. Resist the devil, and he will flee from you. Come near to God and he will come near to you. Wash your hands, you sinners, and purify your hearts, you double-minded. Grieve, mourn and wail. Change your laughter to mourning and your joy to gloom. Humble yourselves before the Lord, and he will lift you up.

Cast: **James, Scripture**

Boasting about Tomorrow
James 4:13–17

James	Now listen, you who say:
Voice 1 (confident)	Today or tomorrow we will go to this or that city, spend a year there, carry on business and make money.
James	Why, you do not even know what will happen tomorrow. What is your life? You are a mist that appears for a little while and then vanishes. Instead, you ought to say:
Voice 2 (humble)	If it is the Lord's will, we will live and do this or that.
James	As it is, you boast and brag. All such boasting is evil. Anyone, then, who knows the good he ought to do and doesn't do it, sins.

Cast: **James, Voice 1, Voice 2**

1 Peter

Praise to God for a Living Hope
1 Peter 1:3–12

Voices 1 and 2 Praise be to the God and Father of our Lord Jesus Christ!

Voice 1 In his great mercy he has given us new birth into a living hope through the resurrection of Jesus Christ from the dead.

Voice 2 And into an inheritance that can never perish, spoil or fade—kept in heaven for you, who through faith are shielded by God's power until the coming of the salvation that is ready to be revealed in the last time.

Voice 1 In this you greatly rejoice, though now for a little while you may have had to suffer grief in all kinds of trials.

Voice 2 These have come so that your faith—of greater worth than gold, which perishes even though refined by fire—may be proved genuine and may result in praise, glory and honor when Jesus Christ is revealed.

Voice 3 Though you have not seen him, you love him.

Voice 1 And even though you do not see him now, you believe in him.

Voice 2 And are filled with an inexpressible and glorious joy.

Voice 3 For you are receiving the goal of your faith, the salvation of your souls.

Voice 2 Concerning this salvation, the prophets, who spoke of the grace that was to come to you, searched intently and with the greatest care—

Voice 3 Trying to find out the time and circumstances to which the Spirit of Christ in them was pointing when he predicted the sufferings of Christ and the glories that would follow.

Voice 2 It was revealed to them that they were not serving themselves but you, when they spoke of the things that have now been told you by those who have preached the gospel to you by the Holy Spirit sent from heaven.

Voice 1 Even angels long to look into these things.

Cast: **Voice 1, Voice 2, Voice 3** (can be the same as Voice 1)

Be Holy
1 Peter 1:13–25

Voice 1 Prepare your minds for action.

Voice 2 Be self-controlled; set your hope fully on the grace to be given you when Jesus Christ is revealed.

Voice 1	As obedient children, do not conform to the evil desires you had when you lived in ignorance.
Voice 2	But just as he who called you is holy, so be holy in all you do; for it is written:
Scripture	Be holy, because I am holy.
Voice 1	Since you call on a Father who judges each man's work impartially, live your lives as strangers here in reverent fear.
Voice 2	For you know that it was not with perishable things such as silver or gold that you were redeemed from the empty way of life handed down to you from your forefathers, but with the precious blood of Christ, a lamb without blemish or defect.
Voice 1	He was chosen before the creation of the world, but was revealed in these last times for your sake.
Voice 2	Through him you believe in God, who raised him from the dead and glorified him, and so your faith and hope are in God. (PAUSE)
Voice 1	Now that you have purified yourselves by obeying the truth so that you have sincere love for your brothers, love one another deeply, from the heart. For you have been born again, not of perishable seed, but of imperishable, through the living and enduring word of God. [For:]

Scripture	All men are like grass,
	    and all their glory is like the flowers of the field;
	the grass withers and the flowers fall,
	    but the word of the Lord stands forever.

Voices 1 and **2** And this is the word that was preached to you.

Cast: **Voice 1, Voice 2, Scripture**

The Living Stone and a Chosen People
1 Peter 2:1–10

Peter	Rid yourselves of all malice and all deceit, hypocrisy, envy, and slander of every kind. Like newborn babies, crave pure spiritual milk, so that by it you may grow up in your salvation—
Psalmist	Now that you have tasted that the Lord is good.
Peter	As you come to him, the living Stone—rejected by men but chosen by God and precious to him—you also, like living stones, are being built into a spiritual house to be a holy priesthood, offering spiritual sacrifices acceptable to God through Jesus Christ. [For in Scripture it says:]

Isaiah	See, I lay a stone in Zion,
	    a chosen and precious cornerstone,
	and the one who trusts in him
	    will never be put to shame.

Peter	Now to you who believe, this stone is precious. But to those who do not believe:
Psalmist	The stone the builders rejected has become the capstone—
[Peter	And:]
Isaiah	A stone that causes men to stumble and a rock that makes them fall.
Peter	They stumble because they disobey the message—which is also what they were destined for. But you are a chosen people, a royal priesthood, a holy nation, a people belonging to God, that you may declare the praises of him who called you out of darkness into his wonderful light. Once you were not a people, but now you are the people of God; once you had not received mercy, but now you have received mercy.

Cast: **Peter, Psalmist, Isaiah**

Submission to Rulers and Masters
1 Peter 2:21–25

Voice 1	[To this you were called, because] Christ suffered for you, leaving you an example, that you should follow in his steps.
Voice 2	He committed no sin, and no deceit was found in his mouth.
Voice 1	When they hurled their insults at him, he did not retaliate.
Voice 2	When he suffered, he made no threats. Instead, he entrusted himself to him who judges justly.
Voices 1 and 2	He himself bore our sins in his body on the tree, so that we might die to sins and live for righteousness.
Voice 2	By his wounds you have been healed.
Voice 1	For you were like sheep going astray, but now you have returned to the Shepherd and Overseer of your souls.

Cast: **Voice 1, Voice 2**

Suffering for Doing Good
1 Peter 3:8–18

Peter	All of you, live in harmony with one another; be sympathetic, love as brothers, be compassionate and humble. Do not repay evil with evil or insult with insult, but with blessing, because to this you were called so that you may inherit a blessing. [For:]

Psalmist	Whoever would love life
	    and see good days
	must keep his tongue from evil
	    and his lips from deceitful speech.
	He must turn from evil and do good;
	    he must seek peace and pursue it.
	For the eyes of the Lord are on the righteous
	    and his ears are attentive to their prayer,
	but the face of the Lord is against those who do evil.

Peter	Who is going to harm you if you are eager to do good? But even if you should suffer for what is right, you are blessed.
Isaiah	Do not fear what they fear; do not be frightened.
Peter	But in your hearts set apart Christ as Lord. Always be prepared to give an answer to everyone who asks you to give the reason for the hope that you have. But do this with gentleness and respect, keeping a clear conscience, so that those who speak maliciously against your good behavior in Christ may be ashamed of their slander. It is better, if it is God's will, to suffer for doing good than for doing evil. For Christ died for sins once for all, the righteous for the unrighteous, to bring you to God.

Cast: **Peter, Psalmist, Isaiah**

2 Peter

Prophecy of Scripture
2 Peter 1:16–21

Voice 1   We did not follow cleverly invented stories when we told you about the power and coming of our Lord Jesus Christ.

Voices 1 and 2   But we were eyewitnesses of his majesty.

Voice 2   For he received honor and glory from God the Father when the voice came to him from the Majestic Glory, saying:

God   This is my Son, whom I love; with him I am well pleased.

Voice 2   We ourselves heard this voice that came from heaven when we were with him on the sacred mountain.

Voice 1   And we have the word of the prophets made more certain, and you will do well to pay attention to it, as to a light shining in a dark place, until the day dawns and the morning star rises in your hearts.

Voice 2   Above all, you must understand that no prophecy of Scripture came about by the prophet's own interpretation. For prophecy never had its origin in the will of man, but men spoke from God as they were carried along by the Holy Spirit.

Cast: **Voice 1, Voice 2, God**

The Day of the Lord
2 Peter 3:3–9

Teacher   You must understand that in the last days scoffers will come, scoffing and following their own evil desires. They will say:

Person 1   Where is this "coming" he promised?

Person 2   Ever since our fathers died, everything goes on as it has since the beginning of creation.

Teacher   But they deliberately forget that long ago by God's word the heavens existed and the earth was formed out of water and by water. By these waters also the world of that time was deluged and destroyed. By the same word the present heavens and earth are reserved for fire, being kept for the day of judgment and destruction of ungodly men.

But do not forget this one thing, dear friends: With the Lord a day is like a thousand years, and a thousand years are like a day. The Lord is not slow in keeping his promise, as some understand slowness. He is patient with you, not wanting anyone to perish, but everyone to come to repentance.

The Lord's Coming
From 2 Peter 3:10–18

Voice 1   The day of the Lord will come like a thief.

Voice 2   The heavens will disappear with a roar.

Voice 1   The elements will be destroyed by fire.

Voice 2   And the earth and everything in it will be laid bare. (PAUSE)

Voice 1   Since everything will be destroyed in this way, what kind of people ought you to be?

Voice 2   You ought to live holy and godly lives as you look forward to the day of God and speed its coming. That day will bring about the destruction of the heavens by fire, and the elements will melt in the heat.

Voice 1   But in keeping with his promise we are looking forward to a new heaven and a new earth, the home of righteousness.

Voice 2   So then, dear friends, since you are looking forward to this, make every effort to be found spotless, blameless and at peace with him. . . . But grow in the grace and knowledge of our Lord and Savior Jesus Christ.

Voices 1 and 2   To him be glory both now and forever! Amen.

1 John

The Word of Life

1 John 1:1–3

Voice 1   That which was from the beginning—

Voice 2   Which we have heard, which we have seen with our eyes—

Voice 1   Which we have looked at and our hands have touched—

Voice 2   This we proclaim concerning the Word of life. The life appeared; we have seen it and testify to it, and we proclaim to you the eternal life, which was with the Father and has appeared to us.

Voice 1   We proclaim to you what we have seen and heard, so that you also may have fellowship with us. And our fellowship is with the Father and with his Son, Jesus Christ.

Cast: **Voice 1, Voice 2**

Walking in the Light

1 John 1:5–10

Voice 1   This is the message we have heard from him and declare to you: God is light; in him there is no darkness at all.

Voice 2   If we claim to have fellowship with him yet walk in the darkness, we lie and do not live by the truth.

Voice 1   But if we walk in the light, as he is in the light, we have fellowship with one another, and the blood of Jesus, his Son, purifies us from all sin.

Voice 2   If we claim to be without sin, we deceive ourselves and the truth is not in us.

Voice 1   If we confess our sins, he is faithful and just and will forgive us our sins and purify us from all unrighteousness.

Voice 2   If we claim we have not sinned, we make him out to be a liar and his word has no place in our lives.

Cast: **Voice 1, Voice 2**

Our Helper, Christ
1 John 2:1–6

Voice 1	[My dear children, I write this to you so that you will not sin. But] if anybody does sin, we have one who speaks to the Father in our defense—Jesus Christ, the Righteous One.
Voice 2	He is the atoning sacrifice for our sins, and not only for ours but also for the sins of the whole world.
Voice 1	We know that we have come to know him if we obey his commands.
Voice 2	The man who says, "I know him," but does not do what he commands is a liar, and the truth is not in him.
Voice 1	But if anyone obeys his word, God's love is truly made complete in him. This is how we know we are in him:
Voice 2	Whoever claims to live in him must walk as Jesus did.

Cast: **Voice 1, Voice 2**

God's Love and Ours
1 John 4:7–21

Voice 1	Dear friends, let us love one another, for love comes from God.
Voice 2	Everyone who loves has been born of God and knows God.
Voice 3	Whoever does not love does not know God.
Voices 1 and 2	Because God *is* love.
Voice 1	This is how God showed his love among us: He sent his one and only Son into the world that we might live through him. This is love:
Voice 3	Not that we loved God—
Voice 2	But that he loved us and sent his Son as an atoning sacrifice for our sins.
Voice 1	Dear friends, since God so loved us, we also ought to love one another. (PAUSE)
Voice 3	No one has ever seen God.
Voice 2	But if we love one another, God lives in us and his love is made complete in us. (PAUSE)
Voice 1	We know that we live in him and he in us, because he has given us of his Spirit.
Voice 2	And we have seen and testify that the Father has sent his Son to be the Savior of the world.

Voice 1	If anyone acknowledges that Jesus is the Son of God, God lives in him and he in God.
Voice 2	And so we know and rely on the love God has for us. (PAUSE)
Voice 1	God is love. Whoever lives in love lives in God, and God in him.
Voice 2	In this way, love is made complete among us so that we will have confidence on the day of judgment, because in this world we are like him. There is no fear in love. But perfect love drives out fear.
Voice 3	Because fear has to do with punishment. The one who fears is not made perfect in love.
Voice 1	We love because he first loved us.
Voice 3	If anyone says, "I love God," yet hates his brother, he is a liar. For anyone who does not love his brother, whom he has seen, cannot love God, whom he has not seen. (PAUSE) And he has given us this command:
Voices 1 and 3	Whoever loves God must also love his brother.

Cast: **Voice 1** (authoritative voice), **Voice 2** (encouraging voice), **Voice 3** (warning voice)

Faith in the Son of God
1 John 5:6–12

Voice 1	[Jesus Christ] is the one who came by water and blood.
Voice 2	He did not come by water only—
Voice 3	But by water and blood.
Voice 1	And it is the Spirit who testifies, because the Spirit is the truth.
Voice 2	For there are three that testify:
Voice 1	The Spirit—
Voice 2	The water—
Voice 3	And the blood.
Voices 1–3	And the three are in agreement. (PAUSE)
Voice 2	We accept man's testimony.
Voice 3	But God's testimony is greater because it is the testimony of God, which he has given about his Son.
Voice 1	Anyone who believes in the Son of God has this testimony in his heart.
Voice 2	Anyone who does not believe God has made him out to be a liar, because he has not believed the testimony God has given about his Son.
Voice 3	And this is the testimony:

Voices 1–3	God has given us eternal life.
Voice 1	And this life is in his Son.
Voice 3	He who has the Son has life.
Voice 2	He who does not have the Son of God does not have life.

Cast: **Voice 1** (authoritative voice), **Voice 2** (warning voice), **Voice 3** (encouraging voice)

Jude

Greetings and Doxology
From Jude

Voice 1	To those who have been called—
Voice 2	Who are loved by God the Father.
Voice 3	And kept by Jesus Christ:
Voice 1	Mercy, peace and love be yours in abundance. . . .
Voice 2	To him who is able to keep you from falling—
Voice 3	And to present you before his glorious presence without fault and with great joy—
Voice 1	To the only God our Savior—
Voice 2	Be glory
Voice 3	Majesty
Voice 1	Power
Voice 2	Authority
Voice 3	Through Jesus Christ our Lord—
Voice 1	Before all ages,
Voices 1 and 2	Now
Voices 2 and 3	and forevermore!
Voices 1–3	Amen.

Cast: **Voice 1, Voice 2, Voice 3**

Revelation

The Revelation to John: Prologue

Revelation 1:1–3

Voice 1   The revelation of Jesus Christ—

Voice 2   Which God gave him to show his servants what must soon take place.

Voice 1   He made it known by sending his angel to his servant John, who testifies to everything he saw—

Voice 2   That is, the word of God and the testimony of Jesus Christ.

Voice 3   Blessed is the one who reads the words of this prophecy, and blessed are those who hear it and take to heart what is written in it—

Voices 1–3   Because the time is near.

Cast: **Voice 1, Voice 2, Voice 3**

Greetings and Doxology

Revelation 1:4–8

Reader   [From] John, to the seven churches in the province of Asia:

John   Grace and peace to you from him who is, and who was, and who is to come, and from the seven spirits before his throne, and from Jesus Christ, who is the faithful witness, the firstborn from the dead, and the ruler of the kings of the earth.

Worshiper   To him who loves us and has freed us from our sins by his blood, and has made us to be a kingdom and priests to serve his God and Father— to him be glory and power for ever and ever! Amen.

John   Look, he is coming with the clouds,
    and every eye will see him,
even those who pierced him;
    and all the peoples of the earth will mourn because of him.
                            So shall it be! Amen.

Voice   I am the Alpha and the Omega.

John   [So] says the Lord God—

Reader	Who is—and who was—
Reader and **John**	And who is to come.
Voice	The Almighty.

Cast: **Reader, John, Worshiper, Voice** (can be the same as Reader)

One Like a Son of Man
Revelation 1:9–20

John I, John, your brother and companion in the suffering and kingdom and patient endurance that are ours in Jesus, was on the island of Patmos because of the word of God and the testimony of Jesus. On the Lord's Day I was in the Spirit, and I heard behind me a loud voice like a trumpet, which said:

Voice Write on a scroll what you see and send it to the seven churches: to Ephesus, Smyrna, Pergamum, Thyatira, Sardis, Philadelphia and Laodicea.

John I turned around to see the voice that was speaking to me. And when I turned I saw seven golden lampstands, and among the lampstands was someone "like a son of man," dressed in a robe reaching down to his feet and with a golden sash around his chest. His head and hair were white like wool, as white as snow, and his eyes were like blazing fire. His feet were like bronze glowing in a furnace, and his voice was like the sound of rushing waters. In his right hand he held seven stars, and out of his mouth came a sharp double-edged sword. His face was like the sun shining in all its brilliance.

When I saw him, I fell at his feet as though dead. Then he placed his right hand on me and said:

Voice Do not be afraid. I am the First and the Last. I am the Living One; I was dead, and behold I am alive for ever and ever! And I hold the keys of death and Hades.

Write, therefore, what you have seen, what is now and what will take place later. The mystery of the seven stars that you saw in my right hand and of the seven golden lampstands is this: The seven stars are the angels of the seven churches, and the seven lampstands are the seven churches.

Cast: **John, Voice**

To the Church in Ephesus
Revelation 2:1–7

Voice 1 To the angel of the church in Ephesus write:

Voice 2	These are the words of him who holds the seven stars in his right hand and walks among the seven golden lampstands:
Voice 3	I know your deeds, your hard work and your perseverance. I know that you cannot tolerate wicked men, that you have tested those who claim to be apostles but are not, and have found them false. You have persevered and have endured hardships for my name, and have not grown weary.
	Yet I hold this against you: You have forsaken your first love. Remember the height from which you have fallen! Repent and do the things you did at first. If you do not repent, I will come to you and remove your lampstand from its place. But you have this in your favor: You hate the practices of the Nicolaitans, which I also hate.
Voices 1 and 2	He who has an ear, let him hear what the Spirit says to the churches.
Voice 3	To him who overcomes, I will give the right to eat from the tree of life, which is in the paradise of God.

Cast: **Voice 1, Voice 2, Voice 3**

To the Church in Smyrna
Revelation 2:8–11

Voice 1	To the angel of the church in Smyrna write:
Voice 2	These are the words of him who is the First and the Last, who died and came to life again.
Voice 3	I know your afflictions and your poverty—yet you are rich! I know the slander of those who say they are Jews and are not, but are a synagogue of Satan. Do not be afraid of what you are about to suffer. I tell you, the devil will put some of you in prison to test you, and you will suffer persecution for ten days. Be faithful, even to the point of death, and I will give you the crown of life.
Voices 1 and 2	He who has an ear, let him hear what the Spirit says to the churches.
Voice 2	He who overcomes will not be hurt at all by the second death.

Cast: **Voice 1, Voice 2, Voice 3**

To the Church in Pergamum
Revelation 2:12–17

Voice 1	To the angel of the church in Pergamum write:
Voice 2	These are the words of him who has the sharp, double-edged sword.

Voice 3	I know where you live—where Satan has his throne. Yet you remain true to my name. You did not renounce your faith in me, even in the days of Antipas, my faithful witness, who was put to death in your city—where Satan lives.
	Nevertheless, I have a few things against you: You have people there who hold to the teaching of Balaam, who taught Balak to entice the Israelites to sin by eating food sacrificed to idols and by committing sexual immorality. Likewise you also have those who hold to the teaching of the Nicolaitans. Repent therefore! Otherwise, I will soon come to you and will fight against them with the sword of my mouth.
Voices 1 and 2	He who has an ear, let him hear what the Spirit says to the churches.
Voice 3	To him who overcomes, I will give some of the hidden manna. I will also give him a white stone with a new name written on it, known only to him who receives it.

Cast: **Voice 1, Voice 2, Voice 3**

To the Church in Sardis
Revelation 3:1–6

Voice 1	To the angel of the church in Sardis write:
Voice 2	These are the words of him who holds the seven spirits of God and the seven stars.
Voice 3	I know your deeds; you have a reputation of being alive, but you are dead. Wake up! Strengthen what remains and is about to die, for I have not found your deeds complete in the sight of my God. Remember, therefore, what you have received and heard; obey it, and repent. But if you do not wake up, I will come like a thief, and you will not know at what time I will come to you.
	Yet you have a few people in Sardis who have not soiled their clothes. They will walk with me, dressed in white, for they are worthy. He who overcomes will, like them, be dressed in white. I will never blot out his name from the book of life, but will acknowledge his name before my Father and his angels.
Voices 1 and 2	He who has an ear, let him hear what the Spirit says to the churches.

Cast: **Voice 1, Voice 2, Voice 3**

To the Church in Laodicea
Revelation 3:14–22

Voice 1	To the angel of the church in Laodicea write:

Voice 2	These are the words of the Amen, the faithful and true witness, the ruler of God's creation.
Voice 3	I know your deeds, that you are neither cold nor hot. I wish you were either one or the other! So, because you are lukewarm—neither hot nor cold—I am about to spit you out of my mouth. You say:
Laodicean	I am rich; I have acquired wealth and do not need a thing.
Voice 3	But you do not realize that you are wretched, pitiful, poor, blind and naked. I counsel you to buy from me gold refined in the fire, so you can become rich; and white clothes to wear, so you can cover your shameful nakedness; and salve to put on your eyes, so you can see.
	Those whom I love I rebuke and discipline. So be earnest, and repent. Here I am! I stand at the door and knock. If anyone hears my voice and opens the door, I will come in and eat with him, and he with me.
	To him who overcomes, I will give the right to sit with me on my throne, just as I overcame and sat down with my Father on his throne.
Voices 1 and 2	He who has an ear, let him hear what the Spirit says to the churches.

Cast: **Voice 1, Voice 2, Voice 3, Laodicean**

The Throne in Heaven
Revelation 4:1–11

John	I looked, and there before me was a door standing open in heaven. And the voice I had first heard speaking to me like a trumpet said:
Voice	Come up here, and I will show you what must take place after this.
John	At once I was in the Spirit, and there before me was a throne in heaven with someone sitting on it. And the one who sat there had the appearance of jasper and carnelian. A rainbow, resembling an emerald, encircled the throne. Surrounding the throne were twenty-four other thrones, and seated on them were twenty-four elders. They were dressed in white and had crowns of gold on their heads. From the throne came flashes of lightning, rumblings and peals of thunder. Before the throne, seven lamps were blazing. These are the seven spirits of God. Also before the throne there was what looked like a sea of glass, clear as crystal.
	In the center, around the throne, were four living creatures, and they were covered with eyes, in front and in back. The first living creature was like a lion, the second was like an ox, the third had a face like a man, the fourth was like a flying eagle. Each of the four living creatures had six wings and was covered with eyes all around, even under his wings. Day and night they never stop saying:

399

Chorus	Holy, holy, holy is the Lord God Almighty, who was, and is, and is to come.
John	Whenever the living creatures give glory, honor and thanks to him who sits on the throne and who lives for ever and ever, the twenty-four elders fall down before him who sits on the throne, and worship him who lives for ever and ever. They lay their crowns before the throne and say:

Chorus	You are worthy, our Lord and God,
	    to receive glory and honor and power,
	for you created all things,
	    and by your will they were created
	    and have their being.

Cast: **John**, **Voice**, **Chorus** (two or more)

The Scroll and the Lamb
Revelation 5:1–14

John	I saw in the right hand of him who sat on the throne a scroll with writing on both sides and sealed with seven seals. And I saw a mighty angel proclaiming in a loud voice:
Angel	Who is worthy to break the seals and open the scroll?
John	But no one in heaven or on earth or under the earth could open the scroll or even look inside it. I wept and wept because no one was found who was worthy to open the scroll or look inside. Then one of the elders said to me:
Elder	Do not weep! See, the Lion of the tribe of Judah, the Root of David, has triumphed. He is able to open the scroll and its seven seals.
John	Then I saw a Lamb, looking as if it had been slain, standing in the center of the throne, encircled by the four living creatures and the elders. He had seven horns and seven eyes, which are the seven spirits of God sent out into all the earth. He came and took the scroll from the right hand of him who sat on the throne. And when he had taken it, the four living creatures and the twenty-four elders fell down before the Lamb. Each one had a harp and they were holding golden bowls full of incense, which are the prayers of the saints. And they sang a new song:

Chorus	You are worthy to take the scroll
	    and to open its seals,
	because you were slain,
	    and with your blood you purchased men for God
	    from every tribe and language and people and nation.
	You have made them to be a kingdom and priests to serve our God,
	    and they will reign on the earth.

John	Then I looked and heard the voice of many angels, numbering thousands upon thousands, and ten thousand times ten thousand. They encircled the throne and the living creatures and the elders. In a loud voice they sang:
Chorus	Worthy is the Lamb, who was slain, to receive power and wealth and wisdom and strength, and honor and glory and praise!
John	Then I heard every creature in heaven and on earth and under the earth and on the sea, and all that is in them, singing:
Chorus	To him who sits on the throne and to the Lamb be praise and honor and glory and power, for ever and ever!
John	The four living creatures said:
Four creatures	Amen!
John	And the elders fell down and worshiped.

Cast: **John**, **Angel**, **Elder**, **Chorus** (two or more—one can be the same as Elder), **Four creatures** (one can be the same as Angel, and the other three can be the same as Chorus)

The Seals
Revelation 6:1–17

John	I watched as the Lamb opened the first of the seven seals. Then I heard one of the four living creatures say in a voice like thunder:
Creature 1	Come!
John	I looked, and there before me was a white horse! Its rider held a bow, and he was given a crown, and he rode out as a conqueror bent on conquest. (PAUSE) When the Lamb opened the second seal, I heard the second living creature say:
Creature 2	Come!
John	Then another horse came out, a fiery red one. Its rider was given power to take peace from the earth and to make men slay each other. To him was given a large sword. (PAUSE) When the Lamb opened the third seal, I heard the third living creature say:
Creature 3	Come!
John	I looked, and there before me was a black horse! Its rider was holding a pair of scales in his hand. Then I heard what sounded like a voice among the four living creatures, saying:
Voice	A quart of wheat for a day's wages, and three quarts of barley for a day's wages, and do not damage the oil and the wine! (PAUSE)
John	When the Lamb opened the fourth seal, I heard the voice of the fourth living creature say:

Creature 4	Come!
John	I looked, and there before me was a pale horse! Its rider was named Death, and Hades was following close behind him. They were given power over a fourth of the earth to kill by sword, famine and plague, and by the wild beasts of the earth. (PAUSE)
	When he opened the fifth seal, I saw under the altar the souls of those who had been slain because of the word of God and the testimony they had maintained. They called out in a loud voice:
Martyrs 1 and 2	How long, Sovereign Lord, holy and true—
Martyr 1	Until you judge the inhabitants of the earth—
Martyr 2	And avenge our blood?
John	Then each of them was given a white robe, and they were told to wait a little longer, until the number of their fellow servants and brothers who were to be killed as they had been was completed
	I watched as he opened the sixth seal. There was a great earthquake. The sun turned black like sackcloth made of goat hair, the whole moon turned blood red, and the stars in the sky fell to earth, as late figs drop from a fig tree when shaken by a strong wind. The sky receded like a scroll, rolling up, and every mountain and island was removed from its place.
	Then the kings of the earth, the princes, the generals, the rich, the mighty, and every slave and every free man hid in caves and among the rocks of the mountains. They called to the mountains and the rocks:
Rulers 1 and 2	Fall on us.
Ruler 1	Hide us from the face of him who sits on the throne.
Ruler 2	And from the wrath of the Lamb!
Ruler 1	For the great day of their wrath has come.
Ruler 2	Who can stand?

Cast: **John, Creature 1, Creature 2, Creature 3, Voice, Creature 4, Martyr 1, Martyr 2** (Martyrs 1 and 2 can be the same as Creatures 1 and 2), **Ruler 1, Ruler 2** (Rulers 1 and 2 can be the same as Creatures 3 and 4)

144,000 Sealed
Revelation 7:1–8

John	I saw four angels standing at the four corners of the earth, holding back the four winds of the earth to prevent any wind from blowing on the land or on the sea or on any tree. Then I saw another angel coming up from the east, having the seal of the living God. He called out in a loud

	voice to the four angels who had been given power to harm the land and the sea:
Angel 1	Do not harm the land or the sea or the trees until we put a seal on the foreheads of the servants of our God.
John	Then I heard the number of those who were sealed: 144,000 from all the tribes of Israel.
Angel 2	From the tribe of Judah were sealed:
Angel 3	Twelve thousand.
Angel 2	From the tribe of Reuben were sealed:
Angel 3	Twelve thousand.
Angel 2	From the tribe of Gad were sealed:
Angel 3	Twelve thousand.
Angel 2	From the tribe of Asher were sealed:
Angel 3	Twelve thousand.
Angel 2	From the tribe of Naphtali were sealed:
Angel 3	Twelve thousand.
Angel 2	From the tribe of Manasseh were sealed:
Angel 3	Twelve thousand.
Angel 2	From the tribe of Simeon were sealed:
Angel 3	Twelve thousand.
Angel 2	From the tribe of Levi were sealed:
Angel 3	Twelve thousand.
Angel 2	From the tribe of Issachar were sealed:
Angel 3	Twelve thousand.
Angel 2	From the tribe of Zebulun were sealed:
Angel 3	Twelve thousand.
Angel 2	From the tribe of Joseph were sealed:
Angel 3	Twelve thousand.
Angel 2	From the tribe of Benjamin were sealed:
Angel 3	Twelve thousand.

Cast: **John, Angel 1, Angel 2, Angel 3** (can be the same as Angel 1)

The Great Multitude in White Robes
Revelation 7:9–17

John	I looked and there before me was a great multitude that no one could count, from every nation, tribe, people and language, standing before the throne and in front of the Lamb. They were wearing white robes and were holding palm branches in their hands. And they cried out in a loud voice:
Voices 1 and 2	Salvation belongs to our God, who sits on the throne, and to the Lamb.
John	All the angels were standing around the throne and around the elders and the four living creatures. They fell down on their faces before the throne and worshiped God, saying:
Voices 2 and 3	Amen!
Voice 1	Praise
Voice 2	Glory
Voice 3	Wisdom
Voice 1	Thanks
Voice 2	Honor
Voice 3	Power
Voice 1	Strength
Voices 2 and 3	Be to our God for ever and ever.
Voices 1–3	Amen!
John	Then one of the elders asked me:
Elder	These in white robes—who are they, and where did they come from?
John	I answered, "Sir, you know."
Elder	These are they who have come out of the great tribulation; they have washed their robes and made them white in the blood of the Lamb. Therefore, they are before the throne of God and serve him day and night in his temple; and he who sits on the throne will spread his tent over them. Never again will they hunger; never again will they thirst. The sun will not beat upon them, nor any scorching heat.

> For the Lamb at the center of the throne will be their shepherd;
> > he will lead them to springs of living water.
> And God will wipe away every tear from their eyes.

Cast: **John, Voice 1, Voice 2, Voice 3, Elder** (can be the same as Voice 3)

The Angel and the Little Scroll
Revelation 10:1–11

John   I saw another mighty angel coming down from heaven. He was robed in a cloud, with a rainbow above his head; his face was like the sun, and his legs were like fiery pillars. He was holding a little scroll, which lay open in his hand. He planted his right foot on the sea and his left foot on the land, and he gave a loud shout like the roar of a lion. When he shouted, the voices of the seven thunders spoke. And when the seven thunders spoke, I was about to write; but I heard a voice from heaven say:

Voice   Seal up what the seven thunders have said and do not write it down.

John   Then the angel I had seen standing on the sea and on the land raised his right hand to heaven. And he swore by him who lives for ever and ever, who created the heavens and all that is in them, the earth and all that is in it, and the sea and all that is in it.

Angel   There will be no more delay! But in the days when the seventh angel is about to sound his trumpet, the mystery of God will be accomplished, just as he announced to his servants the prophets.

John   Then the voice that I had heard from heaven spoke to me once more:

Voice   Go, take the scroll that lies open in the hand of the angel who is standing on the sea and on the land.

John   So I went to the angel and asked him to give me the little scroll. He said to me:

Angel   Take it and eat it. It will turn your stomach sour, but in your mouth it will be as sweet as honey.

John   I took the little scroll from the angel's hand and ate it. It tasted as sweet as honey in my mouth, but when I had eaten it, my stomach turned sour. Then I was told:

Voice   You must prophesy again about many peoples, nations, languages and kings.

Cast: **John, Voice, Angel**

The Seventh Trumpet
Revelation 11:15–19

John   The seventh angel sounded his trumpet, and there were loud voices in heaven, which said:

Elder 1   The kingdom of the world has become—

Elders 1 and 2 The kingdom of our Lord and of his Christ.

Elder 2   And he will reign for ever and ever.

John   And the twenty-four elders, who were seated on their thrones before God, fell on their faces and worshiped God, saying:

Elder 1   We give thanks to you, Lord God Almighty,
              the One who is and who was,
              because you have taken your great power
              and have begun to reign.

Elder 2   The nations were angry;
              and your wrath has come.

Elder 1   The time has come for judging the dead,
              and for rewarding your servants the prophets
              and your saints and those who reverence your name,
              both small and great—
              and for destroying those who destroy the earth.

John   Then God's temple in heaven was opened, and within his temple was seen the ark of his covenant. And there came flashes of lightning, rumblings, peals of thunder, an earthquake and a great hailstorm.

Cast: **John, Elder 1, Elder 2**

The Beast out of the Sea [and the Beast out of the Earth]
Revelation 13:1–10 [11–12, 15–18]

John   The dragon stood on the shore of the sea.

              And I saw a beast coming out of the sea. He had ten horns and seven heads, with ten crowns on his horns, and on each head a blasphemous name. The beast I saw resembled a leopard, but had feet like those of a bear and a mouth like that of a lion. The dragon gave the beast his power and his throne and great authority. One of the heads of the beast seemed to have had a fatal wound, but the fatal wound had been healed. The whole world was astonished and followed the beast. Men worshiped the dragon because he had given authority to the beast, and they also worshiped the beast and asked:

Worshiper   Who is like the beast? Who can make war against him?

406

John	The beast was given a mouth to utter proud words and blasphemies and to exercise his authority for forty-two months. He opened his mouth to blaspheme God, and to slander his name and his dwelling place and those who live in heaven. He was given power to make war against the saints and to conquer them. And he was given authority over every tribe, people, language and nation. All inhabitants of the earth will worship the beast—all whose names have not been written in the book of life belonging to the Lamb that was slain from the creation of the world.
Voice	He who has an ear, let him hear.

	If anyone is to go into captivity,
	    into captivity he will go.
	If anyone is to be killed with the sword,
	    with the sword he will be killed.

	This calls for patient endurance and faithfulness on the part of the saints.
[John	Then I saw another beast, coming out of the earth. He had two horns like a lamb, but he spoke like a dragon. He exercised all the authority of the first beast on his behalf, and made the earth and its inhabitants worship the first beast, whose fatal wound had been healed. . . . He was given power to give breath to the image of the first beast, so that it could speak and cause all who refused to worship the image to be killed. He also forced everyone, small and great, rich and poor, free and slave, to receive a mark on his right hand or on his forehead, so that no one could buy or sell unless he had the mark, which is the name of the beast or the number of his name.
	This calls for wisdom. If anyone has insight, let him calculate the number of the beast, for it is man's number. His number is 666.]

Cast: **John, Worshiper, Voice**

The Three Angels
Revelation 14:6–13

John	I saw another angel flying in midair, and he had the eternal gospel to proclaim to those who live on the earth—to every nation, tribe, language and people. He said in a loud voice:
Angel 1	Fear God and give him glory, because the hour of his judgment has come. Worship him who made the heavens, the earth, the sea and the springs of water.
John	A second angel followed and said:
Angel 2	Fallen! Fallen is Babylon the Great, which made all the nations drink the maddening wine of her adulteries.

John	A third angel followed them and said in a loud voice:
Angel 3	If anyone worships the beast and his image and receives his mark on the forehead or on the hand, he, too, will drink of the wine of God's fury, which has been poured full strength into the cup of his wrath. He will be tormented with burning sulfur in the presence of the holy angels and of the Lamb. And the smoke of their torment rises for ever and ever. There is no rest day or night for those who worship the beast and his image, or for anyone who receives the mark of his name.
John	This calls for patient endurance on the part of the saints who obey God's commandments and remain faithful to Jesus. Then I heard a voice from heaven say:
Voice	Write: Blessed are the dead who die in the Lord from now on.
John	[The Spirit says:]
Spirit	Yes, they will rest from their labor, for their deeds will follow them.

Cast: **John, Angel 1, Angel 2, Angel 3, Voice, Spirit**

The Harvest of the Earth
Revelation 14:14–19

John	I looked, and there before me was a white cloud, and seated on the cloud was one "like a son of man" with a crown of gold on his head and a sharp sickle in his hand. Then another angel came out of the temple and called in a loud voice to him who was sitting on the cloud:
Angel 1	Take your sickle and reap, because the time to reap has come, for the harvest of the earth is ripe.
John	So he who was seated on the cloud swung his sickle over the earth, and the earth was harvested.
	Another angel came out of the temple in heaven, and he too had a sharp sickle. Still another angel, who had charge of the fire, came from the altar and called in a loud voice to him who had the sharp sickle:
Angel 2	Take your sharp sickle and gather the clusters of grapes from the earth's vine, because its grapes are ripe.
John	The angel swung his sickle on the earth, gathered its grapes and threw them into the great winepress of God's wrath.

Cast: **John, Angel 1, Angel 2**

Seven Angels with Seven Plagues
Revelation 15:1–8

John	I saw in heaven another great and marvelous sign: seven angels with the seven last plagues—last, because with them God's wrath is completed.

And I saw what looked like a sea of glass mixed with fire and, standing beside the sea, those who had been victorious over the beast and his image and over the number of his name. They held harps given them by God and sang the song of Moses the servant of God and the song of the Lamb:

Saint 1   Great and marvelous are your deeds,
Lord God Almighty.

Saint 2   Just and true are your ways,
King of the ages.

Saint 3   Who will not fear you, O Lord—

Saint 1   And bring glory to your name?

Saint 2   For you alone are holy.

Saint 3   All nations will come
and worship before you,
for your righteous acts have been revealed.

John   After this I looked and in heaven the temple, that is, the tabernacle of the Testimony, was opened. Out of the temple came the seven angels with the seven plagues. They were dressed in clean, shining linen and wore golden sashes around their chests. Then one of the four living creatures gave to the seven angels seven golden bowls filled with the wrath of God, who lives for ever and ever. And the temple was filled with smoke from the glory of God and from his power, and no one could enter the temple until the seven plagues of the seven angels were completed.

Cast: **John, Saint 1, Saint 2, Saint 3**

The Fall of Babylon
From Revelation 18:1–19

John   I saw another angel coming down from heaven. He had great authority, and the earth was illuminated by his splendor. With a mighty voice he shouted:

Angel   Fallen! Fallen is Babylon the Great!
She has become a home for demons
and a haunt for every evil spirit,
a haunt for every unclean and detestable bird.
For all the nations have drunk
the maddening wine of her adulteries.
The kings of the earth committed adultery with her,
and the merchants of the earth grew rich from her excessive luxuries.

John   Then I heard another voice from heaven say:

409

Voice	Come out of her, my people,
	    so that you will not share in her sins,
	    so that you will not receive any of her plagues;
	for her sins are piled up to heaven,
	    and God has remembered her crimes. . . .
	Therefore in one day her plagues will overtake her:
	    death, mourning and famine.
	She will be consumed by fire,
	    for mighty is the Lord God who judges her.

John	When the kings of the earth who committed adultery with her and shared her luxury see the smoke of her burning, they will weep and mourn over her. Terrified at her torment, they will stand far off and cry:
King 1	Woe!
King 2	Woe!
King 1	O great city, O Babylon, city of power!
King 2	In one hour your doom has come!
John	The merchants of the earth will weep and mourn over her because no one buys their cargoes any more—cargoes of gold, silver, precious stones and pearls; fine linen, purple, silk and scarlet cloth; every sort of citron wood, and articles of every kind made of ivory, costly wood, bronze, iron and marble; cargoes of cinnamon and spice, of incense, myrrh and frankincense, of wine and olive oil, of fine flour and wheat; cattle and sheep; horses and carriages; and bodies and souls of men. They will say:
Merchant 1	The fruit you longed for is gone from you.
Merchant 2	All your riches and splendor have vanished, never to be recovered.
John	The merchants who sold these things and gained their wealth from her will stand far off, terrified at her torment. They will weep and mourn and cry out:
Merchant 1	Woe!
Merchant 2	Woe, O great city.
Merchant 1	Dressed in fine linen, purple and scarlet, and glittering with gold, precious stones and pearls!
Merchant 2	In one hour such great wealth has been brought to ruin!
John	Every sea captain, and all who travel by ship, the sailors, and all who earn their living from the sea, will stand far off. When they see the smoke of her burning, they will exclaim:
Sailor 1	Was there ever a city like this great city? . . .
Sailor 2	Woe!

Sailor 1	Woe, O great city,
	    where all who had ships on the sea
	      became rich through her wealth!

Sailor 2	In one hour she has been brought to ruin!

Cast: **John, Angel, Voice, King 1, King 2, Merchant 1** (can be the same as Angel), **Merchant 2** (can be the same as Voice), **Sailor 1** (can be the same as King 1), **Sailor 2** (can be the same as King 2)

Hallelujah!
Revelation 19:5–10

John	A voice came from the throne, saying:

Voice	Praise our God,
	    all you his servants,
	you who fear him,
	    both small and great!

John	Then I heard what sounded like a great multitude, like the roar of rushing waters and like loud peals of thunder, shouting:
Saints 1 and 2	Hallelujah!
Saint 1	For our Lord God Almighty reigns.
Saint 2	Let us rejoice and be glad.
Saint 1	And give him glory!
Saint 2	For the wedding of the Lamb has come, and his bride has made herself ready.
Saint 1	Fine linen, bright and clean, was given her to wear.
John	(Fine linen stands for the righteous acts of the saints.) (PAUSE) Then the angel said to me:
Angel	Write: "Blessed are those who are invited to the wedding supper of the Lamb!"
John	And he added:
Angel	These are the true words of God.
John	At this I fell at his feet to worship him. But he said to me:
Angel	Do not do it! I am a fellow servant with you and with your brothers who hold to the testimony of Jesus. Worship God!
John	For the testimony of Jesus is the spirit of prophecy.

Cast: **John, Voice, Saint 1, Saint 2, Angel**

411

The Rider on the White Horse
Revelation 19:11–16

John   I saw heaven standing open and there before me was a white horse, whose rider is called Faithful and True. With justice he judges and makes war. His eyes are like blazing fire, and on his head are many crowns. He has a name written on him that no one knows but he himself. He is dressed in a robe dipped in blood, and his name is:

Voice (slowly)   The Word of God.

John   The armies of heaven were following him, riding on white horses and dressed in fine linen, white and clean. Out of his mouth comes a sharp sword with which to strike down the nations. "He will rule them with an iron scepter." He treads the winepress of the fury of the wrath of God Almighty. On his robe and on his thigh he has this name written:

Voice (boldly)   KING OF KINGS AND LORD OF LORDS.

Cast: **John, Voice**

A New Heaven and a New Earth
Revelation 21:1–7 [8]

John   I saw a new heaven and a new earth, for the first heaven and the first earth had passed away, and there was no longer any sea. I saw the Holy City, the new Jerusalem, coming down out of heaven from God, prepared as a bride beautifully dressed for her husband. And I heard a loud voice from the throne [saying]:

Voice   Now the dwelling of God is with men, and he will live with them. They will be his people, and God himself will be with them and be their God. He will wipe every tear from their eyes. There will be no more death or mourning or crying or pain, for the old order of things has passed away.

John   He who was seated on the throne said:

God   I am making everything new!

John   Then he said:

God   Write this down, for these words are trustworthy and true.

John   He said to me:

God   It is done. I am the Alpha and the Omega, the Beginning and the End. To him who is thirsty I will give to drink without cost from the spring of the water of life. He who overcomes will inherit all this, and I will be his God and he will be my son. [But the cowardly, the unbelieving, the vile, the murderers, the sexually immoral, those who practice magic arts, the idolaters and all liars—their place will be in the fiery lake of burning sulfur. This is the second death.]

Cast: **John, Voice, God**

Jesus Is Coming
Revelation 22:6–17 [18–19], 20–21

John   The angel said to me:

Angel   These words are trustworthy and true. The Lord, the God of the spirits of the prophets, sent his angel to show his servants the things that must soon take place.

Jesus (voice)   Behold, I am coming soon! Blessed is he who keeps the words of the prophecy in this book.

John   I, John, am the one who heard and saw these things. And when I had heard and seen them, I fell down to worship at the feet of the angel who had been showing them to me. But he said to me:

Angel   Do not do it! I am a fellow servant with you and with your brothers the prophets and of all who keep the words of this book. Worship God!

               Do not seal up the words of the prophecy of this book, because the time is near. Let him who does wrong continue to do wrong; let him who is vile continue to be vile; let him who does right continue to do right; and let him who is holy continue to be holy.

Jesus (voice)   Behold, I am coming soon! My reward is with me, and I will give to everyone according to what he has done. I am the Alpha and the Omega, the First and the Last, the Beginning and the End.

John   Blessed are those who wash their robes, that they may have the right to the tree of life and may go through the gates into the city. Outside are the dogs, those who practice magic arts, the sexually immoral, the murderers, the idolaters and everyone who loves and practices falsehood.

Jesus (voice)   I, Jesus, have sent my angel to give you this testimony for the churches. I am the Root and the Offspring of David, and the bright Morning Star.

John   The Spirit and the bride say:

Voices 1
  and 2   Come!

John   And let him who hears say:

Cast
  (except
  Jesus)   Come!

John   Whoever is thirsty, let him come; and whoever wishes, let him take the free gift of the water of life.

[I warn everyone who hears the words of the prophecy of this book: If anyone adds anything to them, God will add to him the plagues described in this book. And if anyone takes words away from this book of prophecy, God will take away from him his share in the tree of life and in the holy city, which are described in this book.]

He who testifies to these things says:

Jesus (voice)   Yes, I am coming soon.

John   Amen.

Cast
(except
Jesus)   Come, Lord Jesus.

John   The grace of the Lord Jesus be with God's people.

Cast
(except
Jesus)   Amen!

Cast: **John, Angel, Jesus** (voice only), **Voice 1, Voice 2** (can be the same as Angel)

Christmas Readings

Sometimes the dramatized Christmas Readings will be used in public at a crowded service where there is little space for a large cast, or where amplification of the cast is needed but only a single directional microphone is available. In such circumstances it will be as well to keep those participating to a minimum. The cast list below (not in order of appearance) is arranged in groupings to allow each reader to take more than one part in the series, but not in the same reading. This is the minimum configuration which also takes into account a male-female balance of voices. Where such a balance is not possible, please ignore the instructions in parentheses.

Cast of Readers
for the dramatized Christmas Readings

First Reader (*strong female voice*)
Narrator—except in "Mary Visits Elizabeth"
Narrator 1—in "The Shepherds Find the Baby"
Elizabeth

Second Reader (*older male voice*)
Commentator
Shepherd 1
Teacher 1
Simeon
Hebrews

Third Reader (*male voice*)
Isaiah
Prophet
Chorus
Magi 1
Colossians

Fourth Reader (*male voice*)
Jeremiah
Chorus
Magi 2
John
Narrator—in "Mary Visits Elizabeth"
Narrator 2—in "The Shepherds Find the Baby"

Fifth Reader (*authoritative male voice*)
Micah
Angel
Shepherd 2
Herod
Philippians

Sixth Reader (*female voice*)
Numbers
Mary
Chorus
Teacher 2
2 Corinthians

Suggested carols to match the Christmas readings will be found at the back of *Carols for Today* (music edition, from Hope Publishing Company). Carols to match the Christmas themes will be found indexed at the back of *Carol Praise* (music edition, from Harper San Francisco).

The Prophets Promise the Savior
From Numbers 24:16–17; Isaiah 7:14; Jeremiah 23:5–6; Micah 5:2, 4; Isaiah 9:6

Numbers
The oracle of one who hears the words of God,
who has knowledge from the Most High,
who sees a vision from the Almighty. . . .
I see him, but not now;
I behold him, but not near.
A star will come out of Jacob;
a scepter will rise out of Israel. . . .

Isaiah
The Lord himself will give you a sign: The virgin will be with child and will give birth to a son, and will call him Immanuel.

Jeremiah
"The days are coming," declares the LORD,
"when I will raise up to David a righteous Branch,
a King who will reign wisely
and do what is just and right in the land. . . .
This is the name by which he will be called:
The LORD Our Righteousness."

Micah
Bethlehem Ephrathah,
though you are small among the clans of Judah,
out of you will come for me
one who will be ruler over Israel,
whose origins are from of old,
from ancient times. . . .
He will stand and shepherd his flock
in the strength of the LORD,
in the majesty of the name of the LORD his God.

Isaiah
To us a child is born,
to us a son is given,
and the government will be on his shoulders.
And he will be called
Wonderful Counselor, Mighty God,
Everlasting Father, Prince of Peace.

The Birth of Jesus Foretold
From Luke 1:26–38

Narrator
In the sixth month, God sent the angel Gabriel to Nazareth, a town in Galilee, to a virgin pledged to be married to a man named Joseph, a descendant of David. The virgin's name was Mary. The angel went to her and said:

Angel
Greetings, you who are highly favored! The Lord is with you.

Narrator
Mary was greatly troubled at his words and wondered what kind of greeting this might be. But the angel said to her:

Angel	Do not be afraid, Mary, you have found favor with God. You will be with child and give birth to a son, and you are to give him the name Jesus. He will be great and will be called the Son of the Most High. The Lord God will give him the throne of his father David, and he will reign over the house of Jacob forever; his kingdom will never end.
[Narrator	Mary asked the angel:]
Mary	How will this be, since I am a virgin?
Angel	The Holy Spirit will come upon you, and the power of the Most High will overshadow you. So the holy one to be born will be called the Son of God. . . .
[Narrator	Mary answered:]
Mary	I am the Lord's servant. May it be to me as you have said.
Narrator	Then the angel left her.

Mary Visits Elizabeth
Luke 1:39–55 [56]

Narrator	Mary got ready and hurried to a town in the hill country of Judea, where she entered Zechariah's home and greeted Elizabeth. When Elizabeth heard Mary's greeting, the baby leaped in her womb, and Elizabeth was filled with the Holy Spirit. [In a loud voice she exclaimed:]
Elizabeth (delighted)	Blessed are you among women, and blessed is the child you will bear! But why am I so favored, that the mother of my Lord should come to me? As soon as the sound of your greeting reached my ears, the baby in my womb leaped for joy. Blessed is she who has believed that what the Lord has said to her will be accomplished!
Narrator	And Mary said:

Mary	My soul glorifies the Lord
	   and my spirit rejoices in God my Savior,
	for he has been mindful
	   of the humble state of his servant.
	From now on all generations will call me blessed,
	   for the Mighty One has done great things for me—
	   holy is his name.
	His mercy extends to those who fear him,
	   from generation to generation.
	He has performed mighty deeds with his arm;
	   he has scattered those who are proud in their inmost thoughts.
	He has brought down rulers from their thrones
	   but has lifted up the humble.
	He has filled the hungry with good things
	   but has sent the rich away empty.

417

He has helped his servant Israel,
   remembering to be merciful
to Abraham and his descendants forever,
   even as he said to our fathers.

[Narrator   Mary stayed with Elizabeth for about three months and then returned home.]

Joseph Learns the Truth
Matthew 1:18-25

Narrator   This is how the birth of Jesus Christ came about: His mother Mary was pledged to be married to Joseph, but before they came together, she was found to be with child through the Holy Spirit. Because Joseph her husband was a righteous man and did not want to expose her to public disgrace, he had in mind to divorce her quietly.

But after he had considered this, an angel of the Lord appeared to him in a dream [and said:]

Angel   Joseph son of David, do not be afraid to take Mary home as your wife, because what is conceived in her is from the Holy Spirit. She will give birth to a son, and you are to give him the name Jesus, because he will save his people from their sins.

Narrator   All this took place to fulfill what the Lord had said through the prophet:

Prophet   The virgin will be with child and will give birth to a son, and they will call him Immanuel—

Narrator   Which means, "God with us." (PAUSE) When Joseph woke up, he did what the angel of the Lord had commanded him and took Mary home as his wife. But he had no union with her until she gave birth to a son. And he gave him the name Jesus.

The Birth of Jesus
Luke 2:1-7

Narrator   In those days Caesar Augustus issued a decree that a census should be taken of the entire Roman world.

Commentator (This was the first census that took place while Quirinius was governor of Syria.) And everyone went to his own town to register.

Narrator   So Joseph also went up from the town of Nazareth in Galilee to Judea, to Bethlehem the town of David.

Commentator Because he belonged to the house and line of David.

Narrator   He went there to register with Mary, who was pledged to be married to him and was expecting a child. While they were there, the time came for the baby to be born, and she gave birth to her firstborn, a son.

Commentator She wrapped him in cloths and placed him in a manger, because there was no room for them in the inn.

The Angels Announce the Birth

Luke 2:8–14

Narrator There were shepherds living out in the fields nearby, keeping watch over their flocks at night. An angel of the Lord appeared to them, and the glory of the Lord shone around them, and they were terrified. But the angel said to them:

Angel Do not be afraid. I bring you good news of great joy that will be for all the people. Today in the town of David a Savior has been born to you; he is Christ the Lord. This will be a sign to you: You will find a baby wrapped in cloths and lying in a manger.

Narrator Suddenly a great company of the heavenly host appeared with the angel, praising God and saying:

Chorus
(cheerfully) Glory to God in the highest,
and on earth peace to men on whom his favor rests.

The Shepherds Find the Baby

Luke 2:15–20

Narrator 1 When the angels had left them and gone into heaven, the shepherds said to one another:

**Shepherds
1 and 2** Let's go to Bethlehem!

Shepherd 1 And see this thing that has happened—

Shepherd 2 Which the Lord has told us about.

Narrator 1 So they hurried off and found Mary and Joseph, and the baby, who was lying in the manger.

Narrator 2 When they had seen him, they spread the word concerning what had been told them about this child, and all who heard it were amazed at what the shepherds said to them.

Narrator 1 But Mary treasured up all these things and pondered them in her heart.

Narrator 2 The shepherds returned, glorifying and praising God for all the things they had heard and seen, which were just as they had been told.

419

The Visit of the Magi
Matthew 2:1–11

Narrator	After Jesus was born in Bethlehem in Judea, during the time of King Herod, Magi from the east came to Jerusalem and asked:
Magi 1	Where is the one who has been born king of the Jews?
Magi 2	We saw his star in the east and have come to worship him.
Narrator	When King Herod heard this he was disturbed, and all Jerusalem with him. When he had called together all the people's chief priests and teachers of the law, he asked:
Herod	Where [is] the Christ . . . to be born?
[Narrator	They replied:]
Teachers 1 and 2	In Bethlehem in Judea.
Teacher 2	For this is what the prophet has written:
Prophet	But you, Bethlehem, in the land of Judah,
	are by no means least among the rulers of Judah;
	for out of you will come a ruler
	who will be the shepherd of my people Israel.
Narrator	Then Herod called the Magi secretly and found out from them the exact time the star had appeared. He sent them to Bethlehem [and said]:
Herod	Go and make a careful search for the child. As soon as you find him, report to me, so that I too may go and worship him.
Narrator	After they had heard the king, they went on their way, and the star they had seen in the east went ahead of them until it stopped over the place where the child was. When they saw the star, they were overjoyed. On coming to the house, they saw the child with his mother Mary, and they bowed down and worshiped him. Then they opened their treasures and presented him with gifts of gold and of incense and of myrrh.

The Escape to Egypt
Matthew 2:13–18

Narrator	When [the Magi] had gone, an angel of the Lord appeared to Joseph in a dream.
Angel	Get up, take the child and his mother and escape to Egypt. Stay there until I tell you, for Herod is going to search for the child to kill him.
Narrator	So he got up, took the child and his mother during the night and left for Egypt, where he stayed until the death of Herod. And so was fulfilled what the Lord had said through the prophet:

Prophet	Out of Egypt I called my son.
Narrator	When Herod realized that he had been outwitted by the Magi, he was furious, and he gave orders to kill all the boys in Bethlehem and its vicinity who were two years old and under, in accordance with the time he had learned from the Magi. Then what was said through the prophet Jeremiah was fulfilled:
Jeremiah	A voice is heard in Ramah, weeping and great mourning, Rachel weeping for her children and refusing to be comforted, because they are no more.

The Return to Nazareth
Matthew 2:19–23

Narrator	After Herod died, an angel of the Lord appeared in a dream to Joseph in Egypt [and said:]
Angel	Get up, take the child and his mother and go to the land of Israel, for those who were trying to take the child's life are dead.
Narrator	So [Joseph] got up, took the child and his mother and went to the land of Israel. (PAUSE) But when he heard that Archelaus was reigning in Judea in place of his father Herod, he was afraid to go there. Having been warned in a dream, he withdrew to the district of Galilee, and he went and lived in a town called Nazareth. So was fulfilled what was said through the prophets:
Prophet	He will be called a Nazarene.

Simeon Recognizes the Messiah
Luke 2:25–35

Narrator	Now there was a man in Jerusalem called Simeon, who was righteous and devout. He was waiting for the consolation of Israel, and the Holy Spirit was upon him. It had been revealed to him by the Holy Spirit that he would not die before he had seen the Lord's Christ. Moved by the Spirit, he went into the temple courts. When the parents brought in the child Jesus to do for him what the custom of the Law required, Simeon took him in his arms and praised God [saying]:
Simeon	Sovereign Lord, as you have promised, you now dismiss your servant in peace. For my eyes have seen your salvation, which you have prepared in the sight of all people, a light for revelation to the Gentiles and for glory to your people Israel.

421

Narrator	The child's father and mother marveled at what was said about him. Then Simeon blessed them and said to Mary, his mother:
Simeon	This child is destined to cause the falling and rising of many in Israel, and to be a sign that will be spoken against, so that the thoughts of many hearts will be revealed. And a sword will pierce your own soul too.

The Apostles Explain the Meaning
From John 1:1, 3, 14; Colossians 1:15, 17; Hebrews 1:1–3; 2 Corinthians 4:6; 8:9; Philippians 2:6–7; John 1:11–12

John	In the beginning was the Word, and the Word was with God, and the Word was God. . . . Through him all things were made. . . .
	The Word became flesh and made his dwelling among us. We have seen his glory, the glory of the One and Only, who came from the Father, full of grace and truth.
Colossians	[Christ] is the image of the invisible God, the firstborn over all creation. . . . He is before all things, and in him all things hold together.
Hebrews	In the past God spoke to our forefathers through the prophets, . . . but in these last days he has spoken to us by his Son, . . . [who] is the radiance of God's glory and the exact representation of his being.
2 Corinthians	God, who said, "Let light shine out of darkness," made his light shine in our hearts to give us the light of the knowledge of the glory of God in the face of Christ. . . . You know the grace of our Lord Jesus Christ, that though he was rich, yet for your sakes he became poor, so that you through his poverty might become rich.
Philippians	[Christ Jesus,] being in very nature God, did not consider equality with God something to be grasped, but made himself nothing, taking the very nature of a servant, being made in human likeness.
John	He came to that which was his own, but his own did not receive him. Yet to all who received him, to those who believed in his name, he gave the right to become children of God.

Passion Readings

The cast is best placed throughout the building. For instance (in a church), Jesus in the pulpit, Narrator at the lectern (if a different reader), and Pilate in a gallery or other place facing Jesus and remote from the Crowd. The Crowd, if well-rehearsed and coordinated, can be placed throughout the congregation. Otherwise its readers are best in a position away from where Pilate and Jesus will be, but close enough to the congregation/audience to implicate them in the cries of "Crucify!" It is most effective if members of the crowd rise from their seats waving clenched fists to play their parts. During worship, the readings can be interspersed with hymns, songs, instrumental music, and prayers.

Passion Readings from Matthew

Cast of Readers
for the dramatized Passion Readings

[*]Narrator

Jesus

Peter

*Mother, Person 3, Pilate's wife, Reader 2

Son 1, Person 1, Man 1

Son 2, Person 2, Man 2

Zechariah, Jeremiah, Voice (*all unseen*), and Reader 1

Children

Chief priest, High priest

Disciple 1, Elder

Disciple 2, Lawyer

Disciple 3, Centurion, Soldier 2

Judas Iscariot

*Girl 1

*Girl 2 (*can be the same as Mother*)

Pilate

Pharisee, Soldier 1

(*indicates women's voices*)

Groupings allow each reader to take more than one part in the series, but not in the same reading.

Jesus Predicts His Death
Matthew 16:21–28; 20:20–28

Narrator   Jesus began to explain to his disciples:

Jesus   [I] must go to Jerusalem and suffer many things at the hands of the elders, chief priests and teachers of the law. [I] must be killed and on the third day be raised to life.

Narrator   Peter took him aside and began to rebuke him.

Peter   Never, Lord! This shall never happen to you!

Jesus (to Peter)   Get behind me, Satan! You are a stumbling block to me; you do not have in mind the things of God, but the things of men.

Narrator   Then Jesus said to his disciples:

Jesus   If anyone would come after me, he must deny himself and take up his cross and follow me. For whoever wants to save his life will lose it, but whoever loses his life for me will find it. What good will it be for a man if he gains the whole world, yet forfeits his soul? Or what can a man give in exchange for his soul? For the Son of Man is going to come in his Father's glory with his angels, and then he will reward each person according to what he has done. I tell you the truth, some who are standing here will not taste death before they see the Son of Man coming in his kingdom. . . .

Narrator   The mother of Zebedee's sons came to Jesus with her sons and, kneeling down, asked a favor of him:

Jesus   What is it you want?

Mother   Grant that one of these two sons of mine may sit at your right and the other at your left in your kingdom.

Jesus (to the sons)   You don't know what you are asking. Can you drink the cup I am going to drink?

Sons 1 and 2   We can.

Jesus   You will indeed drink from my cup, but to sit at my right or left is not for me to grant. These places belong to those for whom they have been prepared by my Father.

Narrator   When the other ten [disciples] heard about this, they were indignant with the two brothers. [So] Jesus called them [all] together:

Jesus   You know that the rulers of the Gentiles lord it over them, and their high officials exercise authority over them. Not so with you. Instead, whoever wants to become great among you must be your servant, and whoever wants to be first must be your slave—just as the Son of Man did not come to be served, but to serve, and to give his life as a ransom for many.

The Triumphal Entry
Matthew 21:1–17

Narrator	As they approached Jerusalem and came to Bethphage on the Mount of Olives, Jesus sent two disciples, saying to them:
Jesus	Go to the village ahead of you, and at once you will find a donkey tied there, with her colt by her. Untie them and bring them to me. If anyone says anything to you, tell him that the Lord needs them, and he will send them right away.
Narrator	This took place to fulfill what was spoken through the prophet:
Zechariah	Say to the Daughter of Zion, "See, your king comes to you, gentle and riding on a donkey, on a colt, the foal of a donkey."
Narrator	The disciples went and did as Jesus had instructed them. They brought the donkey and the colt, placed their cloaks on them, and Jesus sat on them. A very large crowd spread their cloaks on the road, while others cut branches from the trees and spread them on the road. The crowds that went ahead of him and those that followed shouted:
Person 1	Hosanna to the Son of David!
Person 2	Blessed is he who comes in the name of the Lord!
Person 3	Hosanna in the highest!
Narrator	When Jesus entered Jerusalem, the whole city was stirred [and asked:]
Person 1	Who is this?
[Narrator	The crowds answered:]
Person 3	This is Jesus, the prophet from Nazareth in Galilee.
Narrator	Jesus entered the temple area and drove out all who were buying and selling there. He overturned the tables of the money changers and the benches of those selling doves. [He said to them:]
Jesus	It is written, "My house will be called a house of prayer," but you are making it a "den of robbers."
Narrator	The blind and the lame came to him at the temple, and he healed them. But when the chief priests and the teachers of the law saw the wonderful things he did and the children shouting in the temple area:
Children	Hosanna to the Son of David!

425

Narrator	They were indignant, [so they asked Jesus:]
Chief priest (to Jesus)	Do you hear what these children are saying?
Jesus	Yes. Have you never read, "From the lips of children and infants you have ordained praise"?
Narrator	[Jesus] left them and went out of the city to Bethany, where he spent the night.

The Lord's Supper
Matthew 26:17–30

Narrator	On the first day of the Feast of Unleavened Bread, the disciples came to Jesus [and asked:]
Disciple 1	Where do you want us to make preparations for you to eat the Passover?
Jesus	Go into the city to a certain man and tell him, "The Teacher says: My appointed time is near. I am going to celebrate the Passover with my disciples at your house." (PAUSE)
Narrator	So the disciples did as Jesus had directed them and prepared the Passover. (PAUSE)
	When evening came, Jesus was reclining at the table with the Twelve. And while they were eating, he said:
Jesus	I tell you the truth, one of you will betray me.
Narrator	They were very sad and began to say to him one after the other:
Disciple 1	[Not I, Lord?]
Disciple 2	[Not I, Lord?]
Disciple 3	Surely not I, Lord?
Jesus	The one who has dipped his hand into the bowl with me will betray me. The Son of Man will go just as it is written about him. But woe to that man who betrays the Son of Man! It would be better for him if he had not been born.
Narrator	Then Judas, the one who would betray him, said:
Judas Iscariot	Surely not I, Rabbi?
Jesus (slowly)	Yes, it is you. (PAUSE)
Narrator	While they were eating, Jesus took bread, gave thanks and broke it, and gave it to his disciples:
Jesus	Take and eat; this is my body.
Narrator	Then he took the cup, gave thanks and offered it to them [saying]:

426

Jesus	Drink from it, all of you. This is my blood of the covenant, which is poured out for many for the forgiveness of sins. (PAUSE) I tell you, I will not drink of this fruit of the vine from now on until that day when I drink it anew with you in my Father's kingdom.
Narrator	When they had sung a hymn, they went out to the Mount of Olives.

(Note: A Psalm version, e.g., Psalm 22, might be used here.)

Jesus Predicts Peter's Denial
Matthew 26:31–56

Narrator	Jesus told [his disciples:]
Jesus	This very night you will all fall away on account of me, for it is written:
Zechariah	I will strike the shepherd, and the sheep of the flock will be scattered.
Jesus	But after I have risen, I will go ahead of you into Galilee.
Peter (to Jesus)	Even if all fall away on account of you, I never will.
Jesus	I tell you the truth, [Peter,] this very night, before the rooster crows, you will disown me three times.
Peter	Even if I have to die with you, I will never disown you. (PAUSE)
Narrator	And all the other disciples said the same. Then Jesus went with his disciples to a place called Gethsemane, and he said to them:
Jesus	Sit here while I go over there and pray.
Narrator	He took Peter and the two sons of Zebedee along with him, and he began to be sorrowful and troubled.
Jesus	My soul is overwhelmed with sorrow to the point of death. Stay here and keep watch with me.
Narrator	Going a little farther, he fell with his face to the ground and prayed:
Jesus	My Father, if it is possible, may this cup be taken from me. Yet not as I will, but as you will.
Narrator	Then he returned to his disciples and found them sleeping. [He asked Peter:]
Jesus	Could you men not keep watch with me for one hour? Watch and pray so that you will not fall into temptation. The spirit is willing, but the body is weak.
Narrator	He went away a second time and prayed:

427

Jesus	My Father, if it is not possible for this cup to be taken away unless I drink it, may your will be done.
Narrator	When he came back, he again found them sleeping, because their eyes were heavy. So he left them and went away once more and prayed the third time, saying the same thing. (PAUSE) Then he returned to the disciples [and said to them:]
Jesus	Are you still sleeping and resting? Look, the hour is near, and the Son of Man is betrayed into the hands of sinners. Rise, let us go! Here comes my betrayer!
Narrator	While [Jesus] was still speaking, Judas, one of the Twelve, arrived. With him was a large crowd armed with swords and clubs, sent from the chief priests and the elders of the people. Now the betrayer had arranged a signal with them:
Judas Iscariot	The one I kiss is the man; arrest him.
Narrator	Going at once to Jesus, Judas said:
Judas Iscariot	Greetings, Rabbi!
Narrator	And kissed him. (PAUSE) Jesus replied:
Jesus	Friend, do what you came for.
Narrator	Then the men stepped forward, seized Jesus and arrested him. With that, one of Jesus' companions reached for his sword, drew it out and struck the servant of the high priest, cutting off his ear.
Jesus	Put your sword back in its place, for all who draw the sword will die by the sword. Do you think I cannot call on my Father, and he will at once put at my disposal more than twelve legions of angels? But how then would the Scriptures be fulfilled that say it must happen in this way?
[Narrator	At that time Jesus said to the crowd:]
Jesus (to Judas and the crowd)	Am I leading a rebellion, that you have come out with swords and clubs to capture me? Every day I sat in the temple courts teaching, and you did not arrest me. But this has all taken place that the writings of the prophets might be fulfilled.
Narrator	Then all the disciples deserted him and fled.

Jesus before the Sanhedrin
Matthew 26:57–75

Narrator	Those who had arrested Jesus took him to Caiaphas, the high priest, where the teachers of the law and the elders had assembled. But Peter followed him at a distance, right up to the courtyard of the high priest. He entered and sat down with the guards to see the outcome.

The chief priests and the whole Sanhedrin were looking for false evidence against Jesus so that they could put him to death. But they did not find any, though many false witnesses came forward. Finally two came forward and declared:

Man 1   This fellow said, "I am able to destroy the temple of God—

Man 2   And rebuild it in three days."

Narrator   Then the high priest stood up and said to Jesus:

High priest
(to Jesus)   Are you not going to answer? (PAUSE) What is this testimony that these men are bringing against you?

Narrator   But Jesus remained silent. (PAUSE) The high priest said to him:

High priest   I charge you under oath by the living God: Tell us if you are the Christ, the Son of God.

Jesus   Yes, it is as you say. But I say to all of you: In the future you will see the Son of Man sitting at the right hand of the Mighty One and coming on the clouds of heaven.

Narrator   Then the high priest tore his clothes [and said:]

High priest   He has spoken blasphemy! Why do we need any more witnesses? Look, now you have heard the blasphemy. What do you think?

Man 1   He is worthy of death.

Man 2   [He must die.]

Narrator   Then they spit in his face and struck him with their fists. Others slapped him [and said:]

Man 1
(cynically)   Prophesy to us, Christ.

Man 2   Who hit you? (PAUSE)

Narrator   Peter was sitting out in the courtyard, and a servant girl came to him. [She said:]

Girl 1   You also were with Jesus of Galilee.

Narrator   But he denied it before them all:

Peter   I don't know what you're talking about.

Narrator   Then he went out to the gateway, where another girl saw him [and said to the people there:]

Girl 2 (to men) This fellow was with Jesus of Nazareth.

Narrator   He denied it again, with an oath:

Peter   I don't know the man!

Narrator	After a little while, those standing there went up to Peter:
Man 1	Surely you are one of them.
Man 2	Your accent gives you away.
[Narrator	Then he began to call down curses on himself and he swore to them:]
Peter	I don't know the man!
Narrator	Immediately a rooster crowed. Then Peter remembered the word Jesus had spoken:
Voice of Jesus (far away)	Before the rooster crows, you will disown me three times.
Narrator	And he went outside and wept bitterly.

Jesus before Pilate
Matthew 27:1–2, 11–26

Narrator	Early in the morning, all the chief priests and the elders of the people came to the decision to put Jesus to death. They bound him, led him away and handed him over to Pilate, the governor. . . .
	Jesus stood before the governor, and the governor asked him:
Pilate	Are you the king of the Jews?
Jesus	Yes, it is as you say.
Narrator	When he was accused by the chief priests and the elders, he gave no answer.
Pilate	Don't you hear the testimony they are bringing against you?
Narrator	But Jesus made no reply, not even to a single charge—to the great amazement of the governor.
	Now it was the governor's custom at the Feast to release a prisoner chosen by the crowd. At that time they had a notorious prisoner, called Barabbas. So when the crowd had gathered, Pilate asked them:
Pilate	Which one do you want me to release to you: Barabbas, or Jesus who is called Christ?
Narrator	For he knew it was out of envy that they had handed Jesus over to him.
	While Pilate was sitting on the judge's seat, his wife sent him this message:
Pilate's wife	Don't have anything to do with that innocent man, for I have suffered a great deal today in a dream because of him.
Narrator	But the chief priests and the elders persuaded the crowd to ask for Barabbas and to have Jesus executed. [Pilate asked the crowd:]

Pilate	Which of the two do you want me to release to you?
Person 1 (calling)	Barabbas.
Pilate	What shall I do, then, with Jesus who is called Christ?
Person 2 (calling)	Crucify him!
Pilate	Why? What crime has he committed?
Narrator	But they shouted all the louder:
Persons 1 and 2	Crucify him!
Narrator	When Pilate saw that he was getting nowhere, but that instead an uproar was starting, he took water and washed his hands in front of the crowd.
Pilate	I am innocent of this man's blood. It is your responsibility!
[Narrator	All the people answered:]
Person 1	Let his blood be on us—
Person 2	And on our children!
Narrator	Then he released Barabbas to them. But he had Jesus flogged, and handed him over to be crucified.

Jesus Is Crucified
Matthew 27:3–10, 27–44

Narrator	When Judas, who had betrayed him, saw that Jesus was condemned, he was seized with remorse and returned the thirty silver coins to the chief priests and the elders.
Judas Iscariot	I have sinned, for I have betrayed innocent blood.
Chief priest	What is that to us?
Elder	That's your responsibility.
Narrator	So Judas threw the money into the temple and left. Then he went away and hanged himself.
	The chief priests picked up the coins and said:
Chief priest	It is against the law to put this into the treasury, since it is blood money.
Narrator	So they decided to use the money to buy the potter's field as a burial place for foreigners. That is why it has been called the Field of Blood to this day. Then what was spoken by Jeremiah the prophet was fulfilled:

431

Jeremiah	They took the thirty silver coins, the price set on him by the people of Israel, and they used them to buy the potter's field, as the Lord commanded me. . . .
Narrator	[Pilate's] soldiers took Jesus into the Praetorium and gathered the whole company of soldiers around him. They stripped him and put a scarlet robe on him, and then twisted together a crown of thorns and set it on his head. They put a staff in his right hand and knelt in front of him and mocked him.
Soldiers 1 and 2	Hail, king of the Jews!
Narrator	They spit on him, and took the staff and struck him on the head again and again. After they had mocked him, they took off the robe and put his own clothes on him. Then they led him away to crucify him. (PAUSE)
	As they were going out, they met a man from Cyrene, named Simon, and they forced him to carry the cross. They came to a place called Golgotha (which means:
Voice (slowly)	The Place of the Skull).
Narrator	There they offered Jesus wine to drink, mixed with gall; but after tasting it, he refused to drink it. When they had crucified him, they divided up his clothes by casting lots. And sitting down, they kept watch over him there. Above his head they placed the written charge against him:
Voice	THIS IS JESUS, THE KING OF THE JEWS.
Narrator	Two robbers were crucified with him, one on his right and one on his left. (PAUSE) Those who passed by hurled insults at him, shaking their heads and saying:
Person 1	You who are going to destroy the temple and build it in three days, save yourself!
Person 2	Come down from the cross, if you are the Son of God!
Narrator	In the same way the chief priests, the teachers of the law and the elders mocked him:
Chief priest (cynically)	He saved others, but he can't save himself!
Lawyer (with sarcasm)	He's the King of Israel?
Elder (mocking)	Let him come down now from the cross, and we will believe in him.
Chief priest (challenging)	He trusts in God. Let God rescue him now if he wants him, for he said, "I am the Son of God."

Narrator
(slowly)

In the same way the robbers who were crucified with him also heaped insults on him.

The Death of Jesus
Matthew 27:45–54

Narrator

From the sixth hour until the ninth hour darkness came over all the land. About the ninth hour Jesus cried out in a loud voice:

Jesus

Eloi, Eloi, lama sabachthani? My God, my God, why have you forsaken me?

Narrator

When some of those standing there heard this, they said:

Person 1

He's calling Elijah.

Narrator

Immediately one of them ran and got a sponge. He filled it with wine vinegar, put it on a stick, and offered it to Jesus to drink. The rest said:

Person 2

Now leave him alone. Let's see if Elijah comes to save him.

Narrator

And when Jesus had cried out again in a loud voice, he gave up his spirit. (PAUSE)

At that moment the curtain of the temple was torn in two from top to bottom. The earth shook and the rocks split. The tombs broke open and the bodies of many holy people who had died were raised to life. They came out of the tombs, and after Jesus' resurrection they went into the holy city and appeared to many people.

When the centurion and those with him who were guarding Jesus saw the earthquake and all that had happened, they were terrified, and exclaimed:

Centurion

Surely he was the Son of God!

The Burial of Jesus (optional reading)
Matthew 27:57–66

Narrator

As evening approached, there came a rich man from Arimathea, named Joseph, who had himself become a disciple of Jesus. Going to Pilate, he asked for Jesus' body, and Pilate ordered that it be given to him. Joseph took the body, wrapped it in a clean linen cloth, and placed it in his own new tomb that he had cut out of the rock. He rolled a big stone in front of the entrance to the tomb and went away. Mary Magdalene and the other Mary were sitting there opposite the tomb. (PAUSE)

The next day, the one after Preparation Day, the chief priests and the Pharisees went to Pilate [and said:]

Chief priest

Sir, we remember that while he was still alive that deceiver said, "After three days I will rise again." So give the order for the tomb to be made secure until the third day.

433

Pharisee	Otherwise, his disciples may come and steal the body and tell the people that he has been raised from the dead. This last deception will be worse than the first.
Narrator	[Pilate told them:]
Pilate	Take a guard. Go, make the tomb as secure as you know how.
Narrator	So they went and made the tomb secure by putting a seal on the stone and posting the guard.

His Saving Work
From Hebrews 9:1–26

Reader 1	The first covenant had regulations for worship and also an earthly sanctuary. A tabernacle was set up. In its first room were the lampstand, the table and the consecrated bread; this was called the Holy Place.
Reader 2	Behind the second curtain was a room called the *Most* Holy Place, which had the golden altar of incense and the gold-covered ark of the covenant. . . . Above the ark were the cherubim of the Glory, overshadowing the atonement cover. . . .
Reader 1	Only the high priest entered the inner room, and that only once a year, and never without blood, which he offered for himself and for the sins the people had committed in ignorance. . . .
Reader 2	When Christ came as high priest of the good things that are already here, he went through the greater and more perfect tabernacle that is not man-made, that is to say, not a part of this creation. He did not enter by means of the blood of goats and calves; but he entered the Most Holy Place once for all by his own blood, having obtained eternal redemption.
Reader 1	The blood of goats and bulls and the ashes of a heifer sprinkled on those who are ceremonially unclean sanctify them so that they are outwardly clean. How much more, then, will the blood of Christ, who through the eternal Spirit offered himself unblemished to God, cleanse our consciences from acts that lead to death, so that we may serve the living God! . . .
Reader 2	For Christ did not enter a man-made sanctuary that was only a copy of the true one; he entered heaven itself, now to appear for us in God's presence. Nor did he enter heaven to offer himself again and again, the way the high priest enters the Most Holy Place every year with blood that is not his own. Then Christ would have had to suffer many times since the creation of the world. But now he has appeared once for all at the end of the ages to do away with sin by the sacrifice of *himself*.

It is suggested that the penultimate entry, "The Burial of Jesus (optional reading)," be omitted if the last entry, above, is to be used. The optional reading is intended as a link directly to the Easter Readings, if both sections are used together.

Passion Readings from Mark

(See note at commencement of the Passion Readings on page 423.)

Cast of Readers
for the dramatized Passion Readings

[*] Narrator (*strong, experienced voice*)

Voice 1

Jesus

Pilate (*authoritative voice*)

Priest, Man, Person 1

High priest, Lawyer 1, Centurion

Disciple, Peter, Commentator

Judas Iscariot, Lawyer 2

Bystander

*Girl, Person 2

Voice 2 (*to contrast with Voice 1*)

Crowd, Soldiers

(*indicates women's voices*)

Jesus Predicts His Death
Mark 10:32–34

Narrator   [Jesus and his disciples] were on their way up to Jerusalem, with Jesus leading the way, and the disciples were astonished, while those who followed were afraid. . . . He took the Twelve aside and told them what was going to happen to him.

Jesus   We are going up to Jerusalem, and the Son of Man will be betrayed to the chief priests and teachers of the law. They will condemn him to death and will hand him over to the Gentiles, who will mock him and spit on him, flog him and kill him. Three days later he will rise.

Jesus Enters Jerusalem and the Temple
Mark 11:1–10, 15–19

Narrator   As they approached Jerusalem and came to Bethphage and Bethany at the Mount of Olives, Jesus sent two of his disciples, [saying to them:]

Jesus   Go to the village ahead of you, and just as you enter it, you will find a colt tied there, which no one has ever ridden. Untie it and bring it here. If anyone asks you, "Why are you doing this?" tell him, "The Lord needs it and will send it back here shortly."

Narrator   They went and found a colt outside in the street, tied at a doorway. As they untied it, some people standing there asked:

Person 1   What are you doing, untying that colt?

435

Narrator	They answered as Jesus had told them to, and the people let them go. When they brought the colt to Jesus and threw their cloaks over it, he sat on it. Many people spread their cloaks on the road, while others spread branches they had cut in the fields. Those who went ahead and those who followed shouted:
Persons 1 and 2	Hosanna!
Person 1	Blessed is he who comes in the name of the Lord!
Person 2	Blessed is the coming kingdom of our father David!
Persons 1 and 2	Hosanna in the highest! . . .
Narrator	On reaching Jerusalem, Jesus entered the temple area and began driving out those who were buying and selling there. He overturned the tables of the money changers and the benches of those selling doves, and would not allow anyone to carry merchandise through the temple courts. And as he taught them, he said:
Jesus	Is it not written: "My house will be called a house of prayer for all nations"? But you have made it "a den of robbers."
Narrator	The chief priests and the teachers of the law heard this and began looking for a way to kill him, for they feared him, because the whole crowd was amazed at his teaching. When evening came, they went out of the city.

The Plot and the Passover
Mark 14:1–2, 10–25

Narrator	Now the Passover and the Feast of Unleavened Bread were only two days away, and the chief priests and the teachers of the law were looking for some sly way to arrest Jesus and kill him.
Priest	But not during the Feast.
Lawyer 1	Or the people may riot. . . .
Narrator	Then Judas Iscariot, one of the Twelve, went to the chief priests to betray Jesus to them. They were delighted to hear this and promised to give him money. So he watched for an opportunity to hand him over. On the first day of the Feast of Unleavened Bread, when it was customary to sacrifice the Passover lamb, Jesus' disciples asked him:
Disciple	Where do you want us to go and make preparations for you to eat the Passover?
[Narrator	So he sent two of his disciples, telling them:]

436

Jesus	Go into the city, and a man carrying a jar of water will meet you. Follow him. Say to the owner of the house he enters, "The Teacher asks: Where is my guest room, where I may eat the Passover with my disciples?" He will show you a large upper room, furnished and ready. Make preparations for us there.
Narrator	The disciples left, went into the city and found things just as Jesus had told them. So they prepared the Passover. (PAUSE) When evening came, Jesus arrived with the Twelve. While they were reclining at the table eating, he said:
Jesus	I tell you the truth, one of you will betray me—one who is eating with me.
Narrator	They were saddened, and one by one they said to him:
Disciple	Surely not I?
Jesus	It is one of the Twelve, one who dips bread into the bowl with me. The Son of Man will go just as it is written about him. But woe to that man who betrays the Son of Man! It would be better for him if he had not been born. (PAUSE)
Narrator	While they were eating, Jesus took bread, gave thanks and broke it, and gave it to his disciples, [saying:]
Jesus	Take it; this is my body.
Narrator	Then he took the cup, gave thanks and offered it to them, and they all drank from it.
Jesus	This is my blood of the covenant, which is poured out for many. I tell you the truth, I will not drink again of the fruit of the vine until that day when I drink it anew in the kingdom of God.

(Note: A Psalm version, e.g., Psalm 22, might be used here.)

Jesus Is Deserted and Arrested
Mark 14:26–52

Narrator	When they had sung a hymn, they went out to the Mount of Olives. Jesus told them:
Jesus	You will all fall away, for it is written: "I will strike the shepherd, and the sheep will be scattered." But after I have risen, I will go ahead of you into Galilee.
Narrator	Peter declared:

Peter	Even if all fall away, I will not.
Jesus (to Peter)	I tell you the truth, today—yes, tonight—before the rooster crows twice you yourself will disown me three times.
Peter (insistently)	Even if I have to die with you, I will never disown you.
Narrator	And all the others said the same. (PAUSE) They went to a place called Gethsemane, and Jesus said to his disciples:
Jesus	Sit here while I pray.
Narrator	He took Peter, James and John along with him, and he began to be deeply distressed and troubled.
Jesus	My soul is overwhelmed with sorrow to the point of death. Stay here and keep watch.
Narrator	Going a little farther, he fell to the ground and prayed that if possible the hour might pass from him.
Jesus	*Abba,* Father, everything is possible for you. Take this cup from me. (PAUSE) Yet not what I will, but what you will.
Narrator	Then he returned to his disciples and found them sleeping.
Jesus (looking around)	Simon, are you asleep? Could you not keep watch for one hour? Watch and pray so that you will not fall into temptation. The spirit is willing, but the body is weak.
Narrator	Once more he went away and prayed the same thing. (PAUSE) When he came back, he again found them sleeping, because their eyes were heavy. They did not know what to say to him. (PAUSE) Returning the third time, he said to them:
Jesus	Are you still sleeping and resting? Enough! The hour has come. Look, the Son of Man is betrayed into the hands of sinners. Rise! Let us go! Here comes my betrayer!
Narrator	Just as he was speaking, Judas, one of the Twelve, appeared. With him was a crowd armed with swords and clubs, sent from the chief priests, the teachers of the law, and the elders. Now the betrayer had arranged a signal with them:
Judas Iscariot	The one I kiss is the man; arrest him and lead him away under guard.
Narrator	Going at once to Jesus, Judas said:
Judas Iscariot	Rabbi!
Narrator	. . . and kissed him. The men seized Jesus and arrested him. Then one of those standing near drew his sword and struck the servant of the high priest, cutting off his ear. [Jesus said:]

438

Jesus	Am I leading a rebellion, that you have come out with swords and clubs to capture me? Every day I was with you, teaching in the temple courts, and you did not arrest me. But the Scriptures must be fulfilled.
Narrator	Then everyone deserted him and fled. (PAUSE) A young man, wearing nothing but a linen garment, was following Jesus. When they seized him, he fled naked, leaving his garment behind.

Jesus before the High Priest
Mark 14:53–72

Narrator	They took Jesus to the high priest, and all the chief priests, elders and teachers of the law came together. Peter followed him at a distance, right into the courtyard of the high priest. There he sat with the guards and warmed himself at the fire.
	The chief priests and the whole Sanhedrin were looking for evidence against Jesus so that they could put him to death, but they did not find any. Many testified falsely against him, but their statements did not agree.
	Then some stood up and gave this false testimony against him:
Man	We heard him say, "I will destroy this man-made temple and in three days will build another, not made by man."
Narrator	Yet even then their testimony did not agree.
	Then the high priest stood up before them and asked Jesus:
High priest	Are you not going to answer? What is this testimony that these men are bringing against you?
Narrator	But Jesus remained silent and gave no answer. Again the high priest asked him:
High priest	*Are* you the Christ, the Son of the Blessed One?
Jesus	I am. And you will see the Son of Man sitting at the right hand of the Mighty One and coming on the clouds of heaven.
Narrator	The high priest tore his clothes.
High priest	Why do we need any more witnesses? You have heard the blasphemy. What do you think?
Narrator	They all condemned him as worthy of death. Then some began to spit at him; they blindfolded him, struck him with their fists, and said:
Man	Prophesy!
Narrator	And the guards took him and beat him. (PAUSE)

439

While Peter was below in the courtyard, one of the servant girls of the high priest came by. When she saw Peter warming himself, she looked closely at him.

Girl	You also were with that Nazarene, Jesus.
[Narrator	But he denied it:]
Peter	I don't know or understand what you're talking about.
Narrator	And he went out into the entryway. (PAUSE) When the servant girl saw him there, she said again to those standing around:
Girl	This fellow is one of them.
Narrator	Again he denied it. (PAUSE)
	After a little while, those standing near said to Peter:
Bystander	Surely you are one of them, for you are a Galilean.
Narrator	[Peter] began to call down curses on himself, and he swore to them:
Peter	I don't know this man you're talking about.
Narrator	Immediately the rooster crowed the second time. Then Peter remembered the word Jesus had spoken to him, "Before the rooster crows twice you will disown me three times." And he broke down and wept.

Jesus before Pilate
Mark 15:1–15

Narrator	Very early in the morning, the chief priests, with the elders, the teachers of the law and the whole Sanhedrin, reached a decision. They bound Jesus, led him away and handed him over to Pilate.
Pilate	Are you the king of the Jews?
Jesus	Yes, it is as you say.
Narrator	The chief priests accused him of many things. So again Pilate asked him:
Pilate	Aren't you going to answer? See how many things they are accusing you of.
Narrator	But Jesus still made no reply, and Pilate was amazed. (PAUSE)
	Now it was the custom at the Feast to release a prisoner whom the people requested. A man called Barabbas was in prison with the insurrectionists who had committed murder in the uprising. The crowd came up and asked Pilate to do for them what he usually did.
Pilate (calling)	Do you want me to release to you the king of the Jews?
Narrator	[He knew] it was out of envy that the chief priests had handed Jesus over to him. But the chief priests stirred up the crowd to have Pilate release Barabbas instead.

Pilate	What shall I do, then, with the one you call the king of the Jews?
Crowd (shouting)	Crucify him!
Pilate	Why? What crime has he committed?
Narrator	But they shouted all the louder:
Crowd (louder)	Crucify him!
Narrator	Wanting to satisfy the crowd, Pilate released Barabbas to them. He had Jesus flogged, and handed him over to be crucified.

The Crucifixion

Mark 15:16–32

Narrator	The soldiers led Jesus away into the palace (that is, the Praetorium) and called together the whole company of soldiers. They put a purple robe on him, then twisted together a crown of thorns and set it on him. And they began to call out to him:
Soldier(s)	Hail, king of the Jews!
Narrator	Again and again they struck him on the head with a staff and spit on him. Falling on their knees, they paid homage to him. And when they had mocked him, they took off the purple robe and put his own clothes on him. Then they led him out to crucify him. (PAUSE)
	A certain man from Cyrene . . . was passing by on his way in from the country.
Commentator	Simon, the father of Alexander and Rufus.
Narrator	They forced him to carry the cross. (PAUSE) They brought Jesus to the place called Golgotha—
Commentator	(Which means The Place of the Skull).
Narrator	Then they offered him wine mixed with myrrh, but he did not take it. And they crucified him. Dividing up his clothes, they cast lots to see what each would get.
	It was the third hour when they crucified him. The written notice of the charge against him read:
Voice of Pilate (slowly)	THE KING OF THE JEWS.

Narrator	They crucified two robbers with him, one on his right and one on his left. Those who passed by hurled insults at him, shaking their heads and saying:
Persons 1 and 2	So!
Person 1	You who are going to destroy the temple and build it in three days—
Person 2	Come down from the cross and save yourself!
Narrator	In the same way the chief priests and the teachers of the law mocked him among themselves.
Lawyer 1	He saved others, but he can't save himself!
Lawyer 2	Let this Christ, this King of Israel, come down now from the cross, that we may see and believe.
Narrator	Those crucified with him also heaped insults on him.

The Death of Jesus
Mark 15:33–39

Narrator	At the sixth hour darkness came over the whole land until the ninth hour. And at the ninth hour Jesus cried out in a loud voice:
Jesus	*Eloi, Eloi, lama sabachthani?*
Narrator	Which means, "My God, my God, why have you forsaken me?"
	When some of those standing near heard this, they said:
Person 1	Listen, he's calling Elijah.
Narrator	One man ran, filled a sponge with wine vinegar, put it on a stick, and offered it to Jesus to drink.
Person 2	Now leave him alone. Let's see if Elijah comes to take him down. (PAUSE)
Narrator	With a loud cry, Jesus breathed his last. (PAUSE)
	The curtain of the temple was torn in two from top to bottom. And when the centurion, who stood there in front of Jesus, heard his cry and saw how he died, he said:
Centurion	Surely this man was the *Son of God!*

Christ and Us
1 Peter 2:21–24

Voice 1	Christ suffered for you, leaving you an example, that you should follow in his steps.
Voice 2	He committed no sin, and no deceit was found in his mouth.

Voice 1   When they hurled their insults at him, he did not retaliate.

Voice 2   When he suffered, he made no threats. Instead, he entrusted himself to him who judges justly.

Voices 1
and 2   He himself bore our sins in his body on the tree, so that we might die to sins and live for righteousness.

Voice 2   By his wounds you have been healed.

Passion Readings from Luke

(See note at commencement of the Passion Readings Gospels on page 423.)

Cast of Readers
for the dramatized Passion Readings

[*] Narrator, Narrator 1

Jesus

Disciple 1, Criminal 1, Leader 1

Disciple 2, Criminal 2, Narrator 2

Disciple 3, Commentator

Peter, Reader 1, Centurion

Owner, Man 1, Guard 1, Person 1, Soldier

Pharisee, Lawyer, Ruler 1

*Girl, Leader 2, Person 3, Reader 2

Man 2, Guard 2, Person 2, Ruler 2

Pilate

(*indicates women's voices)

Peter's Confession of Christ
Luke 9:18–24

Narrator   Once when Jesus was praying in private and his disciples were with him, he asked them:

Jesus   Who do the crowds say I am?

Narrator   They replied:

Disciple 1   Some say John the Baptist.

Disciple 2   Others say Elijah.

Disciple 3   And still others, that one of the prophets of long ago has come back to life.

Jesus   But what about you? Who do you say I am?

Narrator	Peter answered:
Peter	The Christ of God.
Narrator	Jesus strictly warned them not to tell this to anyone. [And he said:]
Jesus (to disciples)	The Son of Man must suffer many things and be rejected by the elders, chief priests and teachers of the law, and he must be killed and on the third day be raised to life.
[Narrator	Then he said to them all:]
Jesus (calling)	If anyone would come after me, he must deny himself and take up his cross daily and follow me. For whoever wants to save his life will lose it, but whoever loses his life for me will save it.

Jesus Goes up to Jerusalem and into the Temple
Luke 18:31–34; 19:28–48

Narrator	Jesus took the Twelve aside:
Jesus	We are going up to Jerusalem, and everything that is written by the prophets about the Son of Man will be fulfilled. He will be handed over to the Gentiles. They will mock him, insult him, spit on him, flog him and kill him. On the third day he will rise again.
Narrator	The disciples did not understand any of this. Its meaning was hidden from them, and they did not know what he was talking about. . . . (PAUSE)
	Jesus . . . went on ahead, going up to Jerusalem. As he approached Beth-phage and Bethany at the hill called the Mount of Olives, he sent two of his disciples, saying to them:
Jesus	Go to the village ahead of you, and as you enter it, you will find a colt tied there, which no one has ever ridden. Untie it and bring it here. If anyone asks you, "Why are you untying it?" tell him, "The Lord needs it."
Narrator	Those who were sent ahead went and found it just as he had told them. As they were untying the colt, its owners asked them:
Owner	Why are you untying the colt?
Disciple 1	The Lord needs it.
Narrator	They brought it to Jesus, threw their cloaks on the colt and put Jesus on it. As he went along, people spread their cloaks on the road. (PAUSE)

444

When he came near the place where the road goes down the Mount of Olives, the whole crowd of disciples began joyfully to praise God in loud voices for all the miracles they had seen:

Disciple 2
(calling)   Blessed is the king who comes in the name of the Lord!

Disciple 3   Peace in heaven and glory in the highest!

Narrator   Some of the Pharisees in the crowd said to Jesus:

Pharisee   Teacher, rebuke your disciples!

Jesus   I tell you, if they keep quiet, the stones will cry out.

Narrator   As [Jesus] approached Jerusalem and saw the city, he wept over it [and said:]

Jesus   If you, even you, had only known on this day what would bring you peace—but now it is hidden from your eyes. The days will come upon you when your enemies will build an embankment against you and encircle you and hem you in on every side. They will dash you to the ground, you and the children within your walls. They will not leave one stone on another, because you did not recognize the time of God's coming to you.

Narrator   Then he entered the temple area and began driving out those who were selling.

Jesus (firmly)   It is written, "My house will be a house of prayer"; but you have made it "a den of robbers."

Narrator   Every day he was teaching at the temple. But the chief priests, the teachers of the law and the leaders among the people were trying to kill him. Yet they could not find any way to do it, because all the people hung on his words.

Judas Agrees to Betray Jesus
Luke 22:1–13

Narrator   Now the Feast of Unleavened Bread, called the Passover, was approaching, and the chief priests and the teachers of the law were looking for some way to get rid of Jesus, for they were afraid of the people. (PAUSE) Then Satan entered Judas, called Iscariot, one of the Twelve. And Judas went to the chief priests and the officers of the temple guard and discussed with them how he might betray Jesus. They were delighted and agreed to give him money. He consented, and watched for an opportunity to hand Jesus over to them when no crowd was present. (PAUSE)

Then came the day of Unleavened Bread on which the Passover lamb had to be sacrificed. Jesus sent Peter and John, saying:

Jesus   Go and make preparations for us to eat the Passover.

445

Peter	Where do you want us to prepare for it?
Jesus	As you enter the city, a man carrying a jar of water will meet you. Follow him to the house that he enters, and say to the owner of the house, "The Teacher asks: Where is the guest room, where I may eat the Passover with my disciples?" He will show you a large upper room, all furnished. Make preparations there.
Narrator	They left and found things just as Jesus had told them. So they prepared the Passover.

The Last Supper
Luke 22:14–34

Narrator	. . . Jesus and his apostles reclined at the table.
Jesus	I have eagerly desired to eat this Passover with you before I suffer. For I tell you, I will not eat it again until it finds fulfillment in the kingdom of God.
Narrator	After taking the cup, he gave thanks and said:
Jesus	Take this and divide it among you. For I tell you I will not drink again of the fruit of the vine until the kingdom of God comes.
Narrator	And he took bread, gave thanks and broke it, and gave it to them [saying:]
Jesus	This is my body given for you; do this in remembrance of me.
Narrator	In the same way, after the supper he took the cup [saying:]
Jesus	This cup is the new covenant in my blood, which is poured out for you. (PAUSE) But the hand of him who is going to betray me is with mine on the table. The Son of Man will go as it has been decreed, but woe to that man who betrays him.
Narrator	They began to question among themselves which of them it might be who would do this.

Also a dispute arose among them as to which of them was considered to be greatest. Jesus said to them: |
| **Jesus** | The kings of the Gentiles lord it over them; and those who exercise authority over them call themselves Benefactors. But you are not to be like that. Instead, the greatest among you should be like the youngest, and the one who rules like the one who serves. For who is greater, the one who is at the table or the one who serves? Is it not the one who is at the table? But I am among you as one who serves. You are those who have stood by me in my trials. And I confer on you a kingdom, just as my Father conferred one on me, so that you may eat and drink at my table in my kingdom and sit on thrones, judging the twelve tribes of Israel. (PAUSE) |

(to Peter)	Simon, Simon, Satan has asked to sift you as wheat. But I have prayed for you, Simon, that your faith may not fail. And when you have turned back, strengthen your brothers.
Peter	Lord, I am ready to go with you to prison and to death.
Jesus	I tell you, Peter, before the rooster crows today, you will deny three times that you know me.

Jesus Prays on the Mount of Olives
Luke 22:35–62

Narrator	Jesus asked [his disciples]:
Jesus	When I sent you without purse, bag or sandals, did you lack anything?
Disciple 1	Nothing.
Disciple 2	Nothing.
Jesus	But now if you have a purse, take it, and also a bag; and if you don't have a sword, sell your cloak and buy one. It is written: "And he was numbered with the transgressors"; and I tell you that this must be fulfilled in me. Yes, what is written about me is reaching its fulfillment.
Disciple 3	See, Lord, here are two swords.
Jesus	That is enough.
Narrator	Jesus went out as usual to the Mount of Olives, and his disciples followed him. On reaching the place, he said to them:
Jesus	Pray that you will not fall into temptation.
Narrator	He withdrew about a stone's throw beyond them, knelt down and prayed.
Jesus	Father, if you are willing, take this cup from me; yet not my will, but yours be done.
Narrator	An angel from heaven appeared to him and strengthened him. And being in anguish, he prayed more earnestly, and his sweat was like drops of blood falling to the ground. (PAUSE)
	When he rose from prayer and went back to the disciples, he found them asleep, exhausted from sorrow.
Jesus	Why are you sleeping? Get up and pray so that you will not fall into temptation.
Narrator	While he was still speaking a crowd came up, and the man who was called Judas, one of the Twelve, was leading them. He approached Jesus to kiss him, but Jesus asked him:
Jesus	Judas, are you betraying the Son of Man with a kiss?

Narrator	Jesus' followers saw what was going to happen.
Disciple 3	Lord, should we strike with our swords?
Narrator	And one of them struck the servant of the high priest, cutting off his right ear.
Jesus	No more of this!
Narrator	And he touched the man's ear and healed him. Then Jesus said to the chief priests, the officers of the temple guard, and the elders, who had come for him:
Jesus	Am I leading a rebellion, that you have come with swords and clubs? Every day I was with you in the temple courts, and you did not lay a hand on me. But this is your hour—when darkness reigns.
Narrator	Then seizing [Jesus], they led him away and took him into the house of the high priest. Peter followed at a distance. But when they had kindled a fire in the middle of the courtyard and had sat down together, Peter sat down with them. A servant girl saw him seated there in the firelight. She looked closely at him.
Girl	This man was with him.
[Narrator	But he denied it.]
Peter	Woman, I don't know him.
Narrator	A little later someone else saw him.
Man 1	You also are one of them.
Peter	Man, I am not!
Narrator	About an hour later another asserted:
Man 2	*Certainly* this fellow was with him, for he is a Galilean.
Peter	Man, I don't know what you're talking about!
Narrator	Just as he was speaking, the rooster crowed. The Lord turned and looked straight at Peter. Then Peter remembered the word the Lord had spoken to him:
Jesus	Before the rooster crows today, you will disown me three times.
Narrator	[Peter] went outside and wept bitterly.

Jesus Is Brought before the Council and before Pilate
Luke 22:63–23:12

Narrator	The men who were guarding Jesus began mocking and beating him. They blindfolded him and demanded:

Guard 1	Prophesy!
Guard 2	Who hit you?
Narrator	And they said many other insulting things to him. (PAUSE)
	At daybreak the council of the elders of the people, both the chief priests and teachers of the law, met together, and Jesus was led before them.
Lawyer	If you are the Christ, tell us.
Jesus	If I tell you, you will not believe me, and if I asked you, you would not answer. But from now on, the Son of Man will be seated at the right hand of the mighty God.
Lawyer	Are you then the Son of God?
Jesus	You are right in saying I am.
Lawyer	Why do we need any more testimony? We have heard it from his own lips.
Narrator	The whole assembly rose and led [Jesus] off to Pilate. And they began to accuse him:
Leader 1	We have found this man subverting our nation.
Leader 2	He opposes payment of taxes to Caesar.
Leader 1	And claims to be Christ, a king.
Pilate (to Jesus)	Are you the king of the Jews?
Jesus	Yes, it is as you say.
Narrator	Then Pilate announced to the chief priests and the crowd:
Pilate	I find no basis for a charge against this man.
Narrator	But they insisted:
Leader 1	He stirs up the people all over Judea by his teaching.
Leader 2	He started in Galilee and has come all the way here.
Narrator	On hearing this, Pilate asked if the man was a Galilean. When he learned that Jesus was under Herod's jurisdiction, he sent him to Herod, who was also in Jerusalem at that time.
	When Herod saw Jesus, he was greatly pleased, because for a long time he had been wanting to see him.
Commentator	From what he had heard about him, he hoped to see him perform some miracle.
Narrator	He plied him with many questions, but Jesus gave him no answer. (PAUSE) The chief priests and the teachers of the law were standing there,

449

vehemently accusing him. Then Herod and his soldiers ridiculed and mocked him. Dressing him in an elegant robe, they sent him back to Pilate.

Commentator That day Herod and Pilate became friends—before this they had been enemies.

Jesus Is Sentenced to Death
Luke 23:13–32

Narrator Pilate called together the chief priests, the rulers and the people:

Pilate You brought me this man as one who was inciting the people to rebellion. I have examined him in your presence and have found no basis for your charges against him. Neither has Herod, for he sent him back to us; as you can see, he has done nothing to deserve death. Therefore, I will punish him and then release him.

Commentator [Now he was obliged to release one man to them at the Feast.]

Narrator With one voice they cried out:

Persons 1–3 Away with this man!

Person 3 Release Barabbas to us!

Commentator (Barabbas had been thrown into prison for an insurrection in the city, and for murder.)

Narrator Wanting to release Jesus, Pilate appealed to them again. But they kept shouting:

Person 1 Crucify him!

Persons 2 and 3 Crucify him!

Narrator For the third time he spoke to them:

Pilate Why? What crime has this man committed? I have found in him no grounds for the death penalty. Therefore I will have him punished and then release him.

Narrator But with loud shouts they insistently demanded that he be crucified, and their shouts prevailed. So Pilate decided to grant their demand. He released the man who had been thrown into prison for insurrection and murder, the one they asked for, and surrendered Jesus to their will. (PAUSE)

As [the soldiers] led Jesus away, they seized Simon from Cyrene, who was on his way in from the country, and put the cross on him and made him carry it behind Jesus. A large number of people followed him, including women who mourned and wailed for him. Jesus turned [and said to them:]

450

Jesus	Daughters of Jerusalem, do not weep for me; weep for yourselves and for your children. For the time will come when you will say, "Blessed are the barren women, the wombs that never bore and the breasts that never nursed!" Then
	"they will say to the mountains, 'Fall on us!' and to the hills, 'Cover us!'"
	For if men do these things when the tree is green, what will happen when it is dry?
Narrator	Two other men, both criminals, were also led out with him to be executed.

Jesus' Death
Luke 23:33–49

Narrator	When they came to the place called the Skull, there they crucified [Jesus], along with the criminals—one on his right, the other on his left. Jesus said:
Jesus	Father, forgive them, for they do not know what they are doing.
Narrator	And they divided up his clothes by casting lots. The people stood watching, and the rulers even sneered at him.
Ruler 1	He saved others; let him save himself—
Ruler 2	If he *is* the Christ of God, the Chosen One.
Narrator	The soldiers also came up and mocked him. They offered him wine vinegar [and said:]
Soldier	If you are the king of the Jews, save yourself.
Narrator	There was a written notice above him, which read:
Commentator	THIS IS THE KING OF THE JEWS.
Narrator	One of the criminals who hung there hurled insults at him:
Criminal 1	Aren't you the Christ? Save yourself and us!
Narrator	But the other criminal rebuked him.
Criminal 2 (to Criminal 1)	Don't you fear God, since you are under the same sentence? We are punished justly, for we are getting what our deeds deserve. But this man has done nothing wrong.
(to Jesus)	Jesus, remember me when you come into your kingdom.
Jesus	I tell you the truth, today you will be with me in paradise. (PAUSE)

451

Narrator	It was now about the sixth hour, and darkness came over the whole land until the ninth hour, for the sun stopped shining. And the curtain of the temple was torn in two.
Jesus (loud voice)	Father, into your hands I commit my spirit.
Narrator	When he had said this, he breathed his last. (PAUSE)
	The centurion, seeing what had happened, praised God and said:
Centurion	Surely this was a righteous man.
Narrator	When all the people who had gathered to witness this sight saw what took place, they beat their breasts and went away. But all those who knew him, including the women who had followed him from Gailiee, stood at a distance, watching these things.

Jesus' Burial
Luke 23:50–56

Narrator 1	There was a man named Joseph, a member of the Council, a good and upright man, who had not consented to their decision and action. He came from the Judean town of Arimathea and he was waiting for the kingdom of God. Going to Pilate, he asked for Jesus' body. Then he took it down, wrapped it in linen cloth and placed it in a tomb cut in the rock, one in which no one had yet been laid. It was Preparation Day, and the Sabbath was about to begin.
Narrator 2	The women who had come with Jesus from Galilee followed Joseph and saw the tomb and how his body was laid in it. Then they went home and prepared spices and perfumes.
Narrator 1	But they rested on the Sabbath in obedience to the commandment.

He Died for Us
From Isaiah 53:1–5 [6–7, 12]

Narrator	Who has believed our message and to whom has the arm of the LORD been revealed?
Reader 1	He grew up before him like a tender shoot, and like a root out of dry ground.
Reader 2	He had no beauty or majesty to attract us to him, nothing in his appearance that we should desire him.
Reader 1	He was despised and rejected by men, a man of sorrows, and familiar with suffering.

Reader 2   Like one from whom men hide their faces
          he was despised, and we esteemed him not.

**Readers 1
and 2**   Surely he took up our infirmities
          and carried our sorrows—

Reader 1   Yet we considered him stricken by God,
          smitten by him, and afflicted.

Reader 2   But he was pierced for our trangressions,
          he was crushed for our iniquities;
    the punishment that brought us peace was upon him,
          and by his wounds we are healed.

**[Readers 1
and 2**   We all, like sheep, have gone astray—

Reader 2   Each of us has turned to his own way.

Reader 1   And the Lord has laid on him
          the iniquity of us all.

Reader 2   He was oppressed and afflicted,
          yet he did not open his mouth.

Reader 1   He was led like a lamb to the slaughter,
          and as a sheep before her shearers is silent,
          so he did not open his mouth. . . .

Reader 2   He poured out his life unto death. . . .
    For he bore the sin of many.]

Passion Readings
from John

(See note at commencement of the Passion Readings on page 423.)

Cast of Readers
for the dramatized Passion Readings

[*] Narrator, Voice 1

Person 1, Philip, John

*Person 2, Voice 2

Zechariah, Voice of God, Psalmist (all
  unseen), and Voice 3

Commentator

Peter

*Girl

Pharisee 1, Pilate

Pharisee 2, Priest, Thomas, Guard

Jesus

Greek 1, Soldier 1

Greek 2, Soldier 2, Witness

(*indicates women's voices)

The Triumphal Entry
John 12:12–19

Narrator The next day the great crowd that had come for the Feast heard that Jesus was on his way to Jerusalem. They took palm branches and went out to meet him, shouting:

Persons 1 and 2 Hosanna!

Person 1 Blessed is he who comes in the name of the Lord!

Person 2 Blessed is the King of Israel!

Narrator Jesus found a young donkey and sat upon it, as it is written:

Zechariah Do not be afraid, O Daughter of Zion;
  see, your king is coming,
  seated on a donkey's colt.

Commentator At first his disciples did not understand all this. Only after Jesus did they realize that these things had been written about him and that they had done these things to him.

Narrator Now the crowd that was with him when he called Lazarus from the tomb and raised him from the dead continued to spread the word. Many people, because they had heard that he had given this miraculous sign, went out to meet him. So the Pharisees said to one another:

Pharisee 1 See, this is getting us nowhere.

Pharisee 2 Look how the whole world has gone after him!

Jesus Predicts His Death
John 12:20–26

Narrator   Now there were some Greeks among those who went up to worship at the Feast. They came to Philip, who was from Bethsaida in Galilee, with a request:

**Greeks 1
and 2**   Sir—

Greek 2   We would like to see Jesus.

Narrator   Philip went to tell Andrew; Andrew and Philip in turn told Jesus. Jesus replied:

Jesus   The hour has come for the Son of Man to be glorified. I tell you the turth, unless a kernel of wheat falls to the ground and dies, it remains only a single seed. But if it dies, it produces many seeds. The man who loves his life will lose it, while the man who hates his life in this world will keep it for eternal life. (PAUSE) Whoever serves me must follow me; and where I am, my servant also will be. My Father will honor the one who serves me.

Jesus Predicts His Death
John 12:27–36

Jesus   Now my heart is troubled, and what shall I say? "Father, save me from this hour"? No, it was for this very reason I came to this hour. Father, glorify your name!

Narrator   Then a voice came from heaven:

Voice of God   I have glorified it, and will glorify it again.

Narrator   The crowd that was there and heard it said it had thundered; others said:

Person 1   An angel [has] spoken to him.

Narrator   Jesus said:

Jesus   This voice was for your benefit, not mine. Now is the time for judgment on this world; now the prince of this world will be driven out. But I, when I am lifted up from the earth, will draw all men to myself.

Commentator   He said this to show the kind of death he was going to die.

Narrator   The crowd spoke up:

Person 1   We have heard from the Law that the Christ will remain forever.

Person 2   So how can you say, "The Son of Man must be lifted up"?

Person 1   Who is this "Son of Man"?

Jesus	You are going to have the light just a little while longer. Walk while you have the light, before darkness overtakes you. The man who walks in the dark does not know where he is going. Put your trust in the light while you have it, so that you may become sons of light.

Jesus Washes His Disciples' Feet
John 13:1–15, 21–30

Narrator	It was just before the Passover Feast. Jesus knew that the time had come for him to leave this world and go to the Father. Having loved his own who were in the world, he now showed them the full extent of his love.
Commentator	The evening meal was being served, and the devil had already prompted Judas Iscariot, son of Simon, to betray Jesus.
Narrator	Jesus knew that the Father had put all things under his power, and that he had come from God and was returning to God; so he got up from the meal, took off his outer clothing, and wrapped a towel around his waist. After that, he poured water into a basin and began to wash his disciples' feet, drying them with the towel that was wrapped around him. He came to Simon Peter, who said to him:
Peter	Lord, are *you* going to wash *my* feet?
Jesus	You do not realize now what I am doing, but later you will understand.
Peter	No, you shall *never* wash my feet.
Jesus	Unless I wash you, you have no part with me.
Peter	Then, Lord, not just my feet but my hands and my head as well!
Jesus	A person who has had a bath needs only to wash his feet; his whole body is clean. And you are clean, though not every one of you.
Commentator	[Jesus] knew who was going to betray him, and that was why he said not every one was clean. (PAUSE)
Narrator	When he had finished washing their feet, he put on his clothes and returned to his place.
Jesus	Do you understand what I have done for you? You call me "Teacher" and "Lord," and rightly so, for that is what I am. Now that I, your Lord and Teacher, have washed your feet, you also should wash one another's feet. I have set you an example that you should do as I have done for you. . . . (PAUSE)
Narrator	Jesus was troubled in spirit and testified:
Jesus	I tell you the truth, one of you is going to betray me.
Narrator	His disciples stared at one another, at a loss to know which of them he meant. One of them, the disciple whom Jesus loved, was reclining next to him. Simon Peter motioned to this disciple **[and said:]**

Peter (to John) Ask him which one he means.

Narrator Leaning back against Jesus, he asked him:

John (to Jesus) Lord, who is it?

Jesus It is the one to whom I will give this piece of bread when I have dipped it in the dish.

Narrator Then, dipping the piece of bread, he gave it to Judas Iscariot, son of Simon. As soon as Judas took the bread, Satan entered into him.

Jesus (to Judas) What you are about to do, do quickly.

Narrator But no one at the meal understood why Jesus said this to him.

Commentator Since Judas had charge of the money, some thought Jesus was telling him to buy what was needed for the Feast, or to give something to the poor.

Narrator As soon as Judas had taken the bread, he went out. (PAUSE) And it was night.

Jesus Comforts His Disciples
John 13:31–14:11, 27–31

Narrator When [Judas] was gone, Jesus said:

Jesus Now is the Son of Man glorified and God is glorified in him. If God is glorified in him, God will glorify the Son in himself, and will glorify him at once.

My children, I will be with you only a little longer. You will look for me, and just as I told the Jews, so I tell you now: Where I am going, you cannot come.

A new command I give you: Love one another. As I have loved you, so you must love one another. By this all [people] will know that you are my disciples, if you love one another.

[Narrator Simon Peter asked him:]

Peter Lord, where are you going?

Jesus (to Peter) Where I am going, you cannot follow now, but you will follow later.

Peter Lord, *why* can't I follow you now? I will lay down my life for you.

Jesus Will you really lay down your life for me? I tell you the truth, before the rooster crows, you will disown me three times! (PAUSE)

(to disciples) Do not let your hearts be troubled. Trust in God; trust also in me. In my Father's house are many rooms; if it were not so, I would have told you. I am going there to prepare a place for you. And if I go and prepare a place for you, I will come back and take you to be with me that you also may be where I am. You know the way to the place where I am going.

457

Thomas	Lord, we don't know where you are going, so how can we know the way?
Jesus (to Thomas)	I am the way and the truth and the life. No one comes to the Father except through me. If you really knew me, you would know my Father as well. From now on, you do know him and have seen him.
Philip	Lord, *show* us the Father and that will be enough for us.
Jesus (to Philip)	Don't you know me, Philip, even after I have been among you such a long time? Anyone who has seen me has seen the Father. How can you say, "Show us the Father"? Don't you believe that I am in the Father, and that the Father is in me? The words I say to you are not just my own. Rather, it is the Father, living in me, who is doing his work. Believe me when I say that I am in the Father and the Father is in me; or at least believe on the evidence of the miracles themselves. . . . (PAUSE) Peace I leave with you; my peace I give you. I do not give to you as the world gives. Do not let your hearts be troubled and do not be afraid.
	You heard me say, "I am going away and I am coming back to you." If you loved me, you would be glad that I am going to the Father, for the Father is greater than I. I have told you now before it happens, so that when it does happen you will believe. I will not speak with you much longer, for the prince of this world is coming. He has no hold on me, but the world must learn that I love the Father and that I do exactly what my Father has commanded me.
(to Thomas and Philip)	Come now; let us leave.

Jesus Prays to the Father
John 17:1–5, 13–19

[Narrator	Jesus . . . looked toward heaven and prayed:]
Jesus	Father, the time has come. Glorify your Son, that your Son may glorify you. For you granted him authority over all people that he might give eternal life to all those you have given him. Now this is eternal life: that they may know you, the only true God, and Jesus Christ, whom you have sent. I have brought you glory on earth by completing the work you gave me to do. And now, Father, glorify me in your presence with the glory I had with you before the world began. . . .
	I am coming to you now, but I say these things while I am still in the world, so that they may have the full measure of my joy within them. I have given them your word and the world has hated them, for they are not of the world any more than I am of the world. My prayer is not that you take them out of the world but that you protect them from the evil one. They are not of the world, even as I am not of it. Sanctify them by the truth; your word is truth. As you sent me into the world, I have sent

them into the world. (PAUSE) For them I sanctify myself, that they too may be truly sanctified.

Jesus Arrested
John 18:1–27

Narrator   When he had finished praying, Jesus left with his disciples and crossed the Kidron Valley. On the other side there was an olive grove, and he and his disciples went into it. (PAUSE)

Now Judas, who betrayed him, knew the place, because Jesus had often met there with his disciples. So Judas came to the grove, guiding a detachment of soldiers and some officials from the chief priests and Pharisees. They were carrying torches, lanterns and weapons. Jesus, knowing all that was going to happen to him, went out and asked them:

Jesus (slowly)   Who is it you want?

Soldier 1   Jesus of Nazareth.

Jesus   I am he.

Narrator   (Judas the traitor was standing there with them.)

Commentator   When Jesus said, "I am he," they drew back and fell to the ground.

[Narrator   Again he asked them:]

Jesus   Who is it you want?

Soldier 2   Jesus of Nazareth.

Jesus   I told you that I am he. If you are looking for me, then let these men go.

Commentator   This happened so that the words he had spoken would be fulfilled: "I have not lost one of those you gave me."

Narrator   Then Simon Peter, who had a sword, drew it and struck the high priest's servant, cutting off his right ear.

Commentator   (The servant's name was Malchus.)

Jesus   Put your sword away! Shall I not drink the cup the Father has given me?

Narrator   Then the detachment of soldiers with its commander and the Jewish officials arrested Jesus. They bound him and brought him first to Annas, who was the father-in-law of Caiaphas, the high priest that year.

Commentator   Caiaphas was the one who had advised the Jews that it would be good if one man died for the people.

Narrator   Simon Peter and another disciple were following Jesus. Because this disciple was known to the high priest, he went with Jesus into the high priest's courtyard, but Peter had to wait outside at the door. The other disciple, who was known to the high priest, came back, spoke to the girl on duty there and brought Peter in. The girl at the door asked Peter:

Girl (to Peter)	*You* are not one of his disciples, are you?
Peter	I am not.
Narrator	It was cold, and the servants and officials stood around a fire they had made to keep warm. Peter also was standing with them, warming himself. (PAUSE)
	Meanwhile, the high priest questioned Jesus about his disciples and his teaching. [Jesus replied:]
Jesus	I have spoken openly to the world. I always taught in synagogues or at the temple, where all the Jews come together. I said nothing in secret. Why question me? Ask those who heard me. Surely they know what I said.
Narrator	When Jesus said this, one of the officials nearby struck him in the face.
Guard	Is this the way you answer the high priest?
Jesus	If I said something wrong, testify as to what is wrong. But if I spoke the truth, why did you strike me?
Narrator	Then Annas sent him, still bound, to Caiaphas the high priest. (PAUSE)
	As Simon Peter stood warming himself, he was asked:
Person 1 (to Peter)	*You* are not one of his disciples, are you?
Narrator	[Peter] denied it, saying:
Peter	I am not.
Narrator	One of the high priest's servants, a relative of the man whose ear Peter had cut off, challenged him:
Person 2 (to Peter)	Didn't I *see* you with him in the olive grove?
Peter	[No!]
Narrator (slowly)	And at that moment a rooster began to crow.

Jesus before Pilate
John 18:28–19:16

Narrator	The Jews led Jesus from Caiaphas to the palace of the Roman governor. By now it was early morning, and to avoid ceremonial uncleanness the Jews did not enter the palace; they wanted to be able to eat the Passover. So Pilate came out to them and asked:
Pilate	What *charges* are you bringing against this man?
Priest	If he were not a criminal, we would not have handed him over to you.

Pilate	Take him yourselves and judge him by your own law.
Person 1	But we have no right to execute anyone. (PAUSE)
Commentator	This happened so that the words Jesus had spoken indicating the kind of death he was going to die would be fulfilled.
Narrator	Pilate then went back inside the palace, summoned Jesus and asked him:
Pilate	*Are* you the king of the Jews?
[Narrator	Jesus asked:]
Jesus	Is that your own idea, or did others talk to you about me?
Pilate	Am *I* a Jew? It was *your* people and *your* chief priests who handed you over to me. What is it you have done?
Jesus	My kingdom is not of this world. If it were, my servants would fight to prevent my arrest by the Jews. But now my kingdom is from another place.
Pilate	You *are* a king, then! (PAUSE)
Jesus	You are right in saying I am a king. In fact, for this reason I was born, and for this I came into the world, to testify to the truth. Everyone on the side of truth listens to me.
Pilate (slowly)	What is truth? (PAUSE)
Narrator	With this, [Pilate] went out again to the Jews [and said:]
Pilate	I find no basis for a charge against him. But it is your custom for me to release to you one prisoner at the time of the Passover. Do you want me to release "the king of the Jews"?
Person 1	No, not *him*!
Person 2	Give us *Barabbas*!
Commentator	Now Barabbas had taken part in a rebellion. (PAUSE)
Narrator	Then Pilate took Jesus and had him flogged. The soldiers twisted together a crown of thorns and put it on his head. They clothed him in a purple robe and went up to him again and again, saying:
Soldiers 1 and 2	Hail, *king of the Jews!*
Narrator	And they struck him in the face.
	Once more Pilate came out and said to the Jews:
Pilate	Look, I am bringing him out to you to let you know that I find no basis for a charge against him.
Narrator	Jesus came out wearing the crown of thorns and the purple robe.

Pilate	Here is the man!
Narrator	As soon as the chief priests and their officials saw him, they shouted:
Priest	Crucify!
Persons 1 and 2	Crucify!
Pilate	*You* take him and crucify him. As for me, I find no basis for a charge against him.
Person 1	We have a law, and according to that law he must die, because he claimed to be the Son of God.
Narrator	When Pilate heard this, he was even more afraid, and he went back inside the palace.
Pilate	Where do you come from?
Narrator	But Jesus gave him no answer. (PAUSE)
Pilate	Do you refuse to speak to me? Don't you realize I have power either to free you or to crucify you?
Jesus	You would have no power over me if it were not given to you from above. Therefore the one who handed me over to you is guilty of a greater sin.
Narrator	From then on, Pilate tried to set Jesus free, but the Jews kept shouting:
Person 2	If you let this man go, you are no friend of Caesar.
Person 1	Anyone who claims to be a king opposes Caesar.
Narrator	When Pilate heard this, he brought Jesus out and sat down on the judge's seat at a place known as the Stone Pavement.
Commentator	(Which in Aramaic is Gabbatha).
Narrator	It was the day of Preparation of Passover Week, about the sixth hour.
Pilate (to all)	Here is your king.
Persons 1 and 2	Take him away!
Soldiers 1 and 2	Take him away!
Priest	Crucify him!
Pilate	Shall I crucify your *king*?
Priest	We have no king but Caesar.
Narrator	Finally Pilate handed him over to them to be crucified.

The Crucifixion
John 19:16–30

Narrator The soldiers took charge of Jesus. Carrying his own cross, he went out to the place of the Skull—

Commentator (Which in Aramaic is called Golgotha).

Narrator Here they crucified him, and with him two others—one on each side and Jesus in the middle.

Pilate had a notice prepared and fastened to the cross. It read:

Commentator JESUS OF NAZARETH, THE KING OF THE JEWS.

Narrator Many of the Jews read this sign, for the place where Jesus was crucified was near the city, and the sign was written in Aramaic, Latin and Greek. The chief priests of the Jews protested to Pilate:

Priest Do not write "The King of the Jews," but that this man *claimed to be* king of the Jews.

Pilate What I have written, I have written.

Narrator When the soldiers crucified Jesus, they took his clothes, dividing them into four shares, one for each of them, with the undergarment remaining. This garment was seamless, woven in one piece from top to bottom. [The soldiers said to one another:]

Soldier 1 (to Soldier 2) Let's not tear it.

Soldier 2 (to Soldier 1) Let's decide by lot who will get it.

Narrator This happened that the scripture might be fulfilled which said:

Psalmist They divided my garments among them
    and cast lots for my clothing.

Narrator So this is what the soldiers did. (PAUSE)

Near the cross of Jesus stood his mother, his mother's sister, Mary the wife of Clopas, and Mary Magdalene. When Jesus saw his mother there, and the disciple whom he loved standing nearby, he said to his mother:

Jesus Dear woman, here is your son.

Narrator And to the disciple:

Jesus Here is your mother.

Narrator From that time on, this disciple took her into his home. (PAUSE)

Later, knowing that all was now completed, and so that the Scripture would be fulfilled, Jesus said:

Jesus	I am thirsty.
Narrator	A jar of wine vinegar was there, so they soaked a sponge in it, put the sponge on a stalk of the hyssop plant, and lifted it to Jesus' lips. When he had received the drink, Jesus said:
Jesus	It is finished. (PAUSE)
Narrator	With that, he bowed his head and gave up his spirit.

The Burial of Jesus (optional reading)
John 19:31–42

Narrator	It was the day of Preparation, and the next day was to be a special Sabbath. Because the Jews did not want the bodies left on the crosses during the Sabbath, they asked Pilate to have the legs broken and the bodies taken down. The soldiers therefore came and broke the legs of the first man who had been crucified with Jesus, and then those of the other. But when they came to Jesus and found that he was already dead, they did not break his legs. Instead, one of the soldiers pierced Jesus' side with a spear, bringing a sudden flow of blood and water.
Witness	The man who saw it has given testimony, and his testimony is true. He knows that he tells the truth, and he testifies so that you also may believe.
Commentator	These things happened so that the scripture would be fulfilled:
Voice 3	Not one of his bones will be broken.
Commentator	And, as another scripture says:
Voice 2	They will look on the one they have pierced.
Narrator	Later, Joseph of Arimathea asked Pilate for the body of Jesus.
Witness	Now Joseph was a disciple of Jesus, but secretly because he feared the Jews.
Narrator	With Pilate's permission, he came and took the body away. He was accompanied by Nicodemus, the man who earlier had visited Jesus at night. Nicodemus brought a mixture of myrrh and aloes, about seventy-five pounds. Taking Jesus' body, the two of them wrapped it, with the spices, in strips of linen.
Commentator	This was in accordance with Jewish burial customs.
Narrator	At the place where Jesus was crucified, there was a garden, and in the garden a new tomb, in which no one had ever been laid. Because it was the Jewish day of Preparation and since the tomb was nearby, they laid Jesus there.

God's Love and Ours

1 John 4:7–19

Voice 1 Dear friends, let us love one another, for love comes from God.

Voice 2 Everyone who loves has been born of God and knows God.

Voice 3 Whoever does not love does not know God.

Voices 1 and 2 Because God *is* love.

Voice 1 This is how God showed his love among us: He sent his one and only Son into the world that we might live through him. This is love:

Voice 3 Not that we loved God—

Voice 2 But that he loved us and sent his Son as an atoning sacrifice for our sins.

Voice 1 Dear friends, since God so loved us, we also ought to love one another. (PAUSE)

Voice 3 No one has ever seen God.

Voice 2 But if we love one another, God lives in us and his love is made complete in us. (PAUSE)

Voice 1 We know that we live in him and he in us, because he has given us of his Spirit.

Voice 2 And we have seen and testify that the Father has sent his Son to be the Savior of the world.

Voice 1 If anyone acknowledges that Jesus is the Son of God, God lives in him and he in God.

Voice 2 And so we know and rely on the love God has for us. (PAUSE)

Voice 1 God is love. Whoever lives in love lives in God, and God in him.

Voice 2 In this way, love is made complete among us so that we will have confidence on the day of judgment, because in this world we are like him. There is no fear in love. But perfect love drives out fear.

Voice 3 Because fear has to do with punishment. The one who fears is not made perfect in love.

Voice 1 We love because he first loved us.

Easter Readings

In the Easter Readings it is important that the person reading the part of Jesus stands in a variety of places. Similarly, the disciples should appear in differing places. The readings, especially if they are used for worship services, can be interspersed with Easter hymns, psalms, songs, instrumental music, and prayers.

Please note: the last nine readings are intended as *alternatives*. They should on no account *all* be read, not least because they are not placed in any theological sequence, but in biblical order. A sensitive choice would be one reading from the Acts and one reading from the Epistles, to complement the narrative readings from the Gospels.

Cast of Readers
for the dramatized Easter Readings

[*] Narrator

Man 1, Angel 1, Disciple, Disciple 1

Man 2, Angel 2, Disciple 2

Commentator, Voice, Voice 1

Priest, Thomas, Scripture

*Mary, Voice 3

Jesus

Cleopas, Paul

[*] Companion, Person

Peter, Voice 2

John, Younger Paul (*younger voice than "Paul"*)

(*indicates women's voices*)

The Resurrection
Luke 24:1–10 [Matthew 28:11–15]

Narrator	On the first day of the week, very early in the morning, the women took the spices they had prepared and went to the tomb. They found the stone rolled away from the tomb, but when they entered, they did not find the body of the Lord Jesus. While they were wondering about this, suddenly two men in clothes that gleamed like lightning stood beside them. In their fright the women bowed down with their faces to the ground, but the men said to them:
Man 1	Why do you look for the living among the dead?
Man 2	He is not here; he has risen!
Man 1	Remember how he told you, while he was still with you in Galilee:
Man 2	The Son of Man must be delivered into the hands of sinful men, be crucified—
Man 1	And on the third day be raised again.

Narrator	Then they remembered [Jesus'] words. (PAUSE) When they came back from the tomb, they told all these things to the Eleven and to all the others.
Commentator	It was Mary Magdalene, Joanna, Mary the mother of James, and the others with them who told this to the apostles.
[Narrator	While the women were on their way, some of the guards went into the city and reported to the chief priests everything that had happened. When the chief priests had met with the elders and devised a plan, they gave the soldiers a large sum of money, telling them:
Priest	You are to say, "His disciples came during the night and stole him away while we were asleep." If this report gets to the governor, we will satisfy him and keep you out of trouble.
Narrator	So the soldiers took the money and did as they were instructed.
Commentator	This story has been widely circulated among the Jews to this very day.]

The Empty Tomb
John 20:1–18

Narrator	Early on the first day of the week, while it was still dark, Mary Magdalene . . . came running to Simon Peter and the other disciple, the one Jesus loved [and said:]
Mary	They have taken the Lord out of the tomb, and we don't know where they have put him!
Narrator	So Peter and the other disciple started for the tomb. Both were running, but the other disciple outran Peter and reached the tomb first. He bent over and looked in at the strips of linen lying there but did not go in. Then Simon Peter, who was behind him, arrived and went into the tomb. He saw the strips of linen lying there, as well as the burial cloth that had been around Jesus' head. The cloth was folded up by itself, separate from the linen. Finally the other disciple, who had reached the tomb first, also went inside. He saw and believed.
Commentator	(They still did not understand from Scripture that Jesus had to rise from the dead.)
Narrator	Then the disciples went back to their homes. (PAUSE) But Mary stood outside the tomb crying. As she wept, she bent over to look into the tomb and saw two angels in white, seated where Jesus' body had been, one at the head and the other at the foot. They asked her:
Angel(s)	Woman, *why* are you crying?
Mary	They have taken my Lord away, and I don't know where they have put him.

Narrator	At this, she turned around and saw Jesus standing there, but she did not *realize* that it was Jesus.
Jesus	Woman, why are you crying? Who is it you are looking for?
Narrator	Thinking he was the gardener, she said:
Mary	Sir, if you have carried him away, tell me where you have put him, and I will get him.
Jesus (gently)	Mary.
Mary (crying out)	Rabboni! Teacher!
Jesus	Do not hold on to me, for I have not yet returned to the Father. Go instead to my brothers and tell them, "I am returning to my Father and your Father, to my God and your God."
Narrator	Mary Magdalene went to the disciples with the news:
Mary	I have seen the Lord!
Narrator	And she told them that he had said these things to her.

On the Road to Emmaus
Luke 24:13–35

Narrator	Now that same day two of [the disciples] were going to a village called Emmaus, about seven miles from Jerusalem. They were talking with each other about everything that had happened. As they talked and discussed these things with each other, *Jesus himself* came up and walked along *with* them; but they were kept from recognizing him. [He asked them:]
Jesus	What are you discussing together as you walk along?
Narrator	They stood still, their faces downcast. One of them, named Cleopas, asked him:
Cleopas	Are you only a *visitor* to Jerusalem and do not know the things that have happened there in these days?
Jesus	What things?
Cleopas	About Jesus of Nazareth.
Companion	He was a prophet, powerful in word and deed before God and all the people.
Cleopas	The chief priests and our rulers handed him over to be sentenced to death, and they crucified him.
Companion	But we had hoped that he was the one who was going to redeem Israel.
Cleopas	And what is more, it is the third day since all this took place.

Companion	In addition, some of our women amazed us. They went to the tomb early this morning but didn't find his body.
Cleopas	They came and told us that they had seen a vision of angels, who said he was alive.
Companion	Then some of our companions went to the tomb and found it just as the women had said.
Cleopas	But him they did not see.
Jesus	How foolish you are, and how slow of heart to believe all that the prophets have spoken! Did not the Christ have to suffer these things and then enter his glory?
Narrator	And beginning with Moses and all the Prophets, he explained to them what was said in all the Scriptures concerning himself. (PAUSE) As they approached the village to which they were going, Jesus acted as if he were going farther. But they urged him strongly:
Companion	Stay with us, for it is nearly evening.
Cleopas	The day is almost over.
Narrator	So he went in to stay with them. (PAUSE) When he was at the table with them, he took bread, gave thanks, broke it and began to give it to them. Then their eyes were opened and they recognized him, and he disappeared from their sight. (PAUSE) They asked each other:
Cleopas	Were not our hearts burning within us while he talked with us on the road . . .
Companion	. . . and opened the Scriptures to us?
Narrator	They got up and returned at once to Jerusalem. There they found the Eleven and those with them, assembled together [and saying:]
Disciple 1	It is true!
Disciple 2	The Lord has risen—
Disciple 1	And has appeared to Simon.
Narrator	Then the two told what had happened on the way, and how Jesus was recognized by them when he broke the bread.

Jesus Appears to His Disciples
John 20:19–23

Narrator	On the evening of that first day of the week, when the disciples were together, with the doors locked for fear of the Jews, Jesus came and stood among them [and said:]
Jesus	Peace be with you!

Narrator	After he said this, he showed them his hands and side. The disciples were overjoyed when they saw the Lord.
Jesus	Peace be with you! As the Father has sent me, I am sending you.
Narrator	And with that he breathed on them:
Jesus	Receive the Holy Spirit. If you forgive anyone his sins, they are forgiven; if you do not forgive them, they are not forgiven.

Jesus Appears to Thomas
John 20:24–29

Narrator	Thomas—
Commentator	(called Didymus),
Narrator	. . . one of the Twelve, was not with the disciples when Jesus came. So the other disciples told him:
Disciple(s)	We have seen the Lord!
Thomas	Unless I see the nail marks in his hands and put my finger where the nails were, and put my hand into his side, I will not believe it.
Narrator	A week later his disciples were in the house again, and Thomas was with them. Though the doors were locked, Jesus came and stood among them [and said:]
Jesus	Peace be with you! (PAUSE)
(to Thomas)	Put your finger here; see my hands. Reach out your hand and put it into my side. Stop doubting and believe.
Thomas	My Lord and my God!
Jesus	Because you have seen me, you have believed; blessed are those who have not seen and yet have believed.

Jesus and the Miraculous Catch of Fish
John 21:1–22

Narrator	Jesus appeared again to his disciples, by the Sea of Tiberias. It happened this way: Simon Peter, Thomas—
Commentator	(called Didymus),
Narrator	Nathanael—
Commentator	From Cana in Galilee—
Narrator	The sons of Zebedee, and two other disciples were together.
Peter	I'm going out to fish.
Disciple	We'll go with you.

Narrator	So they went out and got into the boat, but that night they caught nothing.
	Early in the morning, Jesus stood on the shore, but the disciples did not realize that it was Jesus. He called out to them:
Jesus (calling)	Friends, haven't you any fish?
Disciple	No.
Jesus (calling)	Throw your net on the right side of the boat and you will find some.
Narrator	When they did, they were unable to haul the net in because of the large number of fish. (PAUSE) Then the disciple whom Jesus loved said to Peter:
John	It is the Lord!
Narrator	As soon as Simon Peter heard him say, "It is the Lord," he wrapped his outer garment around him—
Commentator	(For he had taken it off)—
Narrator	And [he] jumped into the water. The other disciples followed in the boat, towing the net full of fish, for they were not far from shore.
Commentator	About a hundred yards.
Narrator	When they landed, they saw a fire of burning coals there with fish on it, and some bread. [Jesus said to them:]
Jesus	Bring some of the fish you have just caught.
Narrator	Simon Peter climbed aboard and dragged the net ashore. It was full of large fish—
Commentator	153!
Narrator	But even with so many the net was not torn. Jesus said to them:
Jesus	Come and have breakfast.
Narrator	None of the disciples dared ask him, "Who are you?" They knew it was the Lord. Jesus came, took the bread and gave it to them, and did the same with the fish.
Commentator	This was now the third time Jesus appeared to his disciples after he was raised from the dead.
Narrator	When they had finished eating, Jesus said to Simon Peter:
Jesus	Simon son of John, do you truly love me more than these?
Peter	Yes, Lord, you know that I love you.
Jesus	Feed my lambs. (PAUSE) Simon son of John, do you truly love me?
Peter	Yes, Lord, you know that I love you.

Jesus	Take care of my sheep. (PAUSE) Simon son of John, do you love me?
Narrator	Peter was hurt because Jesus asked him the third time, "Do you love me?"
Peter	Lord, you know all things; you know that I love you.
Jesus	Feed my sheep. (PAUSE) I tell you the truth, when you were younger you dressed yourself and went where you wanted; but when you are old you will stretch out your hands, and someone else will dress you and lead you where you do not want to go.
Commentator	Jesus said this to indicate the kind of death by which Peter would glorify God.
Narrator	(PAUSE) Then he said to him:
Jesus	Follow me!
Narrator	Peter turned and saw that the disciple whom Jesus loved was following them.
Commentator	(This was the one who had leaned back against Jesus at the supper and had said, "Lord, who is going to betray you?")
Narrator	When Peter saw him, he asked:
Peter	Lord, what about *him*?
Jesus	If I want him to remain alive until I return, what is that to you? *You* must follow me.

The Great Commission
Matthew 28:16–20

Narrator	Then the eleven disciples went to Galilee, to the mountain where Jesus had told them to go. When they saw him, they worshiped him; but some doubted. Then Jesus came to them [and said:]
Jesus	All authority in heaven and on earth has been given to me. Therefore go and make disciples of all nations, baptizing them in the name of the Father and of the Son and of the Holy Spirit, and teaching them to obey everything I have commanded you. And surely I am with you always, to the very end of the age.

Peter Speaks of Christ the Son of David*
Acts 2:22–24, 32–33

Peter	Men of Israel, listen to this: Jesus of Nazareth was a man accredited by God to you by miracles, wonders and signs, which God did among you through him, as you yourselves know. This man was handed over to you by God's set purpose and foreknowledge; and you, with the help of wicked men, put him to death by nailing him to the cross. But God

raised him from the dead, freeing him from the agony of death, because it was impossible for death to keep its hold on him. . . .God has raised this Jesus to life, and we are all witnesses of the fact. Exalted to the right hand of God, he has received from the Father the promised Holy Spirit and has poured out what you now see and hear.

*Normally, only one or two of these final readings would be used.

Paul Preaches in Antioch*

From Acts 13:29–41

Paul When [the people of Jerusalem and their rulers] had carried out all that was written about [Jesus,] they took him down from the tree and laid him in a tomb. But God raised him from the dead, and for many days he was seen by those who had traveled with him from Galilee to Jerusalem. They are now his witnesses to our people.

We tell you the good news: What God promised our fathers he has fulfilled for us, their children, by raising up Jesus. As it is written in the second Psalm:

Voice You are my Son;
today I have become your Father.

Paul The fact that God raised him from the dead, never to decay, is stated in these words:

Voice I will give you the holy and sure
blessings promised to David.

Paul So it is stated elsewhere:

Voice You will not let your Holy One see decay.

Paul For when David had served God's purpose in his own generation, he fell asleep; he was buried with his fathers and his body decayed. But the one whom God raised from the dead did not see decay.

Therefore, my brothers, I want you to know that through Jesus the forgiveness of sins is proclaimed to you. Through him everyone who believes is justified from everything you could not be justified from by the law of Moses. Take care that what the prophets have said does not happen to you:

Voice Look, you scoffers,
wonder and perish,
for I am going to do something in your days
that you would never believe,
even if someone told you.

The Resurrection of Christ*
From 1 Corinthians 15:1–11

Paul   Now, brothers, I want to remind you of the gospel I preached to you, which you received and on which you have taken your stand. By this gospel you are saved, if you hold firmly to the word I preached to you. Otherwise, you have believed in vain.

For what I received I passed on to you as of first importance:

Younger Paul   Christ died for our sins according to the Scriptures, . . . he was buried, . . . he was raised on the third day according to the Scriptures, and . . . he appeared to Peter, and then to the Twelve. After that, he appeared to more than five hundred of the brothers at the same time, most of whom are still living, though some have fallen asleep. Then he appeared to James, then to all the apostles.

Paul   Last of all he appeared to me also, as to one abnormally born. For I am the least of the apostles and do not even deserve to be called an apostle, because I persecuted the church of God. But by the grace of God I am what I am, and his grace to me was not without effect. No, I worked harder than all of them—yet not I, but the grace of God that was with me. Whether, then, it was I or they, this is what we preach, and this is what you believed.

The Resurrection Body*
From 1 Corinthians 15:35–57

Paul   Someone may ask:

Person   How are the dead raised? With what kind of body will they come?

Paul   How foolish! What you sow does not come to life unless it dies. When you sow, you do not plant the body that will be, but just a seed, perhaps of wheat or of something else. But God gives it a body as he has determined, and to each kind of seed he gives its own body. . . . If there is a natural body, there is also a spiritual body. So it is written:

Scripture   The first man Adam became a living being.

Paul   The last Adam [is] a life-giving spirit. The spiritual did not come first, but the natural, and after that the spiritual. The first man was of the dust of the earth, the second man from heaven. (PAUSE) As was the earthly man, so are those who are of the earth; and as is the man from heaven, so also are those who are of heaven. And just as we have borne the likeness of the earthly man, so shall we bear the likeness of the man from heaven.

I declare to you, brothers, that flesh and blood cannot inherit the kingdom of God, nor does the perishable inherit the imperishable. (PAUSE) Listen, I tell you a mystery: We will not all sleep, but we will all be

474

changed—in a flash, in the twinkling of an eye, at the last trumpet. For the trumpet will sound, the dead will be raised imperishable, and we will be changed. For the perishable must clothe itself with the imperishable, and the mortal with immortality. When the perishable has been clothed with the imperishable, and the mortal with immortality, then the saying that is written will come true:

Scripture Death has been swallowed up in victory.

Where, O death, is your victory?
  Where, O death, is your sting?

Paul The sting of death is sin, and the power of sin is the law. But thanks be to God! He gives us the victory through our Lord Jesus Christ.

God's Power and the Church*
Ephesians 1:19–23; 3:20–21

Voice 1 [God's] power is like the working of his mighty strength, which he exerted in Christ when he raised him from the dead and seated him at his right hand in the heavenly realms.

Voice 2 Far above all rule and authority, power and dominion, and every title that can be given, not only in the present age but also in the one to come.

Voice 3 And God placed all things under his feet and appointed him to be head over everything for the church,

Voice 1 Which is his body, the fullness of him who fills everything in every way. . . .

Voice 2 Now to him who is able to do immeasurably more than all we ask or imagine, according to his power that is at work within us,

Voice 3 To him be glory in the church and in Christ Jesus throughout all generations, for ever and ever!

Voices 1–3 Amen.

The Coming of the Lord*
1 Thessalonians 4:13–18

Voice 1 We do not want you to be ignorant about those who fall asleep, or to grieve like the rest of men, who have no hope.

Voice 2 We believe that Jesus died and rose again and so we believe that God will bring with Jesus those who have fallen asleep in him.

Voice 1 According to the Lord's own word, we tell you that we who are still alive, who are left till the coming of the Lord, will certainly not precede those who have fallen asleep.

Voice 2	For the Lord himself will come down from heaven, with a loud command, with the voice of the archangel and with the trumpet call of God.
Voice 1	And the dead in Christ will rise first.
Voice 2	After that, we who are still alive and are left will be caught up together with them in the clouds to meet the Lord in the air.
Voice 1	And so we will be with the Lord forever.
Voices 1 and 2	Therefore encourage each other with these words.

The Great Secret*
1 Timothy 3:14–16

Paul	Although I hope to come to you soon, I am writing you these instructions so that, if I am delayed, you will know how people ought to conduct themselves in God's household, which is the church of the living God, the pillar and foundation of the truth. Beyond all question, the mystery of godliness is great:
Voice 1	He appeared in a body.
Voice 2	Was vindicated by the Spirit.
Voice 3	Was seen by angels.
Voice 1	Was preached among the nations.
Voice 2	Was believed on in the world.
Voice 3	Was taken up in glory.

Praise to God for a Living Hope*
1 Peter 1:3–12

Voices 1 and 2	Praise be to the God and Father of our Lord Jesus Christ!
Voice 1	In his great mercy he has given us new birth into a living hope through the resurrection of Jesus Christ from the dead.
Voice 2	And into an inheritance that can never perish, spoil or fade.
Voice 3	Kept in heaven for you.
Voice 2	Who through faith are shielded by God's power until the coming of the salvation that is ready to be revealed in the last time.
Voice 3	In this you greatly rejoice, though now for a little while you may have had to suffer grief in all kinds of trials.

Voice 1	These have come so that your faith—of greater worth than gold, which perishes even though refined by fire—may be proved genuine and may result in praise, glory and honor when Jesus Christ is revealed.
Voice 3	Though you have not seen him, you love him.
Voice 1	And even though you do not see him now, you believe in him—
Voice 2	And are filled with an inexpressible and glorious joy.
Voice 1	For you are receiving the goal of your faith, the salvation of your souls.
Voice 2	Concerning this salvation, the prophets, who spoke of the grace that was to come to you, searched intently and with the greatest care—
Voice 3	Trying to find out the time and circumstances to which the Spirit of Christ in them was pointing when he predicted the sufferings of Christ and the glories that would follow.
Voice 2	It was revealed to them that they were not serving themselves but you, when they spoke of the things that have now been told you by those who have preached the gospel to you by the Holy Spirit sent from heaven.
Voice 1	Even angels long to look into these things.

The Glory of the Son of Man*
From Revelation 1:9–18

John	I, John, your brother and companion in the suffering and kingdom and patient endurance that are ours in Jesus, was on the island of Patmos because of the word of God and the testimony of Jesus. On the Lord's Day I was in the Spirit, and I heard behind me a loud voice like a trumpet:
Voice	Write on a scroll what you see and send it to the seven churches. . . .
John	I turned around to see the voice that was speaking to me. And when I turned I saw seven golden lampstands, and among the lampstands was someone "like a son of man" dressed in a robe reaching down to his feet and with a golden sash around his chest. His head and hair were white like wool, as white as snow, and his eyes were like blazing fire. His feet were like bronze glowing in a furnace, and his voice was like the sound of rushing waters. In his right hand he held seven stars, and out of his mouth came a sharp double-edged sword. His face was like the sun shining in all its brilliance.
	When I saw him, I fell at his feet as though dead. Then he placed his right hand on me and said:
Voice	Do not be afraid. I am the First and the Last. I am the Living One; I was dead, and behold I am alive for ever and ever! [And I hold the keys of death and Hades.]

Subject Index

481

Scripture Index

485